John Forster

The Life and Times of Oliver Goldsmith Vol. 1

John Forster

The Life and Times of Oliver Goldsmith Vol. 1

ISBN/EAN: 9783742839824

Manufactured in Europe, USA, Canada, Australia, Japa

Cover: Foto ©Thomas Meinert / pixelio.de

Manufactured and distributed by brebook publishing software (www.brebook.com)

John Forster

The Life and Times of Oliver Goldsmith Vol. 1

EACH VOLUME SOLD SEPARATELY.

COLLECTION

OF

BRITISH AUTHORS

TAUCHNITZ EDITION.

VOL. 1332.

THE LIFE AND TIMES OF OLIVER GOLDSMITH
BY
JOHN FORSTER.

IN TWO VOLUMES. — VOL. 1.

LEIPZIG: BERNHARD TAUCHNITZ.

PARIS: C. REINWALD & Cᵢₑ, 15, RUE DES SAINTS PÈRES.

This Collection

COLLECTION

OF

BRITISH AUTHORS

TAUCHNITZ EDITION.

VOL. 1332.

OLIVER GOLDSMITH'S
LIFE, ADVENTURES, AND TIMES BY J. FORSTER.
IN TWO VOLUMES.
VOL. I.

THE LIFE AND TIMES

OF

OLIVER GOLDSMITH.

·BY

JOHN FORSTER.

COPYRIGHT EDITION.

IN TWO VOLUMES.—VOL.

L E I P Z I G
BERNHARD TAUCHNITZ
1873.

TO

CHARLES DICKENS.

———

GENIUS AND ITS REWARDS ARE BRIEFLY TOLD:

    A LIBERAL NATURE AND A NIGGARD DOOM,

    A DIFFICULT JOURNEY TO A SPLENDID TOMB.

NEW-WRIT, NOR LIGHTLY WEIGHED, THAT STORY OLD

IN GENTLE GOLDSMITH'S LIFE I HERE UNFOLD:

    THRO' OTHER THAN LONE WILD OR DESERT-GLOOM,

    IN ITS MERE JOY AND PAIN, ITS BLIGHT AND BLOOM,

ADVENTUROUS.   COME WITH ME AND BEHOLD,

    O FRIEND WITH HEART AS GENTLE FOR DISTRESS,

    AS RESOLUTE WITH WISE TRUE THOUGHTS TO BIND

    THE HAPPIEST TO THE UNHAPPIEST OF OUR KIND,

THAT THERE IS FIERCER CROWDED MISERY

    IN GARRET-TOIL AND LONDON LONELINESS

THAN IN CRUEL ISLANDS 'MID THE FAR-OFF SEA.

JOHN FORSTER.

March, 1848.

PREFACE.

When this work first appeared, twenty-three years ago, it was made the subject of an attack by the author of a former "Life of Goldsmith" so unprovoked and inexcusable that even literary history affords hardly a parallel to it. I at once published a reply, to which no rejoinder was ever attempted; and all the subsequent editions of my book were prefaced by it. Sir James Prior is now dead, and I do not print it here. It is, however, necessary to retain some remark on the principle involved in his complaint.

It implied on his part nothing less than the claim to an absolute property in facts. Mr. Prior (he was not Sir James until many years later) complained that facts relating to Goldsmith discovered by him had been used by me without authority or permission. It was not pretended that my book contained a line of his writing. Not even the monomania that suggested the charge could extend it into an imputation that a single word of original comment or criticism, literary or personal, had been appropriated by me; or that I had adopted a thought, an expression, a view of character, a construction of any particular circumstances, or a decision on any doubtful point, which my predecessor had suggested or made. The specific and sole offence was the use in my narrative of matter which a previous biographer had used, which he assumed to have discovered, and the repetition of which he would prohibit to all coming after him. The question broadly raised was, whether any man who may have published a biography, contributing to it certain facts as the result of his own research, can from that instant lay claim to the entire beneficial interest in those facts, nay, can appropriate to himself the subject of them, and from the ground so seized turn all others off as trespassers.

Upon the reason or common sense of such a proposition one is ashamed to waste a word. Taking for granted the claim of discovery to the fullest extent, any claim to exclusive use of such discovery is sheer folly. Not without out excuse perhaps a new biographer may ask some brief interval for public judgment before any successor shall occupy his ground; but even this in courtesy only; and when Mr. Washington Irving, within as many weeks after the appearance of my book as I had waited years before encroaching on Mr. Prior's, "expanded into its present form "from the additions of Forster" (*Life and Letters of Irving*), a sketch which he had written for one of the Galignani editions, it never for a moment occurred to me to call that pleasant writer to account. No man can hold a patent in biography or history except by a mastery of execution unapproached by competitors. He only may hope to have possessed himself of a subject who has exhausted it, or to have established his originality in dealing with facts who has so happily disposed and applied them as to preclude the chances of more successful treatment by any subsequent writer. If I had thought that Mr. Prior had done this, the present book would not have been written.

The reader who examines both will probably admit that two so unlike each other have seldom been produced on the same theme. Any claim to merit which my own may possess is indeed grounded on the completeness of its contrast to its predecessor. For what had led me to the subject was the knowledge that I could illustrate it not alone by addition of facts and letters that would be new, but by a new handling of those that were old. It seemed no unworthy task to rescue one of the most fascinating writers in the language from one of its least lively books, from a posthumous admiration more harassing than any spite that vexed poor Goldsmith while he lived, from an indiscriminate and incessant exaltation which he would probably have found harder to bear than Hawkins's absurd contempt or the amusing slights of Boswell. But the new matter I found myself also able to contribute, both of narrative and letters, proved to be very considerable; and the plan adopted in the present edition will enable the reader to judge of its importance, and to measure its comparative value by that of the previous discoveries of others. Not only are very numerous corrections to every former publication relating to Goldsmith here made, and a great many new facts brought forward, but each fact, whether new or old, is given from its first authority, and no quotation has been made at second-hand. An unerring test is thus applied to Mr. Prior's extravagant claim of originality in research; and, to even a small fraction of the matter alleged to have been first set forth by him, his title as its discoverer is found to be as little established as his right to its exclusive ownership. The real truth is, that except as to bibliography, where the books themselves furnished easy hints for the supply of every defect, the most important particulars of Goldsmith's life had been made public, long before either of us, by Cooke, Glover, Percy, Davies, Hawkins, and Boswell.

It only remains to say, as to the title of my book, that while the Times as well as the Life are meant to be comprised, the persons introduced appear always, as far as possible, in the character and proportions which they bore to the society of their day *during* the life, and not beyond it;

that Burke is not yet the impeacher of Hastings, nor Boswell the biographer of Johnson; and that in thus bringing
within the circle of view not a little of the social as well
as literary characteristics of the arts, the theatres, and the
politics, of this fragment of the eighteenth century, still the
object strictly has been to show in more vivid lights from
each the central figure of GOLDSMITH himself, not exaggerated, not unduly exalted, but with all that there was
in him to admire and love, and all there was around him
to suggest excuse or pity.

 · PALACE GATE HOUSE, KENSINGTON,
   April, 1871.

NOTICE OF THE PUBLISHER.

Having had the privilege to see a letter which the late Mr. Charles Dickens wrote to the author of this work upon its first appearance, and which there was no intention to publish in England, it became my lively wish to make it known to the readers of my edition.

I therefore addressed an earnest request to Mr. Forster that he would permit the letter to be prefixed to a reprint not designed for circulation in England; where I could understand his reluctance to sanction its publication. Its varied illustration of the subject of the book, and its striking passages of personal feeling and character, led me also to request that I might be allowed to present it in facsimile.

Mr. Forster complied; and I am most happy to be thus enabled to give to my public on the following pages, so attractive and so interesting a letter, reproduced in the exact form in which it was written, by the most popular and admired of writers—too early gone.

Kleinzschocher near Leipzig,
        May, 23, 1873.

                                TAUCHNITZ.

Devonshire Terrace
Saturday Evening Second April 1848.

My Dear Forster.

I finished the Goldsmith yesterday, after dinner; having read it from the first page to the last with the greatest care and attention.

As a picture of the time, I really think it impossible to give it too much praise. It seems to me the very essence of all about the time that I have ever seen in biography or fiction, presented in most wise and humane lights, and in a thousand new and just aspects. I have never liked the Johnson half so well. Nobody's contempt for Boswell ought to be

capable if necessary, but I have never seen him
in my mind's eye half so plainly. The introduction
of him is quite a masterpiece — I should
point to that, if I did not know the author
as being close by somebody, with a remarkable
vivid conception of what he narrated, and
a most admirable and fanciful power of
communicating it to another. All about
Reynolds, is charming; and the first account
of the Literary club, and of Beauclerc, as
excellent a piece of description as ever I
read in my life. But to read the book, is
other in the kind. It lives again in us
fresh and lively a manner, as if it were
presented on an uncommonly good stage by
the very best actors that ever lived, or by
the real actors come out of their graves
on purpose

   and as Mr. Goldsmith himself,

and his life, and the tracing of it out in
his own writings, and the mature and
dignified account of him without any
ists, whines, or convulsions of any sort. It is
throughout a noble achievement, of which,
apart from any private and personal affection
for you, I think (and really think) I should
feel proud as one who had no indifferent
perception of these books of his — & the
test of remembrance — when little more
than a child. I was a little afraid
in the beginning, when he committed
those very discouraging imprudences
that you were going to champion
him somewhat indiscreetly; but
I very soon got over that fear, and
found reason in every page to
admire the sense, calmness, and
moderation, with which you make

the love & admiration of the reader cluster
about him in prose with his youth, and strengthen
with his strength — and weakness too, which is
better still.

I don't quite agree with you in two
small respects. 1st I question very much whether
it would have been a good thing for every great
man to have had his ~~~~~~ Boswell, inasmuch as I think that two Boswells, or three
utmost, would have made great men extraor-
dinarily false, and would have set them on
always playing a part, and would have
made distinguished people about them, for
ever restless and distrustful. I can
imagine a succession of Boswells bringing
about a tremendous state of falsehood
in society, and playing the very devil with
confidence and friendship. 2nd I cannot
keep objecting to what I think (upon I
think, or great funlaught, I think) of
italicizing lines and words and whole

perhaps in extracts, without some very special
reason indeed. It does appear to be a kind
of annoyance of the editor over the reader
—almost over the author himself —which
grates upon me. ~~[deletion]~~ The author might almost
as well do it himself, by thinking, as a
disagreeable thing; and it is such a sharp
contrast to the modest, quiet, ...
... if the ... Killarney, for
instance, that I should almost as soon
hear the 'town crier speak the lines. The
... always reminds me of a man
seeing a beautiful view, and not thinking
of how beautiful it is, but so much
as what he shall say about it.

In that picture at the close of
the third book (a most beautiful one) of
Goldsmith sitting looking out [window]
at the Temple Trees, you 'speak of the
'grey-eyed' rooks. Are you sure they are
grey-eyed? The raven's eye is a deep
lustrous black; and so, I suspect, is

the works, except where the light shines full
into it.

I have reviewed for my purpose — though
I don't mean be eloquent about it: being far
too much in earnest — the admirable
manner in which the case of the literary
man is stated throughout this book. It
is splendid. I don't believe that any
book was ever written, or anything ever
done or said, half so conducive to
the dignity and honor of literature, as
the life and adventures of Oliver Goldsmith
by J. F. of the Inner Temple. The gratitude
of every man who is content to rest his
station and claims quietly on literature, and
to make no parade of living by writing
things is your due, for evermore. I have often
said, here and there, where you have seen
at work upon the book, that [this] was only

atonned the . and Irish shall insist on that
debt being due Upon (though there will be
no need for insisting about it) as long as
I have my tediousness and obstinacy to
bestow on anybody. As of, I never will
hear the biography compared with Boswell's,
except under vigorous protest. Yet I do
say that it is mere folly to put into
opposite scales, a book, however
amusing and curious, written by one
ingenuous coxcomb like that, and
one which surveys and so grandly
understands the characters of all the
illustrious company that move
in it.

My dear Leslie I cannot sufficiently
say how much I am of what you have
done, or how sensible I am of

things so tenderly connected with it. When I look over this note, I feel as if I had said no part of what I think — and yet if I were to write another, I should say no more, for I can't get it out. I desire no better for my fame, when my personal dustyness shall be past the control of my loving editors, than such a biographer and such a critic. And again I say most solemnly, that literature in England has never had, and probably never will have, such a champion as yourself, in right of this book.

Ever affectionately

Charles Dickens

John Forster Esquire

TABLE OF CONTENTS OF VOL. I.

ANALYTICAL AND CHRONOLOGICAL.

BOOK I. 1728 to 1757.

THE SIZAR, STUDENT, TRAVELLER, APOTHECARY'S JOURNEYMAN, USHER, AND POOR PHYSICIAN. Pages 5 to 69.

CHAPTER VI.

1746-1757.

Peckham School and Grub-Street.

BOOK II. 1757 to 1759.

AUTHORSHIP BY COMPULSION. Pages 70 to 146.

CHAPTER I.

1757.

Reviewing for Mr. and Mrs. Griffiths.

Book III. 1759 to 1767.

CHAPTER VIII.
1763.
The Club and its First Members.

CHAPTER IX.
1763-1764.
The Arrest and what preceded it.

CHAPTER X.
1764-1765.
The Traveller and what followed it.

TABLE OF CONTENTS.

APPENDIX.

For INDEX *to entire work see close to Second Volume.*

THE AUTHOR TO THE READER OF GOLDSMITH'S LIFE, ADVENTURES, AND TIMES.

———

"IT *seems rational to hope,*" says *Johnson in the* Life of Savage, "*that minds qualified for great attainments should* "*first endeavour their own benefit; and that they who are most* "*able to teach others the way to happiness, should with most* "*certainly follow it themselves: but this expectation, however* "*plausible, has been very frequently disappointed.*" *Perhaps not so frequently as the earnest biographer imagined. Much depends on what we look to for our benefit, and much on what we follow as the way to happiness. It may not be for the one, and may have led us far out of the way of the other, that in the pursuit we had acted on a mere worldly estimate, and to that directed our endeavour. So may we have blocked up, ourselves, the path it was our hope to have pointed out to others, and in straits of a selfish profit made wreck of the great attainments.*

OLIVER GOLDSMITH, *whose life and adventures should be known to all who know his writings, must be held to have succeeded in nothing that his friends would have had him succeed in. He was intended for a clergyman, and was rejected when he applied for orders; he practised as a physician, and never made what would have paid for a degree. What he was not asked or expected to do, was to write: but he wrote, and paid the penalty. His existence was a continued privation. The days were few, in which he had resources for the night, or dared to look forward to the morrow. There was not any miserable want, in the long and sordid catalogue, which in its turn and in all its bitterness he did not feel. He had shared the experience of those to whom he makes affecting reference in his* Animated Nature, *"people who die really of hunger, in "common language of a broken heart;" and when he succeeded at the last, success was but a feeble sunshine on a rapidly approaching decay, which was to lead him, by its flickering light, to an early grave.*

Self-benefit seems out of the question here, and the way to happiness very distant indeed. But if we look a little closer, we shall see that he has passed through it all with a child-like purity of heart unstained. Much of the misery vanishes when this is known; and when it is remembered that in spite of it the Vicar of Wakefield *was written, nay, that without it, in all human probability, a book so delightful and wise could not have been written. Fifty-six years after its author's death, the greatest of Germans recounted to a friend how much he had been indebted to the celebrated Irishman. "It is not to be "described," wrote Goethe to Zelter in* 1830, *"the effect that "Goldsmith's* Vicar *had upon me, just at the critical moment "of mental development. That lofty and benevolent irony, that "fair and indulgent view of all infirmities and faults, that "meekness under all calamities, that equanimity under all "changes and chances, and the whole train of kindred virtues, "whatever names they bear, proved my best education; and in "the end," he added with sound philosophy, "these are the "thoughts and feelings which have reclaimed us from all the "errors of life."*

And why were they so enforced in that charming book, but because the writer had undergone them all; because they had reclaimed himself, not from the world's errors only but also from its suffering and care; and because his own life and adventures had been the same beautiful romance of the triumph of good over evil.

Though what is called worldly success, then, was not attained by Goldsmith, it may be that the way to happiness was yet not wholly missed. The sincere and sad biographer of Savage might have profited by the example. His own benefit he had not successfully "endeavoured," when the gloom of his early life embittered life to the last, and the trouble he had endured was made excuse for a sorrowful philosophy, and for manners that were an outrage to the kindness of his heart. What had fallen to Johnson's lot, fell not less· heavily to Goldsmith's. Of the calamities to which the literary life was then exposed,

"Toil, Envy, Want, the Patron, and the Gaol,"

none were spared to the subject of these pages. But they found and left him gentle and unspoiled; and though the discipline that taught him charity entailed some personal disadvantage, his genuine unaffectedness and simplicity of heart contributed to every social enjoyment. When his conduct least agreed with his writings, these characteristics did not fail him. What he gained, was others' gain; what he lost, concerned only himself; he suffered pain, but never inflicted it; and it is amazing to think how small an amount of mere insensibility to other people's opinions would have exalted "Doctor" Goldsmith's position in the literary circles of his day. He lost caste because he could not acquire it; and could as little assume the habit of indifference, as trade upon the gravity of the repute he had won. "Admirers in a room," said Northcote, repeating what had been told him by Sir Joshua, "whom his en-"trance had struck with awe, might be seen riding out upon "his back." It was hard, he said himself to Reynolds, that fame and its dignities should intercept people's liking and fondness; and for his love of the fondness, he forfeited doubtless not a little of the fame. "He is an inspired idiot," cried Walpole. "He does not know the difference of a turkey from "a goose," said Cumberland. "Sir," shouted Johnson, "he

1 *

"knows nothing, he has made up his mind about nothing." Few cared to think or speak of him but as little Goldy, honest Goldy; and every one laughed at him for the oddity of his blunders, or the awkwardness of his manners.

But I invite the reader to his life and adventures, and to the times they illustrate. No uninstructive explanation may possibly await us there, if together we review each scene, and move among the actors as they play their parts.

BOOK THE FIRST.

OLIVER

AS

THE SIZAR, STUDENT, TRAVELLER, APOTHECARY'S JOURNEYMAN, USHER, AND POOR PHYSICIAN.

1728 TO 1757.

CHAPTER I.

School Days and Holidays.
1728–1745.

THE marble in Westminster Abbey is correct in the place, but not in the time, of the birth of 1728. OLIVER GOLDSMITH. He was born at a small old parsonage house (supposed afterwards to be haunted by the fairies, or good people of the district, who could not however save it from being levelled to the ground) in a lonely, remote, and almost inaccessible Irish village on the southern banks of the river Inny, called Pallas * or Pallasmore, the property of the Edgeworths of Edgeworthstown, in the county of Longford, on the 10th of November 1728: a little 1728. more than three years earlier than the date upon his epitaph. *

* Pallas is often written Pallice, or Pallis, and seems to have been so written by Goldsmith's father. The rev. Mr. Mangin believed the latter to be the proper name, having seen it in Charles Goldsmith's handwriting. (*Parlour Window*, 4.) So did the rev. Mr. Graham, who supposed indeed that Dr. Johnson, in writing it Pallas, had simply laid a trap for the too classical biographer who

afterwards translated the line of his epitaph, "In loco cui nomen Pallas," "at a "place where Pallas had set her name!" *Gent. Mag.* xc. 620. Pilgrims to the birthplace must make the latter part of their journey on foot. "The hamlet," says Macaulay, "lies far from any highroad, "on a dreary plain, which in wet weather "is often a lake. The lanes would break "any jaunting-car to pieces; and there "are ruts and sloughs through which "the most strongly built wheels cannot "be dragged." *Biog. contrib. to Encyclo. Britt.* 51 (1860).

* The year of his birth was first correctly given in the *Percy Memoir* (1 and 116), and in Mr. Shaw Mason's *Statistical Account or Parochial Survey of Ireland*, iii. 357; but Mr. Prior settled the date of the month by reference to the fly-leaf of Charles Goldsmith's family Bible, still preserved by one of his descendants in Athlone (*Life*, i. 11). The exact year does not now appear upon the leaf, but Mr. Mason has stated it correctly.

His father, the reverend Charles Goldsmith, descended from a family which had long been 1728. settled in Ireland, and held various offices or dignities in connection with the established church,* was a protestant clergyman with an uncertain stipend, which, with the help of some fields he farmed, and occasional duties performed for the rector of the adjoining parish of Kilkenny-west (the reverend Mr. Green) who was uncle to his wife, averaged forty pounds a year. In May 1718 he had married Anne, the daughter of the reverend Oliver Jones, who was master of the school at Elphin to which he had gone in boyhood; and before 1728 four children had been the issue of the marriage. A new birth was but a new burthen; and little dreamt the humble village preacher, then or ever, that from the date of that tenth of November on which his Oliver was born his own virtues and very foibles were to be a legacy of pleasure to many generations of men. For they who have loved, laughed, or wept with the father of the man in black in the *Citizen of the World*, the preacher of the *Deserted Village*, or the hero of the *Vicar of Wakefield*, have given laughter, love, and tears, to the reverend Charles Goldsmith.

The death of the rector of Kilkenny-west improved his fortunes. He succeeded in 1730 to this living of his wife's uncle;* his income of forty pounds was raised to nearly two hundred; and Oliver had not completed his second year when the family moved from Pallasmore to a respectable house and farm on the verge of the pretty little village of Lissoy, "in the "county of Westmeath, barony "of Kilkenny-west," some six miles from Pallasmore, and about midway between the towns of Ballymahon and Athlone.** The first-born, Margaret (22nd August, 1719), appears to have died in childhood; and the family, at this time consisting of Catherine (13th January, 1721), Henry (9th February, 17—***), Jane (9th February, 17—), and Oliver, born at Pallasmore, was in the next ten years increased by Maurice

1730.
———
Æt. 2.

* *Percy Memoir*, 2.

** Here Charles Goldsmith seems to have procured a lease of about 70 acres at an eight shillings rent, renewable for ever on the payment of half a year's rent for every new life, the first lives being those of himself, his eldest son Henry, and his daughter Catherine; a property which remained in the family till sold in 1802 by Henry Goldsmith's son, then a settler in America. *Prior*, 1. 16, 17.

*** The leaf of the family Bible recording these dates is unfortunately so torn that, as in the case of Oliver's birth, the precise year of the births of Henry and Jane is not discernible from it; but it seems to me quite decisive, from the fact of the same day specified in both cases, coupled with the distinct assurance of Mrs. Hodson that there was a childless interval of seven years before the birth of Oliver, that Henry and Jane were twins, and both born in 1722. The month of John's birth is also erased.

* Many particulars of them will be found in Mr. Shaw Mason's volume quoted above, "drawn up from the communica-"tions of the clergy."

(7th July, 1736), Charles (16th August, 1737), and John (23rd ——, 1740), born at Lissoy. The youngest, as the eldest, died in youth; Charles went in his twentieth year, a friendless adventurer, to Jamaica, and after long self-exile died, soon after the opening of the present century (1803-4), in a poor lodging in Somers'-town; Maurice was put to the trade of a cabinet-maker, kept a meagre shop in Charlestown in the county of Roscommon, and "departed from a miser-" "able life" in 1792; Henry followed his father's calling, and died as he had lived, a humble village preacher and schoolmaster, in 1768; Catherine married a wealthy husband, Mr. Hodson, Jane a poor one, Mr. Johnstone, and both died in Athlone, some years after the death of that celebrated brother to whose life, adventures, and times these pages are devoted.

A trusted dependant in Charles Goldsmith's house, a young woman related to the family, afterwards known as Elizabeth Delap and schoolmistress of Lissoy, first put a book into Oliver Goldsmith's hands. She taught him his letters; lived till it was matter of pride to remember; often talked of it to Doctor Strean, Henry Goldsmith's successor in the curacy of Kilkenny-west; and at the ripe age of ninety, when the great writer had been thirteen years in his grave, boasted of it with her last breath. That her success in the task had not been much to boast of, she at other times admitted. "Never "was so dull a boy: he seemed impenetrably stu-" "pid,"* said the good Elizabeth Delap, when she bored her friends, or answered curious enquirers, about the celebrated Doctor Goldsmith. "He was a plant "that flowered late," said Johnson to Boswell; "there appeared "nothing remarkable about him "when he was young."** This, if true, would have been only another confirmation of the saying that the richer a nature is, the more slow its development is like to be; but, in the meaning it would ordinarily bear, it may here be of doubtful application, for all the charms of Goldsmith's later style are to be traced in even the letters of his youth, and his sister expressly tells us that he not only began to scribble verses when he could scarcely write, but otherwise showed a fondness for books and learning, and what she calls "signs of genius." ***

At the age of six, Oliver was handed over to the village school, kept by Mr. Thomas Byrne. Looking back from this distance of time, and penetrating through greater obscurity than its own cabin smoke into that Lissoy academy, it is to

1731.
Æt. 3.

1734.
Æt. 6.

---

* The rev. Edward Mangin's *Essay on Light Reading* (1808), 144. And see *Prior*, i. 22.

** *Boswell's Life* (Ed. 1839), vi. 309.

*** *Percy Memoir*, 4.

be discovered that this excellent Mr. Byrne, retired quarter-master of an Irish regiment that had served in Marlborough's Spanish wars, was more given to "shoulder a crutch "and show how fields were won," and certainly more apt to teach wild legends of an Irish hovel, or hold forth about fairies and rapparees, than to inculcate what are called the humanities. Little Oliver came away from him much as he went, in point of learning; but there were certain wandering unsettled tastes, which his friends thought to have been here implanted in him, * and which, as well as a taste for song, one of his later essays might seem to connect with the vagrant life of the blind harper Carolan, whose wayside melodies he had been taken to hear. ** Unhappily

also something more and other than this remained, in the effects of a terrible disease which assailed him at the school, and were not likely soon to pass away.

An attack of confluent small-pox that nearly proved mortal had left deep and indelible traces on his face, for ever settled his small pretension to good-looks, and exposed him to jest and sarcasm. Kind-natured Mr. Byrne might best have reconciled him to it, used to his temper as no doubt he had become; and it was doubly unfortunate to be sent at such a time away from home, to a school among strangers, at once to taste the bitterness of those school-experiences which too early and sadly teach the shy, ill-favoured, backward boy, what tyrannies the strong have to inflict, and what sufferings the weak must be prepared to endure. But to the reverend Mr. Griffin's superior school of Elphin in Roscommon it was resolved to send him; and at the house of an uncle John, * at Ballyoughter in the neighbourhood of Elphin, he was lodged and boarded. ** The knowledge

---

* See his sister Mrs. Hodson's narrative contributed to the *Percy Memoir*, 3, 4. She does not give the name of the schoolmaster, but this was supplied by Dr. Strean. Mangin's *Essay*, 142.

** *Essay* xx. Thorlogh O'Carolan, who was born at Nobber in 1670, and brought up at Carrick O'Shannon, where Oliver's uncle Contarine first settled, died in 1738 at Roscommon, to which Contarine had removed. To his patroness in whose house he died, the wife of the Mac-Dermott of Alderwford, he owed the "horse, harp, and gossoou," with which, renewed as his needs dictated, he had meanwhile wandered about for half a century from house to house, a guest always welcome, improvising music and songs. The harp had been his amusement up to the age of manhood, when, being struck with blindness, he thus made it his profession. For curious anecdotes of Carolan, and other Irish poets, see Nichols's *Illustrations of Lit. Hist. of XVIIIth Century*, VII. 688.

* His father's brother, "who, with "his family," Mrs. Hodson tells us, "considered him as a prodigy for his age." *Percy Memoir*, 6.

** "At the age of seven or eight," says Mrs. Hodson, "he discovered a natural "turn for rhyming, and often amused his "father and his friends with early poetical attempts. When he could scarcely "write legibly, he was always scribbling "verses which he burnt as he wrote "them. Observing his fondness for books

of *Ovid* and *Horace*, introduced to him here, was the pleasantest as well as the least important, though it might be by far the most difficult, of what he had now to learn. It was the learning of bitter years, and not taught by the schoolmaster but by the school-fellows of this poor little, thick, pale-faced, pock-marked boy. "He was considered by his "contemporaries and school-fel-"lows, with whom I have often "conversed on the subject," said Doctor Strean,* who succeeded, on the death of Charles Gold-smith's curate and eldest son, to his pastoral duty and its munifi-cent rewards, "as a stupid, heavy "blockhead, little better than a "fool, whom every one made fun "of."**

This was early to trample fun out of any one; and Oliver bore marks of it to his dying day. It had not been his least qualifica-tion as game for laughter, that all confessed his nature to be kind and affectionate, and knew his temper to be cheerful and agree-able; but feeling as well as fun he could hardly be expected to supply unintermittingly, and, pre-cisely as in after years it was said

of him that he had the most un-accountable alternations of gaiety and gloom, and was subject to the most particular humours, even so his elder sister de-scribed his school-days to Doctor Percy, bishop of Dro-more, when that divine and his friends were gathering materials for his biography. That he seemed to possess two natures, was the comment on both his childhood and his manhood;* and there was sense in it, so far as it repre-sented the continued struggle, happily always unavailing, car-ried on against feelings that God had given him by fears he had to thank the world for.

"Why Noll!" exclaimed a visi-tor at uncle John's, "you are be-"come a fright! When do you "mean to get handsome again?" Oliver moved in silence to the window. The speaker, a reck-less and notorious scapegrace of the Goldsmith family, repeated the question with a worse sneer: and "I mean to get better, sir, "when you do!"** was the boy's

1737.
Æt. 9.

"and learning, his mother, with whom "he was always a favourite, pleaded with "his father to give him a liberal educa-"tion: but his own narrow income, the "expense attending the education of his "oldest son, and his numerous family, "were strong objections." *Percy Memoir,* 4, 5.

* See Appendix (A. "DR. STREAN AND "THE REV. EDWARD MANGIN") at the close of this volume.

** Mangin's *Essay,* 149.

* "Oliver was from his earliest in-"fancy," writes his sister to Dr. Percy, "very different from other children, sub-"ject to particular humours, for the most "part uncommonly serious and reserved, "but when in gay spirits none ever so "agreeable as he." *Percy Memoir,* 4. "He was such a compound of absurdity, "envy, and malice, contrasted with the "opposite virtues of kindness, generosity, "and benevolence," says Mr. Thomas Davies (who, bad actor as he was, seems to have been a worse philosopher), "that "he might be said to consist of two dis-"tinct souls, and influenced by the "agency of a good and bad spirit." *Life of Garrick,* ii. 117-8.

** *Prior,* i. 29, 30.

retort, which has delighted his biographers for its quickness of repartee. It was probably something more than smartness. Another example of precocious wit occurred also at uncle John's, when his nephew was still a mere child. There was company one day, to a small dance; and the fiddler engaged on the occasion, thinking himself entitled to assume the airs of a wit, was made conscious suddenly of an Oliver to his Rowland for which he was wholly unprepared. During a pause between two country dances, the party had been greatly surprised by little Noll quickly jumping up and dancing impromptu a *pas seul* about the room; whereupon, seizing the opportunity of the lad's ungainly look and grotesque figure, the jocose fiddler promptly exclaimed, "Æsop!" A burst of laughter rewarded him, which however was rapidly turned the other way by Noll stopping his hornpipe, looking round at his assailant, and giving forth, in audible voice and without hesitation, the couplet thought worth preserving as the first formal effort of his genius by Percy, Malone, Campbell, and the rest who compiled that biographical preface * to the *Miscellaneous Works*

1737.
Æt. 9.

on which the subsequent biographies have been founded:

led to an angry dispute on its being handed to the publishers of the *Miscellaneous Works*. Other causes of disagreement sprang up afterwards with Mr. Rose (Cowper's friend), employed as their editor, and Percy ultimately declined to sanction the publication. His correspondence with Steevens, Malone, and other friends, shows ample traces of this quarrel, and of his dissatisfaction with Mr. Rose, whom he accuses of impertinently tampering with the Memoir. "I never," writes Malone to Percy, in corroboration of such complaints, "ob-"served any of those grimaces or fooleries "that the interpolator talks of!" "In "going over Goldsmith's life," writes Dr. Anderson to Percy, "I will thank you to "point out the particular passages which "were thrust into your narrative." Nichols's *Illustrations*, vii. 213. Substantially, however, the narrative doubtless remained in its leading details what it is stated to be in the advertisement, "com-"posed from the information of persons "who were intimate with the poet at an "early period, and who were honoured "with a continuance of his friendship till "the time" of his death. For proof of Percy's unceasing reference to it as the authentic account of Goldsmith, even after its interpolation by Rose, see Nichols's *Illustrations*, vii. 102, where he recommends it to Dr. Anderson's notice. In a letter to Mr. Nichols (*Illustrations*, vi. 584), Percy also expressly describes it as compiled under his direction. I refer to it throughout my volume, therefore, as the *Percy Memoir;* and in an Appendix to the second volume of this biography ("WHAT WAS PROPOSED AND WHAT WAS "DONE FOR THE RELATIVES OF GOLD-"SMITH"), I have entered more largely into the delays and disputes connected with its composition. It should be added that many of the materials for a life which Percy had obtained from Goldsmith himself, were lost by being intrusted to Johnson, when the latter proposed to be his friend's biographer; and some were lost by Percy himself. But the failure of Johnson's design arose less from his own dilatoriness than from a difficulty started by Francis Newbery's surviving partner (Carnan, the older New-

---

* The biographical preface, or Memoir, for which the materials had been collected by Percy, Malone, and other friends, was drawn up in the first instance by Percy's friend, Dr. Campbell; it then received ample correction from Percy, whose interlineations were engrafted into the text; but circumstances

Heralds! proclaim aloud! all saying,
See Æsop dancing, and his *Monkey*
　　playing. *

1738.
———
Æt. 10. Yet these things may stand for more than quick- ness of repartee. It is even possible that the secret might be found in them, of much in Goldsmith which has been harshly characterised as vanity. It may have been that; but it sprang from a source very sel- dom connected with any of the ordinary forms of personal con- ceit. Fielding describes a class of men who feed upon their own hearts; who are egotists, as he says, the wrong way; and if Gold- smith was vain, it was the wrong way. It arose, not from over- weening self-complacency in sup- posed advantages, but from what the world had forced him since his earliest youth to feel, intense uneasy consciousness of sup- posed defects. His resources of boyhood went as manhood came. There was no longer the cricket- match, the hornpipe, an active descent upon an orchard, or a game of fives or foot-ball, to purge unhealthy humours and "clear out the mind." There was no old dairy- 1738.
———
Æt. 10. maid, no Peggy Golden, to beguile childish sorrows, or, as he tells us in one of his essays, to sing him into pleasant tears with Johnny Armstrong's Last Good Night, or the Cruelty of Barbara Allen. It was his ardent wish, as he grew to manhood, to be on good terms with the society around him; and, finding it es- sential first of all to be on good terms with himself, he would have restored by fantastic dress and other innocent follies what his friends till then had done their best to banter him out of. It was to no purpose he made the attempt. So unwitting a con- trast to gentleness, simplicity, and an utter absence of disguise in his real nature, could but make an absurdity the mo.e. "Why, "what wouldst thou have, dear "Doctor!" said Johnson, laugh- ing at a squib in the *St. James's Chronicle* which had coupled him- self and his friend as the pedant and his flatterer in *Love's Labour's Lost*, and at which poor Gold- smith was fretting and foam- ing; "who the plague is hurt "with all this nonsense? and "how is a man the worse I won- "der, in his health, purse, or "character, for being called Ho- "lofernes?" "How you may re- "lish being called Holofernes," replied Goldsmith, "I do not "know; but I do not like at least

bery's son-in-law), who held the copy- right of *She Stoops to Conquer*, and who refused to join the other possessors of Goldsmith's writings in the "Edition and "Memoir" which Johnson had under- taken. "I know he intended to write "Goldsmith's Life," says Malone, "for I "collected some materials for it by his "desire."

* In proof that they missed, neverthe- less, the correct version of what they thought so clever, I have quoted the couplet as above (of which the first line is tamely given in the *Percy Memoir*, 5—
　　"Our herald hath proclaimed this
　　　　saying")
from Mr. Shaw Mason's *Statistical Ac- count*, III. 369.

"to play Goodman Dull."* It was the part he was set down for from the first, very much against his will.

1738.
———
Æt. 10. But were there not still the means, at the fireside of his good-hearted father, of returning these childish rebuffs to something of a wholesome discipline? Alas! little; there was little of worldly wisdom in the home circle of the kind but simple preacher, to make a profit of this worldly experience. "My "father's education," says the man in black, and no one ever doubted who sat for the portrait, "was above his fortune, and his "generosity greater than his "education. . . He told the story "of the ivy-tree, and that was "laughed at; he repeated the jest "of the two scholars and one "pair of breeches, and the com-"pany laughed at that; but the "story of Taffy in the sedan-"chair was sure to set the table "in a roar: thus his pleasure in-"creased in proportion to the "pleasure he gave; he loved all "the world, and he fancied all "the world loved him. As his "fortune was but small, he lived "up to the very extent of it: he "had no intentions of leaving his "children money, for that was "dross; he was resolved they "should have learning, for learn-"ing, he used to observe, was "better than silver or gold. For "this purpose he undertook to "instruct us himself; and took as

"much pains to form our morals "as to improve our understand-"ing. We were told, that uni-"versal benevolence was what "first cemented society; we were "taught to consider all the wants "of mankind as our own; to re-"gard the human face divine with "affection and esteem; he wound "us up to be mere machines of "pity, and rendered us incapable "of withstanding the slightest "impulse made either by real or "fictitious distress: in a word, "we were perfectly instructed in "the art of giving away thou-"sands, before we were taught "the more necessary qualifica-"tions of getting a farthing."*

Acquisitions highly primitive, and supporting what seems to have been the common fame of the Goldsmith race. "The Gold-"smiths were always a strange "family," confessed three different branches of them, in as many different quarters of Ireland, when inquiries were made by a recent biographer of the poet. "They rarely acted like "other people: their hearts were "always in the right place, but "their heads seemed to be "doing anything but what they "ought."** It is very commonly to be remarked, however, as to opinions or confessions of this kind, that if the heart's right place were better discriminated, the head itself might come to be more favourably regarded. Worthy Doctor Strean expressed

* Mrs. Piozzi's Anecdotes, (1786), 180, 181.

* Citizen of the World, xxvii.
** Prior, i. 101.

himself more correctly when Mr. Mangin was making his inquiries more than forty years ago. "Several of the family and "name," he said, "live near El- "phin, who, as well as the poet, "were and are remarkable for "their worth, but of no clever- "ness in the common affairs of "the world." *

If cleverness in the common affairs of the world is what the head should be always versed in, to be meditating what *it ought*, poor Oliver was a grave de- faulter. We are all of us related to chaos, more or less; and with him, to the last, much lay unre- deemed from its void. Sturdy boys who work a gallant way through school, are the picked men of their colleges, grow up to thriving eminence in their several callings, and found re- spectable families, are seldom troubled with this relationship till chaos reclaims them, and they die and are forgotten. All men have their advantages, and that is theirs. But it shows too great a pride in what they have, to put the whole world under penalties to possess it too, and to set up so many doleful lamen- tations over the poor, confused, erratic, Goldsmith nature. Their tone will not be taken here, the writer making no pretension to its moral dignity. Consideration will be had for the harsh lessons this boy so early and bitterly en- countered; it will not be for- gotten that feeling, not always

under right control or free from extravagance and excess,* must often of necessity be his who has a privilege by such means largely to diffuse it among others; and in the endea- vour to show that the heart of Oliver Goldsmith was in the best sense rightly placed, it may ap- pear that his head also profited by so good an example.

1738.
Æt. 10.

At the age of eleven he was removed from Mr. Griffin's, and put to a school of repute at Athlone, about five miles from his father's house, and kept by a reverend Mr. Camp- bell. **   At about the same time

1739.
Æt. 11.

* "A lad whose passions are not "strong enough in youth to mislead him "from that path of science which his "tutors, and not his inclination, have "chalked out, by four or five years' per- "severance probably obtains every ad- "vantage and honour his college can "bestow. I forget whether the simile has "been used before, but I would compare "the man whose youth has been thus "passed in the tranquillity of dispas- "sionate prudence, to liquors that never "ferment, and consequently continue al- "ways muddy. Passions may raise a "commotion in the youthful breast, but "they disturb only to refine it. How- "ever this be, mean talents are often "rewarded in colleges with an easy sub- "sistence." *Enquiry into the Present State of Polite Learning*, chap. x. So, too, in his *Life of Bolingbroke*, he excuses the youthful excesses and irregularities of the statesman by the remark that this period of his career might have been compared to that of fermentation in liquors, which grow muddy before they brighten; "but it must also be confessed "that those liquors which never ferment "are seldom clear." *Miscell. Works* (Ed. 1837), III. 383. The same observation (as usual with anything that is a favourite with him) again and again recurs in his various writings.

** *Percy Memoir*, 6.

* Mangin's *Essay*, 149.

his brother Henry went as a pensioner to Dublin University, and it was resolved that in due course Oliver should follow him: a determination, his sister told Doctor Percy, which had replaced that of putting him to a common trade * on those evidences of a certain liveliness of talent which had broken out at uncle John's being discussed among his relatives and friends. He remained at Athlone two years; and, when Mr. Campbell's ill-health obliged him to resign his charge, was removed to the school of Edgeworthstown kept by the reverend Patrick Hughes. Here he stayed more than three years, and was long remembered by the school acquaintance he formed; among whom were Mr. Beatty, Mr. Nugent, Mr. Roach, and Mr. Daly, to whom we are indebted for some traits of that early time. They recollected Mr. Hughes's special kindness to him, and "thinking well" of him, as matters not then to be accounted for.** The good

1741.
Æt. 13.

1743.
Æt. 15.

master, it appeared, had been Charles Goldsmith's friend. They dwelt upon his ugliness and awkward manners; they professed to recount even the studies he liked or disliked (*Ovid* as well as *Horace* he welcomed eagerly, hating *Cicero*, delighting in *Livy*, and finding in *Tacitus* a source of deeper interest);* they described his temper as ultra-sensitive, but added that though quick to take offence he was feverishly ready to forgive. They also said, that though at first diffident and backward in the extreme, he in time mustered sufficient boldness to take even a leader's place in the boyish sports, and particularly at fives or ball-playing.** Whenever an exploit was proposed or a trick was going forward, "*Noll* "*Goldsmith*" was certain to be in it; an actor or a victim.

Of his holidays, Ballymahon was the central attraction; and here too recollection was vivid and busy, as soon as his name grew famous. An old man who directed the sports of the place, and kept the ball-court in those

* "Oliver was his second son, and "born. very unexpectedly after an in-"terval of seven years from the birth of "the former child, and the liberal educa-"tion which their father was then be-"stowing on his eldest son bearing hard "upon his small income, he could only "propose to bring up Oliver to some "mercantile employment." Mrs. Hodson's narrative, in the *Percy Memoir*, 3. In the next page she adds, "he began at "so early a period to show signs of genius "that he quickly engaged the notice of "all the friends of the family, many of "whom were in the church."
** We learn from a note to Mrs. Hodson's narrative that Mr. Hughes conversed with him on a footing. very different from that of master and scholar. "This circumstance Dr. Goldsmith al-"ways mentioned with respect and gra-"titude." *Percy Memoir*, 6.

* It is less easy to believe what is added, that a reproof from his elder brother first turned his attention to style in writing; for that, having sent Henry some short and confused letters from school, he was told in reply that "If he "had but little to say, he should en-"deavour to say it well."
** Doctor Strean, in Mangin's *Essay*, 149, 150.

days, long subsisted on his stories of "Master Noll." The narrative masterpiece of this ancient Jack Fitzsimmons related to a raid or foray made upon the orchard of Tirlicken, by the youth and his companions.* Fitzsimmons also vouched to the reverend John Graham for the entire truth of the adventure so currently and confidently told by his Irish acquaintance which offers an agreeable relief to the excess of diffidence heretofore noted in him, and on which, if true, the leading incident of *She Stoops to Conquer* was founded.

1744. Æt. 16. At the close of his last holidays, then a lad of nearly seventeen, he left home for Edgeworthstown mounted on a borrowed hack which a friend was to restore to Lissoy, and with a guinea, store of unaccustomed wealth, in his pocket. The delicious taste of independence beguiled him to a loitering, lingering, pleasant enjoyment of the journey; and instead of finding himself under Mr. Hughes's roof at nightfall, night fell upon him some two or three miles out of the direct road, in the middle of the streets of Ardagh. But nothing could disconcert the owner of the guinea, who, with a lofty confident air, inquired of a person passing the way to the town's best house of entertainment. The man addressed was the wag of Ardagh, a humorous fencing-master, Mr. Cornelius Kelly, and the schoolboy swagger was irresistible provocation to a jest. Submissively he turned back with horse and rider till they came within a pace or two of the great Squire Featherston's, to which he respectfully pointed as the "best "house," of Ardagh. Oliver rang at the gate, gave his beast in charge with authoritative rigour, and was shown, as a supposed expected guest, into the comfortable parlour of the squire. Those were days when Irish innkeepers and Irish squires more nearly approximated than now; and Mr. Featherston, unlike the excellent but explosive Mr. Hardcastle, is said to have seen the mistake and humoured it. Oliver had a supper which gave him so much satisfaction, that he ordered a bottle of wine to follow; and the attentive landlord was not only forced to drink with him, but, with like familiar condescension, the wife and pretty daughter were invited to the supper-room. Going to bed, he stopped to give special instructions for a hot cake to breakfast; and it was not till he had dispatched this latter meal, and was regarding his guinea with a pathetic last look, that the truth was told him by the good-natured

1744. Æt. 16.

---

* "In this adventure," Mr. Graham writes, "which Jack detailed minutely, "both he and Oliver were engaged; de-"tection, however, either at the moment "or soon afterwards, ensued; and had it "not been for the respectability of Gold-"smith's connections, which secured im-"munity also to his companions, tho "consequences might have been unplea-"sant."

squire.* The late Sir Thomas Featherston, grandson to the supposed inn-keeper, had faith in the adventure; and told Mr. Graham that as his grandfather and Charles Goldsmith had been college acquaintance, it might the better be accounted for.**

1744.
Æt. 16.

It is certainly, if true, the earliest known instance of his disposition to swagger with a grand air which afterwards displayed itself in other forms, and strutted about in clothes noted rather for fineness than fitness.

CHAPTER II.

College.
1745—1749.

BUT the school-days of Oliver Goldsmith are now to close. Within the last year there had been some changes at Lissoy, which not a little affected the family fortunes. Catherine, the elder sister, had privately married a Mr. Daniel Hodson, "the son of a gentle-"man of good property, residing "at St. John's, near Athlone." The young man was at the time availing himself of Henry Goldsmith's services as private tutor; Henry having obtained a scholarship two years before', and as-

1745.
Æt. 17.

sisting the family resources with such employment of his college distinction. The good Charles Goldsmith was greatly indignant at the marriage, and on reproaches from the elder Hodson "made a sacrifice detrimental "to the interests of his family." He entered into a legal engagement, still registered in the Dublin Four Courts and bearing date the 7th of September 1744, "to pay to Daniel Hodson, Esq. "of St. John's, Roscommon, £400 "as the marriage portion of his "daughter Catherine, then the "wife of the said Daniel Hod-"son." But it could not be effected without sacrifice of his tithes and rented land; and it was a sacrifice, as it seems to me, made in a spirit of very simple and very false pride. The writer who discovered this marriage settlement attributes it to "the highest sense of honour;"* but it must surely be doubted if an act which, to elevate the pretensions of one child, and adapt them to those of the man she had married, inflicted beggary on the rest, should be so referred to. Oliver was the first to taste its bitterness. It was announced to him that he could not go to college as Henry had gone, a pensioner; but must consent to enter it, a sizar.

The first thing exacted of a sizar in those days (it has been altered since) was to give proof of classical attainments. He was to show himself, to a

---

* *Percy Memoir*, 6, 7.

** "The story," said Mr. Graham, at a public meeting in Ballymahon for a monument to the Poet (reported in the *Gent. Mag.* for 1820, xc. 620), "was con-"firmed to me by the late Sir Thomas "Featherston Bart. a short time before "his death."

* *Prior*, i. 49.

certain reasonable extent, a good scholar; in return for which, being clad in a black gown of coarse stuff without sleeves, he was marked with the servant's badge of a red cap, and put to the servant's offices of sweeping courts in the morning, carrying up dishes from the kitchen to the fellows' dining-table in the afternoon, and waiting in the hall till the fellows had dined. This, commons, teaching, and chambers, being on the other hand greatly reduced, is called by one of Goldsmith's biographers "one "of those judicious and con- "siderate, arrangements of the "founders of such institutions, "that gives to the less opulent "the opportunity of cultivating "learning at a trifling expense;"* but it is called by Goldsmith himself, in his *Enquiry into the Present State of Polite Learning,* ** a contradiction suggested by motives of pride and a passion which he thinks absurd, "that "men should be at once learning "the liberal arts, and at the same "time treated as slaves; at once "studying freedom and practis- "ing servitude."

To this contradiction he is now himself doomed; and that which to a stronger judgment and more determined purpose *** might have prompted only the struggle that triumphs over the meanest circumstance, proved to him the hardest lesson yet in his life's hard school. He re- sisted with all his strength; for little less than a whole year, it is said, he made a resolute stand against the new contempts and loss of worldly consideration thus bitterly set before him. He would rather have gone to the trade chalked out for him as his rough alternative,—when uncle Contarine interfered.

1745.
Æt. 17.

This was an excellent man; and with some means, though very far from considerable, to do justice to his kindly impulses. In youth he had been the college companion of Bishop Berkeley,* and was worthy to have had so divine a friend. He too was a clergyman; and held the living of Kilmore near Carrick-on-Shannon, which he afterwards changed to that of Oran near Roscommon; where he built the house of Emblemore, changed to that of Tempe by its subsequent possessor Mr. Edward Mills, Goldsmith's relative and contemporary. Mr. Contarine had married Charles

---

* *Prior,* i. 59.

** Chap. XIII. Johnson himself condemns the practice not less severely; and as pompously, on the other hand, Sir John Hawkins supports it.

*** Such judgment and purpose, for example, as animated Bishop Watson (Llandaff), who, himself a sizar at Cambridge exactly ten years after this date, thus writes in the *Anecdotes* of his Life:— "Perceiving that the sizars were not so "respectfully looked upon by the pen- "sioners and scholars of the house, as "they ought to have been, inasmuch as "the most learned and leading men in "the University have ever arisen from "that order, I offered myself for a "scholarship a year before the usual "time of the sizars sitting, and suc- "ceeded, &c., &c."

* See note to *Percy Memoir,* 17. 18.

Goldsmith's sister (who died at about this time, leaving one child), and was the only member of the Goldsmith family of whom we have solid evidence that he at any time took pains with Oliver, or felt anything like a real pride in him. He bore the greater part of his school expenses;* and was used to receive him with delight in holidays, as the playfellow of his daughter Jane, a year or two older than Oliver, and some seven years after this married to a Mr. Lawder. How little the most charitable of men will make allowance for differences of temper and disposition in the education of youth, is too well known: Mr. Contarine told Oliver that he had himself been a sizar, and that it had not availed to withhold from *him* the friendship of the great and the good.

His counsel prevailed. The youth went to Dublin, showed by passing the necessary examination that his time at school had not been altogether thrown away, and on the 11th of June 1745 was admitted, last in the list of eight who so presented themselves, a sizar of Trinity College;**—

there most speedily to learn that experience, which, on his elder brother afterwards consulting him as to the education of his son, prompted him to answer thus: "If he has ambition, strong "passions, and an exquisite sen- "sibility of contempt, do not "send him to your college, unless "you have no other trade for him "except your own."*

Flood was then in the college, and being some years younger than Goldsmith, and a fellow commoner, it is not surprising that they should have held no intercourse; but a greater than Flood, though himself little notable at college, said he perfectly recollected his old fellow-student when they afterwards met at the house of Mr. Reynolds. Not that there was much for an Edmund Burke to recollect of him. Little went well with Goldsmith in his student course. He had a menial position, a learned savage for his tutor, and few inclinations to the study exacted. He was not indeed, as perhaps never living creature in this world was, without his consolations; he could sing a song well, and, at a new insult or outrage, could blow off excitement through his flute with a kind of desperate "mechanical "vehemence." At the worst he had, as he describes it himself, a "knack at hoping;" and at all times, it must with equal cer-

* "The Rev. Mr. Greene," the son of the rector of Kilkenny West, "also "liberally assisted, as Dr. Goldsmith "used to relate, in this beneficent pur- "pose." *Percy Memoir*, 6.

** *Percy Memoir*, 14, 15. "His being ad- "mitted a sizar in Trinity College, "Dublin, at that early age, denotes a re- "markable proficiency. Sizars there are "expected to come better prepared than "other boys, and therefore usually apply "for admission somewhat later in life." A

sizarship might in other words be called an inferior scholarship, disposed of in like manner to the best answerer.

* See *post*, Book II. Chap. v.

tainty be affirmed, a knack at getting into scrapes. Like Samuel Johnson at Oxford, he avoided lectures when he could, and was a lounger at the college gate.* The popular picture of him in these Dublin University days is little more than of a slow, hesitating, somewhat hollow voice, heard seldom and always to great disadvantage in the class-rooms; and of a low-sized, thick, robust, ungainly figure, lounging about the college courts on the wait for misery and ill-luck.

His Edgeworthstown schoolfellow, Beatty, had entered among the sizars with him, and for a time shared his rooms. They were the top-rooms adjoining the library of a building numbered 35, where might be seen, until the building itself was taken down, the name of Oliver Goldsmith scratched by himself upon a window-pane. Visible still indeed is the actual piece of glass, on which, with the name, appears the date of "March "1746;" for I saw it not long ago, when the University did me the honour to make me one of its doctors of laws, framed and placed in the manuscript room of the college library. Marshall, also a sizar, is said to have been another of Oliver's chums. Among his occasional associates, were certainly Edward Mills, his relative; Robert Bryanton, a Ballymahon youth, also his relative, of whom he was fond; Charles

1746. Æt. 18.

and Edward Purdon, whom he lived to befriend; James Willington, whose name he afterwards in London had permission to use for low literary work he was ashamed to put his own to;* Wilson ** and Kearney, subsequently doctors and fellows of the college; Wolfen, also well known; *** and Lauchlan Macleane, whose political pamphlets, unaccepted challenge to Wilkes, and general party exertions made a noise in the world twenty or thirty years later. When a man becomes famous it is to be expected that wonderful feats of memory should be performed respecting him; but it seems tolerably evident that, with the exception of perhaps Bryanton and Beatty, not one owner of the names recounted had ever put himself in friendly relation with the sizar, to cheer or help him on. Richard Malone, afterwards Lord Sunderlin, Barnard and Marlay, afterwards worthy bishops of Killaloe and Waterford; found nothing more pleasant than to talk of "their "old fellow-collegian Doctor "Goldsmith," in the painting-room of Reynolds: but nothing I suspect more difficult, thriving lads as they were in even these

1746. Æt. 18.

---

* See *post*, Book II. Chap. II.

** Wilson communicated to Malone the various entries to be found respecting him.

*** Wolfen told Dr. Percy that translations from the classics occasionally made by his fellow-student at this period were long remembered by his contemporaries with applause. *Percy Memoir,* 16, 17.

* *Percy Memoir,* p. 19.

earlier days, than to vouchsafe recognition to the unthriving, depressed, insulted Oliver.*

1747.
Æt. 19.

A year and a half after he had entered college, at the commencement of 1747, his father suddenly died. The scanty sums required for his support had been often intercepted, but this stopped them altogether. It may have been the suffering incident to that sorrow for which he cared the least, but "squalid "poverty," relieved by occasional gifts according to his small means from uncle Contarine, by petty loans from Bryanton or Beatty, or by desperate pawning of his books of study, was Goldsmith's lot thenceforward. Yet even in depths like these arose the consciousness of faculties reserved for better fortune than continual contempt and failure. He would write street-ballads to save himself from actual starving; sell them at the Reindeer repository in Mountrath-court for five shillings a-piece; and steal out of the college at night to hear them sung.**

* "When he had got high in fame," said Johnson to Boswell, "one of his "friends began to recollect something of "his being distinguished at college. Gold-"smith in the same manner recollected "more of that friend's early years, as he "grew a greater man," *Boswell*, vi. 310. This, we must admit, is the general rule. Barnard, Dean of Derry, who held the bishoprics successively of Killaloe and Limerick, and who was upwards of eighty when he died at Wimbledon in 1806, will frequently appear in these pages. Marlay became bishop of Waterford, and is described by Malone as an amiable, benevolent, and ingenious man.
** *Prior*, i. 75.

Happy night, worth all the dreary days! Hidden by some dusky wall, or creeping within darkling shadows of the ill-lighted streets, the poor neglected sizar watched and waited there, lingering and listening, for the only effort of his life that had not wholly failed. Few and dull perhaps the beggar's audience at first, but more thronging, eager, and delighted, as he shouted his newly-gotten ware. Cracked enough, I doubt not, were those ballad-singing tones; very harsh, extremely discordant, and passing from loud to low without meaning or melody; but not the less fell with them on the ear of Goldsmith the sweetest music that this earth affords. Gentle faces pleased, old men stopping by the way, young lads venturing a purchase with their last remaining farthing; why, here was a world in little, with its fame at the sizar's feet! "The greater "world will be listening one "day" perhaps he muttered, as he turned with a lighter heart to his dull home.

It is said to have been a rare occurrence when the five shillings of the Reindeer repository reached home along with him. It was more likely, when he was at his utmost need, to stop with some beggar on the road who had seemed to him more destitute even than himself. Nor this only. The money gone, he had often, for the naked shivering wretch, slipped off a portion of the scanty clothes he wore, to patch a misery he could not otherwise relieve. To one starving creature, with five crying children, he gave at one time the blankets off his bed, and crept himself into the ticking for shelter from the cold. For this anecdote Mr. Edward Mills, Goldsmith's relative and fellow-student, is the authority. He occasionally furnished Oliver, when in college, with small supplies, and gave him a breakfast now and then; for which kindly purpose having gone to call him one morning, Goldsmith's voice from within his own room shouted out that he was a prisoner, and they must force the door to help him out. Mills did this; and found him so fastened in the ticking of his bed, into which he had taken shelter from the cold, that he could not escape unassisted. Late on the previous winter night, unable otherwise to relieve a woman and her five children who seemed all perishing with cold, he had brought out his blankets to the college-gate and given them to her.

It is not meant to insist on these things as examples of conduct. "Sensibility is not Bene-"volence;" nor will this kind of agonised sympathy with distress, even when graced by that active self-denial of which there is here small proof, supply the solid duties or satisfactions of ·life. There are distresses, vast and remote, with which it behoves us still more to sympathise than with those, less really terrible,

which only more attract us by intruding on our senses; and the conscience is too apt to discharge itself of the greater duty by instant and easy attention to the less. Let me observe also, that, in the case of a man dependent on others, the title to such enjoyment as this largeness and looseness of sympathy involves, has very obvious and controlling limits. So much it is right to interpose when anecdotes of this description are told. To Goldsmith, all the circumstances considered, they are really very creditable; and it is well to recollect them when the "neglected opportunities" of his youth are spoken of. Doubtless there were better things to be done, by a man of stronger purpose. But the nature of men is not different from that of other living creatures; it gives the temper and disposition, but not the nurture or culture. These Goldsmith never rightly had, except in such sort as he could himself provide; and now, assuredly, he had not found them in his college. "That strong steady "disposition which alone makes "men great," he avowed himself deficient in:* but were other dispositions not worth the caring for? "His imagination might "have been too warm to relish "the cold logic of Burgersdicius, "or the dreary subtleties of "Smiglesius:"** but with no-

1747. ———— Æt. 19.

---

* See *post*, Book II. Chap. IV. Letter to his brother-in-law Hodson.

** Such is his remark, with probable

thing less cold or dreary might a warm imagination have been cherished? When, in after years 1747. Æt. 19. at the house of Burke, he talked these matters over with Edmund Malone, he said that though he made no great figure in mathematics, which was a study in much repute there, he could turn an ode of Horace into English better than any of them.* His tutor, Mr. Theaker Wilder, thought him fitter to turn a lathe.

This tutor, this reverend instructor of youth, was the same who, on one occasion in Dublin streets, sprang at a bound from the pavement on a hackney-coach which was passing at its swiftest pace, and felled to the ground the driver who had accidentally touched his face with the whip. So, mathematics being Mr. Theaker Wilder's intellectual passion, the same strength, agility, and ferocity which drove him into brawls with hackney-coachmen, he carried to the demonstrations of Euclid; and for this, all his life afterwards, even more than poet Gray, did poor Goldsmith wage war with mathematics.**

Never had he stood up in his class that this learned savage did not insult him. Having a comic as well as tragic side, and such wit as he possessed being part of his malice, Mr. Wilder made for himself continual mirth out of the misery he occasioned to this awkward, ugly, "ignorant," most sensitive young man.*

reference to himself, on Parnell's want of success at Dublin University. *Miscellaneous Works*, iii. 358. See also the seventeenth of his *Essays* (on a Taste for the Belles Lettres), in which he contrasts Swift's failure at college with his success in after-life.

* *Boswell*, ii. 189. Watkins's *Anecdotes of Men of Learning and Genius*, 513.

** Gray, while yet as young as Goldsmith, complained from Cambridge to West in much the same language that Goldsmith might have employed in Dublin, if at this early time of life he had been blessed with such a friend. All the letter is good, but I quote only a line or two:—"It is very possible that two and "two make four, but I would not give "four farthings to demonstrate this ever "so clearly; and if these be the profits of "life, give me the amusements of it. The "people I behold all around me, it seems, "know all this and more, and yet I do "not know one of them who inspires me "with any ambition of being like him." *Works*, Ed. Mitford (1835), ii. 7—9. "Gray "regretted his want of mathematical "knowledge," says Norton Nicholls, "yet "he would never allow that it was neces- "sary, in order to form the mind to a "habit of reasoning or attention. Does "not Locke require as much attention as "Euclid?" *Works*, v. 52. On the other hand, Goldsmith has taken occasion to put into the mouth of the Man in Black a wiser explanation than he gave in talking to friends of his own early dislike of mathematics, and this I will presently quote. In his *Enquiry* he characterizes them as too much studied at our universities, and "a science to which the meanest "intellects are equal." Chap. xii.

* "Theaker Wilder, a man of the most "morose and merciless temper, thence- "forth persecuted him with unremitting "cruelty, especially at the quarterly ex- "aminations, when he would insult him "before his fellow-students by sarcastic "taunts and ironical applauses of the "severest malignity." *Percy Memoir*, 15. "He was a younger son," says Mr. Shaw Mason, "of the family of Castle Wilder, "in the county of Longford." *Statistical Account*, iii. 357. "I well remember," writes Dr. Wilson to Malone, "for he "was in the class below me, that his "tutor (Wilder), examining him in the "Sen. Soph. Class, commenced his judg-

There came to be no limit or pause to the strife between them. The tutor's brutality rose even to personal violence; the pupil's shame and resentment hardened into reckless idleness; and the college career of Oliver Goldsmith was a proclaimed, and wretched failure.

Let us be thankful that it was no worse, and that participation in a college riot was after all the gravest of his college crimes. Twice indeed he was cautioned for neglecting even his Greek lecture, but he was also thrice commended for diligence in attending it, and Doctor Kearney said he once got a prize at a Christmas examination in classics. The latter seems doubtful; but at any rate the college riot was the worst to allege against him, and in this there was no very active sin. A scholar had been arrested, though the precincts of the university had always been held privileged from the intrusion of bailiffs, and the students resolved to take rough revenge. It was in the summer of 1747. They explored every bailiff's den in Dublin, found the offender by whom the arrest was made, brought him naked to the college pump, washed his delinquency thoroughly out of him; and were so elated with the triumph, and everything that bore affinity to law, restraint, or authority looked so ludicrous in the person of this drenched bailiff's-runner, their miserable representative, that it was on the spot proposed to consummate and crown success by breaking open Newgate, and making a general jail delivery. The Black Dog, as the prison was called, stood on the feeblest of legs, and with one small piece of artillery must have gone down for ever; but the cannon was with the constable, the assailants were repulsed, and some townsmen attracted by the fray unhappily lost their lives. Five of the ringleaders were discovered, and expelled the college; and among five lesser offenders who were publicly admonished for being present aiding and abetting,* the name of Oliver Goldsmith occurs.

1747.
Æt. 19.

More galled by formal University admonition than by Wilder's insults, and anxious to wipe out a disgrace that seemed not so undeserved, Goldsmith tried in the next month for a scholarship. He lost the scholarship, but gained an exhibition:** a

---

"ments with a *Mole*, and concluded them "with a *Fable Rene*. 'Twas a mistake that "the good tutor often fell into, to think "he was witty when he was simply mali- "cious." Wilder published in 1768, when he was D.D. and a senior fellow, an elaborate edition of Sir Isaac Newton's *Universal Arithmetic*, in the preface to which, expressing likes and dislikes in a characteristically peremptory way, he describes himself as having been appointed, when a junior fellow, to succeed Mr. Maguire as "teacher of the "mathematicks to the undergraduates of "the university." See *post*, Book III. Chap. VI.

* "Quod seditioni favisset et tumul- "tuantibus opem tulisset." See *Percy Memoir*, 16.

** *Percy Memoir*, 16.

very small exhibition truly, worth some thirty shillings, of which there were nineteen in number and his was seventeenth in the list. In the way of honour or glory this was trifling enough; but, little used to anything in the shape of even such a success, he let loose his unaccustomed joy in a dancing party of the humblest description at his rooms, which had more of tragical than trifling issue.

Wilder heard of the affront to discipline, suddenly showed himself in the middle of the festivity, and knocked down the poor triumphant exhibitioner. [*] It seemed an irretrievable disgrace. Goldsmith sold his books next day, scraped together a small sum, ran away from college, lingered fearfully about Dublin till his money was spent, and then with a shilling in his pocket set out for Cork. He did not know where he would have gone, he said, but he thought of America. For three days he lived upon the shilling; parted by degrees with nearly all his clothes to save himself from famine; and long afterwards told Reynolds, what his sister relates in her narrative, that of all the exquisite meals he had ever tasted the most delicious was a handful of grey peas given him by a girl at a wake after twenty-four hours' fasting. [**] The vision of America sank before this reality, and he turned his feeble steps to Lissoy. His brother had private intimation of his state, went to him, clothed him, and carried him back to college. "Something of a reconciliation," says Mrs. Hodson, was effected with the tutor.

Probably the tutor made so much concession as to promise not to strike him to the ground again; for certainly no other improvement is on record. An anecdote, "often told in conver-"sation" to Bishop Percy, exhibits the sizar at his usual disadvantage. Wilder called on Goldsmith, at a lecture, to explain the centre of gravity; which, on getting no answer, he proceeded himself to explain: calling out harshly to Oliver at the close, "Now, blockhead, where "is *your* centre of gravity?" The answer, which was delivered in a slow, stammering, hollow voice, and began "Why, Doctor, by "your definition, I think it must "be" — disturbed every one's centre of gravity in the lecture room; and, turning the laugh against Wilder, *turned down* poor Oliver. [*] And so the insults, the merciless jests, the "Oliver Goldsmith turned "down," continue as before. We still trace him less by his fame in the class-room than by his fines in the buttery-book. The

*1747.
Æt. 19.*

*1748.
Æt. 20.*

---

[*] *Percy Memoir*, 7, 8. For later news of Dr. Wilder see *post*, Book III. Chap. vi.
[**] *Ibid*, 5.

[*] Mr. Prior found the latter brief record duly entered under the date of May 9, 1748, on consulting the senior lecturer's book in Dublin University. I. 90.

only change is in that greater submission of the victim which marks unsuccessful rebellion. He offers no resistance; makes no effort of any kind; sits, for the most part, indulging day-dreams. A Greek *Scapula* has been identified * which he used at this time, scrawled over with his writing. "Free. Oliver Goldsmith;" "I promise to pay, &c. Oliver "Goldsmith;" * are among the autograph's musing shapes. Perhaps one half the day he was with Steele or Addison in parliament; perhaps the other half in prison with Collins or with Fielding. We should be thankful, as I have said, that a time so dreary and dark bore no worse fruit than this. The shadow cast over his spirit, the uneasy sense of disadvantage which obscured his manners in later years, affected himself singly; but how many they are whom such suffering, and such idleness, would have wholly and for ever corrupted. **

Spirits hardly less generous, cheerful, or self-supported than Goldsmith's, have been broken by them utterly.

He took his degree of $\frac{1749.}{\textit{Æt. 21.}}$ bachelor of arts on the 27th February, 1749; * and, as his name stood lowest in the list of sizars with whom he was originally admitted, so it stands also lowest in a list still existing of the graduates who passed on the same day and became thereby entitled to use the college library. ** It would yet be needless to recount the names that appear above his, for the public merits of their owners ended with their college course, and oblivion has received them. Nor does the low position of his name indicate necessarily his place in the examination; it being then the

---

* *Prior*, I. 94.

** Who can possibly doubt the original from whom the man in black's experiences were taken? *Citizen of the World*, XXVII. "The first opportunity he "[my father] had of finding his expectations disappointed, was in the middling "figure I made at the university; he had "flattered himself that he should soon see "me rising into the foremost rank in "literary reputation, but was mortified "to find me utterly unnoticed and unknown. His disappointment might have "been partly ascribed to his having over-"rated my talents, and partly to my dislike of mathematical reasonings at a time "when my imagination and memory, yet "unsatisfied, were more eager after new "objects than desirous of reasoning upon "those I knew. This, however, did not "please my tutor, who observed indeed "that I was a little dull; but at the same "time allowed that I seemed to be very "goodnatured, and had no harm in "me."

* *Percy Memoir*, 17.

** Shaw Mason's *Statistical Account*, III. 358. "Feb. 27, 1749, he was admitted "bachelor of arts, two years after the re-"gular time. In the roll of those quali-"fied for admission to the college library, "it appears that Oliver Goldsmith took "the oaths necessary to those who desire "that privilege. The time for this is im-"mediately after obtaining the degree of "bachelor of arts." Mr. Shaw Mason's reference to the date of the degree as "two years after the regular time," would imply that the date 1749 was in reality (computing the opening of the year, as was usual then and for a little while longer, from the 25th of March) 1750. But as the error in the text, if it be one, involves nothing more material than a slight shortening of the interval of idleness that follows, I leave it as originally written.

usage to regulate the mere college standing of a student through the whole of his course, by his position obtained at starting. But be this as it might, Mr. Wilder and his pupil now parted for ever: and when the friend of Burke, Johnson, and Reynolds heard in later years the name of his college tyrant, a violent death had overtaken him in a disreputable brawl. *

1749.
—
Æt. 21.

CHAPTER III.

Three Years of Idleness.
1719—1752.

GOLDSMITH returned to his mother's house. There were great changes. She had removed, in her straitened circumstances, to a cottage at Ballymahon, "situated "on the entrance to Ballymahon "from the Edgeworthstown-road "on the left-hand side." ** His brother Henry had gone back to his father's little parsonage house at Pallas; and, with his father's old pittance of forty pounds a year, was serving as curate to the living of Kilkenny-west, and was master of the village school, which after shifting about not a little had become ultimately fixed at Lissoy. His eldest sister, Mrs. Hodson, for whom the sacrifice was made that impoverished the family resources, was mistress of the old and better Lissoy parsonage house in which his father had lived his latter life. All en-

treated Oliver to qualify himself for orders; and when they joined uncle Contarine's request, his own objection was withdrawn. But he is only twenty-one; he must wait two years; and they are passed at Ballymahon.

It is the sunny time between two dismal periods of his life. He has escaped one scene of misery; another is awaiting him; and what possibilities of happiness lie in the interval, it is his nature to seize and make the most of. He assists his brother Henry in the school; runs household errands for his mother, as if he were still what the village gossips called him, "Master "Noll;" * brings her green tea by the ounce, the half-ounce, and the quarter-ounce, for which the charges respectively are sevenpence, threepence-halfpenny, and

* I subjoin a curious passage from Mr. Shaw Mason's volume already quoted, in which what appears to be a misstatement of dates is either to be explained by supposing that the entries as to "Master "Noll" refer to a period before the family had removed from Lissoy, or by the suggestion in the text that the young bachelor of arts still ran the errands of his boyhood, and retained its familiar name. "The writer of this account pur- "chased some old books a few years ago, "at an auction in Ballymahon; and "among them an account-book, kept by "a Mrs. Edwards, and a Miss Sarah "Shore, who lived in the next house to "Mrs. Goldsmith. In this village record, "were several shop accounts from the "year 1740 to 1756. Some of the entries "in the earliest of those accounts ran "thus;—'Ten by Master Noll—Cash by "'ditto;'—from which it appears, that "the young poet was then perhaps his "mother's only messenger. One of the "accounts, in 1756, may be considered a "statistical curiosity, ascertaining the

* Prior, i. 67-8.
** Shaw Mason's *Statistical Account*, iii. 357.

twopence; writes scraps of verse to please his uncle Contarine; and, to please himself, gets cousin Bryanton and Tony Lumpkins of the district, with wandering bear-leaders of genteeler sort, to meet at an old inn by his mother's house, and be a club for story-telling, for an occasional game of whist, and for the singing of songs. First in these accomplishments, great at Latin quotations, as admirer of happy human faces greatest of all,—Oliver presides. Cousin Bryanton had seen his disgrace in college, and thinks this a triumph indeed. So seems it to the hero of the triumph, on whose taste and manners, still only forming as yet in these sudden and odd extremes, many an amusing shade of contrast must have fallen in after-life from the storms of Wilder's class-room and the sunshine of George Conway's inn.

Thus the two years passed. In the day-time occupied, as I have said, in the village school; on the winter nights, at Conway's; and, in the evenings of summer, taking solitary walks among the rocks and wooded islands of the Inny, strolling up its banks to fish or play the flute, otter-hunting by the course of the Shannon,* learning French from the Irish priests, or winning a prize for throwing the sledge-hammer at the fair of Ballymahon.** "A lady who "died lately in this neighbour-"hood, and who was well ac-"quainted with Mrs. Goldsmith, "mentioned that it was one of "Oliver's habits to sit in a win-"dow of his mother's lodgings, "and amuse himself by playing "the flute."***

1749.
Æt. 21.

Two sunny years, with sorrowful affection long remembered;† storing up his mind with many a thought and fancy turned to profitable use in after-life; but

* In the *Animated Nature*, after giving Buffon's description of the otter coupling in winter and bringing forth in the beginning of spring, he adds: "It is cer-"tainly different with us, for its young "are never found till the latter end of "summer; and I have frequently, when a "boy, discovered their retreats, and pur-"sued them at that season." III. 240. A curious account follows of his personal experience as to their being trained for hunting fish. 242-3.

** "A blacksmith, who boasted to the "rev. Mr. Handcock of having taught him "the art, still survived about the year "1787." *Prior*, I. 116.

*** *Shaw Mason*, III. 358.

† "Those who have walked in an even-"ing by the sedgy sides of unfrequented "rivers, must remember a variety of "notes from different water-fowl; the "loud scream of the wild goose, the "croaking of the mallard, the whining of "the lapwing, and the tremulous neigh-"ing of the jack snipe. But of all these "sounds, there is none so dismally hol-"low as the booming of the bittern . . . I

"use and price of green tea in this part "of the country, sixty years ago." (Mr. Mason wrote in 1818.)

"Mrs. Goldsmith, to Sarah Shore, *Dr.*
"Brought forward . . . . 15s. 5d.
"Jan. 16, Half an ounce of
  "green tea 0 3½
"A quarter of a pound of
  "lump sugar 0 3
"A pound of Jamaica sugar . 0 8
"An ounce of green tea . . . 0 7
"Half a pound of rice. 0 2
"A quarter of an ounce of
  "green tea . . . . 0 2."
        Statistical Account, III. 358.

hardly better than his college course to help him through the world. So much even occurred to himself when eight years were gone, and, in the outset of his London distresses, he turned back with wistful looks to Ireland. "Un-"accountable fondness for coun-"try, this *Maladie du Pais*, as the "French call it!" he exclaimed, writing to his brother-in-law Hodson. "Unaccountable that he "should still have an affection "for a place who never received "when in it above common civi-"lity; who never brought any-"thing out of it except his brogue "and his blunders. Surely my "affection is equally ridiculous "with the Scotchman's, who re-"fused to be cured of the itch "because it made him unco' "thoughtful of his wife and bonny "Inverary. But to be serious, "let me ask myself what gives "me a wish to see Ireland again? "The country is a fine one per-"haps? No. There are good "company in Ireland? No. The "conversation there is generally "made up of a smutty toast or a "bawdy song; the vivacity sup-"ported by some humble cousin, "who has just folly enough to "earn his dinner. Then perhaps "there's more wit and learning "among the Irish? Oh, lord!

1749
Æt. 21.

"no! There has been more "money spent in the encourage-"ment of the Padareen mare "there one season, than given in "rewards to learned men since "the times of Usher. All their "productions in learning amount "to perhaps a translation, or a "few tracts in divinity; and all "their productions in wit, to just "nothing at all. Why the plague "then so fond of Ireland? Then "all at once, because you, my "dear friend, and a few more, "who are exceptions to the "general picture, have a re-"sidence there. This it is that "gives me all the pangs I feel in "separation. I confess I carry "this spirit sometimes to the "souring the pleasures I at pre-"sent possess." *

But perhaps the secret escaped without his knowledge, when, in that same year, he was writing to a more intimate friend. "I "have disappointed your neg-"lect," he said to Bryanton, "by "frequently thinking of you. "Every day do I remember the "calm anecdotes of your life, "from the fireside to the easy "chair; recal the various adven-"tures that first cemented our "friendship, the school, the col-"lege, or the tavern; pre-"side in fancy over your "cards, and am displeased "at your bad play when the "rubber goes against you, though "not with all that agony of soul "as when I once was your

1750
Æt. 22.

"remember in the place where I was a "boy, with what terror this bird's note "affected the whole village." *Animated Nature*, (Ed. 1816) iv. 316-18.
  "Among thy glades, a solitary guest,
  "The hollow sounding bittern guards
    "Its nest."   *Deserted Village*.

* *Percy Memoir*, 42, 43. The rest of the letter is printed *post*, Book II. Chap. ii.

"partner." *   Let the truth then be confessed; and that it was the careless idleness of fireside and easy chair, that it was the tavern excitement of the game at cards, to which Goldsmith so wistfully looked back from those first hard London struggles.

It is not an example I would wish to inculcate; nor is this narrative written with that purpose. To try such a process for the chance of another Goldsmith would be a dangerous attempt. The truth is always to be kept in view, that genius, representing the health as well as victory of the mind, is in no respect allied to these weaknesses, although, when unhappily connected with them, it is itself a means to avert their most evil consequence. Of the associates of Goldsmith in these happy, careless years, perhaps not one emerged to better fortune, and many sank to infinitely worse. "Pray give my love to Bob "Bryanton, and entreat him from "me not to drink," is a passage from one of his later letters to his brother Henry.** The habit of drinking he never suffered to overmaster himself; if the love of gaming to some extent continued, it led at least to many thoughts that may have saved others from like temptation;***

and if these irregular early years unsettled him for the pursuits his friends would have had him follow, and sent him wandering, with no pursuit, to mix among the poor and happy of other lands, it is very certain that he brought back some secrets both of poverty and happiness which were worth the finding, and, having paid for his errors by infinite personal privation, turned all the rest to the comfort and instruction of the world. There is a providence that shapes our ends, rough-hew them how we will; and to charming issues did the providence of Goldsmith's genius shape these rough-hewn times. What it received in mortification or grief, it gave back in cheerful humour or whimsical warning. It was not alone that it made him wise enough to know what infirmities he had, but it gave him the rarer wisdom of turning them to entertainment and to profit. Through the pains and obstructions of his childhood, through the uneasy failures of his youth, through the desperate struggles of his manhood, it lighted him to those last uses of experience and suffering which have given him an immortal name.

Let it be observed, too, that this Ballymahon idleness could lay claim to a certain activity in one

1750.
ÆT. 22.

---

* See *post*, Book II. Chap. III.

** See *post*, Book II. Chap. V.

*** "If it were necessary that practice "square with precept, our monitors "would be but few. The conduct of the "individual can affect but a small circle "beyond himself; the permanent good or "evil that he works to others lies rather "in the sentiments he can diffuse. His "acts are limited and momentary; his "sentiments may pervade the universe, "and inspire generations till the day of "doom." Lord Lytton's *Zanoni*.

respect. It was always cheerful; and this is no unimportant part of education, if heart and head are to go together. "Rely upon it, sir," said Johnson to Boswell, "viva- "city is much an art, and de- "pends greatly on habit."* Nor in this view will it be other than well with many of us when habits of cheerfulness are as much inculcated as habits of study; and when the foolish argument will be heard no longer, that these things, being in nature's charge, may be left exclusively to her. Nature in all things asks help and culture, and to their solicitation will reveal what might otherwise perish unknown. It was an acute remark of Goldsmith's, in respect to literary efforts, that the habit of writing will give a man justness of thinking; and that he may get from it a mastery of manner, which holiday writers, though with ten times his genius, will find it difficult to equal.** It is the same in temper as in mind: habit comes in aid of all deficiencies. The reader may be therefore not unprepared to find, as well in these sunny Irish years, as in other parts of the apparently vagrant and idle career to be now described, some points of even general beneficial example.

The two years are passed; and Oliver must apply for orders. "For the clerical profession," says Mrs. Hodson, "he had no "liking." It is not very wonder-

ful; after having seen, in his father and his brother, how much learning and labour were rewarded in the church by forty pounds a year. But he had yet another, and to him perhaps a stronger motive; though I do not know if it has not been brought against him as an imputation of mere vanity or simplicity, that he once said, "he did not deem himself good "enough for it." His friends, however, though not so resolutely as at first, still advised him to the family profession. "Our friends," says the man in black, "always "advise, when they begin to de- "spise us." He made application to the Bishop of Elphin, and was refused; sent back as he went; in short, plucked: but the story is told in various ways, and it is hard to get at the truth. His sister says that his youth was the objection; while it was a tradition "in the diocese" that either Mr. Theaker Wilder had given the bishop an exaggerated report of his college irregularities, or (which is more likely, and indeed is the only reasonable account of the affair) that he had neglected the preliminary professional studies. Doctor Strean on the other hand fully believed, from rumours he picked up, that "Mr. Noll's" offence was the having presented himself before his right reverence in scarlet breeches;* and if this last reason

---

* *Life,* vi. 95.

** See *post,* Book II. Chap. iv.

* Mangin's *Essay,* 150. "To be obliged," says the man in black, "to wear a long "wig when I liked a short one, or a black

be the true one, it is certainly our first ominous experience of that misplaced personal finery which is to find reiterated mention in this veritable history. In truth, however, the rejection is the only absolute certainty. The man in black, it will be remembered, undergoes something of the same kind, remarking, "my "friends were now perfectly satis- "fied I was undone; and yet "they thought it a pity, for one "that had not the least harm in "him, and was so very good- "natured."

Uncle Contarine, however, was far from thinking this. He found a gentleman of his county, a Mr. Flinn, in want of a tutor, and re-commended Oliver. The en-gagement continued for a year, and ended, as it might have been easy to anticipate, unsatisfac-torily. His talent for card-play-ing as well as for teaching is said to have been put in requisi-tion by Mr. Flinn; and the separa-tion took place on Goldsmith's accusing one of the family of un-fair play.* But when he left this excellent Irish family and returned to Ballymahon, he had thirty pounds in his pocket, it is to be hoped the produce of fairer play; and was undisputed owner of a good plump horse. Within

a few days, so furnished and mounted, he again left his mo-ther's house (where, truth to say, things do not by this time seem to have been made $\frac{1751.}{\text{Æt. 23.}}$ very comfortable to him), and started for Cork, with an-other floating vision of America. He returned in six weeks, with nothing in his pocket, and on a lean beast to which he had given the name of Fiddleback. The nature of his reception at Bally-mahon appears from the simple remark he is said to have made to his mother. "And now, my "dear mother, after having "struggled so hard to come home "to you, I wonder you are not "more rejoiced to see me." *

He afterwards addressed a clever though somewhat cavalier letter to her from his brother's house; which is open to the ob-jection that no copy exists in his handwriting, but which has great internal evidence of his facility, grace, and humour. Nor is there anything more signally worth re-mark in connection with the vagabond vicissitudes to be re-corded in these pages, than that, out of all the accidents which befell the man, the poverty he had to undergo, the companions with whom he associated, the sordid necessities that lead so often unavoidably into miry ways, no single speck or stain ever fell

"coat when I generally dressed in brown, "I thought was such a restraint upon my "liberty that I absolutely rejected the "proposal ... I rejected a life of luxury, "indolence, and ease, from no other "consideration but that boyish one of "dress." *Citizen of the World*, xxvn.

* Mrs. Hodson's narrative in the *Percy Memoir*, 9. And see *Prior*, i. 118.

* "His mother," says Mrs. Hodson, "as might be expected, was highly of-"fended; but his brothers and sisters "had contrived to meet him there, and at "length effected a reconciliation." *Percy Memoir*, 9.

on that enchanting beauty of style. Wherever he might be, or with whatever clowns for play-fellows; in the tavern, in the garret, or among citizens in the Sunday gardens; when he took the pen in hand, he was a gentleman. Everything coarse or vulgar dropped from it instinctively. It reflected nothing, even in its descriptions of things vulgar or coarse in themselves, but the elegance and sweetness which, whatever might be the accident or meanness of his external lot, remained pure in the last recesses of his nature.

1751.

Æt. 23.

In substance this letter to his mother confessed that his intention was to have sailed for America: that he had gone to Cork for that purpose; converted the horse which his mother prized so much higher than Fiddleback into cash; paid for his passage in an American ship; and, the wind threatening to detain them some days, had taken a little country excursion in the neighbourhood of the city: but that, the wind suddenly serving in his absence, his friend the captain never inquired after him, setting sail with as much indifference as if he had been on board. "You know, mother," he remarks, "that no one can "starve while he has money in "his pocket:" and, being reduced by the practice of this apophthegm to his last two guineas, he bought the generous beast, Fiddleback, for one pound

seventeen, and with five shillings in his pocket turned homewards. Then had come one of those sudden appeals to a sharp and painful susceptibility, when, as he afterwards described them to his brother, charitable to excess, he forgot the rules of justice, and placed himself in the situation of the wretch who was thanking him for his bounty. Penniless in consequence, he bethought him of a college acquaintance on the road, to whose house he went. With exquisite humour he describes this most miserly acquaintance, who, to allay his desperate hunger, dilated on the advantages of a diet of slops, setting him down to a porringer of sour milk and a heel of musty cheese; and on being asked for the loan of a guinea, earnestly recommended the sale of Fiddleback, producing what he called a much better nag to ride upon which would cost neither price nor provender, in the shape of a stout oaken cudgel. His adventures ended a little more agreeably at last however, in a more genial abode, where an acquaintance of the miser entertained him. He had "two sweet "girls to his daughters, who "played enchantingly on the "harpsichord; and yet it was but "a melancholy pleasure I felt the "first time I heard them; for, that "being the first time also that "either of them had touched "the instrument since their mo-"ther's death, I saw the tears in

"silence trickle down their fa-
"ther's cheeks." *

Law was the next thing thought
of, and the good Mr. Con-
1752. tarine came forward with
Æt. 24. fifty pounds. It seems a
small sum wherewith to travel
to Dublin and London, to defray
expenses of entrance at inns of
court, and to live upon till a
necessary number of terms are
eaten. But with fifty pounds
young Oliver started; on a luckless journey. A Roscommon
friend laid hold of him in Dublin,
seduced him to play, and the
fifty pounds he would have raised
to a hundred he reduced to fifty
pence. In bitter shame, after
great physical suffering, he wrote
to his uncle, confessed, and was
forgiven.

On his return to Ballymahon,
it is probable that his mother
objected to receive him; ** since
after this date we find him living
wholly with his brother. It was
but for a short time, however;
disagreement followed there too;
and we see him next by
Mr. Contarine's fireside, 1752.
again talking literature to Æt. 24.
his good-natured uncle, writing
new verses to please him (alleged
copies of which are not sufficiently authentic to be quoted),
and joining his flute to Miss Contarine's harpsichord.

CHAPTER IV.

Preparing for a Medical Degree.
1752—1755.

THE years of idleness must
nevertheless come to a close. To
do nothing, no matter how me-
lodiously accompanied by flute
and harpsichord, is not what a
man is born into this world to
do; and it required but a casual
word from a not very genial visitor to close for ever Goldsmith's
happy nights at uncle Contarine's.
There was a sort of cold grandee
of the family, Dean Goldsmith
of Cloyne, who did not think it
unbecoming his dignity to visit
the good clergyman's parsonage
now and then; and Oliver having
made a remark which showed
him to be no fool, the dean gave
it as his opinion to Mr. Contarine
that his young relative would
make an excellent medical man.
The hint seemed a good one,
and was the dean's contribution
to his young relative's fortune.
The small purse was contributed
by Mr. Contarine; and in the
autumn of 1752, Oliver Gold-

---

* The letter descriptive of this adventure, as printed in various editions of
Goldsmith's works, is in all respects con-
firmatory of the narrative as given by
Mrs. Hodson; and it is only for the
reason mentioned in the text that I do
not quote it in detail. I have thought it
right, however, to include it in the Appendix (B) to the present volume.

** Mrs. Hodson's narrative, from which
these facts are derived, after remarking
that "his own distress and disgrace may
"readily be conceived," adds, "to make
"short of the story, he was again for-
"given;" but Mr. Prior states the tradition of the neighbourhood to be, that
though forgiven by his uncle he was less
readily forgiven by his mother, so that
he ceased to live with her, and went to
his brother Henry, until a quarrel, arising from some trifling cause, for a time
terminated intercourse between the brothers also. 1. 129.

smith started for Edinburgh, a medical student.

Anecdotes of amusing simplicity and forgetfulness in this new character are, as usual, more rife than notices of his course of study. But such records as have been preserved of the period rest upon authority too obviously doubtful to require other than a very cursory mention here. On the day of his arrival he is reported to have set forth for a ramble round the streets, after leaving his luggage at hired lodgings where he had forgotten to inquire the name either of the street or the landlady, and to which he only found his way back by the accident of meeting the porter who had carried his trunk from the coach.* He is also said to have obtained, in this temporary abode, a knowledge of the wondrous culinary expedients with which three medical students might be supported for a whole week on a single loin of mutton, by a brandered chop served up one day, a fried steak another, chops with onion sauce a third, and so on till the fleshy parts should be quite consumed, when finally, on the seventh day, a dish of broth manufactured from the bones would appear, and the ingenious landlady rested from her labours.** It is moreover recorded, in proof of his careless habits in respect to money, that being in company with several fellow-students on the first night of a new play, he suddenly proposed to draw lots with any one present which of the two should treat the whole party to the theatre; when the real fact was, as he afterwards confessed in speaking of the secret joy with which he heard them all decline the challenge, that had it been accepted, and he had proved to be the loser, he must have pledged a part of his wardrobe in order to raise the money.* This last anecdote, if true, reveals to us at any rate that he had a wardrobe to pledge. Such resource in the matter of dress is one of his peculiarities found generally peeping out in some form or other: and, unable to confirm any other fact in these recollections, I can at least establish that.

But first let me remark that no traditions remain of the character or extent of his studies. It seems tolerably certain that any learned celebrity he may have got in the schools paled an ineffectual fire before his amazing social repute, as inimitable teller of a humorous story and capital singer of Irish songs.** He be-

* _Percy Memoir_, 19.

** _Ibid._ And see preface to the Glasgow edition of the _Works_ published in 1816.

* _Prior_, i. 137.

** We may afford to smile at his first biographer's notice of this fact, which forms one of the "interpolations" complained of by Malone. "These endeavours to amuse, it must be con-"fessed, were however, from an in-"ordinate desire of gaining applause,

came a member of the Medical Society, and on his admission appears to have been exempted from the usual condition of reading a paper on a medical subject.* But he was really fond of chemistry, and was remembered favourably by the celebrated Black; other well-known fellow-students, as William Farr, and his whilome college acquaintance, Lauchlan Macleane, conceived a regard for him, which somewhat later Farr seems to have had the opportunity of showing; certainly so much is without contradiction to be said of kind quaker Sleigh, known afterwards as the eminent physician of that name, painter Barry's first patron, Burke's friend, and one of the many victims of Foote's witty malice;** and it may therefore be supposed that Oliver's eighteen months' residence in Edinburgh was, on the whole, not unprofitable. It had its mortifications, of course; for all his life had these. "An ugly "and a poor man is society only "for himself; and such society "the world lets me enjoy in "great abundance:" "nor do I "envy my dear Bob his blessings, "while I may sit down and laugh

"at the world; and at myself, the "most ridiculous object in it:" are among his expressions of half bitter, half goodnatured candour, in a letter to his cousin Bryanton.*

1752.
Æt. 24.

There is another confession, in a later letter to his uncle, which touches him in a nearer point, and suggests perhaps more than it reveals. It would seem as though, to eke out his resources, he had for some part of his time accepted employment in a great man's house: probably as tutor. "I have spent," he says, "more than a fortnight "every second day at the Duke "of Hamilton's; but it seems "they like me more as a jester "than as a companion; so I dis-"dained so servile an employ-"ment." To those with whom, on equal terms, he could be both jester and companion, Bryanton was charged with every kind of remembrance. "You cannot send "me much news from Bally-"mahon, but such as it is, send "it all; everything you send will "be agreeable to me. Has "George Conway put up a sign "yet? or John Fineely left off "drinking drams? or Tom Allen "got a new wig?" To the plea-

---

"and of setting the table in a roar, too "often blended with grimace and buf-"foonery, from which defects, notwith-"standing he was afterwards introduced "into the politest company, his conversa-"tion was never wholly exempt." *Percy Memoir,* 19.

* This is manifest from an entry in the books of the Medical Society of Edinburgh, 13th January, 1754.

** See Burke's *Correspondence,* i. 35.

* The letter to Bryanton quoted above was first printed in the *Anthologia Hibernica* of 1793, and thence transferred to the London magazines of the same year. A mutilated copy was afterwards printed in the *Percy Memoir,* (22—26). The reader will find the letter correctly printed in the Appendix (C) to this volume, but the discrepancies from the copies as ordinarily printed are not material.

sant and whimsical satire of the Scotch he at the same time wrote to Bryanton, I need scarcely refer, because in all the editions of his works (except the Scotch) it is commonly printed: but on the whole I think it best to include these various letters in an appendix without pledging myself to any special belief in the accuracy of all their statements. As a generally humorous picture drawn from various sources, rather than a strictly veracious record of his own experience, it will be safest to regard them; but this remark applies less strongly to those two of the three letters to his uncle Contarine, the earliest in date and least important in contents, which have been recently discovered.

1752.
Æt. 24.

In the first, dated May-day 1753,* and in which he alludes to a description of himself by his uncle, as "the "philosopher who carries all his "goods about him," he describes Munro as the one great professor, and the rest of the doctor-teachers as only less afflicting to their students than they must be to their patients. He makes whimsical mention of a trip to the Highlands, for which he had hired a horse about the size of a ram, who "walked away "(trot he could not) as pensive "as his master."** Other pas-

1753.
Æt. 25.

sages have a tendency to show within what narrow limits he had brought his wants; with how

* Appendix (C) to this volume.

** My friend Mr. Gavan Duffy sent me lately an alleged unpublished incident in Goldsmith's life, related in the Mel- bourne *Argus* on the authority of a Scotch settler in Australia, Mr. Alexander Dick; not sufficiently authentic to claim a place in my text, but which it might yet be unsafe to omit altogether. Its closing allusion may connect it with one of the excursions which he tells his uncle he had made from Edinburgh during the two years he lived there; but the whole story is probably a confused tradition of the incident glanced at in a previous page (31-2), and described by Goldsmith himself in the famous letter to his mother there referred to (printed in Appendix B.) "On his farm near Falkirk, and about "the year 1750, my grandfather, William "Dick, was caught by the press-gang, "and compelled to serve in the regiment "of Picardy. My grandmother, Mary "Dalgleish or Douglass, joined him. The "regiment passed to Ireland, and it was "ordered on foreign service. Mary was "debarred from accompanying her hus- "band. They had three children—Adam, "Willie (my father), and Jeannie. It "was now 1752, and the children were "seven, five, and three years of age. "Mary resolved to return from Ireland to "Edinburgh. She had not travelled a "fortnight when she was robbed, as she "slept, of her money, clothes, and chil- "dren's clothes. It was a lone house, and "the people had no fresh clothing to "bestow. Mary and her children went "forth in their night-dresses. Despond- "ing, despairing, she travelled on, but a "ministering angel was at hand, and "saved her. Oliver Goldsmith, on horse- "back, met her. No salutation passed. "Willie and Jeannie were behind. "Jeannie—now three years old—was "ashamed of her dress, and to hide from "the gentleman who got close to Willie. "He pushed her into a ditch, and ran. "Goldsmith cried, 'What sort of a wo- "'man are you, that you do not look "'better after your children?' Mary "turned round, and saw her daughter "getting to her feet quietly. Goldsmith "drew near, and Mary replied, 'I am the "'wife of an impressed soldier, and on "'my way to Edinburgh, but last night I "'was robbed of our money and our "'clothes, and I am almost distracted.'

little he was cheerfully 'content'; and that, for whatever advances he had, though it was desirable he should have turned them to more practical use, he at least overflowed with gratitude.

There have been harsh judgments of Goldsmith for the money thus wasted on abortive professional undertakings: but

"Goldsmith saw that she was an edu-"cated lady, and he begged pardon for "the harsh manner in which he had "spoken to her, and said, 'I am sorry "'that I cannot give you more than £1: "'but I won't leave you till I see you all "'better clothed.' He turned back some "miles. They came to a mansion. "Goldsmith addressed the inmates, told "them his name, begged clothes for his "companions, and said that he would "return and pay for all that they could "give. The inmates gave Mary decent "material to make clothes for herself "and her children. Mary got to Muir-"avonside, but she did not go to Edin-"burgh. The friend that she had lodged "with there had died. She was a widow "that kept a small shop at the foot of the "Canongate, and my grandfather's bro-"ther had occasion to call on her suc-"cessor. Goldsmith arrived subsequently "in Edinburgh, and called frequently at "the shop to inquire after Mary's welfare. "He was informed that William had "been bought off for 40l. that he was "working at Cathcart for 8d. a day, and "that Mary was sewing, and the children "knitting, to pay off the money by in-"stalments. He sent them a few pounds. "Honoured be the memory of Gold-"smith. He said that it was the informa-"tion that Mary gave him of Edinburgh "College that made him make up his "mind to come to it. Goldsmith set out "on a tour to the North and West High-"lands, and to visit Mary at Cathcart; "but his money failed him, and he had to "cut his tour short. He expressed himself "greatly disappointed that he had not "seen the Loch Lomond district, and "that he had not seen Mary. He spoke "constantly of taking another tour, but "he did not set out a second time."

the sacrifices cannot fairly be called great. Burke had an allowance of £200 a year for leisure to follow studies to which he never paid the least attention; and when his father anxiously expected to hear of his call to the bar, he might have heard, instead, of a distress that forced him to sell his books: yet for this, quite rightly, we none of us visit Burke with pains or penalties. Poor Goldsmith's supplies were on the other hand small, irregular, uncertain, and, in some two years at the furthest, exhausted altogether.

1753.
———
Æt. 25.

Here, in this letter to his uncle, he says that he has drawn for six pounds, and that his next draft, five months after this date, will be for but four pounds; pleading in extenuation of these light demands that he has been obliged to buy everything since he came to Scotland, "shirts not "even excepted:" while, in another letter at the close of the same year, he accounts for money spent by the remark that he has "good store of clothes" to accompany him on his travels. Yet there was decided moderation even in the direction sartorial; nor does the wardrobe, to which allusion was made a few pages back, appear to have been by any means extensive in the proportion of the variety of its colours. Upon the latter point our evidence is not to be gainsayed. What will have to be remarked of Goldsmith in this respect at Mr. Boswell's or Mr. Reynolds's, is already to be said of him in the lodging-house and lecture - room at Edinburgh; and on the same proof of old tailors' bills, the very ghosts of which continue to flutter about and plague his memory.

1753.
Æt. 25.

The leaf of an Edinburgh ledger of 1753 has fallen into my hands, from which it would appear that one of his fellow-students, Mr. Honner, had introduced him at the beginning of that year to a merchant tailor with whom he dealt for sundry items of hose, hats, silver lace, satin, allapeen, fustian, durant, shalloon, cloth, and velvet; which materials of adornment are charged to him, from the January to the December of the year, in the not very immoderate sum of £9 11s. 2¼d., the first entries of which, to the amount of £3 15s. 9¼d., were in November duly paid in full, and what remained at the year's end carried to a folio in the same ledger, unluckily destroyed before it was discovered to whom the page related. The earlier leaf had not been found when "folio 424" was burnt.

P. 383.

Mr. Oliver Goldsmith, Student, pr. Mr. Honner.

1753.			£	s.	d.
Jany. 24.	To 2½ yds. rich Sky-Blew sattin, 12s.		1	10	0
"	To 1½ yds. white Allapeen, 2s.			3	0
"	To 1½ yds. Do. Fustian, 1s. 4d.			2	4
"	To 4 yds. Blew Durant, 1s. 4d.			5	4
"	To ½ yds. fine Sky-Blew Shalloon, 1s. 9d.			1	3½
Febry. 23.	To 2½ yds. fine Priest's Grey cloth, 10s. 6d.		1	3	7½
"	To 2 yds. Black shalloon, 1s. 6d.			3	0
"	To a pair fine 3-thd Black worsed Hose			4	6
"	To ½ yds. rich Ditto Genoa velvett, 22s.			2	9
			3	15	9½
Novr. 23.	By Cash in full		£3	15	9½
"	To 1 oz. 6½ drs. silver Hatt-Lace, 8s.			11	4½
"	To 1 drs. silver chain, 6d., and plate button, 2d.				8
"	To lacing your Hatt, 6d., and a new lyning, 6d.			1	0
"	To a sfine small Hatt			14	0
"	To 3½ yds. best sfine high Clarett-colour'd Cloth, 19s.	3	6	6
"	To 5½ yds. sfine best White shalln., 2s.			11	0
"	To 4 yds. white Fustian, 16d.			5	4
Decr. 6.	To a pr sfine Best Blk worsed hose.			5	6
			£5	15	4½

To Folio 424.

Such is the old leaf exactly copied;* and glowing as it is, through all its age and dinginess, with a name bright and familiar since to many generations in almost every department of literary research. Mentioning the fact of the top of "folio 424," Mr. Laing adds: "Neither "was there any indication of the name of "the merchant-tailor."

* I owe this curious little document to the kindness of Mr. David Laing of the signet library in Edinburgh, whose readiness to communicate information to all who are in want of it has been equalled only by the value of his discoveries in

tions of boys and men in the good merchant-tailor's city, is it not also in every part still radiant with its rich sky-blue satin, its fine sky-blue shalloon, its super-fine silver-laced small hat, its rich black Genoa velvet, and that very best superfine high claret-coloured cloth in which the odd little clumsy figure thus early had arrayed itself? For all which the gravest reader will not unwillingly spare a smile before he returns with me to the letters that preceded student Oliver's departure for the continent.

1754.
Æt. 26.
    In that first letter he had professed himself pleased with his studies, and expressed a hope that when he should have heard Munro for another year he might go "to hear "Albinus, the great professor at "Leyden." The whole of the letter gives evidence of a most grateful affection. In the second,* written eight months later, where he describes his preparations for travel, and, confirming his intentions as to Leyden in the following winter, says that he shall pass the intervening months in Paris, the same feeling is not less apparent: "Let me here ac-"knowledge," he says, "the "humility of the station in which "you found me; let me tell how "I was despised by most, and "hateful to myself. Poverty, "hopeless poverty, was my lot, \"and Melancholy was beginning "to make me her own. When

"you . . . ." This good man did not live to know the entire good he had done, or that his own name would probably live with the memory of it as long as the English language lasted. "Thou best of "men!" exclaims his nephew in the third of these letters, to which I shall presently make larger reference, "may Heaven guard "and preserve you, and those "you love!" It is the care of Heaven that actions worthy of itself should in the doing find reward, not waiting for it even on such thanks and prayers as Goldsmith's. Another twenty pounds are acknowledged on the eve of departure from Edinburgh, as the last he will ever draw for; and it was the last, of which we have record. But Goldsmith had drawn his last breath before he forgot his uncle Contarine.

1754.
Æt. 26.
    The old vicissitudes attended him at this new move in his game of life, for which, according to his own account, his sole provision was a capital or stock in hand of exactly thirty-three pounds. Land rats and water rats were at his heels as he quitted Scotland; bailiffs hunted him for security given to a fellow-student (for which he was arrested, says the Percy Memoir, but soon released by the liberal assistance of the "friends Mr. Lauchlan "Macleane and Dr. Sleigh, who were then in college"), and shipwreck he only escaped by a fortnight's imprisonment on a false political charge. Bound for

* See Appendix (C) to this volume.

Leyden, and his purpose to interpose Paris for some reason or other laid aside, with characteristic oddity or carelessness he had secured his passage in a ship bound for Bordeaux; but, taken for a Jacobite in Newcastle-on-Tyne, and in Sunderland arrested by a tailor, the ship sailed on without him, and sank at the mouth of the Garonne. He tells the tale very explicitly: "I embarked for "Bordeaux on board a Scotch "ship, called the St. Andrews, "Captain John Wall, master. "The ship made a tolerable ap-"pearance, and, as another in-"ducement, I was let to know "that six agreeable passengers "were to be my company. Well, "we were but two days at sea, "when a storm drove us into a "city of England called New-"castle-upon-Tyne. We all went "ashore to refresh us after the "fatigue of our voyage. Seven "men and I were one day on "shore, and on the following "evening, as we were all very "merry, the room door bursts "open: enter a serjeant and "twelve grenadiers, with their "bayonets screwed, and put us "all under the king's arrest. It "seems my company were Scotch-"men in the French service, and "had been in Scotland to enlist "soldiers for the French army. "I endeavoured all I could to "prove my innocence; however, "I remained in prison with "the rest a fortnight, and with "difficulty got off even then."

The facts are thus stated on his own authority; but whether they are all exactly credible, or whether credit may not rather be due to the suggestion that they were mere fanciful modes of carrying off the loss, in other ways, of money given to enable him to carry on studies in which it cannot now be supposed that he took any great interest, I shall leave to the judgment of the reader.

Certain it is that at last he got safe to the learned city; and wrote off to his uncle, among other sketches of character obviously meant to give him pleasure, what he thought of the three specimens of womankind he had now seen, out of Ireland. "A Dutch woman and Scotch "will well bear an opposition. "The one is pale and fat, the "other lean and ruddy: the one "walks as if she were straddling "after a go-cart, and the other "takes too masculine a stride. "I shall not endeavour to "deprive either country of "its share of beauty; but I "must say, that of all objects on "this earth, an English farmer's "daughter is most charming." In the same delightful letter he observingly corrects the vulgar notion of the better kind of Dutchman, amusingly comparing him with the downright Hollander, while in equally happy vein he contrasts Scotland and Holland. The playful tone of these passages, the amusing touch of satire, and the incomparably easy style, so compact and graceful, were announcements, properly first vouchsafed to the delight of good Mr. Contarine, of powers that were one day to give unfading delight to all the world.*

Little is known of his pursuits at Leyden, beyond the fact that, in his *Enquiry into Polite Learning*, he mentions himself as in the habit of familiar intercourse with Gaubius, the chemical professor.** But by this time he would seem to have applied himself, with little affectation of disguise, to general knowledge more than to professional. The one was available in immediate wants; the other pointed to but a distant hope which those very wants made, daily, more obscure; and the narrow necessities of self-help now crowded on him. His principal means of support were as a teacher; but the difficulties and disappointments of his own philosophic vagabond, when he went to Holland to teach the natives English, himself knowing nothing of Dutch, appear to have made it a sorry calling. Then, it is said, he borrowed, and again resorted to play, winning even largely, but losing all he won;*** and it is at least certain that he encountered every form of distress. Unhappily, though he wrote many letters to Ireland, some of them described from recollection as compositions of singular ease and humour, all are lost. But Doctor Ellis, an Irish physician of eminence and ex-student of Leyden, remembered his fellow-student when years had made him famous, and said (much, it may be confessed, in the tone of ex-post-facto prophecy) that in all his peculiarities it was remarked there was about him an elevation of mind, a philosophical tone and manner, and the language and information of a scholar.*.Being much in want of the philosophy, it is well that his friends should have given him credit for it; though his last known scene in Leyden showed greatly less of the philosophic mind than of the gentle, grateful heart. Bent upon leaving that city, where he had now been nearly a year without an effort for a degree, he called upon Ellis, and asked his assistance in some trifling sum. It was given; but, as his evil or

1755. ————— ÆL. 27.

* See Appendix (C) to this volume.

** See the ninth chapter, in which they discuss the subject of professors' salaries at Edinburgh.

*** "One morning he came to a fellow-"student" (this was the Doctor Ellis, clerk of the Irish house of commons, mentioned in the text) "with his pockets "literally full of money, and with exulta-"tion counted out to him a large sum, "which he had won the preceding even-"ing. His friend earnestly pressed him "to play no more, but to secure his "present gains as a fund for completing "his medical studies. Oliver, who could "always see what was right, though he "could not always pursue it, highly ap-"proved this advice, and declared his "firm resolution to make it the rule of "his future conduct. But the seductions "of the gaming table were irresistible, "and he was soon after stripped of every "shilling." *Percy Memoir*, 55.

* *Prior*, 1. 170.

(some might say) his good genius
would have it, he passed a
florist's garden on his return,
and seeing some rare and
high-priced flowers which
his uncle Contarine, an
enthusiast in such things, had
often spoken and been in search
of, he ran in without other
thought than of immediate pleasure to his kindest friend, bought
a parcel of the roots, and sent
them off to Ireland.*   He left
Leyden next day, it is stated on
the same authority, with a guinea
in his pocket, one shirt to his
back, and a flute in his hand.

1755.
Æt. 27.

CHAPTER V.

Travels.

1755—1756.

To understand what was probably passing in Goldsmith's
mind at this curious point of
his fortunes when, without any
settled prospect in life, and de-
void even of all apparent means
of self-support, he quitted Leyden, the *Enquiry into the Present
State of Polite Learning*, the first
literary piece which a few years
afterwards he published on his
own account, will in some degree
serve as a guide. The Danish
writer, Baron de Holberg, was
much talked of at this time, as a
celebrated person recently dead.
His career had greatly impressed
Goldsmith. It was that of a man
of obscure origin, to whom literature, other sources having failed,
had given high fame and station.

* *Percy Memoir*, 33, 34.

On the death of his father, Holberg found himself involved in
"all that distress which is com-
"mon among the poor, and of
"which the great have scarcely
"any idea:" but, persisting in a
determination to be *something*, he
resolutely begged his learning
as well as his bread, and so succeeded that "a life begun in con-
"tempt and penury ended in
"opulence and esteem." Goldsmith had his thoughts more
especially directed to this career,
when at Leyden, by the accident
of its sudden close in that city;
and the desire of extensive travel,
his sister told Mr. Handcock,
had from his own boyhood been
a passion with him. "Being of
"a philosophical turn," says
Oliver's later associate and friend,
Doctor Glover, "and at that time
"possessing a body capable of
"sustaining every fatigue and a
"heart not easily terrified at
"danger, this ingenious unfor-
"tunate man became an en-
"thusiast to the design he had
"formed of seeing the manners
"of different countries."*   An
enthusiast also to the same design, with precisely the same
means of indulging it, Holberg
himself had been. "His ambi-
"tion," I turn again to the *Polite
Learning*, "was not to be re-
"strained, or his thirst of know-
"ledge satisfied, until he had
"seen the world. Without money,
"recommendations, or friends,

* Malone's edition of the *Poems* (1777),
p. iii. And see the *Annual Register*, xvii.
29, 30.

"he undertook to set out upon "his travels, and make the tour "of Europe on foot. A good "voice, and a trifling skill in "music, were the only finances "he had to support an under- "taking so extensive; so he tra- "velled by day, and at night "sung at the doors of peasants' "houses to get himself a lodging. "In this manner, while yet very "young, Holberg passed through "France, Germany, and Hol- "land."* With exactly the same resources, still also very young, Goldsmith quitted Leyden, bent upon the travel which his *Traveller* has made immortal.

It was in February, 1755. For the exact route he took, the na- ture of his adventures, and the course of thought they sug- gested, it is necessary to resort for the most part to his published writings. Though he wrote to his cousin Contarine from Ley- den, from Louvain, and from Rouen, his letters to her, and others of the period to other friends, have perished. It was common talk at the dinner table of Reynolds that the wanderings of the philosophic vagabond in the *Vicar of Wakefield* had been suggested by his own, and he often admitted at that time, to various friends, the accuracy of special details. "He frequently "used to talk," says one who be- came very familiar with him in

later life,* "of his distresses on "the continent, such as living on "the hospitalities of the friars "in convents, sleeping in "barns, and picking up a "kind of mendicant liveli- "hood by the German flute, with "great pleasantry."** And if he did not make this confession more openly than to private friends, it was to please the booksellers only; who could not bear that any one so popular with their customers as Doctor Goldsmith had become, should lie under the horrible imputation of a poverty so deplorable. "Countries wear very different "appearances," he had written in the first edition of the *Polite Learning,* "to travellers of dif- "ferent circumstances. A man "who is whirled through Europe "in a post-chaise, and the pilgrim "who walks the grand tour on "foot, will form very different "conclusions. *Haud inexpertus lo-* "*quor.*" In the second edition, the *haud inexpertus loquor* disap- peared; but the experience had been already set down in the *Vicar of Wakefield.*

Louvain attracted him of course,

1755.
Æt. 27.

* *Enquiry into Polite Learning,* chap. vi. This parallel to his own adventures has before been pointed out; but no reader of Goldsmith could fail to be struck by it.

* This was a young Irish law student named Cooke, who had chambers near him in the Temple, who will have fre- quent mention in the course of my nar- rative, who wrote among other things a life of Foote, and who contributed to the *European Magazine* not long after Gold- smith's death a series of papers from which I have derived many highly interest- ing and quite authentic details. It is surprising to me that they should have escaped the attention of the compilers and editor of the *Percy Memoir.*

** *European Magazine,* xxiv. 91.

as he passed through Flanders; and here, according to his first biographer,* he took the degree of medical bachelor, which, as early as 1763, is found in one of the Dodsley agreements appended to his name. Though this is by no means certain, it is yet likely enough. The records of Louvain University were destroyed in the revolutionary wars, and the means of proof or disproof lost; but it is improbable that any false assumption of a medical degree would have passed without question among the distinguished friends of his later life, even if it escaped the exposure of his enemies. Certain it is, at any rate, that he made some stay at Louvain, became acquainted with its professors, and informed himself of its modes of study. "I "always forgot the meanness of "my circumstances when I could "converse upon such subjects." Some little time he also seems to have passed at Brussels. Of his having examined at Maestricht an extensive cavern, or stone quarry, at that time much visited by travellers, there is likewise trace. It must undoubtedly have been at Antwerp (a "fortification "in Flanders") that he saw the maimed, deformed, chained, yet cheerful slave, to whom he refers in that charming essay wherein he argues that happiness and pleasure are in ourselves, and

1755.
———
Æt. 27.

not in the objects offered for our amusement.* ' And he afterwards remembered, and made it the subject of a striking allusion, how, as he approached the coast of Holland, he looked down upon it from the deck, as into a valley; so that it seemed to him at once a conquest from the sea, and in a manner rescued from its bosom.** He did not travel to see that all was barren. He did not merely outface the poverty, the hardship, and fatigue, but made them his servants and ministers to entertainment and wisdom.

Before he passed through Flanders good use had been made of his flute; and when he came to the poorer provinces of France, he found it greatly serviceable. "I had some know-"ledge of music," says the vaga-bond, "with a tolerable voice; "I now turned what was once "my amusement into a present "means of subsistence. I passed "among the harmless peasants "of Flanders, and among such "of the French as were poor "enough to be very merry; for I "ever found them sprightly in "proportion to their wants. "Whenever I approached a pea-"sant's house towards night-fall, "I played one of my most merry "tunes, and that procured me "not only a lodging, but sub-"sistence for the next day. I "once or twice attempted to play "for people of fashion; but they

* *Life of Dr. O. Goldsmith* printed for Swan 1771. 8vo. And *Annual Register*, XVII. 20.

* *The Bee*, ii.
** *Anim. Nat.* i. 230.

"always thought my performance "odious, and never rewarded me "even with a trifle." In plain words he begged, as Holberg had done; supported by his cheerful spirit, and the thought that Holberg's better fate might also yet be his. Not, we may be sure, the dull round of professional labour, but intellectual distinction, popular fame, the applause and wonder of his old Irish associates, were now within the sphere of Goldsmith's vision; and what these will enable a man joyfully to endure, he afterwards bore witness to. "The perspec-"tive of life brightens upon us "when terminated by objects so "charming. Every intermediate "image of want, banishment, or "sorrow, receives a lustre from "their distant influence. With "these in view, the patriot, phi-"losopher, and poet, have looked "with calmness on disgrace and "famine, and rested on their "straw with cheerful serenity." Straw, doubtless, was his own peasant-lodging often; but from it arose the wanderer, refreshed and hopeful, and bade the melody and sport resume, and played with a new delight to the music of enchanting verse already dancing in his brain.

Gay sprightly land of mirth and social ease,
Pleas'd with thyself, whom all the world
    can please—
How often have I led thy sportive choir,
With tuneless pipe, beside the murmur-
    ing Loire,
Where shading elms along the margin
    grow,
And, freshen'd from the wave, the zephyr
    flew!

And haply, though my harsh touch, falter-
    ing still,
But mock'd all tune, and marr'd the
    dancer's skill—
Yet would the village praise my
    wondrous power,
And dance forgetful of the noon-
    tide hour.
Alike all ages: dames of ancient days
Have led their children through the
    mirthful maze;
And the gay grandsire, skill'd in gentle
    lore,
Has frisk'd beneath the burden of three-
    score.
So bless'd a life these thoughtless realms
    display;
Thus idly busy rolls their world away.
Theirs are those arts that mind to mind
    endear,
For honour forms the social temper here;
Honour, that praise which real merit
    gains,
Or e'en imaginary worth obtains,
Here passes current—paid from hand to
    hand,
It shifts, in splendid traffic, round the
    land;
From courts to camps, to cottages it
    strays,
And all are taught an avarice of praise—
They please, are pleas'd, they give to get
    esteem,
Till, seeming bless'd, they grow to what
    they seem.

1755.
———
Æt. 27.

Arrived in Paris, he rested some brief space, and, for the time, a sensible improvement is to be observed in his resources. This is not easily explained; for, as will appear a little later on, many applications to Ireland of this date remained altogether without answer, and a sad fate had fallen suddenly on his best friend. But in subsequent communication with his brother-in-law Hodson he remarked, with that strange indifference to what was implied in such obligations which is not the agreeable side of his character, that there was hardly a kingdom in Europe in which he was not a debtor;[*] and in Paris, if anywhere, he would find many hearts made liberal by the love of learning. His early memoir-writers assert with confidence, that in at least some small portion of these travels he acted as companion to a young man of large fortune, nephew to a pawnbroker and ex-articled-clerk to an attorney;[**] and there are passages in the philosophic vagabond's adventures, which, if they did not themselves suggest the assertion (as they certainly supply the language) of those first biographers, would tend to bear it out. "I was to be the "young gentleman's governor, "with a proviso that he should "always be permitted to govern "himself. He was heir to a for- "tune of two hundred thousand "pounds, left him by an uncle in "the West Indies; and all his "questions on the road were, "how much money could be "saved. Such curiosities as could "be seen for nothing, he was

1755.
Æt. 27.

"ready enough to look at, but if "the sight of them was to be paid "for, he usually asserted that he "had been told they were not "worth seeing; and he never "paid a bill that he would not "observe how amazingly expen- "sive travelling was."

Poor Goldsmith could not have profited much by so thrifty a young gentleman, but he certainly seems to have been present, whether as a student or a mere visitor, at the fashionable chemical lectures of the day ("I "have seen as bright a circle of "beauty at the chemical lectures "of Rouelle as gracing the court "at Versailles");[*] to have seen and admired the celebrated actress Mademoiselle Clairon (of whom he speaks in an essay at the close of the second number of the *Bee*); and to have had leisure to look quietly around him, and form certain grave and settled conclusions on the political and social state of France. He says, in his *Animated Nature*, that he never walked about the environs of Paris that he did not look upon the immense quantity of game running almost tame on every side of him, as a badge of the slavery of the people.[**] What they wished him to observe as an object of triumph, he adds, he regarded with a secret dread and compassion. Nor was it the badge of slavery alone that had arrested his attention. If on every side he saw this, he

* See *post*, Book II. Chap. II.

** *Annual Register*, XVII. 30. *Perry Memoir*, 35, 36. I may here remark that, some thirty years after Goldsmith's death, the *Annual Register* printed what purported to be "a letter of the late Doctor "Goldsmith, when about twenty-five "years old, to a young gentleman, whom "he had for a short time instructed in "different branches of learning," which is so manifestly *not* genuine that I should not have thought it worth even this mention, if Mr. Mitford had not strangely given it some authority by inserting it at the close of his sketch of Goldsmith's life prefixed to the Aldine edition of the *Poems*.

* *Polite Learning*, chap. VII.
** IV. 158-9.

saw liberty at but a little distance beyond; and more than ten years before the *Animated Nature* was written he had predicted, in words really very remarkable, the issue, terrible and yet glorious, which changed the face of the world. The remark* might suffice of itself to reveal to us the advantage derived by Goldsmith from the rude, strange, wandering life to which his nature for a time impelled him. It was the education so picked up from personal experience, and by actual collision with many varieties of men, which not only placed him in advance of his contemporaries on several social questions, but occasionally gave him very much the advantage over greatly more learned, and, so to speak, educated men. It was thus, in short, he became a Citizen of the World. "As the "Swedes are making concealed "approaches to despotism, the "French, on the other hand, are "imperceptibly vindicating themselves into freedom. When I "consider that those parliaments "(the members of which are all "created by the court, the pre- "sidents of which can only act "by immediate direction) presume even to mention privi- "leges and freedom, who, till of "late, received directions from "the throne with implicit humility; when this is considered, "I cannot help fancying that the "genius of freedom has entered "that kingdom in disguise. If

"they have but three weak "monarchs more successively on "the throne, the mask will be laid "aside, and the country "will certainly once more "be free."* Some thirty years after this was written, and when the writer had been fifteen years in his grave, the crash of the falling Bastille resounded over Europe.

1755.
Æt. 27.

Before Goldsmith quitted Paris, he is said by his biographers to have seen and become known to Voltaire. But at Paris this could not have been.** The great wit

* It occurs in the *Citizen of the World.*

* *Citizen of the World*, Letter LVI. The passage did not fail to attract notice when the revolution broke out. It ran the round of the London magazines in 1792; and it may be taken for proof that Goldsmith never could have used the argument maintained by Johnson in his dispute with Sir Adam Ferguson: "Sir, I "would not give half a guinea to live "under one form of government rather "than another. It is of no moment to "the happiness of an individual. Sir, "the danger of the abuse of power is no- "thing to a private man. What French- "man is prevented from passing his life "as he pleases? SIR ADAM: But, Sir, in "the British constitution it is surely of "importance to keep up a spirit in the "people, so as to preserve a balance against "the crown. JOHNSON: Sir, I perceive "you are a vile whig. Why all this "childish jealousy of the power of the "crown? The crown has not power "enough." *Boswell*, III. 202-3. This was in 1772; and in 1789 the Bastille came down. See Macaulay's *Essays*, I. 390. Tauchn. ed.

** *Prior*, I. 181. After my first edition was published, an octogenarian of Cork, the late Mr. Roche, who, by his own account, had talked to Gibbon in Switzerland, narrowly missed talking with Montesquieu, was entitled to call Vergniaud "friend," had heard Mirabeau's speech on national bankruptcy, paid afterwards at a Paris chop-house 14000 francs (in assignats) for his dinner, and finally had

was then self-exiled from the capital, which he had not seen from the luckless hour in which he accepted the invitation of Frederick of Prussia. The fact is alleged, it is quite true, on Goldsmith's own authority; but the passage is loosely written, does not appear in a work which bore the writer's name, and may either have been tampered with by others, or even mistakenly set down by himself in confusion of memory. The error does not vitiate the statement in an integral point, for that the meeting actually took place may not unfairly be inferred. The time when Goldsmith certainly passed through the Genevese territory, is the time when Voltaire had settled himself, in greater quiet than he had known for years, in his newly-purchased house of *Les Délices,* his first residence in Geneva. He is now in a certain sort admitted president of the European intellectual republic, and from his president's chair is laughing quietly at his own follies, heartily at the kings of his acquaintance, and particularly at Frederick and his "*Œuvres des Poeshies.*" It is the time when, according to his own letters, he is resolved to have on every occasion and to invite to himself by all inducements, "the society of agreeable "and clever people."* Goldsmith flute in hand, or Goldsmith learned and poor companion to a rich young fool, in either position or character a youth yearning to literature, its fame, and its awe-inspiring professors, could hardly find himself near *Les Délices* without finding perhaps easy passage to its illustrious owner; and there at any rate, by whatever chance or design, he seems really to have been. A large party was present, and conversation turned upon the English; of whom, as he afterwards observed in a letter to the *Public Ledger,* Goldsmith recollected Voltaire

1755.
Æt. 27.

---

the honour in company with Malesherbes to be put in prison by Robespierre,—made much, in a book of published anecdotes, of his supposed detection of this error: Mr. Irving having repeated it in the interval, and Lord Brougham having also given currency to it in a *Life of Voltaire.* "Take for instance," said a fellow-townsman of Mr. Roche, enlarging at the time on the cleverness of his octogenarian friend, "Brougham, "Washington Irving, Mr. Prior, and "Oliver Goldsmith, all of whom are con-"victed of a gross conspiracy to cir-"culate a fraud of which honest Noll was "the original fabricator, the others hav-"ing only endorsed the forgery. Gold-"smith could not by chance have con-"versed with Voltaire in Paris during "the year 1754, as he impudently says he "did, for the simple reason that Voltaire "quitted Paris in 1750, and never set "foot in the capital till twenty-eight "years afterwards, in 1778. The two "lives by Irving and Prior still hold this "falsehood, but"—and the writer ("Fa-"ther Prout" in the *Globe*) went on to say that I appeared not only to have entertained some suspicion of it, but to have doubted the veracity of my hero, and that in consequence I had omitted the anecdote altogether. My text in this passage, nevertheless, stands now precisely as it did on the first publication of my book.

* See the autobiographical fragment written on that quarrel with the great king which is explained (with how much else!) in Mr. Carlyle's *History of Frederick.*

to have remarked, that at the battle of Dettingen they exhibited prodigies of valour, but lessened their well-bought conquest by lessening the merit of those they had conquered.

In a *Life of Voltaire* afterwards begun, but not finished, in one of the magazines of the day, Goldsmith recalled this conversation in greater detail, to illustrate the general manner of the famous Frenchman. "When he "was warmed in discourse, and "had got over a hesitating manner "which sometimes he was "subject to, it was rapture to hear "him. His meagre visage seemed "insensibly to gather beauty, "every muscle in it had meaning, "ing, and his eye beamed with "unusual brightness." Among the persons alleged to be present, though this might be open to question if anything of great strictness were involved, the names are used of the vivid and noble talker, Diderot, and of Fontenelle, then on the verge of the grave that waited for him nigh a hundred years.* The last, Goldsmith says, reviled the English in everything; the first, with unequal ability, defended them; and, to the surprise of all, Voltaire long continued silent. At last he was roused from his reverie; a new life pervaded his frame; he flung himself into an animated defence of England; strokes of the finest raillery fell thick and fast on his antagonist, and he spoke almost without intermission for three hours. "I never was so "much charmed," Oliver adds; "nor did I ever remember so absolute "a victory as he gained in "this dispute."*

1753.
Æt. 27.

Goldsmith here was a worshipper at the footstool, and Voltaire was on the throne; yet it is possible that when the great Frenchman heard in later years the name of the celebrated Englishman he may have remembered this night at *Les Délices*, and the enthusiasm of his young admirer. He may have recalled, with a smile for its fervent zeal, the pale, somewhat sad face, with its two great wrinkles between the eyebrows, but redeemed from ugliness or contempt by its kind expression of simplicity, as his own was by its wonderful intellect and look of unutterable mockery. For, though Voltaire was upwards of sixty-one when they met, and Goldsmith was not twenty-seven, it happened that when (in 1778) the Frenchman's popularity returned, and all the fashion and all the intellect of Paris were again at the feet of the phi-

* In the *Animated Nature* Goldsmith takes special occasion to interpose (ii. 63), amid the remarks of Buffon on old age and death, a mention of his own about Fontenelle. "Fontenelle, the celebrated "writer, was naturally of a very weak "and delicate habit of body. He was "affected by the smallest irregularities: "and had frequently suffered severe fits "of illness from the slightest causes. "But the remarkable equality of his "temper, and his seeming want of passion, "lengthened out his life to above a "hundred, &c."

* *Miscellaneous Works*, iii. 221, 225.

losopher of Ferney; our English Johnsons, Burkes, Gibbons, Wartons, Sheridans, and Reynoldses were discussing the inscription for the marble tomb of the author of the *Vicar of Wakefield*.

1755.
Æt. 27.

The lecture-rooms of Germany are so often referred to in his prose writings, that, as he passed to Switzerland, he must have taken them in his way. In the *Polite Learning*,[*] one is painted admirably: its Nego, Probo, and Distinguo, growing gradually loud till denial, approval, and distinction are altogether lost; till disputants grow warm, moderator is unheard, audience take part in the debate, and the whole hall buzzes with false philosophy, sophistry, and error. Passing into Switzerland, he saw Schaffhausen frozen quite across, and the water standing in columns where the cataract had formerly fallen. His *Animated Nature*, in which this is noticed, contains also masterly description, from his own experience, of the wonders that present themselves to the traveller over lofty mountains; and he adds that "nothing "can be finer or more exact "than Mr. Pope's description of "a traveller straining up the "Alps."[**] Geneva was his resting-place in Switzerland; but he visited Basle and Berne; ate a "savoury" dinner on the top of the Alps;[***] flushed wood-

cocks on Mount Jura;[*] wondered to see the sheep in the valleys, as he had read of them in the old pastoral poets, following the sound of the shepherd's pipe of reed;[**] and, poet himself at last, sent off to his brother Henry[***] the first sketch of what was afterwards expanded into the *Traveller*. Who can doubt that it would contain the germ of these exquisite lines?—

Eternal blessings crown my earliest
    friend,
And round his dwelling guardian saints
    attend:
Bless'd be that spot, where cheerful guests
    retire
To pause from toil, and trim their even-
    ing fire;
Bless'd that abode, where want and pain
    repair
And every stranger finds a ready chair:
Bless'd be those feasts, with simple plenty
    crown'd,
Where all the ruddy family around
Laugh at the jests or pranks that never
    fall,
Or sigh with pity at some mournful
    tale,
Or press the bashful stranger to his
    food,
And learn the luxury of doing good.

Remembering thus his brother's humble kindly life, he had set in pleasant contrast before

---

[*] *Animated Nature*, IV. 338.

[**] *Ib.* 252-3. The description is very pretty.

[***] Glover, who related many anecdotes on Goldsmith's own authority, distinctly tells us (Malone's Dublin edition of the *Poems*, p. IV: and see *Annual Register*, XVII. 30) that it was here he first tried a sustained flight in verse, and that he sent from Switzerland the first sketch of the *Traveller* to his brother Henry. Expressly indeed he states himself in the dedication that a part of it had been sent to his brother from Switzerland, and Mrs. Hodson tells us: "she hath seen letters "to his friends, which he wrote from

---

[*] Chap. v.
[**] *Animated Nature*, I. 130.
[***] *Ib.* I. 273.

him the weak luxuriance of Italy, and the sturdy enjoyment of the rude Swiss home. Observe in this following passage with what an exquisite art of artlessness, if I may so speak, an unstudied character is given to the verses by the recurring sounds in the rhymes; by the use that is made of particular words and their repetition; and by the personal feeling, the natural human pathos, which invests the lines with a charm so rarely imparted to mere descriptive poetry. These extracts are given thus early because there is every reason to believe that much of the poem was written before his return to England, and that certainly he had, while himself a traveller, conceived the simple and extremely striking design of bringing into contrast the varieties of scenery and character observed by him, only the more decisively to show that it is not by such varieties, or by any particular institutions, the happiness of individuals is determined, so much as by their own self-government in mind and temper.

My soul, turn from them, turn we to survey
Where rougher climes a nobler race display—

Where the bleak Swiss their stormy man-
　sions tread,
And force a churlish soil for scanty
　bread.
No product here the barren hills
　afford,
But man and steel, the soldier
　and his sword;
No vernal blooms their torpid rocks ar-
　ray,
But winter lingering chills the lap of
　May;
No zephyr fondly sues the mountain's
　breast,
But meteors glare, and stormy glooms
　invest.
Yet still, even here, content can spread a
　charm,
Redress the clime, and all its rage dis-
　arm.
Though poor the peasant's hut, his feasts
　though small,
He sees his little lot the lot of all;
Sees no contiguous palace rear its head
To shame the meanness of his humble
　shed—
No costly lord the sumptuous banquet
　deal
To make him loathe his vegetable meal—
But calm, and bred in ignorance and toil,
Each wish contracting, fits him to the
　soil.
Cheerful at morn, he wakes from short
　repose,
Breasts the keen air and carols as he
　goes; *
With patient angle trolls the finny deep;
Or drives his venturous plough-share to
　the steep;
Or seeks the den where snow-tracks mark
　the way,
And drags the struggling savage into day.
At night returning, every labour sped,
He sits him down the monarch of a
　shed:

1755.
———
Æt. 27.

"Switzerland, Germany, and Italy." Narrative in *Percy Memoir*, 14. These letters have been supposed to be still in existence; and another in more humorous vein, written from Paris and describing his necessities, is also alleged to have been preserved; but none of them have yet risen to the surface, and it is my own belief, as I lately said, that they have perished.

* The sixth edition of the *Traveller*, published in 1770, is undoubtedly the best. "Mansion" in the third line of the above extract, is the reading of the earlier editions, but "mansions" is obviously better. In the twenty-second line, the word "breasts," which is in every edition published while Goldsmith lived, was corrupted into "breathes" in the editions afterwards printed, and is so given in Prior's (or rather Wright's) edition of 1837. The superiority of the original word is very marked.

4*

Smiles by his cheerful fire, and round
    surveys
His children's looks that brighten at the
    blaze —
      While his loved partner, boastful
        of her board,
Displays her cleanly platter on
    the board:
And haply too some pilgrim, thither led,
With many a tale repays the nightly bed.
Thus every good his native wilds impart,
Imprints the patriot passion on his heart:
And e'en those hills, that round his man-
    sion rise,
Enhance the bliss his scanty fund sup-
    plies:
Dear is that shed to which his soul con-
    forms,
And dear that hill which lifts him to the
    storms;
And as a child, when scaring sounds
    molest,
Clings closer and closer to the mother's
    breast —
So the loud torrent, and the whirlwind's
    roar,
But bind him to his native mountains
    more.

1755.
Æt. 27.

Such was the education of thought and heart now taking the place of a more learned discipline in the truant wanderer; such the wider range of sympathies and enjoyment opening out upon his view; such the larger knowledge that awakened in him, as the subtle perceptions of genius arose. More than ever was he here, in the practical paths of life, a loiterer and laggard; yet as he passed from place to place, finding for his foot no solid resting-ground, no spot of all the world that he might hope to call his own, there was yet sinking deep into the heart of the homeless vagrant that power and possession to which all else on earth subserves and is obedient, and which out

of the very abyss of poverty and want gave him right and title over all.

For me your tributary stores combine;
Creation's heir, the world, the world is
    mine!

Descending into Piedmont he observed the floating bee-houses of which he speaks so pleasantly in the *Animated Nature.* * "As "the bees are continually choos- "ing their flowery pasture along "the banks of the stream, they "are furnished with sweets be- "fore unrifled; and thus a single "floating bee-house yields the "proprietor a considerable in- "come. Why a method similar "to this has never been adopted "in England, where we have "more gentle rivers, and more "flowery banks, than any other "part of the world, I know not." After this, proofs of his having seen Florence, Verona, Mantua, and Milan, are apparent; and in Carinthia the incident occurred with which his famous couplet has too hastily reproached a people, when, sinking with fatigue, after a long day's toilsome walk, he was turned from a peasant's hut at which he implored a lodging. At Padua he is supposed to have stayed some little time;** and here, it has been as-

* vi. 100. In the same narrative (ii. 171) he mentions what he had observed of the tarantula in Italy. "A friend of "mine had a servant who suffered him- "self to be bit, &c."

** The *Percy Memoir* (35) says six months, and adds that, "descending to Italy he "made his description of that country "so much more vigorous and picturesque "than that of Addison, though they both

serted, though in this case also the official records are lost, he received his degree. Here, or at Louvain, or at some other of these foreign universities where he always boasted of himself as hero in the disputations to which his philosophic vagabond refers, there can hardly be a question that the degree, a very simple and accessible matter at any of them, was actually conferred. "Sir," said Boswell to Johnson, "he *disputed* his passage through "Europe."* Of his having also taken a somewhat close survey of those countless academic institutions of Italy in the midst of which Italian learning at this time withered, evidence is not wanting; and he always thoroughly discriminated the character of that country and its people.

But small the bliss that sense alone
        bestows,
And sensual bliss is all the nation
        knows;

In florid beauty groves and fields ap-
        pear—
Man seems the only growth that dwindles
        here!
Contrasted faults through all his
        manners reign:
Though poor, luxurious; though
        submissive, vain:
Though grave, yet trifling; zealous, yet
        untrue—
And even in penance planning sins
        anew.

1755.

Æt 27.

It is a hard struggle to return to England; but his steps are now bent that way. "My skill "in music," says the philo- sophic vagabond, whose account there will be little danger in ac- cepting as at least some certain reflection of the truth, "could "avail me nothing in Italy, "where every peasant was a "better musician than I: but by "this time I had acquired an- "other talent which answered "my purpose as well, and this "was a skill in disputation. In "all the foreign universities and "convents there are, upon cer- "tain days, philosophical theses "maintained against every ad- "ventitious disputant; for which, "if the champion opposes with "any dexterity, he can claim a "gratuity in money, a dinner, "and a bed for one night. In "this manner, then, I fought my "way towards England; walked "along from city to city; ex- "amined mankind more nearly; "and, if I may so express it, "saw both sides of the pic- "ture."

"viewed it through pretty much the same "political optics." The same authority informs us (36) that Goldsmith, after his travels, landed at Dover in 1756; and there is a passage in the first number of the *Bee*, written in the assumed character of a traveller, which no doubt fairly describes his own restless and desultory wanderings. "When will my restless "disposition give me leave to enjoy the "present hour? When at Lyons I thought "all happiness lay beyond the Alps; "when in Italy, I found myself still in "want of something, and expected to "leave solicitude behind me by going "into Roumelia; and now you find me "turning back, still expecting ease every- "where but where I am. It is now seven "years since I saw the face of a single "creature who cared a farthing whether "I was dead or alive."
    * *Life*, n. 189.

CHAPTER VI.

Peckham School and Grub Street.
1756—1757.

1756.
Æt. 28. IT was on the 1st of February, 1756, just at the breaking out of the war, that Oliver Goldsmith stepped upon the shore at Dover, and stood again among his country-men.

Stern o'er each bosom reason holds her
    state,
With daring aims irregularly great.
Pride in their port, defiance in their eye,
I see the lords of human kind pass by,
Intent on high designs. . .

The comfort of seeing it must have been nearly all the comfort to him. At this moment, there is little doubt, he had not a farthing in his pocket; and from the lords of human kind, intent on looking in any direction but his, it was much more difficult to get one than from the care-less good-humoured peasants of France or Flanders. In the struggle of ten days or a fort-night which it took him to get to London, there is reason to suspect that he attempted a "low "comedy" performance in a country barn; and, at one of the towns he passed, had implored to be hired in an apothecary's shop.* In the middle of February he was wandering without friend or acquaintance, without the knowledge or comfort of even one kind face, in the lonely, ter-rible, LONDON streets.

He thought he might find em-ployment as an usher; and there is a dark uncertain kind of story, of his getting a bare subsistence in this way for some few months, under a feigned name: which would have involved him in a worse distress but for the judi-cious silence of the Dublin Doc-tor (Radcliff), fellow of the col-lege and joint-tutor with Wilder, to whom he had been suddenly obliged to refer for a character, and whose good-humoured ac-quiescence in his private appeal saved him from suspicion of im-posture. Goldsmith showed his gratitude by a long, and, it is said, a most delightful letter to Radcliff, descriptive of his travels; now unhappily destroyed.* He

---

* In one of the newspaper notices which appeared after his death, the writer stated that he had once set up as an apothecary in a country town. This was immediately denied, on the assump-tion that Ireland was referred to; where-upon the writer rejoined (*St. James' Chronicle*, April 12, 14, 1771), "We never "said that he set up in Ireland. The "country town alluded to is an English "town, the name of which is forgotten. "But the writer of this and the former "paragraph assures the public that he "had the anecdote from the Doctor's "own mouth." Mr. Prior has quoted this, I. 201.

* Percy's friend, Campbell (in his *Phi-losophical Survey of the South of Ireland*, in a series of letters to John Watkinson, M.D. London, 1777, 286-9), gives an ac-count of this incident from the recollec-tions of Radcliff's widow, but in ante-dating it before his foreign travel makes an evident mistake, which is silently cor-rected in the *Percy Memoir*, 37, where re-ference is made to Campbell's book. I now quote the latter: "She mentioned to "me a very long letter from him (Gold-"smith), which she had often heard her "husband read to his friends, upon "the commencement of Goldsmith's "celebrity. But this, with other things

also wrote again to his more familiar Irish friends, but his letters were again unanswered. He went among the London apothecaries, and asked them to let him spread plaisters for them, pound in their mortars, run with their medicines: but they, too, asked him for a character, and he had none to give.* At last a chemist of the name of Jacob took compassion upon him, and the late Conversation Sharp used to point out a shop at the corner of Monument-yard on Fish-street-hill, shown to him in his youth as this benevolent Mr. Jacob's. Some dozen years later, Goldsmith startled a brilliant circle at Bennet Langton's or Reynolds's with an anecdote of "When I lived among "the beggars in Axe-lane,"** just as Napoleon, fifty years later, appalled the party of crowned heads at Dresden with his story of "When I was lieutenant in the "regiment of La Fère." The experience with the beggars will of course date before that social

[margin: 1756. Æt. 28.]

"of more value, was unfortunately lost "by accidental fire since her husband's "death. Upon his first going to England, "he was in such distress, that he would "gladly have become an usher to a "country school; but so destitute was he "of friends to recommend him, that he "could not without difficulty obtain even "this low department. The master of "the school scrupled to employ him "without some testimonial of his past "life. Goldsmith referred him to his "tutor at college for a character; but all "this while he went under a feigned "name. From this resource, therefore, "one would think that little in his favour "could be ever hoped for; but he only "wanted to serve a present exigency; an "ushership was not his object. In this "strait, he wrote a letter to Dr. Radcliff, "imploring him, as he tendered the wel- "fare of an old pupil, not to answer a "letter which he would probably re- "ceive, the same post with his own, from "the schoolmaster. He added that he "had good reasons for concealing both "from him and the rest of the world "his name, and the real state of the "case; every circumstance of which he "promised to communicate on some fu- "ture occasion. His tutor, embarrassed "enough before to know what answer he "should give, resolved at last to give "none. And thus was poor Goldsmith "snatched from between the horns of "his present dilemma, and suffered to "drag on a miserable life for a few pro- "bationary months." Letter from Athlone, dated November 1775. Campbell goes on to state that the promised letter of thanks to Radcliff "contained a "comical narrative of his adventures "from leaving Ireland to that time; his "musical talents having procured him a "welcome reception wherever he went. "My authority says, her husband ad- "mired this letter more than any part of "his works. But she would not venture "to trust her memory in detailing par- "ticulars, which after all could not ap- "pear very interesting, but from his own "manner of stating them." Isaac Reed quotes the passage (Life prefixed to *Poems by Goldsmith and Parnell*, 1795, p. xi-xii.) with belief in it.

* "His threadbare coat, his uncouth "figure, and Hibernian dialect, caused "him to meet with repeated refusals." *Percy Memoir*, 38. "His broad Irish ac- "cent," says Isaac Reed, "and his un- "couth appearance, operated against his "reception."

** "George Langton told me that he "was present one day" (it could not have been George, but no doubt was Bennet) "when Goldsmith (Dr. Oliver), "in a circle of good company, began "with, 'When I lived among the beggars "'in Axe Lane,'—— Every one present "was well acquainted with the varied "habits of Goldsmith's life, and with the "naiveté of his character; but this sudden "trait of simplicity could not but cause a "momentary surprise." Best's *Personal and Literary Memorials*, 76.

elevation of mixing and selling drugs on Fish-street-hill. For doubtless the latter brought him into the comfort and good society on which he afterwards dwelt with such unction, in describing an elegant little lodging at three shillings a week, with its lukewarm dinner served up between two pewter plates from a cook's-shop.

1756.
Æt. 28.

Thus employed among the drugs, he heard one day that Sleigh, an old fellow-student of the Edinburgh time, was lodging not far off, and he resolved to visit him. He had to wait, of course, for his only holiday; "but notwithstand-"ing it was Sunday," he said afterwards in relating the anec-dote, "and it is to be supposed "I was in my best clothes, Sleigh "did not know me. Such is the "tax the unfortunate pay to "poverty." He did not fail to leave to the unfortunate the lessons they should be taught by it. Doctor Sleigh (Foote's *Doctor Sligo*, honourably named in an earlier page of this narrative) recollected at last his friend of two years gone; and when he did so, added Goldsmith, "I found his "heart as warm as ever, and he "shared his purse and friendship "with me during his continuance "in London."* With the help of this warm heart and friendly purse, seconded also by the good apothecary Jacob ("who," says Cooke, "saw in Goldsmith

1757.
Æt. 29.

"talents above his condition"), he now "rose from the apothe-"cary's drudge to be a physician "in a humble way," in Bankside, Southwark.* It was not a thriving business: poor physician to the poor: but it seemed a change for the better, and hope was strong in him.

An old Irish acquaintance and school-fellow (Beatty) met him at this time in the streets. He was in a suit of green and gold, miserably old and tarnished; his shirt and neckcloth appeared to have been worn at least a fortnight; but he said he was practising physic, and doing very well!** It is hard to confess failure to one's school-fellow.

Our next glimpse, though not more satisfactory, is more professional. The green and gold have faded quite out, into a rusty full-trimmed black suit: the pockets of which, like those of the poets in innumerable farces, overflow with papers. The coat is second-hand velvet, cast-off legacy of a more successful brother of the craft; the cane, and the wig, have served more fortunate owners; and the humble practitioner of Bankside is feeling the pulse of a patient humbler than himself, whose courteous entreaties to be allowed to relieve him of the hat he keeps pressed over his heart, he more courteously but firmly declines. Beneath the hat is a large patch

* Cooke's Narrative. Europ. Mag. XXIV. 91.

* Percy Memoir, 38.
** Prior, I. 215.

in the rusty velvet, which he thus conceals.

But he cannot conceal the starvation which is again impending. Even the poor printer's workman he attends, can see how hardly in that respect it goes with him; and finds courage one day to suggest that his master has been kind to clever men before now, has visited Mr. Johnson in sponging-houses, and might be serviceable to a poor physician. For his master is no less than Mr. Samuel Richardson, of Salisbury-court and Parson's-green, printer, and author of *Clarissa*. The hint is successful; and Goldsmith, appointed reader and corrector to the press* in Salisbury-court,—admitted now and then even to the parlour of Richardson himself, and there grimly smiled upon by its chief literary ornament, great poet of the day, the author of the *Night Thoughts*, **—sees hope in litera-

tare once more. He begins a tragedy. With what modest expectation, with what cheerful, simple hearted deference to critical objection, another of his Edinburgh fellow-students, Doctor Farr, will relate to us.

1757.
Æt. 29.

"From the time of Goldsmith's leaving Edinburgh, in the year 1754, I never saw him till 1756, when I was in London, attending the hospitals and lectures; early in January" [1756 is an evident mistake for 1757] "he called upon me one morning before I was up, and on my entering the room I recognised my old acquaintance, dressed in a rusty full-trimmed black suit, with his pockets full of papers, which instantly reminded me of the poet in Garrick's farce of *Lethe*. After we had finished our breakfast, he drew from his pocket a part of a tragedy; which he said he had brought for my correction; In vain I pleaded inability when he began to read, and every part on which I expressed a doubt as to the propriety was immediately blotted out. I then more earnestly pressed him not to trust to my judgment, but to the opinion of persons better qualified to decide on dramatic compositions, on which he told me he had submitted his production, so far as he had written, to Mr. Richardson, the author of *Clarissa*, on which I peremptorily declined offering another criticism on the performance. The name and subject of the tragedy have unfortunately escaped my memory, neither do I recollect with exactness how much he had written, though I am inclined to believe that he had not completed the third act; I never heard whether he afterwards finished it. In this visit I remember his relating a strange Quixotic scheme he had in contemplation of going to decipher the inscriptions on the *written mountains*,*

* Boswell's enumeration of the employments of his adversity is strictly correct, as far as it goes. "As I once observed to Dr. Johnson, he *disputed* his "passage through Europe. He then came "to England, and was employed successively in the capacities of usher to an "academy, a corrector of the press, a "reviewer, and a writer for a news-"paper." *Life*, II. 189.

** Not that Young's smiles were always "grim." He is said to have been very pleasant in conversation; and I am glad to remember that his parish was indebted to the good-humour of the poet for an assembly and a bowling-green. Since this note was written I find a passage of Moore's *Diary* (VI. 11) wherein Rogers remarks to Moore, on this very subject of Young's mirth in conversation, "I dare say that people who *act* mel-"ancholy as he did, must have a vent in

"some way or other. Now, mutes at "funerals—I can imagine them, when "they throw off their cloaks, playing "leap-frog together."

* Accounts of the written mountains may be seen in Burckhardt's *Syria*, 606-13 (Ed. 1822); they are also referred to in Irby and Mangles' *Travels* (Ed. 1844),

though he was altogether ignorant of Arabic, or the language in which they might be supposed to be written. The salary of £300 per annum, which had been left for the purpose, was the temptation!"*

Temptation indeed! The head may well be full of projects of any kind, when the pockets are only full of papers. But not, alas, to decipher inscriptions on the written mountains, only to preside over pot-hooks at Peckham, was doomed to be the lot of Goldsmith. One Doctor Milner, known still as the author of Latin and Greek grammars useful in their day, kept a school there; his son ** was among these young Edinburgh fellow-students with Oliver, come up, like Farr, Sleigh, and others, to their London examinations; and thus it happened that the office of assistant at the Peckham academy befell. "All my ambition now is to live," he may fairly be supposed to have said, in the words he afterwards placed in the mouth of young Primrose. He seems to have been installed at about the beginning of 1757. An attempt has been made to show that it was an earlier year, but on grounds too unsafe to oppose to known dates in his life. The

good people of Peckham have also cherished traditions of *Goldsmith House*, as what was once the school is now fondly designated, which may not safely be admitted here. Broken window-panes have been religiously kept, for the supposed treasure of his handwriting;* and old gentlemen, once Doctor Milner's scholars, have claimed, against every reasonable evidence, the honour of having been whipped by the author of the *Vicar of Wakefield*. But nothing is with certainty known, save what a daughter of the schoolmaster has related.

At the end of the century Miss Hester Milner, "an intelligent "lady, the youngest, and only "remaining of Doctor Milner's "ten daughters," was still alive, and very willing to tell what she recollected of their old usher. An answer he had given her one day to a question of her own, which, as it interested her youth, had happily not ceased to occupy and interest her old age, seemed to have retained all the strong impression that it first made upon her. Her father being a presbyterian divine, she could hardly fail to hear many arguments and differences in doctrine or dogma discussed; and, in connection with these, it appears to have occurred to her one day to ask Mr. Goldsmith

---

126; and by many other writers on the East; see also Lady Sundon's *Memoirs*, ii. p. 8. The inscriptions cover the rocks, some of them twelve or fifteen feet high, along a range of nearly three leagues, written from right to left, in short lines.

* *Percy Memoir*, 31, 40.

** Afterwards a physician in large practice at Maidstone, where his ten sisters kept house for him until all died but the youngest.

* I derived this from a History of Islington lent to me by Mr. Jerrold, but I omitted at the time to make a more exact reference.

what particular commentator on the Scriptures *h·* would recommend; when after a pause the usher replied, with much earnestness, that in his belief commonsense was the best interpreter of the sacred writings.*

What other reminiscences she indulged took a lighter and indeed humorous tone. He was very goodnatured, she said; played all kinds of tricks on the servants and the boys, of which he had no lack of return in kind; told entertaining stories; "was "remarkably cheerful, both in "the family and with the young "gentlemen of the school"; and amused everybody with his flute. Two of his practical jokes on Doctor Milner's servant, or footboy, were thought worth putting in a notebook by the worthy gentleman,** a neighbour of Miss Milner's at Islington, to whom she related them, and who had already himself made some name in the world. Thinking that the old lady's recollections somewhat pleasantly illustrated the "humour and cheerfulness of "Goldsmith," he was careful, after "receiving them from Miss "Milner on drinking tea with "her," to write them down immediately on his return home. And as even biography has its critics jealous for its due and proper dignity, the present writer had perhaps better anticipate a possible objection to these and other anecdotes which in this narrative will first be read, by pleading also the apology of Miss Milner's friend, that "however trivial they "may be, there are some young "persons to whom they may "prove acceptable."

William was the name of the schoolmaster's servant, and his duty being to wait on the young gentlemen at table, clean their shoes, and so forth, he was not, in social position, so very far removed from the usher but that much familiarity subsisted between them. He was weak, but good-tempered, and one of Goldsmith's jokes had for its object to cure him of a hopeless passion with which a pretty servant-girl in the neighbourhood had inspired him. This youthful Phillis seems to have rather suddenly quitted service and gone back to her home in Yorkshire, leaving behind her a sort of half-promise that she would some day send William a letter; which everybody but William of course knew was only her goodnatured way of getting rid of importunity: he, however, having a fixed persuasion that the letter would come, every morning would watch the

1757.
Æt. 29.

---

* *Gent. Mag.* LXXXVII. 277.

** Mr. John Evans, of Pullin's Row, Islington: at this time a popular preacher in the Baptist persuasion, and known as the writer of a *Brief Sketch of the Denominations*, &c. He conducted a school in Pullin's Row; and his high character is an additional voucher for the authenticity of what he relates. He was a very prolific writer. See a list of his works in *Biographical Dictionary of Living Authors* (1816), 110; and in the *London Catalogue* (1846), 161. He sent his anecdotes to the fifty-third volume of the *European Magazine* (373-375).

postman as he passed, and became at last so wretched with disappointment that Goldsmith goodnaturedly devised an attempt to cure these unfounded expectations. In a servant-girl's hand elaborately imitated, and with such language and spelling as would exactly hit off the longed-for letter out of Yorkshire ("the lady who told me "the anecdote," interposes the narrator, "saw it before it was "sent"), Goldsmith prepared an epistle from Phillis which was to convey to William, in effect, that she had for various reasons delayed writing, but was now to inform him that a young man, by trade a glass-grinder, was repaying his addresses to her, that she had not given him much encouragement, but her relations were strongly for the match, that she, however, often thought of William, and must conclude by saying that something must now be done one way or another, &c. &c. Properly sealed and directed, one of the young gentlemen had it in charge from Goldsmith to take in the letters on the postman's next visit, place this among them, and hand them all to the footboy; "the young gentlemen "being in the habit of running "towards the door whenever the "postman made his appearance." Everything fell out as desired; the letter was seized, read, and secreted by its supposed owner; and though nothing was said of its contents to anybody, the fact of something having happened

1757.
Æt. 29.

as plainly revealed itself in William's increased air of importance, as formerly was shadowed forth in the young lady of Mr. Bickerstaff's acquaintance, who held up her head higher than ordinary from having on (as was afterwards discovered) a pair of striped garters. Nevertheless, for the rest of the day, Goldsmith let the potion work which was to effect the cure; and not till night did he disturb it by the startling question, addressed to the servant-man on his walking into the kitchen, "So, William, "you *have* had a letter from York- "shire? Well, what does she "say to you? Come, now, tell "me all about it." William recovered his surprise, confessed the letter, but would say nothing more. "Yes," nodding his head; "but I shall not tell you, Mr. "Goldsmith, anything about it; "no, no, that will never do." "What, nothing?" No. "Not "if she says she'll marry you?" No. "Not if she has married "anybody else?" No. "Well "then," says Goldsmith, "sup- "pose, William, *I* tell *you* what "the contents of the letter are. "Come," he added, looking at a newspaper he held in his hand, "I will *read* you your letter just "as I find it here;" and he read it accordingly, word for word, to his amazed listener, who at last cried out very angrily, "You use "me very ill, Mr. Goldsmith! you "have opened my letter." The sequel was a full explanation by the goodnatured usher, and such kindly advice not in future to expect any letter more real than that which had been written to cure him of his folly, that, according to Miss Milner, "poor "William was then induced to "believe it the wisest way."

This anecdote sufficiently implies that poor William had obstinate notions of his own, which it was not very easy to dissipate by ordinary modes of persuasion. One of these, Miss Milner told our informant, was a preposterous estimate of his capacity to do astonishing things, which nobody else could attempt, in the eating and drinking way. The whole kitchen laughed at him; but of course refused to accept his challenge for a trial at some poisonous draught, or fare unfit for a Christian. They enlisted Goldsmith at last, however, who, having promised to administer correction to this very eccentric vanity, thus commenced preparations. He procured a piece of uncoloured Cheshire cheese, rolled it up in the form of a candle about an inch in length, and, twisting a bit of white paper to the size of a wick, and blacking its extremity, thrust it into one of the ends of the cheese, which he then put into a candlestick over the kitchen fireplace, taking care that in another, by the side of it, there should be placed the end of a real candle, in size and appearance exactly the same. Everything thus ready, in came William, and was straightway challenged by the usher to display what he had so often boasted of, in a trial with himself. "You "eat yonder piece of "candle," said he, taking down the cheese, "and I "will eat this." William assented rather drily. "I have no "objection to begin," continued Goldsmith, "but both must finish "at the same time." William nodded, took his portion of candle, and, still reluctant, looked ruefully on with the other servants while Goldsmith began gnawing away at *his* supposed share, making terrible wry faces. With no heart or stomach for a like unsavoury meal, his adversary beheld with amazement the progress made, and not till Goldsmith had devoured all but the very last morsel, did he take sudden courage, open his mouth, and "fling his own piece down "his throat in a moment." This had the seeming effect of a sudden triumph over the challenger, which made the kitchen ring with laughter; and William, less distressed with his real sufferings, now that all was over, than elated by his fancied victory, took upon him to express sympathy for the defeated usher, and really wondered why he had not, like himself, swallowed so nauseous a morsel all at once. "Why truly," replied the usher, with undisturbed gravity, "my bit of candle, Wil-"liam, was no other than a bit "of very nice Cheshire cheese, "and therefore, William, I was

1757.

Æt. 29.

"unwilling to lose the relish "of it."

Nor were these the only stories related of the obscure usher at Doctor Milner's school. Others were told, though less distinctly remembered, having less mirth and more pathos in their tone; but the general picture conveyed by Miss Milner's recollections was that of a teacher as boyish as the boys he taught. With his small salary, it would seem, he was always in advance. It went for the most part, Miss Milner said, on the day he received it, in relief to beggars, and in sweetmeats for the younger class. Her mother would observe to him at last: "You had better, Mr. Gold- "smith, let me keep your money "for you, as I do for some of the "young gentlemen:" to which he would goodhumouredly answer, "In truth, madam, there is "equal need." *

All this, at the same time, is very evidently putting the best face upon the matter, as it was natural Miss Milner should. But in sober fact, and notwithstanding the tricks on William, notwithstanding these well-remembered childish or clownish games, and a certain cheerfulness of temper even in gravest things, it was Goldsmith's bitterest time, this Peckham time. He could think in after years of his beggary, but not of his slavery, without shame. "Oh, that is all a "holiday at Peckham," said an old friend very innocently one day, in a common proverbial phrase; but Goldsmith reddened, and asked if he meant to affront him. * Nor can we fail to recall the tone in which he afterwards alluded to this mode of life. When, two years later, he tried to persuade people that a schoolmaster was of more importance in the state than to be neglected and left to starve, he described what he had known too well. "The usher," he wrote, in the sixth number of the *Bee*, "is "generally the laughing-stock of

* Watkins's *Literary Anecdotes*, 515.

* *Europ. Mag.* xxiv. 92. He would tell many stories of his own distresses, says Cooke, "but the *little story of Peckham* "*school* he always carefully avoided." Let me not quit these recollections of Mrs. Hester Milner without allusion to what was written of her by Mr. Evans in the *Gentleman's Magazine*, on the occasion of her death at a most advanced age, in January 1817. His mention of the fact of her attending the discourses of two dissenting ministers, "not alike in their "religious creed," but with neither of whom she quarrelled, seems to imply that she had profited by the early advice of her father's old usher in these matters, and put it to practical use. "She never "troubled herself much with speculative "points, and was most commendably dis- "posed to receive instruction from good "men of every denomination." Mr. Evans adds that she had also a talent for poetical composition, had gracefully translated many of Petrarch's sonnets, was well acquainted both with French and Italian, and showed the singularity and excellence of her taste by the books she selected to read. For instance, he had himself purchased at her request, for her amusement on winter nights at Islington, the works of Lord Bacon, Paley's writings, Samuel Richardson's and Anna Seward's *Correspondence*, Fuller's *Worthies*, and Raleigh's *History of the World*. She left very considerable property, the most part for charitable purposes. *Gent. Mag.* LXXXVII. 178.

"the school. Every trick is "played upon him; the oddity of "his manners, his dress, or his "language, is a fund of eternal "ridicule; the master himself "now and then cannot avoid join- "ing in the laugh, and the poor "wretch, eternally resenting this "ill-usage, lives in a state of war "with all the family. This is a "very proper person, is it not, "to give children a relish for "learning? They must esteem "learning very much, when they "see its professors used with "such ceremony!" So, too, and with more direct reason, it was understood to refer to the Peck- ham discomforts, when he talked of the poor usher obliged to sleep in the same bed with the French teacher, "who disturbs "him for an hour every night in "papering and filleting his hair; "and stinks worse than a carrion "with his rancid pomatums, when "he lays his head beside him on "the bolster." Who will not think, moreover, of George Prim- rose and his cousin? "Ay," cried he, "this is indeed a very "pretty career that has been "chalked out for you. I have "been an usher at a boarding- "school myself; and may I die "by an anodyne necklace, but I "had rather be under-turnkey in "Newgate. I was up early and "late: I was browbeat by the "master, hated for my ugly face "by the mistress, worried by the "boys." Finally, in the only anecdote that rests on other safe authority than Miss Milner's,

there is quite sufficient reason in fact for adoption of the same tone.

Mr. Samuel Bishop, whose sons have had dis- tinction in the church, was a Peckham scholar, and the story is told as it was received from one of the sons.* "When amus- "ing his younger companions "during play-hours with the flute, "and expatiating on the plea- "sures derived from music, in "addition to its advantages in "society as a gentlemanlike ac- "quirement, a pert boy, looking "at his situation and personal "disadvantages with something "of contempt, rudely replied to "the effect that *he* surely could "not consider himself a gentle- "man: an offence which, though "followed by chastisement, dis- "concerted and pained him ex- "tremely." That the pain of this period of his life, which even at its time of pressure we have seen relieved by the love of jest and game, could also on occa- sion be forgotten in what a happy nature found better worth re- membering, may be gathered from the same authority. When the despised usher was a cele- brated man, young Bishop, walk- ing in London with his newly- married wife, met his old teacher. Goldsmith recognised him in- stantly, as a lad he had been fond of at Peckham, and em- braced him with delight. His joy increased when Mr. Bishop made known his wife; but the

1757.
————
Æt. 29.

* *Prior*, i. 219, 220.

introduction had not unsettled the child's image in the kind man's heart. It was still the boy before him; still Master Bishop; the lad he used to cram with fruit and sweetmeats, to the judicious horror of the Milners. "Come, "my boy," he said, as his eye fell upon a basket-woman standing at the corner of the street, "come, Sam, I am delighted to "see you. I must treat you to "something. What shall it be? "Will you have some apples? "Sam," added Goldsmith, suddenly, "have you seen my pic-"ture by Sir Joshua Reynolds? "Have you seen it, Sam? Have "you got an engraving?" Not to appear negligent of the rising fame of his old preceptor, says the teller of the story, "my father "replied that he had not yet pro-"cured it; he was just furnishing "his house, but had fixed upon "the spot the print was to oc-"cupy as soon as he was ready "to receive it." "Sam," returned Goldsmith with some emotion, "if your picture had been "published, I should not have "waited an hour without having "it."

But let me not anticipate these better days. He is still the Peckham usher, and humble sitter at Doctor Milner's board, where it chanced that Griffiths the bookseller, who had started the *Monthly Review* eight years before, dined one day. Doctor Milner was one of his contributors; there was opposition in the field; Archibald

1757.
Æt. 29.

Hamilton the bookseller, with the powerful aid of Smollett, had set afloat the *Critical Review;* the talk of the table turned upon this, and some remarks by the usher attracted the attention of Griffiths. He took him aside: "Could "he furnish a few specimens of "criticism?" The offer was accepted, and the specimens;* and before the close of April 1757, Goldsmith was bound by Griffiths in an agreement for one year. He was to leave Doctor Milner's, to board and lodge with the bookseller, to have a small regular salary, and to devote himself to the *Monthly Review.***

One sees something like the transaction in the pleasant talk of George Primrose and his friend. "Come, I see you are a "lad of spirit and some learning, "what do you think of com-"mencing author, like me? You "have read in books, no doubt, "of men of genius starving at the "trade; at present I'll show you "forty very dull fellows about "town that live by it in opulence. "All honest, jog-trot men, who

* The most important of these sent was a notice of a book by Professor Mallet, to be hereafter described, which was printed in the April number of the review, with this note prefixed: "The following paper "was sent in by the gentleman who signs "D, and who, we hope, will excuse our "striking out a few paragraphs, for the "sake of brevity." In the next number of the review Goldsmith's contribution is of course not marked by any signature or prefatory notice. He had become part of the establishment.

** The agreement is correctly enough described in the *Percy Memoir* (60), but is dated a year later than when it was really entered into.

"go on smoothly and dully, and "write history and politics, and "are praised: men, sir, who, had "they been bred cobblers, would "all their lives have only mended "shoes, but never made them." On which George makes up his mind. "Finding that there was "no great degree of gentility "affixed to the character of an "usher, I resolved to accept his "proposal; and having the highest "respect for literature, hailed the "*antiqua mater* of Grub-street with "reverence. I thought it my "glory to pursue a track which "Dryden and Otway trod before "me." The difference of fact and fiction here will be, that glory had nothing to do with the matter. Griffiths and glory were not to be thought of together. The sorrowful road seemed the last that was left to the hero of my narrative: and he entered it.

On this "track," then, trod by few successfully, trod happily by fewer still, though not on that account less freely or fearlessly chosen by men of genius, we see Goldsmith in his twenty-ninth year, with only the liberty of choice that was left him by sheer necessity, calling after calling having slipped from him, launched for the first time. The unusual gloom of the prospect might have damped the ardour of a more cheerful adventurer.

Fielding had died in shattered hope and fortune, at what should have been his prime of life, three years before. Within the next two years, poor and mad, Collins was fated to descend to his early grave. Smollett was toughly fighting for his every-day's existence; and Johnson had but the other day been tenant of a sponging-house. Only a few months before, on the author of the *English Dictionary* presenting himself to bookseller Wilcox with a plan for obtaining livelihood as a writer, the other, eyeing his powerful frame with a significant shrug, told him he had better buy a porter's knot. No man throve that was connected with letters unless also connected with their trade and merchandise, and, like Richardson, able to print books as well as write them.

"Had some of those," cried Smollett in his bitterness, "who "were pleased to call themselves "my friends, been at any pains "to deserve the character, and "told me ingenuously what I had "to expect in the capacity of an "author, when I first professed "myself of that venerable fra- "ternity, I should in all proba- "bility have spared myself the "incredible labour and chagrin I "have since undergone."* "I "don't think," said Burke, in one of his first London letters to his Irish friends, written seven years before this date, "there is "as much respect paid to a man of "letters on this side the water as "you imagine. I don't find that "Genius, the

'rathe primrose, which forsaken dies,'

---

* Preface to the *Regicide.*

"is patronised by any of the "nobility ... writers of the first "talents are left to the capricious "patronage of the public.

1757.
———
Æt. 29.

"After all, a man will make "more by the figures of "arithmetic than the figures of "rhetoric, unless he can get into "the trade wind, and then he "may sail secure over Pactolean "sands."*

It was in truth one of those times of transition which press hardly on all whose lot is cast in them. The patron was gone, and the public had not come. The seller of books had as yet exclusive command over the destiny of those who wrote them: and he was difficult of access; without certain prospect of the trade wind, hard to move. "The "shepherd in *Virgil*," wrote Johnson to Lord Chesterfield, "grew "at last acquainted with Love, "and found him a native of the "rocks." Nor had adverse circumstances been without their effect upon the literary character itself.** Covered with the blanket of Boyse, and sheltered by the night-cellar of Savage, it had less forfeited its honour and self-respect than as the paid client of the ministries of Walpole and Henry Pelham. As long as its political services were acknow-ledged by offices in the state; as long as Prior's wit could be paid by an embassy, or Addison's humour win its way to a secretaryship; while not Swift only, but Steele and Congreve and Gay sat at ministers' tables, and were not without weight in their councils; though its slavery might not be less real than in later years, yet all outwardly went well with it. Though flat apostacy then might lift literature in rank, while unpurchasable independence depressed it into ruin; though, for the mere hope of gain to be got from it, mere nobodies were worth propitiating by dignified public employments; still, it *was* esteemed by the crowd, because not altogether shut out from prosperity and worldly station. "The middle ranks," said Goldsmith truly, in speaking of that period,* "generally imitate "the great, and applauded from "fashion if not from feeling." But when another state of things succeeded; when politicians had too much shrewdness to despise the help of the pen and too little intellect to recognise its claims or influence, when it was thought that to strike at its dignity was to command its more complete subservience, when undisguised corruption had become the agent of all political intrigue, and votes were never wanting to the minister who would give hard cash in return for them; Literature, or the craft so called, was thrust

* Letter to his school-fellow, Matthew Smith.

** If any one would see a sketch, by the hand of a master, of what the career of the man generally was who lived by literature in this wretched interval, let him turn to Macaulay's *Essays*, I. 379-81. Tauchn. ed.

* In his *Enquiry into Polite Learning*, Chap. x.

from the house of commons into its lobbies and waiting-rooms, and ordered to exchange the honours of the council-table for the comforts of the great man's kitchen.

The order did not of necessity make the man of genius a servant or a parasite: upon him its sentence was simply that he must descend in the social scale, and peradventure starve. But though it could not degrade the genuine writer, it called writers into existence whose vices were a degradation to him; who lowered his pursuits, and made the name of man-of-letters the synonyme for a dishonest hireling. Of the fifty thousand pounds which the secret committee found to have been expended by Walpole's ministry on daily scribblers for their daily bread, not a sixpence was received, either then or when the Pelhams afterwards followed the example, by an author whose name is now enviably known. All went to the Guthries, the Amhersts, the Arnalls, the Ralphs, and the Oldmixons; and while a Mr. Cook was pensioned, a Harry Fielding solicited Walpole in vain. What the man of genius received, unless the man of rank had wisdom to adorn it by befriending him, was nothing but the shame of being confounded, as one who lived by using the pen, with those who lived by its prostitution and abuse.

It was in vain he strove to escape this imputation; it increased, and it fastened itself upon him. To become author was to be treated as adventurer: a man had only to write, to be classed with what Johnson calls the lowest of all human beings, the scribbler for party. One of Fielding's remarks, under cover of a grave sneer, conveys a bitter sense of this injustice. "An author, in a "country where there is no public "provision for men of genius, is "not obliged to be a more dis-"interested patriot than any "other. Why is he, whose liveli-"hood is in his pen, a greater "monster in using it to serve "himself, than he who uses his "tongue for the same purpose?"* Nor was the injustice the work of the vulgar or unthinking, for it was strongest in the greatest of living statesmen. If any one had told William Pitt that a new man of merit, called Goldsmith, was about to try the profession of literature, he would have turned aside in scorn. It had been sufficient to throw doubt upon the career of Edmund Burke, that, in this very year, he opened it

1757.
———
Æt. 29.

---

* But not the less did his manly spirit resent and denounce the shame brought by this class of men on the calling they disgraced. "The malice I bore this fel-"low," says Fielding's poet of his contemporary poet, "is inconceivable to any "but an author, and an unsuccessful one. "I never could bear to hear him well "spoken of; and I writ anonymous "satires against him, though I had re-"ceived obligations from him." This is not an inapt quotation on the threshold of Goldsmith's literary life, for he suffered as much as any man, through the whole of it, from the kind of creature, thus satirized by Fielding.

with the writing of a book.* It was Horace Walpole's vast surprise, four years later, that so sensible a man as "young "Mr. Burke" should not have "worn off his au-"thorism yet. He thinks there "is nothing so charming as "writers, and to be one. He "will know better one of these "days."**

1757.

Æt. 29.

Such was the worldly account of Literature, when, as I have said, deserted by the patron and not yet supported by the public, it was committed to the mercies of the bookseller. They were few and rare. It was the mission of Johnson to extend them, and to replace the writer's craft, in even its worldliest view, on a dignified and honourable basis; but Johnson's work was just beginning. He was yet, as I have said, one of the meaner workers for hire; and though already author of the *Dictionary*, was too glad in this very year to have Robert Dodsley's guinea for writing paragraphs in the *London Chronicle.* "Had you, sir, been "an author of the lower class, "one of those who are paid by "the sheet," remonstrated worthy printer Bowyer with an author who could pay, who did not need to be paid, and who would not be trifled with by the man of types.* Of the lower class, unlike that dignitary Mr. John Jackson, still was Samuel Johnson; he was but a Grub-street man, paid by the sheet, when Goldsmith entered Grub-street, periodical writer and reviewer.

Periodicals were the fashion of the day. They were the means of those rapid returns, of that perpetual interchange of bargain and sale, so fondly cared for by the present arbiters of literature; and were now, universally, the favourite channel of literary speculation. Scarcely a week passed in which a new magazine or paper did not start into life, to perish or survive as might be. Even Fielding had turned from his *Jonathan Wild the Great*, to his *Jacobite's Journal* and *True Patriot;* and, from his *Tom Jones* and *Amelia*, sought refuge in his *Covent Garden Journal.* We have the names of fifty-five papers of the date of a few years before this, regularly published every week.** A more important literary venture, in the nature of a review, and with a title expressive of the fate of letters, the *Grub-street Journal*, had been brought to a close in 1737. Six years earlier than that, for a longer life, Cave had issued the first number of the *Gentleman's Magazine.* Griffiths, aided by Ralph, Kippis, Langhorne, Grainger, and others, followed with the earliest

* The *Vindication of Natural Society*, in imitation of Lord Bolingbroke.

** Horace Walpole's *Correspondence*, (Ed. 1840; to which I shall in future refer as the *Collected Letters* of Walpole), IV. 160.

* Nichols's *Literary Anecdotes of the Eighteenth Century* (1812), II. 630.

** See the curious and complete list in Nichols's *Literary Anecdotes*, IV. 38-97.

regular *Review* which can be said to have succeeded, and in 1749 began, on whig principles, that publication of the *Monthly* which lasted till our own day. Seven years later, the tories opposed it with the *Critical*, which, with slight alteration of title, existed to a very recent date, more strongly tainted with high-church advocacy and principles quasi-popish than when the first number, sent forth under the editorship of Smollett in March 1756, was on those very grounds assailed.*\
In the May of that year of Gold-smith's life to which I have now arrived, another *Review*, the *Universal*, began a short existence of three years, its principal contributor being Samuel Johnson, at this time wholly devoted to it.

1757.\
ÆL. 29.

Such were a few of the examples that, if the least liberty of choice had been his, might have raised or depressed the sanguine heart of Oliver Goldsmith, when, under the watchful eye of Mr. and Mrs. Griffiths, now providers of his bed and board, he sat down in the bookseller's parlour in Paternoster-row faced appropriately with the sign of The Dunciad, to begin his engagement on the *Monthly Review*.

* The *Critical Review*, altered afterwards to the *British Critic*, became in still later years, for reasons connected with its advocacy of extreme "Anglican" views, the *Christian Remembrancer*; under which title it is still published.

END OF BOOK THE FIRST.

BOOK THE SECOND.

AUTHORSHIP BY COMPULSION.

1757 TO 1759.

CHAPTER I.

Reviewing for Mr. and Mrs. Griffiths.
1757.

THE means of existence, long sought, seemed thus to be found, when, in his twenty-ninth year,

1757. Æt. 29. Oliver Goldsmith sat down to the precarious task-work of Author by Profession. He had exerted no control over the circumstances in which he took up the pen: nor had any friendly external aid, in an impulse of kindness, offered it to his hand. To be swaddled, rocked, and dandled into authorship is the lot of more fortunate men: with Goldsmith it was the stern and last resource of his struggle with adversity. As in the country-barn he would have played Scrub or Richard; as he prescribed for the poorer than himself at Bankside, until worse than their necessities drove him to herd with the beggars in Axe-lane; as in Salisbury-court he corrected the press among Mr. Richardson's workmen, on Tower-hill doled out physic over Mr. Jacob's counter, and at Peckham dispensed the more nauseating dose to young gentlemen of Doctor Milner's academy: he had here entered into Mr. Griffiths's service, and put on the livery of the *Monthly Review.*

He was man-of-letters, then, at last; but had gratified no passion, and attained no object of ambition. The hope of greatness and distinction, day-star of his wanderings and his privations, was at this hour, more than it had ever been, dim, distant, cold. A practical scheme of literary life had as yet struck no root in his mind; and the assertion of later years, that he was past thirty before he was really attached to literature and sensible that he had found his vocation in it, is no doubt true. What the conditions of his present employment were, he knew well: that if he had dared to indulge any hopes of finer texture, if he had shown the fragments of his poem, or if he had produced the acts of the tragedy read to Richardson, Mr. and Mrs. Griffiths must have taken immediate counsel on the expenses of his board. He was there, as he had been in other places of servitude, because the dogs of hunger were at his heels.* He was not a strong man, as I have said; but neither was his weakness such that he shrank from the responsibilities it brought. When suffering came, in whatever form, he met it with a quiet, manful endurance: without gnashing of the teeth, or wringing of the hands. Among

1757.
Æt. 29.

* In an essay by Mr. De Quincey on the first edition of this biography, so different an opinion is formed from that which I offer of this Griffiths-agreement, as well as of my contrast between the position of the man-of-letters in Goldsmith's day and that of the men of Queen Anne, while the grounds of difference are so amusingly expressed, that the reader will probably thank me for quoting the passage. I should premise that Smart's agreement, alluded to in the outset, will be found described, *post*, Book III. Chap. I. "The pauperised (or Grub "Street) section of the literary body, at "the date of Goldsmith's taking service "amongst it, was (in Mr. Forster's "estimate) at its very lowest point of de-"pression. And one comic presumption "in favour of that notion was that Smart, "the prose translator of Horace, and a "well-built scholar, actually let himself "out to a monthly journal on a regular "lease of ninety-nine years. What could "move the rapacious publisher to draw "the lease for this monstrous term of "years, we cannot conjecture. Surely "the villain might have been content "with three score years and ten. But "think, reader, of poor Smart two years "after, upon another publisher's apply-"ing to him vainly for contributions, and "angrily demanding what possible ob-"jection could be made to offers so "liberal, being reduced to answer—'No "'objection, sir, whatever, except an "'unexpired term of ninety-seven years "'yet to run.' The bookseller saw that "he must not apply again in *that* cen-"tury; and, in fact, Smart could no "longer let himself, but must be sub-let "(if let at all) by the original lessee. "Query now—was Smart entitled to vote "as a freeholder, and Smart's children "(if any were born during the currency "of the lease) would they be serfs, and "*ascripti prælo?* Goldsmith's own terms "of self-conveyance to Griffiths—the "terms we mean on which he 'con-"'veyed' his person and free-agency to "the uses of the said Griffiths (or his as-"signs?)—do not appear to have been "much more dignified than Smart's in "the quality of the *conditions*, though "considerably so in the duration of the "*term;* Goldsmith's lease being only for "one year, and not for ninety-nine, so "that he had (as the reader perceives) a "clear ninety-eight years at his own dis-"posal. We suspect that poor Oliver, in "his guileless heart, never congratulated "himself on having made a more felici-"tous bargain. Indeed, it was not so "bad, if everything be considered: Gold-"smith's situation at that time was bad; "and for that very reason the lease "(otherwise monstrous) was *not* bad. He "was to have lodging, board, and 'a "'small salary,' *very* small, we suspect; "and in return for all these blessings, he "had nothing to do, but to sit still at a "table, to work hard from an early hour "in the morning until 2 P.M. (at which "elegant hour we presume that the "parenthesis of dinner occurred), but also "—which, not being an article in the "lease, might have been set aside, on a "motion before the King's Bench—to "endure without mutiny the correction "and the revisal of all his MSS. by *Mrs.* "Griffiths, wife to Dr. G. the lessee. This "affliction of Mrs. *Dr.* G. surmounting his "shoulders, and controlling his pen, "seems to us not at all less dreadful than "that of Sindbad, when indorsed with "the old man of the sea; and we, in "Goldsmith's place, should have tried "how far Sindbad's method of abating "the nuisance had lost its efficacy by "time, viz. the tempting our oppressor to

the lowest of human beings he could take his place, as he afterwards proved his right to sit

1757.
Æt. 29.

among the highest, by the strength of his affectionate sympathies with the nature common to all. And so sustained through the scenes of wretchedness he passed, he had done more, though with little consciousness of his own, truly to achieve his destiny, than if, transcending the worldly plans of wise Irish friends, he had clambered to the bishops' bench or

"get drunk once or twice a-day, and
"then suddenly throwing Mrs. Dr. G. off
"her perch. From that 'bad eminence,'
"which she had audaciously usurped,
"what harm could there be in thus dis-
"mounting this old *woman* of the sea?....
"Certainly these conditions—the hard
"work, the being chained by the leg to
"the writing-table, and, above all, the
"having one's pen chained to that of Mrs.
"Dr. Griffiths, *do seem* to countenance
"Mr. Forster's idea, that Goldsmith's
"period was the purgatory of authors.
"And we freely confess that excepting
"Smart's ninety-nine years' lease, or the
"contract between the Devil and Dr.
"Faustus, we never heard of a harder
"bargain driven with any literary man.
"Smart, Faustus, and Goldsmith, were
"clearly over-reached. Yet, after all,
"was this treatment in any important
"point (excepting as regards Dr. Faustus)
"worse than that given to the whole col-
"lege of Grub Street, in the days of
"Pope? The first edition of the *Dunciad*
"dates from 1727; Goldsmith's matricula-
"tion in Grub Street dates from 1757—just
"thirty years later; which is one genera-
"tion. And it is important to remember
"that Goldsmith, at this time in his
"twenty-ninth year, was simply an usher
"at an obscure boarding-school; had
"never practised writing for the press,
"and had not even himself any faith
"at all in his own capacity for writ-
"ing." De Quincey's *Works,* vi. 212-15
(Ed. 1857).

out-practised the whole college of physicians.

The time is at hand in his history, when all this becomes clear. Outside the garret window of Mr. Griffiths, by the light which the miserable labour of the *Monthly Review* will let in upon the heartsick labourer, it may soon be seen. Stores of observation, feeling, and experience, hidden from himself at present, are by that light to be revealed. It is a thought to carry us through this new scene of suffering, with new and unaccustomed hope.

Goldsmith never publicly avowed what he had written in the *Monthly Review,* any more than the Roman poet talked of the millstone he turned in his days of hunger. Men who have been at the galleys, though for no crime of their own committing, are wiser than to brag of the work they performed there. All he stated was, that all he wrote was tampered with by Griffiths or his wife. Smollett has depicted this lady as an antiquated female critic; and when "il-"literate, bookselling" Griffiths declared unequal war against that potent antagonist, protesting that the *Monthly Review* was not written by "physicians with-"out practice, authors without "learning, men without decency, "gentlemen without manners, "and critics without judgment," Smollett retorted in a few broad unscrupulous lines on the whole party of the rival publication. "The *Critical Review* is not "written," he said, "by a parcel "of obscure hirelings, under the "restraint of a bookseller and his "wife, who presume to revise, "alter, and amend the articles "occasionally. The principal "writers in the *Critical Review* are "unconnected with booksellers, "unawed by old women, and in-"dependent of each other."* Commanded by a bookseller, awed by an old woman, and miserably dependent, one of these obscure hirelings desired and resolved, as far as it was

* * *Critical Review*, vii. 151: In a notice of Dr. Grainger's *Letter to Dr. Smollett Occasioned by his Criticism upon a late Translation of Tibullus.* The first attack by Griffiths had been made in reviewing a pamphlet by some irritated author (an Occasional Critic) abusive of Smollett. "By their reciprocal defamation, they "appear to be physicians without prac-"tice; authors without learning; men "without decency; and (notwithstanding "he has made some lucky discoveries of "their mistakes, yet, if their critical "merit be no greater than his, the public "will, probably, be ready to add) critics "without judgment." To which Smollett ultimately retorted as in the text; but he had meanwhile also, in an address to "the Old Gentlewoman who directs the "*Monthly Review*," indulged in an im-mediate onslaught. "There is to be "sure great elegance in this long, draw-"ling, disjointed, paralytic sentence, "that, propped upon the crutch of paren-"thesis, drags its slow length along. But "good, now, Gammer, will you tell us "how you discovered that what we said "of the Occasional Critic was defama-"tion? Have we said anything of him, "but what you yourself have expressly "confirmed? .... Have you found out "by his defamation, that we are phy-"sicians without practice; authors with-"out learning; men without decency; "gentlemen without manners; and critics "without judgment? Defamation im-"plies slander, Goody, and slander is "founded upon falsehood," &c.

possible, to remain in his ob-scurity; but a copy of the *Monthly* which belonged to Griffiths, and in which he had privately marked the authorship of $\frac{1757.}{\text{Æt. 29.}}$ most of the articles, with-draws the veil. It is for no pur-pose that Goldsmith could have disapproved, or I should scorn to assist in calling to memory what he would himself have com-mitted to neglect. The best writers can spare much; it is only the worst who have nothing to spare.

The first subject I may men-tion first, though it takes us back a little. It was the specimen-review which had procured Gold-smith his engagement; and if the book was furnished from the bookseller's stores, it was pro-bably the least common-place of all they contained. This was the year (1757) in which, after six centuries of neglect, the great, dark, wonderful field of northern fiction began to be explored. Professor Mallet of Copenhagen had translated the *Edda*, direct-ing attention strongly to the "re-"mains" of Scandinavian poetry and mythology: and Goldsmith's first effort in the *Monthly Review* was to describe the fruits of these researches, to point out resemblances to the inspiration of the East, and to note the pic-turesqueness and sublimity of the fierce old Norse imagination. "The learned on this side the "Alps," he began, "have long "laboured at the antiquities of "Greece and Rome, but almost "totally neglected their own; like "conquerors, who, while they "have made inroads into the ter-

^{1757.} "ritories of their neigh-
Æt. 29. "bours, have left their own "natural dominions to de-"solation."* This was a lively interruption to the ordinary *Monthly* dulness, and perhaps the Percys, and intelligent subscribers of that sort, opened eyes a little wider at it. It was not long after, indeed, that Percy first began to dabble in *Runic Verses from the Icelandic;* before eight years were passed he had published his famous *Reliques;* and in five years more, during intimacy with the writer of this notice of Mallet, he produced his translation of Mallet's *Northern Antiquities.* In all this there was probably no connection: yet it is wonderful what a word in season from a man of genius may do, even when the genius is hireling and obscure and only labouring for the bread it eats.

More common-place was the respectable-looking thin duodecimo with which Mr. Griffiths's workman began his next month's labour, but a duodecimo which at the time was making noise enough for every octavo, quarto, and folio in the shop. This was *Douglas, a Tragedy, as it is acted at the Theatre Royal in Covent-garden.* It was not acted at the Theatre Royal in Drury-lane, because Garrick, who shortly afterwards so complacently exhibited him-

self in *Agis,* in the *Siege of Aquileia,* and other ineffable dulness from the same hand (wherein his quick suspicious glance detected no Lady Randolphs), would have nothing to do with the character of Douglas. What would come with danger from the full strength of Mrs. Cibber, he knew might be safely left to the enfeebled powers of Mrs. Woffington; whose Lady Randolph would leave him no one to fear but Barry at the rival house. But despairing also of Covent-garden when refused by Drury-lane, and crying plague on both their houses, to the north good parson Home had returned, and after eight months were gone, had sent back his play endorsed by the Scottish capital. *There* it had been acted; and from the beginning of the world, from the beginning of Edinburgh, the like of that play had not been known. The gentlemen who became afterwards the Poker Club* made

* *Monthly Review,* xvi. 377, April 1757. See *ante,* 64.

* The Poker Club was not so named till five years later. But the men spoken of in the text were precisely that select section of Edinburgh society already existing as a club, which, on Scotland being refused a militia, called itself the Poker, "to stir up the fire of the nation." See an account of it in Scott's notice of Home in his *Prose Works* (ed. 1835), xix. 283, in Burton's *Life of Hume,* ii. 456, and in Campbell's *Chancellors,* vi. 29-30. To these authorities I have now (1870) to add the *Autobiography of Alexander* (Jupiter) *Carlyle:* edited by Mr. Burton in 1860. See the 11th chapter of that book; and for various notices of the leading Scotchmen, and of what was done and suffered by Carlyle himself in connection with Home and his tragedies, the 7th and 8th chapters especially, and others, *passim.* Carlyle was born six years before Gold-

their ecstasies felt from Hunter-square to Grub-street and St. James's, for no rise in the price of claret had yet imperilled the continuance of those social gatherings. Without stint or measure to their warmth the cooling beverage flowed; and bottle after bottle (at eighteen-pence a quart *) disappeared in honour of the Scottish Shakespeare, whom the most illustrious of the Pokers pronounced better than the English because free from "un-"happy barbarism." Yes, refined from the unhappy barbarism of our southern Shakespeare, and purged from the licentiousness of our poor London-starved Otway, here at last was a master-piece of the stage. It was David Hume's opinion, and still stands prefixed to the *Four Dissertations* he was bringing out at the time, that "Johnny Home" had all the theatric genius of those two poets so refined and purged. But little was even a philosopher's exalta-tion, to the persecution of a

presbytery. No man better than Hume knew that. The first volume of his *History* had lain hopelessly on Millar's shelves after sale of forty-five copies in a twelve-month, when, on inquisitorial proceedings of the General Assembly against Lord Kames and himself, the public in turn became inquisitive and began to buy. And surely as the *History* of Hume must even puffery of Home have languished, but for that resolve of the presbytery to eject from his pulpit a parson who had written a play. This carried *Douglas* to London for a nine nights' frantic wonder; and the numbers and noise of the carriages on their way to the Norval of silver-tongued Barry at Covent-garden, were now giving sudden headaches to David Garrick in Drury-lane, and suggest-ing strange comparisons of silver tongues to the hooting of owls.

But out of reach of every influence to raise or to depress, unless it be a passing thought now and then to his own tragic fragments, sits the critic with the thin duodecimo before him. The popular stir affects even quiet Gray in his cloistered nook of Pembroke-hall; but the sharp, clear, graceful judgment now lodged and boarded at The Dunciad, shows itself quite unmoved. "When the town," it began, "by a tedious succession "of indifferent performances, has "been long confined to censure, "it will naturally wish for an

---

smith, and outlived him thirty-one years; travelled to Leyden, as he did, after leaving the Edinburgh class-rooms; visited London from time to time, on familiar terms with Garrick, Smollett, and other friends common also to Goldsmith, up to within four years of the death of the latter, when his auto-biography closes; yet he never, from first to last, mentions Goldsmith's name.

* Let me borrow here that exquisite burst of humour with which Johnson met Boswell's grave assurances that Scotch claret could really make a man drunk. "I assure you, sir, there was a great deal "of drunkenness." "No, sir, there were "people who died of dropsies, which they "contracted in trying to get drunk." *Life*, IV. 273.

"opportunity of praise."* That is, as I understand it, the town, sick of Doctor Brown's *Athelstan* and *Barbarossa*, of Mr. Whitehead's *Creusa*, of Mr. Crisp's *Virginia*, of Mr. Glover's *Boadicea*, of Doctor Francis's *Eugenia*, of Mr. Aaron Hill's *Merope*, of the *Regulus* of Mr. Havard, and the *Mahomet* of Mr. Miller, on which lean fare it has had perforce to diet itself for several seasons, turns to anything of the reasonable promise of a *Douglas* with disposition to enjoy it if it can. But the more marked, Goldsmith felt, was the critical folly that could obtrude such a work as "perfect:" in proof of which he made brief but keen mention of its leading defects; while to those who would plead in arrest particular beauties of diction, he directed a remark which seems to belong to a subtler style of criticism than his own. "In works of this nature, "general observation often char- "acterises more strongly than a "particular criticism could do; "for it were an easy task to "point out those passages in "any indifferent author where he "has excelled himself, and yet "these comparative beauties, if "we may be allowed the ex- "pression, may have no real "merit at all. Poems, like build- "ings, have their point of view; "and too near a situation gives "but a partial conception of the "whole."** Southey, not know-

ing the writer, said that all this was malignant;* but really no such spirit is apparent in it. Very goodnaturedly does Goldsmith close with quotation of two of the best passages in the poem, emphatically marking with excellent taste five lines of allusion to the wars of Scotland and England.

Gallant in strife, and noble in their ire,
The Battle is their pastime. They go forth
Gay in the morning, as to Summer sport:
When evening comes, the glory of the morn,
The youthful warrior, is a clod of clay.'

If Boswell, on Johnson's challenge to show any good lines out of *Douglas*, had mustered sense and discrimination to offer these, the Doctor could hardly have exploded his emphatic *pooh!* Goldsmith differed little from Johnson in the matter, it is true: but his pooh was more polite.

A Scottish Homer in due time followed the Shakespeare: Mr. Griffiths submitting to his boarder, in a very thick duodecimo, *The Epigoniad, A Poem in Nine Books.* Doctor Wilkie's** laboured ver-

---

* *Monthly Review*, XVI. 426, May 1757.
** *Ibid*, XVI. 428, May 1757.

* *Common-Place Book*, III. 713. He was at the time out of humour with the *Monthly*, in which he had himself become a writer. In the same passage he calls Griffiths's shop "the appropriate sign of "the Dunciad."

** There are several allusions to him in *Carlyle's Autobiography*, and notably in the description of a magistrate's feast at Musselburgh when Charles Townshend was present, and among the company, besides Wilkie, were Home, Robertson, Ferguson, and (I may add) a gallant Col. Parr who "literally wept and shed bitter "tears" because the haunch of venison that Townshend had given to the feast

sification of the adventures of the descendants of the Theban warriors got into Anderson's collection, the editor being a Scotchman: though candid enough to say of it, that "too antique to "please the unlettered reader, "and too modern for the scholar, "it was neglected by both, read "by few, and soon forgotten by "all."* Yet this not very profound editor might have been more candid, and told us that his sentence was stolen and adapted from the *Monthly Review.* After discussion of the claims justly due and always conceded to a writer of genuine learning, Goldsmith remarked: "on the con-"trary, if he be detected of "ignorance when he pretends to "learning, his case will deserve "our pity: too antique to "please one party, and too "modern for the other, he "is deserted by both, read by "few, and soon forgotten by all, "except his enemies." Perhaps if his friends had forgotten him, the Doctor might have profited. "The *Epigoniad*," continued Goldsmith, "seems to be one of those "new old-performances; a work "that would no more have pleased "a peripatetic of the academic "grove, than it will captivate the "unlettered subscriber to one "of our circulating libraries." *

Nevertheless the Scottish clique made a stand for their rough Homeric doctor. Smith, Robertson, and Home were vehement in laudation; Charles Townshend ("who," writes Hume to Adam Smith,** "passes for the cleverest "fellow in England") said aye to all their praises; and when, some months afterwards, Hume came up to London to bring out the Tudor volumes of his *History*, he published puffs of Wilkie under assumed signatures both in the *Critical Review* and in various magazines, and reported progress to the Edinburgh circle. It was somewhat "uphill work," he told Adam Smith;*** and with much mortification hinted to Robertson that the verdict of

1757.
——
Æt. 29.

---

was sent up anderson. "Townshend "said to me afterwards that he had "never met with a man who approached "so near the two extremes of a god and "a bruto as Wilkie did." p. 394. For a very curious account of Wilkie, who was the son of a farmer near Edinburgh, and is said to have conceived the subject of his poem while he stood as a scarecrow against the pigeons in one of his father's fields of wheat, see a letter of Hume in his *Life* by Burton, II. 25-9. "Wilkie," adds Hume at the close of his letter (dated 3rd July, 1757), "is now a settled "minister at Ratho, within four miles of "the town. He possesses about £80 or £90 "a-year, which he esteems exorbitant "riches. Formerly, when he had only "£20 as helper, he said that he could "not conceive what article, either of "human convenience or pleasure, he was "deficient in, nor what any man could "mean by desiring more money. He "possesses several branches of erudition, "besides the Greek poetry; and par-"ticularly is a very profound geome-"trician. . . . Yet this man, who has "composed the second epic poem in our "language, understands so little of ortho-"graphy," &c. &c. The great painter of the Rent Day was his nephew.

* *British Poets*, xi. Prefatory notice to Wilkie.

* *Monthly Review*, XVII. 228, September 1757.
** Burton's *Life*, II. 58.
*** Ibid. 56.

the *Monthly Review* (vulgarly interpolated, I should mention, by Griffiths himself*) would have upon the whole to stand. "However," he adds, in his letter to Robertson, "if you want a little flattery to "the author (which I own is very "refreshing to an author), you "may tell him that Lord Chester- "field said to me he was a great "poet. I imagine that Wilkie "will be very much elevated by "praise from an English earl, "and a knight of the garter, and "an ambassador, and a secretary "of state, and a man of so great "reputation. For I observe that "the greatest rustics are com- "monly most affected with such "circumstances."** It is to be hoped he was, and proportionately forgetful of low abuse from obscure hirelings in booksellers' garrets.

"An Irish gentleman," Hume in another letter told Adam Smith, "wrote lately a very pretty "treatise on the Sublime."*** This Irish gentleman had indeed written so pretty a treatise on the Sublime that the task-work of our critic became work of praise. "When I was beginning "the world," said Johnson in his old age to Fanny Burney, "and "was nothing and nobody, the "joy of my life was to fire at all "the established wits." Perhaps it is a natural infirmity when one is nothing and nobody, and when

Goldsmith became something and somebody his friends still charged it upon him. They may have had some reason, for he was never subtle and seldom even reliable in literary judgments; but as yet, at any rate, the particular weakness does not appear. A critic of the profounder sort he never was; criticism of that order was little known and seldom practised in his day, and he seems to have had even less than falls to the lot of most men of letters of the clear insight and keen relish so essential to it. But as it is less the want of depth, than the presence of envy, which it has been the fashion to urge against him, it will become us in fairness to observe that at least from the latter vice he is here, in the garret of Griffiths, tolerably free. Whether it is to seize him in the drawing-room of Reynolds, will be matter of later inquiry. He has no pretension yet to enter himself brother or craftsman of the guild of literature, and we find him in his censures just and temperate, and liberal as well as candid in his praise: glad to give added fame to established wits, as even the youths Bonnell Thornton and George Colman were beginning already to be esteemed; and eager, in such a case as Burke's, to help that the wit should be established. In the same number of the Review he noticed the collection into four small volumes of the *Connoisseur*, and the appearance in its three-shilling

* See *Prior*, i. 231.
** Burton's *Life*, ii. 55.
*** *Ibid.*

pamphlet of *A Philosophical Enquiry into the Origin of our Ideas of the Sublime and Beautiful.* The *Connoisseur* he honoured with the title of friend of society, wherein reference was possibly intended to the defective side of that lectureship of society to which the serious and resolute author of the *Rambler* had been lately self-appointed perpetual professor. "He rather converses," said Goldsmith, "with the ease of a "cheerful companion, than dic- "tates, as other writers in this "class have done, with the af- "fected superiority of an Author. "He is the first writer since "*Bickerstaff* who has been per- "fectly satirical yet perfectly "goodnatured; and who never, "for the sake of declamation, "represents simple folly as ab- "solutely criminal. He has so- "lidity to please the grave, and "humour and wit to allure the "gay." * Our author by compulsion seemed to be here anticipating his authorship by choice, and with indistinct yet hopeful glance beyond his Dunciad and its deities perhaps he turned with better faith to Burke's essay on the *Beautiful.* His criticism ** was elaborate and well-studied; he objected to many parts of the theory, and especially to the materialism on which it founded the connection of objects of pleasure with a necessary relaxation of the nerves; but these objections, discreet and thoroughly considered, gave strength as well as relish to its praise, and Burke spoke to many of his friends of the pleasure it had given him.

1757.
Æt. 29.

And now appeared, in three large quarto volumes, followed within six months by a fourth, the *Complete History of England, deduced from the Descent of Julius Cæsar to the Treaty of Aix la Chapelle in* 1748. *Containing the Transactions of One Thousand Eight Hundred and Three Years. By T. Smollett, M.D.* The wonder of this performance had been its incredibly rapid production: the author of *Random* and *Pickle* having in the space of fourteen months scoured through those eighteen centuries. It was a scheme of the London booksellers to thwart the success of Hume, which promised just then to be too considerable for an undertaking in which the craft had no concern. His Commonwealth volume, profiting by religious outcry against its author, was selling vigorously; people were inquiring for the preceding Stuart volume; and Paternoster-row, alarmed for its rights and properties in standard history-books, resolved to take the field before the promised Tudor volumes could be brought to

* *Monthly Review,* XVI. 444, May 1757.
** *Ibid.,* 473. I may add, that besides these and other detailed and important articles in this May number, he contributed also twenty-three notices of minor works to the department of the review styled the Monthly Catalogue (for which indeed he wrote largely every month), and a compilation of literary news from Italy, *dated from Padua!*

market. They backed their best man, and succeeded. The *Complete History*, we are told, "had a "very disagreeable effect "on Mr. Hume's perform- "ance." It had also, it would appear, a very disagreeable effect on Mr. Hume's temper. "A Frenchman came to me," he writes to Robertson, "and spoke "of translating my new volume "of history: but as he also men- "tioned his intention of translat- "ing Smollett, I gave him no en- "couragement to proceed."* It had besides, it may be added, a very disagreeable effect on the tempers of other people. Warburton heard of its swift sale while his own *Divine Legation* lay heavy and quiet at his publisher's; and "the Vagabond Scot who "writes nonsense," was the character vouchsafed to Smollett by the vehement proud priest.** But Goldsmith keeps his temper, notwithstanding Smollett's great and somewhat easily-earned good fortune; and, in this as in former instances, there is no disposition to carp at a great success or

*2757.
Æt. 29.*

* "I am afraid," he writes in a letter to Millar (6th April, 1758), "the extra- "ordinary run upon Dr. Smollett has a "little hurt your sales; but these things "are only temporary." Burton's *Life*, 11. 135.

** "It was well observed that nobody "in the Augustan age could conceive "that so soon after, a Horse should be "made Consul; and yet matters were so "well prepared by the time of Caligula, "that nobody was surprised at the mat- "ter. So, when Clarendon and Temple "wrote History, they little thought the "time was so near when a vagabond Scot "should write nonsense ten thousand "strong." *Letters to Hurd*, 278.

quarrel with a celebrated name. His notice has evident marks of the interpolation of Griffiths, though that worthy's more deadly hostility to Smollett had not yet begun; but even as it stands, in the *Review* which had so many points of personal and political opposition to the subject of it, it is manly and kind. The weak places were pointed out with gentleness, while Goldsmith strongly seized on what he felt to be the strength of Smollett. "The style "of this Historian," he said, "is "in general clear, nervous, and "flowing; and we think it impos- "sible for a reader of taste not "to be pleased with the per- "spicuity and elegance of his "manner."*

For the critic's handling in lighter matters, I will mention what he said of a book by Jonas Hanway. This was the Jonas of whom Doctor Johnson affirmed that he acquired some reputation by travelling abroad, but lost it all by travelling at home: not a witticism, but a sober truth. His book about Persia was excellent, and his book about Portsmouth indifferent. But though an eccentric, he was a very benevolent and earnest man; and though he made the common mistake of thinking himself wise when he was only good, he had too much reason to complain, which he was always doing, of a general want of earnestness and seriousness in his age. His larger schemes of benevolence

* *Monthly Review*, xvi. 532, June 1757.

have connected his name with the Marine Society and the Magdalen, both of which he originated, as well as with the Foundling, which he was active in improving; and to his courage and perseverance in smaller fields of usefulness (his determined contention with extravagant vails to servants* not the least), the men of Goldsmith's day were indebted for liberty to use an umbrella. Gay's pleasant *Trivia*, and Swift's masterly description of a city shower, commemorate its earlier use by poor women, by "tuck'd-up sempstresses" and "walking maids;"** but with even this class it was a winter privilege, and woe to the woman of a better sort, or to the man whether rich or poor, who dared at any time so to invade the rights of coachmen and chairmen. But Jonas steadily underwent the staring, laughing, jeering, hoot-

1757.
——
Æt. 29.

"The tuck'd-up sempstress walks
"with hasty strides,
"While streams run down her oil'd
"umbrella sides."
Swift's City Shower.

Since this biography first appeared, Mr. Bolton Corney has produced some lines a century earlier in date which might seem to prove that the "umbrella" had been in use in Michael Drayton's time, even by the high-born mistress of the sempstress and the maid. "Of doves," says the old poet,

"I have a dainty paire
"Which, when you please to take
"the aier . .
". . with their nimble wings shall
"fan you,
"That neither cold nor heate shall
"tan you,
"And, like vmbrellas, with their
"feathers
"Sheuld you in all sorts of weathers."
Notes and Queries, II. 523.

But neither these nor any similar lines invalidate in any respect what is said in my text as to the use of the umbrella. Clearly, only heat and dust were guarded against in fans and umbrellas before the time of Gay and Hanway (see Coryat's *Crudities*, i. 134); and Drayton's lines must be held simply to refer to a protection from sun and wind. What Wolfe writes from Paris to his mother in 1752 bears out exactly what I say of the custom in Hanway's time. "The people," he says, "here use umbrellas in hot "weather to defend them from the sun, "and something of the same kind to "secure them from snow and rain. I "wonder a practice so useful is not in- "troduced in England, where there are "such frequent showers; and especially "in the country, where they can be ex- "panded without any inconveniency." I

---

* "When I sat to Hogarth," said Mr. Cole, "the custom of giving vails to ser- "vants was not discontinued. On taking "leave of the painter at the door I of- "fered his servant a small gratuity, but "the man very politely refused it, telling "me it would be as much as the loss of "his place if his master knew it. This "was so uncommon and so liberal in a "man of Hogarth's profession at that "time of day, that it much struck me, as "nothing of the kind had happened to "me before." My old friend Allan Cunningham, after quoting this in his *Lives of the Painters*, i. 176, adds: "Nor is it likely "that such a thing would happen again. "Sir Joshua Reynolds gave his servant "£6 annually of wages, and offered him "£100 a-year for the *door!*" I doubt whether this latter statement rests on good authority; for it is the defect of an otherwise pleasant book to do very scant and grudging justice to Reynolds, and too readily to believe everything said against him. The biographer took such earnest part with Hogarth that he became unconscious how unfairly he was treating Sir Joshua.

** "Britain in winter only knows its
"aid
"To guard from chilly showers the
"walking maid." Gay's *Trivia*.
How easily recognised is the stronger hand—

ing, and bullying; and having punished some insolent knaves who struck him with their whips as well as tongues, he finally established a privilege which, when the *Journal des Débats* gravely assured its readers that the king of the barricades (that king whose throne has since been burnt at the top of fresh barricades on the site of the Bastille) was to be seen walking the streets of Paris with an umbrella under his arm, had reached its culminating point and was playing a part in state affairs. Excellent Mr. Hanway, having settled the use of the umbrella, made a less successful move when he would have written down the use of tea.

1757.
Æt. 29

This is one of the prominent subjects in the *Journey from Portsmouth:* the book which Griffiths had now placed in his workman's hands. Doctor Johnson's review of it for the *Literary Magazine* is widely known, and Goldsmith's deserved notoriety as well. It is more kindly and as effectively written. He saw what allowance could be made for a writer, however mistaken, who "shows great "goodness of heart, and an "earnest concern for the welfare "of his country." Where the book was at its worst, the man

may add that Southey quotes this letter in his *Common-Place Book* (i. 574), and accompanies it with the remark: "My "mother was born in the year when this "was written. And I have heard her "say she remembered the time when any "person would have been hooted for "carrying an umbrella in Bristol."

might be at his best, he very agreeably undertakes to prove. "The appearance of an inn on "the road, suggests to our phi- "losopher an eulogium on tem- "perance; the confusion of a dis- "appointed landlady gives rise "to a letter on resentment; and "the view of a company of "soldiers furnishes out materials "for an essay on war." As to the anti-souchong mania, Goldsmith laughs at it; and this was doubtless the wisest way. "He," Jonas had exclaimed in horror, "who should be able to drive "three Frenchmen before him, "or she who might be a breeder "of such a race of men, are to "be seen sipping their Tea! . . . "What a wild infatuation is this! "... The suppression of this "dangerous custom depends en- "tirely on the example of ladies "of rank in this country. . . . "Some indeed have resolution "enough in their own houses to "confine the use of Tea to their "own table, but their number is "so extremely small, amidst a "numerous acquaintance I know "only of Mrs. T. . . . whose name "ought to be written out in letters "of gold." "Thus we see," is Goldsmith's comment upon this, "how fortunate some folks are. "Mrs. T. . . . is praised for con- "fining luxury to her own table: "she earns fame, and saves some- "thing in domestic expenses into "the bargain!" In subsequent serious expostulation with Mr. Hanway on some medical assumptions in his book, the reviewer lays aside his humble patched-velvet of Bankside, and speaks as though with nothing less invested than the president's gold-headed cane: after which he closes with this piece of quiet good sense. "Yet after all, why "so violent an outcry against "this devoted article of modern "luxury? Every nation that is "rich hath had, and will have, its "favourite luxuries. Abridge the "people in one, they generally "run into another; and the reader "may judge which will be most "conducive to either mental or "bodily health, the watery bever- "age of a modern fine lady or "the strong beer and stronger "waters of her great-grand- "mother?"*

This paper had appeared in July, and in the same number there was also from the same hand a clever notice of Dobson's translation of the first book of Cardinal de Polignac's Latin poem of *Anti-Lucretius:* ** the poem whose ill success stopped Gray in what he playfully called his *Master Tommy Lucretius* *** ("De "Principiis Cogitandi"). The Cardinal's work I may mention as a huge monument of misapplied learning and enormous vanity; the talk of the world in those days, now forgotten. It was the work of a life; could boast of having been corrected by Boileau and altered by Louis the Fourteenth; and was kept in

manuscript so long, and so often with inordinate self-complacency publicly recited from by the author in a kind earnest of what the world was one day to expect, that some listeners with good memories (Le Clerc among them) stole its best passages, and published them for the world's earlier benefit as their own. This drove the poor cardinal at last to premature delivery, and an instalment of thirteen thousand lines appeared;* of which certainly one line (*Eripuitque Jovi fulmen, Phœboque sagittas*, which the worthy cardinal had himself stolen from Marcus Manilius), having since suggested Franklin's epitaph (*Eripuit cælo fulmen sceptrumque tyrannis*), ** has a good chance to live. To the August number of the *Review*, among other matters, Goldsmith contributed a lively paper*** on those new

1757.
Æt. 29

* Monthly Review, xvii. 50-4, July 1757.
** Ibid, 44.
*** Works, ii. 101.

* Grimm's *Anecdotes*, i. 455. I may add, that, ten years after the present date, "George Canning of the Middle "Temple Esq," father of the statesman, published a poor translation of the Cardinal's first three books. See *Monthly Review*, xxxvi. 190 (March 1767).

** Turgot's biographer, Condorcet, quotes this line as the only Latin verse composed by the great French economist; but Turgot had only "adapted" it, and from Polignac no doubt, to place under a portrait of Franklin. The line of Manilius, the bar from which both wires are drawn, is that in which he speaks of Epicurus, "Eripuitque Jovi fulmen, vires- "que Tonanti." *Astron.* lib. v. line 104.

*** In the form of a letter to the authors of the *Monthly Review* (xvii. 154, August 1757). Gray disliked Voltaire's opinions generally, "but this," says Mr. Nichols, "did not prevent his paying the "full tribute of admiration due to his

volumes of Voltaire's *Universal History* which so delighted Walpole and Gray; but in the September number, where he remarks on *Odes by Mr. Gray*, I find opinions which place in lively contrast the obscure Oliver and the brilliant Horace.

1757.
Æt. 29.

Walpole called himself a whig, in compliment to his father; but except in very rare humours he hated, while he envied, all things popular. "I am more humbled," was his cry, when thirsting for every kind of notoriety, "I am "more humbled by any applause "in the present age, than by "hosts of such critics as Dean "Milles."* He was very steady in his fondness for Gray (though Gray himself appears never to

have quite thrown aside the recollection of an early disagreement*), because there was that real indifference to popular influences in the poet which the wit and fine gentleman was anxious to have credit for. This liking he proclaimed on all occasions. He had written the short advertisement which prefaced the first edition of the *Elegy;* he had himself taken the risk of publishing, four years before, "a fine edition "of six poems of Mr. Gray with "prints from designs of Mr. R. "Bentley;"** and when he heard, in the July of this year, that Gray had left his Cambridge retreat for a visit to Dodsley the

"genius. He was delighted with his "pleasantry; appproved his historical "compositions, particularly his *Essai sur* "*l'Histoire Universelle;* and placed his "tragedies next in rank to those of "Shakspeare." *Works*, v. 32, 33. In a letter to Wharton (July 10, 1764) he talks of his having been reading "half-a-dozen "new works of that inexhaustible, "eternal, entertaining scribbler Voltaire, "who at last (I fear) will go to Heaven, "for to him entirely it is owing that the "king of France and his council have "reviewed and set aside the decision of "the parliament of Thoulouse in the "affair of Calas ... you see a scribbler "may be of some use in the world." *Works*, iv. 35, 36. Let me add to this note that Gray's high opinion of Voltaire's tragedies is shared by one of our greatest authorities on such a matter now living. Sir Edward Bulwer (Lord Lytton), whom I have often heard maintain the marked superiority of Voltaire over all his countrymen in the knowledge of dramatic art, and the power of producing theatrical effects.

* *Coll. Lett.* v. 323.

* For Walpole's account of their difference when travelling on the continent together in their youth, see *Coll. Lett.* v. 340, 341; but Mr. Mitford, in his edition of Gray, has explained the matter differently on the authority of Mr. Isaac Reed. Fom this it would seem that the quarrel arose out of a suspicion on Walpole's part that Gray had spoken ill of him to some friends in England, which impelled him to open clandestinely and re-seal one of Gray's letters. This was discovered and resented. *Works*, ii. 175, *note*. It is right to add, however, that this account is not borne out by what Gray said to Nichols on the latter questioning him about the quarrel. "Wal- "pole," replied Gray, "was son of the first "minister, and you may easily conceive "that on this account he might assume "an air of superiority, or do or say some- "thing which perhaps I did not bear as well "as I ought." *Works*, v. 48. This, substantially, would bear out Walpole, who takes all that kind of blame frankly to himself.

** See his own Short Notes of his life, *Letters to Mann* (1843, 1844, concluding series), iv. 343. See also his brief Memoir of Gray, and the letters to Brown and Mason, in Mitford's *Correspondence of Gray and Mason* (1853), xxxiii. 89, and 92.

bookseller, he managed, as he says himself, to "snatch" away the new *Odes* to confer grace on the newly started types at Strawberry-hill.* These were the *Bard* and the *Progress of Poesy;* two noble productions, it must surely be admitted, whatever objection can be urged against them for the want of clearness or of ease: though not to be admired after the manner of Walpole, who held their weakness to be their strength, set exaggerated value on every obscure allusion in them, would have encouraged to greater excesses the remoteness and violent effort that detract so gravely from their beauty, and would have closed the appreciation of them, if he could, to all but the circles he moved in. Already Gray's flight into the higher heaven of poetry had been checked by too fastidious fears, and to these his friend would completely have enslaved him. Nor does Walpole ever praise him without showing dislike of others much more than love of Gray. "You are very particular, I can "tell you," he says to Montague, "in liking Gray's *Odes:* but you "must remember that the age "likes Akenside, and did like "Thomson! can the same people "like both? Milton was forced "to wait till the world had done "admiring Quarles."* It was a habit of depreciation too much the manner of the time. Even the enchanting genius of Collins struck no responsive chord in Gray himself; nor had the *Elegies* of Shenstone, the *Imagination* of Akenside, or even the *Castle of Indolence* itself found always grateful welcome amid the learned idleness of the poet of Pembroke-hall.**

But Goldsmith, for the present, was not to this manner born; and though he might perhaps

1757.
———
Æt. 29.

---

* "I snatched them out of Dodsley's "hands, and they are to be the first fruits "of my press." *Coll. Lett.* III. 304. "Odes "by Mr. Gray, Printed at Strawberry "Hill, for R. and J. Dodsley in Pall Mall. "1757. 4to." The publishing price was a *shilling.* "I yet reflect with pain," wrote Wharton to Mason in 1781, when their friend had been ten years in the grave, "upon the cool reception which "those noble odes, The Progress of "Poetry and The Bard, met with at their "first publication; it appeared that there "were not twenty people in England who "liked them." *Correspondence of Gray and Mason,* 405. Nevertheless it would seem, from passages in the same correspondence (89, 101) that Dodsley had had the courage to print 2000 copies; and he told Gray, in little more than a month after the publication that "about 12 or "1300 were gone." The formal assignment, dated 29th June 1757, and showing the sum received by the poet to have been forty guineas for the two odes, brought eight guineas at a public sale in 1835 (*Times* of Dec. 23 of that year).

* *Coll. Lett.* III. 313.

** Nothing surprises me so much as these little heterodoxies in Gray, whose taste for poetry was in other respects exquisite,—always generous, almost always right. To Shenstone, Akenside, and Thomson he makes objection indeed only as to special poems, admitting the beauties of others; but Collins he classes generally with Thomas Warton, as "both "writers of odes;" and continues, "It is "odd enough, but each is the half of a "considerable man, and one the counter-"part of the other . . . . They both de-"serve to last some years, but will not." Gray to Wharton, Dec. 1746. *Works,* III. 28-9.

more freely have acknowledged the splendour of Gray's imagination and the deep humanity of his feeling, his exquisite pathos, the melancholy grandeur of his tone, his touching thoughts and delicately chosen words,—yet was he at least not disposed, when Mr. Griffiths laid Messrs. Dodsley's shilling quarto before him, to any comparison or test less fair than his own feeling of the objects and aims of poetry. And this he stated with a strength and plainness which mark with personal interest what was said of Gray. Portions of a poem he had himself already written, fragments possessing the charm of refined simplicity; and, in the tenor and the tone of his criticism, we see what will one day give to those attempts the unity and design that are to raise them into structures likely to endure. We observe the gradual development of settled views; the better defined thoughts which the rude beginnings of literature are breeding in him; the rich upturning of the soil of his mind, as Mr. Griffiths passes with his harrow. The sufferings of the past are now not only yielding fruit to him, but teaching him how it may be gathered.

The lesson is very simple, but of inappreciable value. It is the reverse of Horace Walpole's. It is to study the people, whom Walpole would disregard; to address those popular sympathies, which he affected to despise; to speak the language of the heart, of which he knew not much; and before all things to study, what so little came within the range of his experience, the joys and the sorrows of the poor. It is the lesson which Roger Ascham would have taught two hundred and fifty years before, to think as a wise man, but to speak as the common people. "We cannot without some re-"gret," Goldsmith wrote, "be-"hold talents so capable of giv-"ing pleasure to all, exerted in "efforts that at best can amuse "only the few: we cannot be-"hold this rising poet seeking "fame among the learned, with-"out hinting to him the same "advice that Isocrates used to "give his scholars, *study the* "*people.* This study it is that has "conducted the great masters "of antiquity up to immortality. "Pindar himself, of whom our "modern lyrist is an imitator, "appears entirely guided by it. "He adapted his works exactly "to the dispositions of his coun-"trymen. Irregular, enthusias-"tic, and quick in transition,— "he wrote for a people incon-"stant, of warm imaginations, "and exquisite sensibility. He "chose the most popular sub-"jects, and all his allusions are "to customs well known, in "his days, to the meanest per-"son."

Admirable rebuke to those who seize the form but not the spirit of an elder time, and mistake the phrase which passes in a century for the heart that is young for ever. The poetical genius of which Goldsmith is already conscious, was in its essential character of a lower grade than that of Gray; but the exquisite uses to which he will direct it, and the wise as well as earnest purpose that will shape and control it, are to be read, as it seems to me, in this capital piece of criticism.

Mr. Gray, continued Goldsmith, wants the Greek writer's advantages. "He speaks to a "people not easily impressed "with new ideas, extremely tena- "cious of the old, with difficulty "warmed and as slowly cooling "again. How unsuited, then, to "our national character is that "species of poetry which rises "upon us with unexpected flights; "where we must hastily catch "the thought, or it flies from us; "and the reader must largely "partake of the poet's enthu- "siasm in order to taste his "beauties! ... Mr. Gray's *Odes*, "it must be confessed, breathe "much of the spirit of Pindar; "but then they have caught the "seeming obscurity, the sud- "den transition, and hazardous "epithet of his mighty master; "all which, though evidently in- "tended for beauties, will pro- "bably be regarded as blemishes "by the generality of his readers. "In short, they are in some mea- "sure a representation of what "Pindar now appears to be, "though perhaps not what he "appeared to the States of "Greece, when they rivalled each "other in his applause, and when "Pan himself was seen dancing "to his melody."* Nothing could be happier than this last allusion.

1757.
Æt. 29.

Of the capabilities of Gray's genius, misdirected as he thus believed it to be, it is satisfactory to mark Goldsmith's strong appreciation. He speaks of him, in the emphatic line of the *Country Churchyard Elegy*, as one whom the muse had marked for her own. He grieves that "such "a genius" should not do justice to itself by trusting more implicitly to its own powers; and quotes passages from the *Bard* to support his belief that they are as great "as anything of that "species of composition which "has hitherto appeared in our "language, the *Odes* of Dryden "himself not excepted." Certainly to the two exceptions therefore, which, while Goldsmith wrote, Gray was describing to Hurd ("my friends tell me "that the *Odes* do not succeed, "and write me moving topics "of consolation on that head: I "have heard of nobody but an "actor and a doctor of divinity "that profess their esteem for "them"**), might with some reason have been added the poor monthly critic of the Dunciad. I wish I could say, that, in later and more successful days, he resisted with equal

* *Monthly Review*, xvii. 239, 240, September 1757.

** *Works*, iii. 166, 169, 177-8.

good taste and good sense the influence of Johnson's habitual and strange dislike to one of the most amiable men and delightful writers to be met with in English literature.

1757.
Æt. 29.

CHAPTER II.

Making Shift to Exist.
1757—1758.

WITH the number of the *Monthly Review* which completed the fifth month of Goldsmith's engagement with Mr. and Mrs. Griffiths, his labours suddenly closed. The circumstances were never clearly explained; but that a serious quarrel had arisen with his employer, there is no reason to doubt. Griffiths accused him of idleness, and said he affected an independence which did not become his condition, leaving his desk before the day was done. Nor would the reproach appear to be groundless, if the amount of his labour for Griffiths were measured by those portions only which have been traced; but this would be altogether a mistake, since the mass of it undoubtedly has perished. For himself Goldsmith retorted, that from the bookseller he had suffered impertinence, and from his wife privation; that Mr. Griffiths withheld common respect, and Mrs. Griffiths the most ordinary comforts;* that they both tampered

with his articles, and as it suited their ignorance or convenience wholly altered them; and finally

effect for good exerted over Goldsmith even by the "antiquated female critic" herself. The passage is supplementary to that which I have quoted *ante*, 71-2. "We "see little to have altered in the lease— "that was fair enough; only as regarded "the execution of the lease, we really "must have protested, under any circum- "stances, against Mrs. Dr. Griffiths. "That woman would have broken the "back of a camel, which must be sup- "posed tougher than the heart of an "usher. There we should have made a "ferocious stand; and should have struck "for much higher wages, before we "could have brought our mind to think "of a capitulation. It is remarkable, "however, that this year of humble ser- "vitude was not only (or, as if by ac- "cident) the epoch of Goldsmith's intel- "lectual development, but also the oc- "casion of it. Nay, if all were known, "perhaps it may have been to Mrs. Dr. "Griffiths in particular that we owe that "revolution in his self-estimation which "made Goldsmith an author by de- "liberate choice. Hag-ridden every day, "he must have plunged and kicked "violently to break loose from his har- "ness; but, not impossibly, the very ef- "fort of contending with the hag, when "brought into collision with his natural "desire to soothe the hag, and the in- "evitable counter-impulse in any con- "tinued practice of composition towards "the satisfaction, at the same time, of his "own reason and taste, must have "furnished a most salutary *palæstra* for "the education of his literary powers. "When one lives at Rome, one must do "as they do at Rome: when one lives "with a hag, one must accommodate "oneself to haggish caprices: besides that "once in a month the hag might be "right; or, if not, and supposing her al- "ways in the wrong, which, perhaps, is "too much to assume even of Mrs. Dr.G, "*that* would but multiply the difficulties "of reconciling *her* demands with the de- "mands of the general reader and of "Goldsmith's own judgment. And in "the pressure of these difficulties would "lie the very value of this rough Spartan "education. Rope-dancing cannot be

---

* In his extreme desire to work out and complete his favourable view of the Griffiths lease or agreement, Mr. De Quincey thus philosophises the probable

that no part of the contract had been broken by himself, he having always worked incessantly every day from nine o'clock till two,[*] and on special days of the week from an earlier hour until late at night. Proof of the most curious part of this counter-statement, as to interpolation of the articles, was in the possession of his first biographers; and, as it now appears from a published letter of Doctor Campbell to Bishop Percy, was at the last moment, in fear of abuse from reviewers, suppressed.[**]

But notwithstanding the quarrel, and Goldsmith's departure from the house, Griffiths retained his hold. Later events will show this; and that probably some small advance was his method of effecting it. It enabled him to keep up the appearance of civility when Goldsmith left his door, and to keep back the purpose of injury and insult till it could fall with heavier effect. The opportunity was not lost when it came, nor did the bookseller's malice end with the writer's death. "*Superintend* the "*Monthly Review!*" cried Griffiths, noticing in the number for August 1774 a brief memoir of Goldsmith professing to have been "written from personal "knowledge," in which his connection with the work was so described. "We are authorised "to say that the author is very "much mistaken in his asser-"tion. The Doctor had his merit, "as a man of letters; but alas! "those who knew him must smile "at the idea of such a super-"intendent of a concern which "most obviously required some "degree of prudence, as well as "a competent acquaintance with "the world. It is however true "that he had, for a while, a seat "at our board; and that, so far "as his knowledge of books ex-"tended, he was not an unuseful "assistant."[*]

And so, without this belauded prudence, without this treasure of a competent acquaintance with the world, into that wide, friendless, desolate world, the poor

1757.
Æt. 29.

"very agreeable in its elementary les-"sons; but it must be a capital process "for calling out the agilities that slumber "in a man's legs. Still, though these "hardships turned out so beneficially to "Goldsmith's intellectual interests, and "consequently so much to the advantage "of all who have since delighted in his "works, not the less on that account "they *were* hardships, and hardships that "imposed heavy degradation. So far, "therefore, they would seem to justify "Mr. Forster's characterisation of Gold-"smith's period by comparison with Ad-"dison's period on the one side, and "our own on the other." *Works*, VI. 215-17.

* *Percy Memoir*, 60.

** "Having mentioned Griffiths," writes Campbell to Percy in the course of his compilation of the *Memoir*, "I will "confess to you that the circumstance of "him and his wife (I mean their altering "and interpolating Goldsmith's criticisms "on books for the *Review*) puzzles me. "It is one of the most valuable anec-"dotes before me, and my conscience "bids me report it, but my fears whisper "to me that all the Reviews will abuse "me for so doing. But who's afraid?" The worthy Dr. Campbell himself was afraid it would seem; for certainly no such anecdote appeared. See Nichols's *Illustrations*, VII. 781.

* *Monthly Review*, LI. 181.

writer, the not unuseful assistant, was launched again. How or where he lived for the next few months is matter of great uncertainty. But his letters were addressed to the Temple-exchange coffee-house near Temple-bar, where the waiter "George," whom he celebrates in the third number of his *Bee*, took charge of them;* the garret where he wrote and slept is supposed to have been in one of the courts near the neighbouring Salisbury-square; Doctor Kippis, one of the Monthly Reviewers, "was impressed by some "faint recollection of his having "made translations from the "French, among others of a tale "from Voltaire;" and the recollection is made stronger by one of his autographs formerly in Heber's collection which purports to be a receipt from Mr. Ralph Griffiths for ten guineas, probably signed a day or two before he left the *Monthly*, for translation of a book entitled *Memoirs of my Lady B.* ** Another writer in the *Review*, Doctor James Grainger, to whom his residence at the sign of the Dunciad had made him known, and of whom the translation of *Tibullus*, the *Ode to Solitude*, the ballad of *Bryan and Pereene*, and the poem of the *Sugar-Cane*, have kept a memory very pleasant though very limited, made the

1757.
Æt. 29

same coffee-house his place of call, and often saw Goldsmith there.* The month in which he separated from Griffiths was that in which Newbery's *Literary Magazine* lost Johnson's services; but this seems the only ground for a surmise that those services were replaced by Goldsmith's. The magazine itself shows little mark of his hand, until his admitted connection with it some months later.

Toiling thus through an obscurity dark as the life itself, the inquirer finds on a sudden a glimpse of light which for an instant places him in that garret near Salisbury-square. Its inmate sits alone in wretched drudgery, when the door opens, and a raw-looking country youth of twenty stands doubtfully on the doleful threshold. Goldsmith sees at once his youngest brother Charles; but Charles cannot bring himself to see, in the

* "My poor worthy friend, Dr. "Grainger, who resided for many years "at St. Christopher's, assured me," &c. &c. *Animated Nature*, v. 155. "An agreeable "man," said Johnson; "a man who would "do any good that was in his power." "One of the most generous, friendly, and "benevolent men I ever knew," said Percy: "it was to him that I owed my "first acquaintance with Johnson." "A "man of modesty and reserve" (said a writer in the *Westminster Magazine* of 1773, who *might* have been Goldsmith); "and, in spite of a broad provincial "dialect, extremely pleasing in his con-"versation. He was tall, and of a lathy "make; plain-featured, and deeply "marked with the small-pox; his eyes "were quiet and keen; his temper "generous and good-natured; and he was "an able man in the knowledge of his "profession."

* Some curious notices of "George's" may be seen in Cunningham's *Handbook of London.*
** *Prior*, i. 279.

occupier of this miserable dwelling, the brother on whose supposed success he had already built his own! Without education, profession, friends, or resource of any kind, it had suddenly occurred to this enterprising Irish lad, as he lounged in weary idleness round Ballymahon, that as brother Oliver had not been asking for assistance lately, but was now a settled author in London, perhaps he had gotten great men for his friends, and a kind word to one of them might be the making of *his* fortune. Full of this he scrambled to London as he could, won the secret of the house from the Temple-exchange waiter to whom he confided his relationship, and found the looked-for architect of wealth and honour, *here!* * "All in good "time, my dear boy," cried Oliver joyfully, to check the bitterness of despair; "all in good "time: I shall be richer bye and "bye. Besides you see, I am "not in positive want. Addison, "let me tell you, wrote his poem "of the *Campaign* in a garret in "the Haymarket three stories

"high; and you see I am not "come to that yet, for I have "only got to the second story." He made Charles sit and answer questions about his Irish friends: but at this point the light is again withdrawn, and for some two months there is greater darkness than before.

1757.
Æt. 29.

Charles quitted London in a few days, suddenly and secretly as he had entered it, and shortly sailed, "in a humble capacity" it is said, for Jamaica: whence he did not return till after four-and-thirty years, to tell this anecdote,* and to be described by

---

* "Having heard of his brother Noll "mixing in the first society in London, "he took it for granted that his fortune "was made, and that he could soon "make a brother's also: he therefore left "home without notice; but soon found, "on his arrival in London, that the picture he had formed of his brother's "situation was too highly coloured, that "Noll would not introduce him to his "great friends, and in fact, that, although "out of a jail, he was also often out of a "lodging." Northcote's *Life of Reynolds*, i. 332-3.

* An interesting notice of that first return may be seen in Northcote's *Life of Reynolds*, i. 331. His object in coming over was to arrange for his ultimate settlement with his family in England. He had not been wholly unsuccessful in his scramble for life in the West Indian Islands; but the unlucky close which awaited him on his second return will be best described by an intelligent correspondent of the *Mirror* (15 Dec. 1832), who knew him well. Mr. R. Roffe thus writes: "Charles, on his coming to this "country from the West Indies, had with "him two daughters, and one son named "Henry; all under 14 years of age. He "purchased two houses in the Polygon, "Somers-town. In one of which he re-"sided; here the older of his girls died; "I attended her funeral; she was buried "in the churchyard of St. Pancras, near "the grave of Mary Wolstoncroft God-"win. Henry was my fellow-pupil; but "not liking the profession of engraving, "after a short trial he returned to the "West Indies. At the peace of Amiens, "Charles Goldsmith sold his houses, and "with his wife (a Creole) and daughter, "and a son christened Oliver, born in "England, he went to reside in France, "where his daughter married. In con-"sequence of the orders of Buonaparte "for detaining British subjects, Charles "again returned home by way of Hol-

Malone as not a little like his celebrated brother in person, speech, and manner. He certainly had no lack of the adventurous spirit; and he so far resembled Oliver that, at the close of a long life of great vicissitude, he said he had met with no such friend in adversity as his flute.

'1757.
_____
Æt. 29.

The next clear view of Oliver is from a letter to his brother-in-law Hodson, with the date of "Temple-exchange coffee-house "(where you may direct an an-"swer), Dec. 27, 1757;" fortunately kept.* The miserable year had brought no happier Christmas to Goldsmith, but he writes with a manly cheerfulness that offers no selfish affront to the unselfish spirit of the season. Some unsuccessful efforts of this Hodson to raise a subscription,

in answer to the supplication for Irish aid during the travel abroad, seem to have been mentioned by Charles; and gratitude, for a little made Goldsmith grateful, prompted the letter. He begins by reminding his kinsman that his last letters to Ireland, and to him in particular, of the date of four years ago, were left unanswered. "Dear Sir, It may "be four years since my last "letters went to Ireland, and to "you in particular. I received "no answer; probably because "you never wrote to me. My "brother Charles however in-"forms me of the fatigue you "were at in soliciting a subscrip-"tion to assist me, not only "among my friends and rela-"tions, but acquaintances in "general. Though my pride "might feel some repugnance at "being thus relieved, yet my "gratitude can suffer no diminu-"tion. How much am I obliged "to you, to them, for such "generosity, or (why should not "your virtues have their proper "name?) for such charity to me "at that juncture. Sure I am "born to ill-fortune to be so "much a debtor and unable to "repay. But to say no more of "this: too many professions of "gratitude are often considered "as indirect petitions for future "favours: let me only add that "my not receiving that supply "was the cause of my present "establishment at London. You "may easily imagine what dif-"ficulties I had to encounter, left

---

"land, much reduced in circumstances, "and died, about 25 years since, at "humble lodgings in Ossulston-street, "Somers-town. Charles Goldsmith had "in his possession a copy from Sir Joshua "Reynolds's portrait of his brother; and I "can vouch his resemblance to this pic-"ture was most striking. Charles, like "the Poet, was a performer on the German "flute, and, to use his own words, found "it in the hour of adversity his best "friend. He only once, I have heard him "say, saw Oliver in England, which was "in his prosperity." The last must have been a brag, if it was not a slip of memory. Mr. Roffe's son has since favoured me with an earlier private letter of his father's containing further notices of Charles, and describing his condition when he died, for which I refer the reader to a paper in the Appendix to the second volume of this biography ("What was proposed and what was "done for the relatives of Goldsmith"). See also Nichols's *Illustrations*, VII. 60.
  * *Percy Memoir*, 40-45.

"as I was without friends, re-
"commendations, money, or im-
"pudence; and that in a country
"where being born an Irishman
"was sufficient to keep me un-
"employed. Many in such cir-
"cumstances would have had re-
"course to the friar's cord or the
"suicide's halter. But, with all
"my follies, I had principle to
"resist the one and resolution to
"combat the other. I suppose
"you desire to know my present
"situation. As there is nothing
"in it at which I should blush,
"or which mankind could cen-
"sure, I see no reason for mak-
"ing it a secret; in short, by a
"very little practice as a phy-
"sician, and a very little reputa-
"tion as a poet, I make a shift
"to live. Nothing is more apt
"to introduce us to the gates of
"the Muses than poverty, but it
"were well if they only left us at
"the door. The mischief is,
"they sometimes choose to give
"us their company at the enter-
"tainment; and Want, instead of
"being gentleman-usher, often
"turns master of the ceremonies.
"Thus, upon hearing I write, no
"doubt you imagine I starve;
"and the name of an author
"naturally reminds you of a gar-
"ret. In this particular I do not
"think proper to undeceive my
"friends. But whether I eat or
"starve, live in a first floor or
"four pair of stairs high, I still
"remember *them* with ardour,
"nay, my very country comes
"in for a share of my affec-
"tion."

This cheery glance at the gloomy aspect of his fortunes would to me be less pathetic if it had been less playful. His Irish friends had shown the charitable wish, however unavailing; and he would not trouble friendly eyes with needless exhibition of his sufferings, or make grim Want the master of other than somewhat cheerful ceremonies. Lightly and quickly he passes from the subject to that unaccountable fondness for Ireland already mentioned in connection with the letter.* What little pleasures he had ever tasted in London, he says, Irish memories had soured. Signora Columba had never poured out for him all the mazes of melody at the opera, that he did not sit and sigh for Lissoy fireside, and Peggy Golden's song of Johnny Armstrong's Last Good Night. "If I climb "Hampstead-hill,** than where "Nature never exhibited a more "magnificent prospect, I confess "it fine; but then I had rather "be placed on the little mount "before Lishoy gate, and there "take in, to me, the most pleas"ing horizon in nature. Be"fore Charles came hither, my "thoughts sometimes found re"fuge from severer studies "among my friends in Ireland. "I fancied strange revolutions at "home; but I find it was the

* See *ante*, 28, for the passage from it here omitted.

** Printed *Hamstead* by mistake in the *Percy Memoir*, and so repeated by Mr. Mitford, and some later biographers.

"rapidity of my own motion that "gave an imaginary one to ob- "jects really at rest. No altera- "tions there. Some friends, "he tells me, are still lean, "but very rich; others very "fat, but still very poor. Nay, "all the news I hear from [of] "you is that you sally out in "visits among the neighbours, "and sometimes make a migra- "tion from the blue bed to the "brown.* I could from my "heart wish that you and she** "and Lishoy and Ballymahon,

* This expression is in the *Vicar of Wakefield*. Goldsmith, as I have already remarked, repeats himself incessantly in his various writings, public and private.

** Mrs. Hodson, of course. I subjoin the closing lines of the letter, as printed in the *Percy Memoir:* "To speak plain "English, as you cannot conveniently "pay me a visit, if next summer I can "contrive to be absent six weeks from "London, I shall spend three of them "among my friends in Ireland. But first, "believe me, my design is purely to visit, "and neither to cut a figure nor levy "contributions, neither to excite envy "nor solicit favour: in fact, my circum- "stances are adapted to neither; I am too "poor to be gazed at, and too rich to need "assistance. You see, dear Dan, how long "I have been talking about myself; but "attribute my vanity to my affection: as "every man is fond of himself, and I "consider you as a second self. I imagine "you will consequently be pleased with "these instances of egotism." [Some mention of private family affairs is here omitted, by the compiler of the *Memoir.*] "My dear sir, these things give me real "uneasiness, and I could wish to redress "them. But at present there is hardly a "kingdom in Europe in which I am not "a debtor. I have already discharged "my most threatening and pressing de- "mands, for we must be just before we "can be grateful. For the rest I need "not say (you know I am) your affec- "tionate kinsman, OLIVER GOLDSMITH."

"and all of you, would fairly "make a migration into Mid- "dlesex: though, upon second "thoughts, this might be attended "with a few inconveniences; "therefore, as the mountain will "not come to Mahomet, why "Mahomet shall go to the moun- "tain." He explains, that if they cannot conveniently now pay him a visit he believes he must go next year to see them; and sub- scribes himself his dear Dan's "affectionate kinsman."

Poet and Physician! the rag- ged livery of Grub-street under one high-sounding name, and wretched fee-less patients beneath the other. He was the poet of Hogarth's print, which the com- mon people then hailed with laughter at every print-shop; he was again, it would seem, the poor physician of the patched velvet among hovels of Bank- side; and yet it was but pleasant colouring for the comfort of brother-in-law Hodson when he said that with both he made a shift to live. With even more he failed to attain that object of humble ambition.

In February 1758 two duodecimos appeared with this most explanatory title: "*The Memoirs of a Protestant con- "demned to the Galleys of France for "his Religion.* Written by him- "self. Comprehending an ac- "count of the various distresses "he suffered in slavery, and his "constancy in supporting almost "every cruelty that bigoted zeal "could inflict, or human nature "sustain. Also a description of "the Galleys, and the service in "which they are employed. The "whole interspersed with anec- "dotes relative to the general "history of the times for a period "of thirteen years, during which "the author continued in slavery "till he was at last set free at the "intercession of the Court of "Great Britain. Translated from "the Original, just published at "the Hague, by James Willing- "ton." James Willington was in reality Oliver Goldsmith.* The property of the book belonged to Griffiths, who valued one name quite as much as the other; and the position of the translator appears in the subsequent assignment of the manuscript by the Paternoster-row bookseller to bookseller Dilly of the Poultry, at no small profit to Griffiths, for the sum of twenty guineas.** But though the translator's name might pass for Willington, the writer could only write as Goldsmith; though with bitterness he calls himself "the obscure pre- "facer," the preface is clear, graceful, and characteristic as in brighter days. The book cannot be recommended, he says, as a grateful entertainment to the readers of reigning romance, for it is strictly true. "No "events are here to astonish, no "unexpected incidents to sur- "prise, no such high-finished pic- "tures as captivate the imagina- "tion and have made fic- "tion fashionable. Our "reader must be content "with the simple exhibition of "truth, and consequently of na- "ture; he must be satisfied to "see vice triumphant and virtue "in distress; to see men punished "or rewarded, not as his wishes "but as Providence has thought "proper to direct; for all here "wears the face of sincerity." Then, with a spirit that shows how strongly he at this time entered into the popular feeling of the day, he contrasts popery and absolute power with the rational religion and moderate constitutionalism of England; glances at the scenes of dungeon, rack, and scaffold through which the narrative will pass; and calls them but a part of the accumulated wretchedness of a miscalled glorious time, "while Louis, sur- "named the Great, was feasting "at Versailles, fed with the in- "cense of flattery or sunk in the "lewd embraces of a prosti- "tute. Could the present per- "formance," he continues, "teach "an individual to value his re- "ligion, by contrasting it with "the furious spirit of Popery; "could it contribute to make him "enamoured of liberty, by show- "ing their unhappy situation "whose possessions are held by "so precarious a tenure as tyran- "nical caprice; could it promote "his zeal in the cause of hu-

1758.
Æt. 30.

* Willington, it would seem, from an entry in the register of Trinity College (*Prior*, i. 253-4), was the name of one of Goldsmith's fellow-students in Dublin.

** *Life* by Isaac Reed (Ed. of *Poems by Goldsmith and Parnell*, 1795), p. xv. Aikin's *Life*, p. xvi.

"manity, by giving him a wish "to imitate the virtues of the "sufferer or redress the injuries

1758. "of oppression; then, in- "deed, the author will not Æt. 30. "have wrote in vain."

But why stood "James Wil-"lington" on the title-page of this book instead of "Oliver "Goldsmith," since the names were both unknown? The question will not admit of a doubtful answer, though a braver I could wish to have given. At this point there is very manifest evidence of despair.

Not without well-earned knowledge had Goldsmith passed through the task-work of the *Monthly Review.* Faculties which lay unused within him were by this time not unknown; and a stronger man, with a higher constancy and fortitude, might with such knowledge have pushed resolutely on, and, conquering the fate of those who look back when their objects are forward, found earlier sight of the singing tree and the golden water. But to him it seemed hopeless to climb any further up the desperate steep; over the dark obstructions which the world is eager to interpose between itself and the least selfish of the labourers in its service, he had not as yet risen high enough to see the glimmerings of light beyond;—even lower therefore than the school-room at Doctor Milner's from which he had been taken to his literary toil, he thought himself now descended;

and in the sudden sense of a misery more intolerable might have cried with Edgar,

O gods! who is't can say "I am at the
worst"?
I am worse than e'er I was.

He returned to Doctor Milner's; — if ever, from thence, again to return to literature, to embrace it for choice and with a braver heart endure its worst necessities.

There came that time; and when, eighteen months after the present date, he was writing the *Bee,* he thus turned into pleasant fiction the incidents now described. "I was once induced to "show my indignation against "the public, by discontinuing my "endeavours to please; and was "bravely resolved, like Raleigh, "to vex them by burning my "manuscripts in a passion. Upon "recollection, however, I con-"sidered what set or body of "people would be displeased at "my rashness. The sun, after "so sad an accident, might shine "next morning as bright as usual; "men might laugh and sing the "next day, and transact business "as before, and not a single "creature feel any regret but my-"self. I reflected upon the story "of a minister, who in the reign "of Charles II. upon a certain "occasion resigned all his posts, "and retired into the country in "a fit of resentment. But, as he "had not given the world en-"tirely up with his ambition, he "sent a messenger to town to "see how the courtiers would

"bear his resignation. Upon the
"messenger's return he was
"asked, whether there appeared
"any commotion at court? To
"which he replied, there were
"very great ones. 'Ay,' says
"the minister, 'I knew my friends
"'would make a bustle; all peti-
"'tioning the king for my resto-
"'ration I presume?' 'No, sir,'
"replied the messenger, 'they
"'are only petitioning his ma-
"'jesty to be put in your place.'
"In the same manner, should I
"retire in indignation, instead of
"having Apollo in mourning,
"or the Muses in a fit of the
"spleen; instead of having the
"learned world apostrophising at
"my untimely decease; perhaps
"all Grub-street might laugh at
"my fall, and self-approving
"dignity might never be able to
"shield me from ridicule." *
Worse than ridicule had he
spared himself, with timely aid
of these better thoughts; but
they came too late. He made
his melancholy journey to Peckham, and knocked at Doctor Milner's door.

The schoolmaster was not an
unkind or unfriendly man, and
would in any circumstances, there
is little doubt, have given Goldsmith the shelter he sought. It
happened now that he had special
need of him, sickness having dis-
abled himself from the proper
school-attendance. So, again installed poor usher, week passed
over week as of old, with suffering, contempt, and many forms
of care. Milner saw what he endured; was moved by it; and
told him that as soon as health
enabled himself to resume
the duties of the school, he
would exert an influence to
place his usher in some medical
appointment at a foreign station.
He knew an East India director,
a Mr. Jones, through whom it
might be done. * Before all
things it was what Goldsmith
fervently desired.]

And now, with something like
the prospect of a settled future
to bear him up against the un-
congenial and uncertain present,
what leisure he had for other
than school-labour he gave to a
literary project of his own designing. This was natural: for
we cling with a strange new fondness to what we must soon
abandon, and it is the strong resolve to separate that most often
has made separation impossible.
Nor, apart from this, is there
ground for the feeling of surprise, or the charge of vacillating
purpose. His daily bread provided here, literature presented
itself again to his thoughts as in
his foreign wanderings; and to
have left better record of himself than the garbled page of
Griffiths's *Review*, would be a
comfort in his exile. Some part
of his late experience, so dearly
bought, should be freely told;
with it could be arranged and
combined such store of literary
fruit as he had gathered in his
travel; and no longer commanded

1758.:
Æt. 30.

____

* The Bee, iv.

Oliver Goldsmith's Life and Times. I.

* Percy Memoir, 45.

by a bookseller, or overawed by an old woman, he might frankly deliver to the world some wholesome truths on the decay

1758.
Æt. 30.

of letters and the rewards of genius. In this spirit he conceived the *Enquiry into the Present State of Polite Learning in Europe:* and if he had reason bitterly to feel, in his own case, that he had failed to break down the barriers which encircled the profession of literature, here might a helping hand be stretched forth to the relief of others, still struggling for a better fate in its difficult environments.

With this design another expectation arose, – that the publication, properly managed, might give him means for the outfit his re appointment would render necessary. And he bethought him of his Irish friends. The zeal so lately professed might now be exerted with effect, and without plaguing overmuch either their pockets or his own pride. In those days, and indeed until the Act of Union was passed, the English writer had no copyright in Ireland: it being a part of the independence of Irish booksellers to steal from English authors, and of the Irish parliament to protect the theft; just as, not twenty years before this date, that excellent native parliament had, on the attempt of a Catholic to recover estates which in the manner of the booksellers a Protestant had seized, voted "all "barristers, solicitors, attorneys "and proctors who should be concerned for him," *public enemies!* But, that serviceable use might be made of the early transmission to Ireland of a set of English copies of the *Enquiry* by one who had zealous private friends there, was Goldsmith's not unreasonable feeling; and he would try this, when the time came. Meanwhile he began the work; and it was probably to some extent advanced, when, with little savings from the school and renewed assurances of the foreign appointment, he was released by Doctor Milner from duties which the necessity (during the Doctor's illness) of flogging the boys as well as teaching them appears to have made quite intolerable to the child-loving usher. The reverend Mr. Mitford knew a lady whose husband had been at this time under Goldsmith's cane; but with no very serious consequence.

Escape from the school might not have been so easy, if the lessening chances of Doctor Milner's recovery had not rendered advisable more permanent arrangements there. Some doubt has been expressed indeed whether the worthy schoolmaster's illness had not already ended fatally, and if the kindness I have recorded should not rather be attributed to his son and successor in the school, Mr. George Milner. But other circumstances clearly invalidate this, and show that it must have been the elder Milner's. In August 1758, however, Goldsmith again had bidden him adieu; and once more had secured a respectable town address for his letters, and, among the Graingers and Kippises and other tavern acquaintance, had obtained the old facilities for correspondence with his friends, at the Temple-exchange coffee-house Temple-bar.

CHAPTER III.

Attempt to Escape from Literature.
1758.

GRAINGER, his friend Percy,[*] and others of the Griffiths connection, were at this time busy upon a new magazine: begun with the present year, and dedicated to the "great Mr. Pitt," whose successful coercion of the king made him just now more than ever the darling of the people. Griffiths was one of the publishing partners in *The Grand Magazine of Universal Intelligence and Monthly Chronicle of our own Times:* and perhaps on this account, as well as for the known contributions of some of his acquaintance,[**] traces of Goldsmith's hand have been sought in the work; in my opinion without success. In truth the first number was hardly out when he went back to the Peckham school;

and on his return to London, though he probably eked out his poor savings by casual writings here and there, it is certain that on the foreign appointment his hopes continued steadily fixed, and that the work which was to aid him in his escape from literature (the completion of the *Enquiry into the State of Polite Learning,* or, as he called it before publication, the *Essay on the Present State of Taste and Literature*) occupied nearly all his thoughts. He was again in London, and again working with the pen; but he was no longer the bookseller's slave, nor was literary toil his impassable and hopeless doom. Therefore, in the confidence of swift liberation, and with hope of a new career brightening in his sanguine heart, he addressed himself cheerily enough to the design in hand, and began solicitation of his Irish friends.

Edward Mills he thought of first, as a person of some influence. He was his relative, had been his fellow-collegian, and was a prosperous wealthy man. "Dear Sir," he begins, in a letter dated from the Temple-exchange coffee-house, on the 7th of August, and published by Bishop Percy:[*]

"You have quitted, I find, that plan of life which you once intended to pursue; and given up ambition for domestic tranquillity. Were I to consult your

---

[*] "My beloved friend," was Percy's description of Grainger, nearly forty years after the present date. Nichols's *Illustrations,* VII. 71.

[**] In the *Grand Magazine* first appeared Grainger's exquisite ballad of Bryan and Pereene, and other contributions which Bishop Percy describes in a letter to Dr. Anderson. Nichols's *Illustrations,* VII. 75.

[*] *Percy Memoir,* 50-2. The date there given is 1759, an obvious misprint for 1758.

satisfaction alone in this change, I have the utmost reason to congratulate your choice; but when I consider my own, I cannot avoid feeling some regret, that one of my few friends has declined a pursuit in which he had every reason to expect success. The truth is, like the rest of the world, I am self-interested in my concern; and do not so much consider the happiness you have acquired, as the honour I have probably lost in the change. I have often let my fancy loose when you were the subject, and have imagined you gracing the bench, or thundering at the bar; while I have taken no small pride to myself, and whispered all that I could come near, that this was my cousin. Instead of this, it seems you are contented to be merely an happy man; to be esteemed only by your acquaintance—to cultivate your paternal acres—to take unmolested a nap under one of your own hawthorns, or in Mrs. Mills's bed-chamber, which even a poet must confess is rather the most comfortable place of the two.

1758.
Æt. 30.

" But however your resolutions may be altered with regard to your situation in life, I persuade myself they are unalterable with regard to your friends in it. I cannot think the world has taken such entire possession of that heart (once so susceptible of friendship), as not to have left a corner there for a friend or two; but I flatter myself that even I have my place among the number. This I have a claim to from the similitude of our dispositions; or, setting that aside, I can demand it as my right by the most equitable law in nature, I mean that of retaliation: for indeed you have more than your share in mine. I am a man of few professions, and yet this very instant I cannot avoid the painful apprehension that my present professions (which speak not half my feelings) should be considered only a pretext to cover a request, as I have a request to make. No, my dear Ned, I know you are too generous to think so; and you know me too proud to stoop to mercenary insincerity. I have a request it is true to make; but, as I know to whom I am a petitioner, I make it without diffidence or confusion. It is in short this, I am going to publish a book in London, entitled An Essay on the Present State of Taste and Literature in Europe. Every work published here the printers in Ireland republish there, without giving the author the least consideration for his copy. I would in this respect disappoint their avarice, and have all the additional advantages that may result from the sale of my performance there to myself. The book is now printing in London, and I have requested Dr. Radcliff, Mr. Lawder, Mr. Bryanton, my brother Mr. Henry Goldsmith, and brother-in-law Mr. Hodson, to circulate my proposals among their acquaintance. The same request I now make to you; and have accordingly given directions to Mr. Bradley, bookseller in Dame-street Dublin, to send you a hundred proposals. Whatever subscriptions pursuant to those proposals you may receive, when collected, may be transmitted to Mr. Bradley, who will give a receipt for the money and be accountable for the books.* I shall not, by a paltry apology, excuse myself for putting you to this trouble. Were I not convinced that you found more pleasure in doing good-natured things, than uneasiness at being employed in them, I should not have singled you out on this occasion. It is probable you would comply with such a request, if it tended to the encouragement of any man of learning whatsoever; what then may not he expect who has claims of family and friendship to enforce his?

"I am, dear Sir, your sincere
"Friend and humble servant,
"OLIVER GOLDSMITH."

What indeed may he not freely expect who is to receive nothing! Nevertheless, there is a worse

* With what chance of success poor Goldsmith was preferring this request may be inferred from what Faulkner, Swift's Dublin printer and publisher, was writing to Derrick three months later. Sending him over his Edition of *Swift's Works* (16 Nov. 1758) he says: "You "know that Dublin is the poorest place in "the world for subscriptions to books. "It is much easier to get a hundred din-"ners, with as many dozen bottles of "claret, than a single guinea for the best "author: few or no people here caring "to subscribe; and reading not being the "prevailing taste." Unpublished Derrick Correspondence, *prints me.*

fool's paradise than that of expectation. To teach our tears the easiest way to flow, should be no unvalued part of this world's wisdom; hope is a good friend, even when the only one; and Goldsmith was not the worse for expecting, though he received nothing. Mr. Mills left his poor requests unheeded, and his letter unacknowledged. Sharking booksellers and starving authors might devour each other before he would interpose; being a man, as his old sizar-relative delicately hinted, with paternal acres as well as boyish friendships to cultivate, and fewer thorns of the world to struggle with than hawthorns of his own to sleep under. He lived to repent it certainly, and to profess great veneration for the distinguished writer to whom he boasted relationship; but Goldsmith had no more pleasant hopes or friendly correspondences to fling away upon Mr. Mills of Roscommon. Not that even this letter, as it seems to me, had been one of very confident expectation. Unusual effort is manifest in it; a reluctance to bring unseemly fancies between the wind and Mr. Mills's gentility; a conventional style of balance between the "pleasure" and the "uneasiness" it talks about; in short, a forced suppression of everything in his own state that may affront the acres and the hawthorns.

Seven days afterwards he wrote to Bryanton, with a curious contrast of tone and manner. Even Bryanton had not inquired for him since the scenes of happier years. The affectionate rememberings of the lonely wanderer, as of the struggling author, he had in carelessness, if not in coldness, passed without return. Yet, here, heart spoke to heart; buoyant, unreserved, and sanguine. That sorrow lay beneath the greetings, was not to be concealed, else had the words which cheerily rose above it been perhaps less sincere; but see, and make profitable use of it,—how, depressed by unavailing labours, and patiently awaiting the disastrous issue of defeat and flight, he shows to the last a bright and cordial happiness of soul unconquered and unconquerable.

1758.
Æt. 30.

The letter, which like that to Mills is also dated* from the Temple coffee-house, was. first printed by permission of Bryanton's son-in-law, the reverend Doctor Handcock of Dublin; and where the paper is torn or has been worn away, there are several erasures that the reader will not find it difficult sufficiently to supply.

"Dear Sir, I have heard it remarked, I believe by yourself, that they who are drunk, or out of their wits, fancy every body else in the same condition: mine is a friendship that neither distance nor time can efface, which is probably the reason that, for the soul of me, I can't avoid thinking yours of the same complexion; and yet I have many reasons for being of a contrary opinion, else why in

* August 14. 1758.

so long an absence was I never made a partner in your concerns? To hear of your successes would have given me the utmost pleasure; and a communication of your very disappointments would divide the uneasiness I too frequently feel for my own. Indeed, my dear Bob, you don't conceive how unkindly you have treated one whose circumstances afford him few prospects of pleasure, except those reflected from the happiness of his friends. However, since you have not let me hear from you, I have in some measure disappointed your neglect by frequently thinking of you. Every day do I remember the calm anecdotes of your life, from the fireside to the easy-chair; recall the various adventures that first cemented our friendship, the school, the college, or the tavern; preside in fancy over your cards; and am displeased at your bad play when the rubber goes against you, though not with all that agony of soul as when I once was your partner.

1758.
Æt. 30.

"Is it not strange that two of such like affections should be so much separated and so differently employed as we are? You seem placed at the centre of fortune's wheel, and let it revolve never so fast, seem insensible of the motion. I seem to have been tied to the circumference, and .... disagreeably round like an whore in a whirligig .... down with an intention to chide, and yet methinks .... my resentment already. The truth is, I am a .... regard to you; I may attempt to bluster, ... Anacreon, my heart is respondent only to softer affections. And yet, now I think on't again, I will be angry. God's curse, sir! who am I? Eh! what am I? Do you know whom you have offended? A man whose character may one of these days be mentioned with profound respect in a German comment or Dutch dictionary; whose name you will probably hear ushered in by a Doctissimus Doctissimorum, or heel-pieced with a long Latin termination. Think how Goldsmithius, or Gubblegurchius, or some such sound, as rough as a nutmeg-grater, will become me! Think of that!—God's curse, sir! who am I? I must own my ill-natured contemporaries have not hitherto paid me those honours I have had such just reason to expect. I have not yet seen my face reflected in all the lively display of red and white paints on any sign-posts in the suburbs. Your handkerchief-weavers seem as yet unacquainted with my merits or my physiognomy, and the very snuff-box makers appear to have forgot their respect. Tell them all from me, they are a set of Gothic, barbarous, ignorant scoundrels. There will come a day, no doubt it will—I beg you may live a couple of hundred years longer only to see the day—when the Scaligers and Daciers will vindicate my character, give learned editions of my labours, and bless the times with copious comments on the text. You shall see how they will fish up the heavy scoundrels who disregard me now, or will then offer to cavil at my productions. How will they bewail the times that suffered so much genius to lie neglected! [*] If ever my works find their way to Tartary or China, I know the consequence. Suppose one of your Chinese Owanowitzers instructing one of your Tartarian Chianobacchhi—you see I use Chinese names to show my own erudition, as I shall soon make our Chinese talk like an Englishman to show his—this may be the subject of the lecture:

"*Oliver Goldsmith flourished in the eighteenth and nineteenth centuries. He lived to be an hundred and three years old .... age may justly be styled the sun of .... and the Confucius of Europe .... learned world, were anonymous, and have probably been lost, because united with those of others. The first avowed piece the world has of his is entitled an Essay on the Present State of Taste and Literature in Europe,—a work well worth its weight in diamonds. In this he profoundly explains what learning is, and what learning is not. In this he proves that blockheads are not men of wit, and yet that men of wit are actually blockheads.*

"But as I choose neither to tire my Chinese Philosopher, nor you, nor myself, I must discontinue the oration, in order to give you a good pause for admiration; and I find myself most violently disposed to admire too. Let me, then, stop my fancy to take a view of my future self; and, as the boys say, light down to see myself on horseback. Well, now I am down, where the devil is *I?* Oh

<hr>

[*] For parallel passages see the fourth number of the *Bee.*

Gods! Gods! here in a garret, writing for bread, and expecting to be dunned for a milk-score! However, dear Bob, whether in penury or affluence, serious or gay, I am ever wholly thine,

"OLIVER GOLDSMITH.

"Give my—no, not compliments neither, but something .... most warm and sincere wish that you can conceive, to your mother, Mrs. Bryanton, to Miss Bryanton, to yourself; and if there be a favourite dog in the family, let me be remembered to it."

"In a garret, writing for bread, "and expecting to be dunned for "a milk-score." Such was the ordinary fate of letters in that age. There had been a Christian religion extant for seventeen hundred and fifty-seven years, the world having been acquainted, for even so long, with its spiritual necessities and responsibilities; yet here, in the middle of the eighteenth century, was the eminence ordinarily conceded to a spiritual teacher, to one of those men who come upon the earth to lift their fellow-men above its miry ways. He is up in a garret, writing for bread he cannot get and dunned for a \milk-score he cannot pay. And age after age,* the prosperous man comfortably contemplates it and decently regrets it, glad to think it no business of this; and in that year of grace and of Gold-

* "There came into my company an "old fellow not particularly smart, so "that he was easily recognised as be- "longing to the class of men of letters, "whom the rich commonly hate. 'I am "'a poet,' said he. 'But why, then, so "'badly dressed?' 'For this reason, the "'love of knowledge never made a man "'rich.'" *Petronius;* who wrote in the reign of Nero.

smith's suffering had doubtless adorned his dining-room with the *Distrest Poet* of the inimitable Mr. Hogarth, inviting laughter from easy guests at the garret and the milk-score. Yet their laughter would not have been so hearty under danger of worldly loss; and it was this, though not discoverable in any of their ledgers, that they had now very gravely to dread. For cheerful hours, for happy thoughts, for fancies that would smooth life's path to their children's children, those very citizens were hereafter to be indebted to Goldsmith; who now, without a friend, with hardly bread to eat, and uncheered by a hearty word or a smile to help him on, sits in his melancholy garret while those fancies die within him. It is but an accident now that the good Vicar shall be born, that the Man in Black shall dispense his charities; that Croaker shall grieve, Tony Lumpkin laugh, or the sweet soft echo of the *Deserted Village* come for ever back upon the heart, in gladness, kindness, and sympathy with the poor. For there is now despair in the garret; and the poet, overmastered by distress, seeks only the means of flight and exile. With a day-dream to his old Irish playfellow, a sigh for the "heavy scoundrels" who disregard him, and a wail for the age to which genius is a mark of mockery; he turns to that first avowed piece, which, being also his last, is to prove that "block-

"heads are not men of wit, and "yet that men of wit are actually "blockheads."

1758.
Æt. 30.

A proposition which men of wit have laboured at from early times; have proved in theory, and worked out in practice. "How many base "men," shrieked one of them in Elizabeth's day who felt that his wit had but made him the greater blockhead, "how many base "men, that want those parts I "have, do enjoy content at will. "and have wealth at command! "I call to mind a cobbler, that is "worth five hundred pounds; an "hostler, that has built a goodly "inn; a carman in a leather "pilche, that has whipt a thou- "sand pounds out of his horse's "tail: and I ask if I have more "than these. Am I not better "born? am I not better brought "up? yea, and better favoured? "And yet am I for ever to sit up "late, and rise early, and con- "tend with the cold, and con- "verse with scarcity, and be a "beggar? How am I crossed, or "whence is this curse, that a "scrivener should be better paid "than a scholar?"* Poor Nash!

he had not even Goldsmith's for- titude, and his doleful outcry for money was a lamentable exhibi- tion out of which no good could come. But the feeling in the miserable man's heart struck at the root of a secret discontent which not the strongest men can resist altogether; and which Gold- smith did not affect to repress, when he found himself, as he says, "starving in those streets "where Butler and Otway starved "before him."

The words are in a letter written the day after that to Bryanton,* bearing the same date of Temple-exchange coffee- house, and sent to Mrs. Lawder, the Jane Contarine of his happy old Kilmore time, to whom he signs himself "her ever affec- "tionate kinsman." Mr. Mills afterwards begged this letter of the Lawders, and from the friend to whom he gave it, Lord Carle- ton's nephew, it was copied for Bishop Percy by Edmund Malone. As in those already given, the style, with its simple air of authorship, is eminently good and happy. The assumption of a kind of sturdy independence, the playful admission of well- known faults, and the incidental slight confession of sorrows, have graceful relation to the per- son addressed, and to the terms

* Thomas Nash, in his *Pierce Pennilesse*. Let me quote, too, that good old English gentleman, whose lamentations had al- ready found earlier record in one of the writings of Wolsey's correspondent, Richard Pace. "Those foolish letters "will end in some bad business. I fairly "wish all this learning at the devil. All "learned men are poor: even the most "learned Erasmus, I hear, is poor; and "in one of his letters calls the vile hag "Poverty his wife. By'r lady I had "rather my son were hanged than that "he should become a man of letters.

"We ought to teach our sons better "things."

* August 15. 1758. Now in possession of Messrs. Griffin the publishers, who, in a recent edition of *Goldsmith*, presented it in a facsimile from which several correc- tions have here been made.

on which they stood of old. His uncle was now in a hopeless state of living death, from which, in a few months, the grave released him; and to this the letter affectingly refers.

"If you should ask, why in an interval of so many years, you never heard from me, permit me, madam, to ask the same question. I have the best excuse in recrimination. I wrote to Kilmore from Leyden in Holland, from Louvain in Flanders, and Rouen in France, but received no answer. To what could I attribute this, please, but to displeasure or forgetfulness? Whether I was right in my conjecture, I do not pretend to determine, but this I must ingenuously own, that I have a thousand times in my turn endeavoured to forget them whom I could not but look upon as forgetting me. I have attempted to blot their names from my memory, and, I confess it, spent whole days in efforts to tear their images from my heart. Could I have succeeded, you had not now been troubled with this renewal of a discontinued correspondence; but, as every effort the restless make to procure sleep serves but to keep them waking, all my attempts contributed to impress what I would forget deeper on my imagination. But this is a subject I would willingly turn from, and yet, for the soul of me, I can't till I have said all. I was, madam, when I discontinued writing to Kilmore, in such circumstances, that all my endeavours to continue your regards might be attributed to wrong motives. My letters might be regarded as the petitions of a beggar, and not the offerings of a friend; while all my professions, instead of being considered as the result of disinterested esteem, might be ascribed to venal insincerity. I believe indeed you had too much generosity to place them in such a light, but I could not bear even the shadow of such a suspicion. The most delicate friendships are always most sensible of the slightest invasion, and the strongest jealousy is ever attendant on the warmest regard. I could not, I own I could not, continue a correspondence where every acknowledgment for past favours might be considered as an indirect request for future ones, and where it might be thought I gave my heart from a motive of gratitude alone, when I was conscious of having bestowed it on much more disinterested principles.

"It is true, this conduct might have been simple enough, but yourself must confess it was in character. Those who know me at all, know that I have always been actuated by different principles from the rest of mankind, and while none regarded the interests of his friends more, no man on earth regarded his own less. I have often affected bluntness to avoid the imputation of flattery, have frequently seemed to overlook those merits too obvious to escape notice, and pretended a disregard to those instances of good nature and good sense which I could not fail tacitly to applaud; and all this lest I should be ranked among the grinning tribe who say very true to all that is said, who fill a vacant chair at a tea-table, whose narrow souls never moved in a wider circle than the circumference of a guinea, and who had rather be reckoning the money in your pocket than the virtues of your breast. All this, I say, I have done, and a thousand other very silly tho' very disinterested things in my time, and for all which no soul cares a farthing about me. God's curse, madam! is it to be wondered that he should once in his life forget you who has been all his life forgetting himself?

1758.
Æt. 30.

"However it is probable you may one of those days see me turn'd into a perfect Hunks, and as dark and intricate as a mouse-hole. I have already given my landlady orders for an entire reform in the state of my finances. I declaim against hot suppers, drink less sugar in my tea, and choak my grate with brickbats. Instead of hanging my room with pictures I intend to adorn it with maxims of frugality. These will make pretty furniture enough, and won't be a bit too expensive; for I shall draw them all out with my own hands, and my landlady's daughter shall frame them with the parings of my black waistcoat. Each maxim is to be inscribed on a sheet of clear paper, and wrote with my best pen; of which the following will serve as a specimen. *Look sharp. Mind the main chance. Money is money now. If you have a thousand pound you can put your hands by your sides and say you are worth a thousand pounds every day of the year. Take a farthing from an hundred pound and it will be an hundred pound no longer.*

1758.
Æt. 30.

Thus, which way soever I turn my eyes, they are sure to meet one of those friendly Monitors; and as we are told of an Actor who hung his room round with looking-glasses to correct the defects of his person, my apartment shall be furnished in a peculiar manner to correct the errors of my mind.

"Faith, madam, I heartily wish to be Rich, if it were only for this reason, to say without a blush how much I esteem you; but, alas! I have many a fatigue to encounter before that happy time comes, when your poor old simple friend may again give a loose to the luxuriance of his nature, sitting by Kilmore fireside recount the various adventures of an hard-fought life, laugh over the follies of the day, join his flute to your harpsichord, and forget that ever he starved in those streets where Butler and Otway starved before him. *

"And now I mention those great names—My uncle—He is no more that soul of fire as when once I knew him. Newton and Swift grow dim with age as well as he. But what shall I say?—his mind was too active an inhabitant not to disorder the feeble mansion of its abode, for the richest jewels soonest wear their settings. Yet who but the fool would lament his condition! He now forgets the calamities of life. Perhaps indulgent heaven has given him a foretaste of that tranquillity here which he so well deserves hereafter.

"But I must come to business; for business, as one of my maxims tells me, must be minded or lost. I am going to publish in London a book entitled *The Present State of Taste and Literature in Europe.* The Booksellers in Ireland republish every performance there without making the author any consideration. I would in this respect disappoint their avarice, and have all the profits of my labours to myself. I must therefore request Mr. Lawder to circulate among his friends and acquaintances an hundred of my Proposals, which I have given the bookseller, Mr. Bradley in Dame-street, directions to send to him. If, in pursuance to such circulation, he should receive any subscriptions, I entreat when collected they may be sent to Mr. Bradley's as aforesaid, who will give a receipt and be accountable for the work or a return of the subscription. If this request (which, so far complied with, will in some measure be an encouragement to a man of learning) should be disagreeable or troublesome, I would not press it; for I would be the last man on earth to have my labours go a-begging; but if I know Mr. Lawder, and sure I ought to know him, he will accept the employment with pleasure. All I can say—if he writes a book I will get him two hundred subscribers, and those of the best wits in Europe.

"Whether this request is complied with or not, I shall not be uneasy; but there is one Petition I must make to him, which I solicit with the warmest ardour, and in which I cannot bear a refusal, I mean, Dear Madam, that I may live

"Your ever affectionate and obliged kinsman,

"OLIVER GOLDSMITH.

"You see how I blot and blunder, * when I am asking a favour.

"*Temple Exchange Coffee House, near Temple Bar, Lond. Aug. 15, 1758.*"

In none of these letters, it will be observed, is allusion made to the expected appointment. To make jesting boast of a visionary influence with two hundred of the best wits in Europe, was pleasanter than to make grave confession of himself as a wit taking sudden flight from the

---

* This passage, coupled with the allusion written at the same date for the first edition of the *Polite Learning* as to its sufficing for one age to have neglected Sale, Savage, Amhurst, and Moore (he struck Savage and Amhurst out of the second edition, though he had meanwhile again introduced them in the 8th number of the *Bee*), seems to connect itself with Dryden's affecting remark in his letter to Lord Rochester, "'Tis enough "for one age to have neglected Mr. Cow-"ley and starved Mr. Butler."

* A line is erased after "kinsman." &c.

scene of defeat and failure. It was the old besetting weakness: but not without excuse. Such allusions as that of the Chinese philosopher introduced to Bryanton, show that, thus prepared for flight as he was, the fancies busiest with him yet had more relation to the wits he was leaving than to the new career he was entering; and whether his unhappy present fortunes were to turn him into a doctor on a foreign station, or some higher ultimate destiny was to connect him with a Chinese philosopher, had been still very far from determined. But shortly after the date of the last letter, the appointment was received. It was that of medical officer to one of the factories on the coast of Coromandel; was forwarded by Doctor Milner's friend Mr. Jones, the East India director; and the worthy schoolmaster did not outlive more than a few weeks this honest redemption of his promise. The desired escape was at last apparently effected, and the booksellers might look around them for another drudge more patient and obedient than Oliver Goldsmith.

CHAPTER IV.

Escape Prevented.

1758.

IT was now absolutely necessary that the proposed change in Goldsmith's life should be broken to his Irish friends; and he wrote to his brother Henry. The letter (which contained also the design of a heroicomical poem at which he had been occasionally working) is lost; but some passages of one of nearly the same date to Mr. Hodson have had a better fortune.

1758.
—
Æt. 30.

It began with obvious allusion to some staid and rather gratuitous reproach from the prosperous brother-in-law.

"Dear Sir, You cannot expect regularity in one who is regular in nothing. Nay, were I forced to love you by rule, I dare venture to say that I could never do it sincerely. Take me, then, with all my faults. Let me write when I please, for you see I say what I please, and am only thinking aloud when writing to you. I suppose you have heard of my intention of going to the East Indies. The place of my destination is one of the factories on the coast of Coromandel, and I go in quality of physician and surgeon; for which the company has signed my warrant, which has already cost me ten pounds. I must also pay 50l. for my passage, and ten pounds for my sea stores; and the other incidental expenses of my equipment will amount to 60l. or 70l. more. The salary is but trifling, namely 100l. per annum; but the other advantages, if a person be prudent, are considerable. The practice of the place, if I am rightly informed, generally amounts to not less than one thousand pounds per annum, for which the appointed physician has an exclusive privilege. This, with the advantages resulting from trade, and the high interest which money bears, viz. 20l. per cent, are the inducements which persuade me to undergo the fatigues of sea, the dangers of war, and the still greater dangers of the climate; which induce me to leave a place where I am every day gaining friends and esteem, and where I might enjoy all the conveniences of life."*

The same weakness that indulged itself with fine clothes when the opportunity offered, is

* *Percy Memoir*, 46-7.

that which prompts these fine words in even such an hour of dire extremity. Of the "friends "and esteem" he was gaining, of the "conveniences "of life" that were awaiting him to enjoy, these pages have told, and have more to tell. But why, in the confident hope of brighter days, dwell on the darkness of the past, or show the squalor that still surrounded him? Of already sufficiently low esteem were wit and intellect in Ireland, to give purse-fed ignorance another triumph over them, or again needlessly invite to himself the contempts and sneers of old.* Yet, though the sadness he almost wholly suppressed while the appointment was but in expectation there was at this moment less reason to indulge, he found it a far from successful effort to seem other than he was, even thus; and it marked with a somewhat painful distraction of feeling and phrase this letter to Mr. Hodson.

1758.
Æt. 30.

"I am certainly wrong not to be contented with what I already possess, trifling as it is; for should I ask myself one serious question.—What is it I want? —what can I answer? My desires are as capricious as the big-bellied woman's, who longed for a piece of her husband's nose. I have no certainty, it is true; but why cannot I do as some men, of more merit, who have lived on more precarious terms? Scarron used jestingly

* "Faulkner is obliged to you," wrote Dr. Wilson of Trinity College to Derrick, in this very month, "but the best Poetry "here, he says, is not worth a farthing a "ream." *Unpublished Derrick MSS. in my possession.*

to call himself the marquis of Quenault, which was the name of the bookseller that employed him; and why may not I assert my privilege and quality on the same pretensions? Yet, upon deliberation, whatever airs I give myself on this side of the water, my dignity, I fancy, would be evaporated before I reached the other. I know you have in Ireland a very indifferent idea of a man who writes for bread; though Swift and Steele did so in the earliest part of their lives. You imagine, I suppose, that every author by profession lives in a garret, wears shabby cloaths, and converses with the meanest company. Yet I do not believe there is one single writer who has abilities to translate a French novel, that does not keep better company, wear finer cloaths, and live more genteelly than many who pride themselves for nothing else in Ireland. I confess it again, my dear Dan, that nothing but the wildest ambition could prevail on me to leave the enjoyment of the refined conversation which I am sometimes admitted to partake in, for uncertain fortune, and paltry shew. You cannot conceive how I am sometimes divided. To leave all that is dear to me gives me pain: but when I consider I may possibly acquire a genteel independance for life, when I think of that dignity which philosophy claims to raise itself above contempt and ridicule, when I think thus, I eagerly long to embrace every opportunity of separating myself from the vulgar as much in my circumstances, as I am already in my sentiments. I am going to publish a book, for an account of which I refer you to a letter which I wrote to my brother Goldsmith. Circulate for me among your acquaintances a hundred proposals, which I have given orders may be sent to you: and if, in pursuance of such circulation, you should receive any subscriptions, let them, when collected, be transmitted to Mr. Bradley, who will give a receipt for the same." [Omitting here, says the *Percy Memoir*, what relates to private family affairs, we add the rest:] "I know not how my desire of seeing Ireland, which had so long slept, has again revived with so much ardour. So weak is my temper, and so unsteady, that I am frequently tempted, particularly when low-spirited, to return home and leave my fortune, though i just beginning to look kinder. But it shall not be. In five or six years I hope to indulge these transports. I find I want constitution, and a strong steady disposition, which alone makes men great. I will however correct my faults, since I am conscious of them." *

With such professions weakness continues to indulge itself, and faults are perpetuated. But some allowances are due. Of the Irish society he knew so well and so often sarcastically painted, these Irish friends were clearly very notable specimens; his prosperous brother-in-law, for whom his youth had been embittered with loss and worldly disadvantage, and whose most solid repayment of help came in shape of a prudent maxim or news of an abortive subscription, being perhaps the best of them. The rest careless yet suspicious, vain whether rich or poor, extravagant, pretending, and vulgar, too evidently prided themselves on nothing so much as the keeping better company, wearing finer clothes, and living more genteelly than their neighbours. Among such there was small chance of decent consideration, if a garret, shabby clothes, and conversation with the meanest company were set hopelessly forth as his inextricable doom. The error lay in giving faith of any kind to such external aid, and so weakening the help that rested in himself. When the claim of ten pounds for his appointment-warrant came upon him, it found him less prepared

* *Percy Memoir*, 48-49.

because of vague expectations raised on these letters to Mills and the Lawders. But any delay might be fatal; and in that condition of extremity whose "wants," alas, are anything but "capricious," he bethought him of the *Critical Review*, saw promise in its rivalry to Griffiths, and went to its proprietor, Mr. Archibald Hamilton.

1758.
Æt. 30.

Soon after he left Griffiths he had written an article for his rival, which appeared in November 1757; and as his contributions then stopped where they began, I am disposed to connect both his joining at that time so suddenly and as suddenly quitting the *Critical Review*, with a letter which Smollett addressed in that same November number "to the Old Gentlewoman who "directs the *Monthly*." * For

* In Carlyle's *Autobiography* (339) there is not a bad description, of himself, Robertson, Home, and Smith dining with Smollett, in the summer of this year, on the one day of the week when he came up from Chelsea to transact his London business at Forrest's coffee-house; where, after dinner, when Smollett had been very "brilliant, he had several of his "minions about him to whom he pre- "scribed tasks of translation, compila- "tion, and abridgment, which, after he "had seen, he recommended to the book- "sellers." An entertainment to the same party by Garrick at Twickenham, with a game at golf on Molesly-hurst, is afterwards pleasantly mentioned. I will add also, from the unpublished correspondence of Derrick, an original glimpse of Smollett making solid addition to our knowledge of him, and otherwise curiously like Carlyle's. Little more than two years from this date, George Faulkner is writing from London to Derrick in Ireland (14 May 1761) of the kindnesses

though Goldsmith might not object to avenge some part of his own quarrel under cover of that *1758.* of Smollett, he would hardly have relished the *Æt. 30.* too broad allusion in which "goody" and "gammer" Griffiths were reminded that "though "we never visited your garrets "we know what sort of doctors "and authors you employ as "journeymen in your manufac- "ture. Did you in your dotage "mistake the application, by "throwing those epithets at us "which so properly belong to "your own understrappers?" * But, whatever may have caused his secession then, he certainly now applied again to Hamilton, a shrewd man who had just made a large fortune out of Smollett's *History*, and, though not very liberal in his payments, ** already not unconscious of the value of Griffiths's discarded

shown him; of attentions from Johnson, Murphy, Sheridan, Foote, and the Delavals; of having dined on turtle with Justice Fielding; and of having met Colman and Lloyd at a dinner at Garrick's, when he counted thirteen dishes on the table: his letter closing thus: "I "often see Lord Southwell, Mr. Mallet, "and Dr. Smollett, who all make friendly "enquiries after you, and last week I "dined with the last gentleman at Sal- "ter's at Chelsea in a very agreeable "sett of company. The Doctor proposes "going to Ireland next summer, and to "spend a year or two in that country, in "order to enable him the better to write "that history. Mr. Sheridan is much "pleased and obliged to you for the "good opinion you have of *Sidney Bid-* "*dulph*."

  * *Critical Review*, iv. 469-71. Nov. 1757.
  ** See Percival Stockdale's *Memoirs* (1809), ii. 57.

writer. The result of the interview was the publication, in the new-year number, of two more papers by Goldsmith apparently in continuation of the first. All three had relation to a special subject; and, as connected with such a man's obscurest fortunes, have an interest hardly less than that of writings connected with his fame. An author is seen in the effulgence of established repute, or discovered by his cries of struggling distress. By both you shall know him.

Ovid was the leading topic in all three. His *Fasti*, translated by a silly master of a Wandsworth boarding-school named Massey; his *Epistles*, translated by a pedantic pedagogue named Barrett (a friend of Johnson and Cave); and an antidote to his *Art of Love* in an *Art of Pleasing* by Mr. Marriott; were the matters taken in hand. The *Art of Pleasing* so far suggested comparison with the Roman poet, "that as "one performance of Ovid was "styled *Tristia* from the subject, "Mr. Marriott's production should "be styled *Tristia* for the execu- "tion;" while the notice of Mr. Massey's *Fasti*, setting out with the statement of its having been "no bad remark of a celebrated "French lady (Madame Lafayette) "that a bad translator was like "an ignorant footman," went on to express much sorrow that "our poor friend Ovid should "send his Sacred Kalendar to us "by the hands of Mr. William "Massey, who like the valet has "entirely forgot his master's message and substituted another in its room very unlike it," and in conclusion asked leave "to remind Mr. Massey of the old Italian proverb" (*Il traduttore traditore*), "and to hope he will never for the future traduce* and injure any of those poor ancients who never injured him by thus pestering the world with such translations as even his own schoolboys ought to be whipped for."** Nor with less just severity was the last of these unhappy gentlemen rebuked. With very lively power Goldsmith dissected the absurdities of Mr. Barrett's version of poor afflicted Ovid's *Epistles* (a classic to all appearance doomed, he humorously interposed, "to successive *Metamorphoses:* being sometimes transposed by schoolmasters unacquainted with English, and sometimes transversed by ladies who knew no Latin);" showed that the translator was a bad critic, and no poet; and passed in his illustrations with amusing effect from lofty to low. Giving two or three instances of Mr. Barrett's skill in parenthetically clapping one sentence within another, this, pursued Goldsmith, "contributes not a little to obscurity, and obscurity, we all know, is nearly al-

"lied to admiration. Thus, when the reader begins a sentence which he finds pregnant with another, which still teems with a third, and so on, he feels the same surprise which a countryman does at Bartholomew fair. Hocus shows a bag, in appearance empty; slap, and out come a dozen new-laid eggs; slap again, and the number is doubled; but what is his amazement, when it swells with the hen that laid them!" The poetry and criticism disposed of, the scholarship shared their fate. Mr. Barrett being master of the thriving grammar-school of Ashford in Kent,* and having the consequence and pretension of a so-called learned man, we are not going, said Goldsmith, "to permit an ostentation of learning pass for merit, nor to give a pedant quarter on the score of his industry alone, even though he took refuge behind Arabic or powdered his head with Hieroglyphics."**

In the garret of Griffiths he would hardly have conceded so much; and since then, the world had not been teaching him literary charity. These Ovid translations had not unnaturally turned his thoughts upon the

1758.
Æt. 30.

* Goldsmith's remark anticipates the French lady, who, being complimented on her English and asked in what manner she had contrived to speak it so well, replied, "I began by *traducing*."
** *Critical Review*, IV. 409, November 1757.

* The second title of his translation runs thus: "Being part of a poetical or "oratorical lecture read in the grammar-"school of Ashford, in the county of "Kent; and calculated to initiate youth "in the first rudiments of taste."
** *Critical Review*, VII. 38, January 1759.

master of the art; on him who was the father of authorship by profession; and the melancholy _1758._ image which arose to a ———— mind so strongly disposed Æt. 30. to entertain it then, of "great Dryden ever poor,"[*] and obliged by his miseries to suffer fleeting performances to be "quartered on the lasting merit "of his name," did not the more entitle to any mercy which truth could not challenge for them, these gentlemen of a more thriving profession who had thrust themselves uninvited and unqualified on the barren land of authorship. "But let not the "reader imagine," he said, "we "can find pleasure in thus ex- "posing absurdities which are "too ludicrous for serious re- "proof. While we censure as "critics, we feel as men, and "could sincerely wish that those "whose greatest sin is perhaps "the venial one of writing bad "verses, would regard their "failure in this respect as we do, "not as faults but foibles: they "may be good and useful mem- "bers of society, without being "poets. The regions of taste "can be travelled only by a few, "and even those often find in- "different accommodation by the "way. Let such as have not got "a passport from nature be con- "tent with happiness, and leave "the poet the unrivalled posses- "sion of his misery, his garret, "and his fame. We have of late "seen the republic of letters "crowded with some who have "no other pretensions to ap- "plause but industry, who have "no other merit but that of read- "ing many books and making "long quotations; these we have "heard extolled by sympathetic "dunces, and have seen them "carry off the rewards of genius; "while others, who should have "been born in better days, felt "all the wants of poverty and "the agonies of contempt.[*]

---

[*] I am glad to record that, amid many heresies that forbid me to claim for Goldsmith the merit of a critical faculty either sound or deep, he had a well-grounded and steady admiration for Dryden, which he often justified in language worthy of it. "The English "tongue," he said, in the eighth number of the _Bee_, "is greatly his debtor. It was "his pen that formed the Congreves, the "Priors, and the Addisons who suc- "ceeded him; and had it not been for "Dryden, we never should have known "a Pope, at least in the meridian lustre "he now displays. But Dryden's ex- "cellencies, as a writer, were not con- "fined to poetry alone. There is, in his "prose writings, an ease and elegance "that have never yet been so well united "in works of taste or criticism."

[*] _Critical Review_, vii. 37-8, January. 1759. Let me add an admirable passage from a later essay (_Citizen of the World_, letter xciii.) in which Goldsmith speaks out for the _profession_ of the writer: "For "my own part, were I to buy a hat, I "would not have it from a stocking- "maker, but a hatter; were I to buy "shoes, I should not go to the tailors for "that purpose. It is just so with regard "to wit: did I, for my life, desire to be well "served, I would apply only to those "who made it their trade, and lived by "it. You smile at the oddity of my "opinion; but be assured, my friend, "that wit is in some measure mechani- "cal, and that a man long habituated to "catch at even its resemblance, will at "last be happy enough to possess the "substance. By a long habit of writing

"Who, then, that has a regard
"for the public, for the literary
"honour of our country, for the
"figure we shall one day make
"among posterity, that would
"not choose to see such humbled
"as are possessed only of talents
"that might have made good
"cobblers, had fortune turned
"them to trade?" So will truth
force its way, when out of Irish
hearing. The friends, the esteem,
and the conveniences of the
poet's life are briefly summed up
here. His misery, his garret,
and his fame.

With part of the money received from Hamilton he moved into new lodgings: took "unrivalled possession" of a fresh garret, on a first floor. The house was number twelve Green-arbour-court, Fleet-street, between the Old Bailey and the site of Fleet-market; and stood in the right hand corner of the court, as the wayfarer approached it from Farringdon-street by an appropriate access of "Break-neck "Steps." Green-arbour-court is now gone for ever; and of its miserable wretchedness, for a little time replaced by the more decent comforts of a stable, not a vestige remains. The houses, crumbling and tumbling in Goldsmith's day, were fairly rotted down some nineteen years since;[*] and it became necessary, for safety sake, to remove what time had spared. But Mr. Washington Irving saw them first, and with reverence had described them for Goldsmith's sake. Through alleys, courts, and blind passages; traversing Fleet-market, and thence turning along a narrow street to the bottom of a long steep flight of stone steps; he made good his toilsome way up into Green-arbour-court. He found it a small square of tall and miserable houses, the very intestines of which seemed turned inside out, to judge from the old garments and frippery that fluttered from every window. "It "appeared," he says in his *Tales of a Traveller*, "to be a region of "washerwomen, and lines were

1758. ———— Æt. 30.

"he acquires a justness of thinking, and
"a mastery of manner which holiday
"writers, even with ten times his genius,
"may vainly attempt to equal. How
"then are they deceived, who expect
"from title, dignity, and exterior cir-
"cumstances, an excellence which is in
"some measure acquired by habit, and
"sharpened by necessity! You have
"seen, like me, many literary reputa-
"tions promoted by the influence of
"fashion which have scarcely survived
"the possessor; you have seen the poor
"hardly earn the little reputation they
"acquired, and their merit only acknow-
"ledged when they were incapable of
"enjoying the pleasures of popularity.
"Such however is the reputation worth
"possessing; that which is hardly earned
"is hardly lost." Most true. He lived
long enough himself to have some foretaste of this in his own case; we all of us
now know it more completely. Let me
not quit this subject without saying that
Johnson held much the same opinion as
Goldsmith about interlopers in literature. Boswell one day was full of regrets that some learned judge had left no
literary monument of himself. "Alas,
"sir," cried Johnson, "what a mass of
"confusion should we have if every
"bishop, and every judge, every lawyer,
"physician, and divine, were to write
"books!" *Life*, vi. 327.

* In 1829.

1758.
—
Æt. 30.

"stretched about the little square, "on which clothes were dangling "to dry." The disputed right to a wash-tub was going on when he entered; heads in mob-caps were protruded from every window; and the loud clatter of vulgar tongues was assisted by the shrill pipes of swarming children, nestled and cradled in every procreant chamber of the hive. The whole scene, in short, was one of whose unchanged resemblance to the scenes of former days I have since found curious corroboration, in an exact magazine-engraving of the place nigh half a century old.* Here were the tall faded houses, with heads out of window at every story; the dirty neglected children; the bawling slipshod women; in one corner, clothes hanging to dry, and in another the cure of smoky chimneys announced. Without question the same squalid, squalling colony, which it then was, it had been in Goldsmith's time. He would compromise with the children for occasional cessation of their noise by frequent cakes or sweetmeats, or by a tune upon his flute for which all the court assembled; he would talk pleasantly with the poorest of his neighbours, and was long recollected to have greatly enjoyed the talk of a working watchmaker in the court; every night, he would risk his neck at those steep stone stairs; * every day, for his clothes had become too ragged to submit to daylight scrutiny, he would keep within his dirty, naked, unfurnished room, with its single wooden chair and window bench. Such was Goldsmith's home.

On a certain night in the beginning of November 1758 his ascent of Break-neck Steps must have had unwonted gloom. He had learnt the failure of his new hope: the Coromandel appointment was his no longer. In what way this mischance so unexpectedly occurred, it would now be hopeless to inquire; no explanation could be had from the dying Dr. Milner; none was given by himself; he always afterwards withheld allusion to it, with even studious care. It is quite possible, though no authority exists for the assertion, that doubts may have arisen of his competence to discharge the duties of the appointment, and

* It appeared as the frontispiece to vol. XLIII. of the *European Magazine*.

* Ward, in his *London Spy*, talks of "returning down stairs with as much "care and caution of tumbling head-fore-"most as he that goes down Green-"arbour-court steps in the middle of "winter." I may quote also from Strype's edition of Stowe, where he speaks of "Seacoal-lane as very ordinary "both as to houses and inhabitants. Out "of this lane is a passage to Snow-hill; "another into Green-arbour, and a third "into Bishop's court, the two last a-"scended up by a great many steps, or a "pair of stairs, made thro' London-wall; "but having their chief entrance out of "the Little Old Bailey." Lord Macaulay speaks of Goldsmith having had to "climb to his garret *from the brink of* "*Fleet Ditch* by a dizzy ladder of flag-"stones," &c. but this is a little misleading, as old Strype shows.

what followed a few months later will be seen to give warrant for such a surmise; but even supposing this to have been the real motive, there is no ground for suspecting that such a motive was alleged. The most likely supposition would probably be, that failure in getting together means for his outfit with sufficient promptitude was made convenient excuse for transferring the favour to another. That it was any failure of his own courage at the prospect of so long an exile, or that he never proposed more by his original scheme than a foreign flight for two or three years, has no other or better foundation than the Hodson letter: on which authority it would also follow that he remained contented with what he already possessed, subdued his capricious wants, and turned to the friends, the esteem, the refined conversation, and all the conveniences of life which awaited him in Green-arbour-court, with a new and virtuous resolve of quiet thankfulness.

Alas! far different were the feelings with which he now ascended Break-neck Steps; far different his mournful conviction, that, but to flee from the misery that surrounded him, no office could be mean, and no possible endurance hard. His determination was taken at once: probably grounded on the knowledge of some passages in the life of Smollett, and of his recent acquaintance Grainger. He would present himself at Surgeons'-hall for examination as a hospital mate: an appointment sufficiently undesirable to be found always of tolerably easy attainment by the duly qualified.

1758.
————
Æt. 30.

But he must have decent clothes to present himself in: the solitary suit in which he crept between the court and the coffee-house being only fit for service after nightfall. He had no resource but to apply to Griffiths, with whom he had still some small existing connection; and from whom his recent acceptance at the *Critical*, increasing his value with a vulgar mind, might help in exacting aid. The bookseller, to whom the precise temporary purpose for which the clothes were wanted does not seem to have been told, consented to furnish them on certain conditions. Goldsmith was to write at once four articles (he had given three to the *Critical*) for the *Monthly Review*. Griffiths would then become security with a tailor for a new suit of clothes; which were either to be returned, or the debt for them discharged, within a given time. This pauper proposal acceded to, Goldsmith doubtless returned to Green-arbour-court with the four books under his arm.

They were: *Some Enquiries Concerning the First Inhabitants of Europe*,* by a member of the society of antiquaries, known

* *Monthly Review*, xix. 513, December 1758.

afterwards as Francis Wise and Thomas Warton's friend; *Anselm Bayly's Introduction to Languages;* * the *Pentalogia* of Doctor Burton;** and a new *Translation of Cicero's Tusculan Disputations.**** The notices of them thus extorted made due appearance as the first four articles of the *Monthly Review* for December 1758. The tailor was then called in, and the compact completed.

1758.
Æt. 30.

Equipped in his new suit, and one can well imagine with what an anxious, hopeful, quaking heart, Goldsmith offered himself for examination at Surgeons'-hall (the new building erected six years before in the Old Bailey) on the 21st December. "The "beadle called my name," says Roderick Random, when he found himself in similar condition at that place of torture, "with a voice "that made me tremble as much "as if it had been the sound of "the last trumpet: however there "was no remedy: I was con- "ducted into a large hall, where "I saw about a dozen of grim "faces sitting at a long table, "one of whom bade me come "forward in such an imperious "tone that I was actually for a "minute or two bereft of my "senses." Whether the same process, conducted through a like memorable scene, bereft

poor Goldsmith altogether of his, cannot now be ascertained. All that is known is told in a dry extract from the books of the college of surgeons. *"At a Court "of Examiners held at the Theatre "21st December, 1758. Present"* . . the names are not given, but there is a long list of the candidates who passed, in the midst of which these occur: *"James "Bernard, mate to an hospital. "Oliver Goldsmith, found not qua- "lified for ditto."* A rumour of this rejection long existed, and on a hint from Maton the king's physician the above entry was found.*

A harder sentence, a more cruel doom than this at the time must have seemed, even the Old Bailey has not often been witness to; yet, far from blaming that worthy court of examiners, should we not rather feel that much praise is due to them? That they really did their duty in rejecting the short, thick, ungainly, over-anxious, over-dressed, simple-looking Irishman who presented himself that memorable day, can hardly, I think, be doubted; but unconsciously they also did a great deal more. They found him not qualified to be a surgeon's mate, and left him quali-fied to heal the wounds and abridge the sufferings of all the world. They found him queru-lous with adversity, given up to irresolute fears, too much blinded with failures and sorrows to see

* *Monthly Review,* xix. 519, December 1758.

** *Ibid,* 522.

*** *Ibid,* 521.

* *Prior,* i. 281-2.

the divine uses to which they tended still; and from all this, their sternly just decision resolutely drove him back. While the door of the Surgeons'-hall was shut upon him that day, the gate of the beautiful mountain was slowly opening. Much of the valley of the shadow he had still indeed to pass; but every outlet save the one was closed upon him, it was idle any longer to strike or struggle against the visions which sprang up in his desolate path, and as he so passed steadily if not cheerily on he saw them fade and become impalpable before him. Steadily, then, if not cheerily, for some months more! "Sir," said Johnson, "the man who has vigour "may walk to the East just as "well as to the West, if he hap- "pens to turn his head that "way."* So, honour to the court of examiners I say, for that, whether Goldsmith would or would not, they turned back his head to the East! The hopes and promise of the world have a perpetual springtime there; and he was hereafter to enjoy them, briefly for himself, but for the world eternally.

CHAPTER V.

Discipline of Sorrow.
1758—1759.

It was four days after the rejection at Surgeons'-hall, the Christmas day of 1758, when to

* Boswell's *Life*, IV. 24.

the ordinary filth and noise of number twelve in Green-arbour-court there was added an unusual lamentation and sorrow. An incident had occurred, of which, painful as were the consequences involved in it, the precise details can only be surmised and guessed at, and must be received with that allowance, though doubtless in the main correct. It would appear that the keeper of this wretched lodging had been suddenly dragged by bailiffs from his home on the previous night, and his wife, with loud wailings, now sought the room of her poorer lodger. He was in debt to the unfortunate couple, who, for the amusement of their children by his flute, had been kind to him according to their miserable means: and it was the woman's sobbing petition that he should try to help them. There was but one way; and in the hope, through Hamilton or Griffiths, to be able still to meet the tailor's debt, the gay suit in which he went to Surgeons'-hall, and in which he was dressed for his doleful holiday, appears to have been put off and carried to the pawnbroker's. Nor had a week passed, before the pangs of his own destitution sharply struck him again; and, without other remaining means of earthly aid, for death had taken in Doctor Milner his apparently last friend, he carried the four books he had recently reviewed for Griffiths to a neighbouring house,

1758.
Æt. 30.

and left them in pledge with an acquaintance for a trifling loan. It was hardly done when a letter from Griffiths was put into his hand, peremptorily demanding the return of the books and the suit of clothes, or instant payment for both.

1758.
Æt. 30.

Goldsmith's answer, and the bookseller's violent retort, are to be presumed from the poor debtor's second letter: the only one preserved of this unseemly correspondence. He appears first to have written in a tone of mixed astonishment, anger, and solicitation; to have prayed for some delay; and to have been met by coarse insult, threats, and the shameless imputation of crime. These forced from him the rejoinder found in the bookseller's papers, endorsed by Griffiths with the writer's name and as "*Recd. in Jany.* "1759;" which passed afterwards into the manuscript collections of Mr. Heber, and is now in my possession. Its appearance harmonises with its contents, for there is nothing of the freedom or boldness of hand in it which one may perceive in his ordinary manuscript. Most interesting of all the Goldsmith papers that have been preserved to our time, it is here printed with the strictest accuracy. The pointing is imperfect and confused, nor is there any break or paragraph from the first line to the signature; but all concealment at least is ended in it, and stern plain truth is told.

"Sir, I know of no misery but a gaol to which my own imprudencies and your letter seem to point. I have seen it inevitable these three or four weeks, and, by heavens! request it as a favour, as a favour that may prevent somewhat more fatal. I have been some years struggling with a wretched being, with all that contempt which indigence brings with it, with all those strong passions which make contempt insupportable. What then has a gaol that is formidable? I shall at least have the society of wretches, and such is to me true society. I tell you again and again I am now neither able nor willing to pay you a farthing, but I will be punctual to any appointment you or the taylor shall make; thus far at least I do not act the sharper, since unable to pay my debts one way I would willingly give some security another. No Sir, had I been a sharper, had I been possessed of less good nature and native generosity I might surely now have been in better circumstances. I am guilty I own of meannesses which poverty unavoidably brings with it, my reflections are filled with repentance for my imprudence, but not with any remorse for being a villain. That may be a character you unjustly charge me with. Your books I can assure you are neither pawn'd nor sold, but in the custody of a friend from whom my necessities oblig'd me to borrow some money; whatever becomes of my person, you shall have them in a month. It is very possible both the reports you have heard and your own suggestions may have brought you false information with respect to my character, it is very possible that the man whom you now regard with detestation may inwardly burn with grateful resentment, it is very possible that upon a second perusal of the letter I sent you, you may see the workings of a mind strongly agitated with gratitude and jealousy. If such circumstances should appear at least spare invective 'till my book with Mr. Dodsley shall be publish'd, and then perhaps you may see the bright side of a mind when my professions shall not appear the dictates of necessity but of choice. You seem to think Dr. Milner knew me not. Perhaps so; but he was a man I shall ever honour. But I have friendship only with the dead! I ask pardon for taking up so much time. Nor shall I add to it by any other professions than that I am Sir your Humble Servt.

"OLIVER GOLDSMITH.

"P.S. I shall expect impatiently the result of your resolutions."

Now, this Ralph Griffiths the bookseller, whom the diploma of some American university as obscure as himself made subsequently *Doctor* Griffiths, was one of the most thriving men of the day. In little more than three years after this he was able to retire from bookselling, and hand over to Becket the publication of his Review. As time wore on, he became a more and more regular attendant at the meeting-house, rose higher and higher in the world's esteem, and at last kept his two carriages, and "lived in style." But he lived, too, to see the changes of thirty years after the grave had received the author of the *Vicar of Wakefield;* and though he had some recollections of the errors of his youth to disturb his decorous and religious peace of mind,—such as having become the proprietor of an infamous novel, and dictated the praise of it in his Review;* such as having

exposed himself to a remark reiterated in Grainger's letters to Bishop Percy, that he was not to be trusted in any verbal agreement upon matters of his trade,*—it may not have been the least bitter of his remembrances, if it ever happened to occur to him, that to Oliver Goldsmith, in the depths of a helpless distress, he had applied the epithets of *sharper* and *villain.*

From Goldsmith himself they fell harmless. His letter is extremely affecting: but the truth is manfully outspoken in it, and for that reason it is less painful to me than those in which the truth is concealed. When such a mind is brought to look its sorrow in the face, and understand clearly the condition in which it is, without further doubling, shrinking, or feeble compromising with false hopes, —it is master of a great gain. With the accession of strength so received it may see the sorrow anyway increase, and calm its worst apprehension. The most touching passage of that letter is the reference to his project, and the bright side of his mind it may reveal. I will date from it the true beginning of Goldsmith's literary career. Not till he was past thirty, he was

1758.
Æt. 30.

---

* See *Monthly Review*, ii. 431, March 1750. For other evidences of the man's taste in such matters, see the *Monthly Review*, v. 4, 70, June 1751; and, at the close of volume VII, the list of books "published by R. Griffiths." The book to which I allude in the text is that which was written by the son of a Colonel Cleland who is generally supposed to have been Pope's Cleland, but is more likely to have been his brother or cousin. Pope's friend is described always as Major Cleland. A letter from his infamous descendant or kinsman is printed in the *Garrick Correspondence*, i. 56-58.

* "You must have little dependence "upon Griffiths. ... Do not go on with "him without a positive bargain," &c. &c. Grainger to Percy, Nichols's *Illustrations*, vii. 259.

wont to say, did he become really attached to literature: not until then was the discipline of his endurance complete, his wandering impulses settled firmly to the right object of their aptitude, or his real destiny revealed to him. He might have still to perish in unconquered difficulties, and with the word that was in him unspoken; but it would be at his post, and in a manly effort to speak the word. Whatever the personal weaknesses that yet remain, and they are neither few nor trifling, his confidence and self-reliance in literary pursuits date from this memorable time. They rise above the cares and cankers of his life, above the lowness of his worldly esteem, far above the squalor of his homes. They take the undying forms which wrong or accident cannot alter or deface; they are the tenants of a world where distress and failure are unknown; and perpetual cheerfulness sings around them. "The night can "never endure so long, but at "length the morning cometh;" and, with these sudden and sharp disappointments of his second London Christmas, there came into Green-arbour-court the first struggling beams of morning. Till all its brightness follows, let him moan and sorrow as he may; the more familiar to himself he makes those images of want and danger, the better he will meet them in the lists where they still await him; the more he cultivates those solitary friendships with the dead, the better he will be armed and strengthened for the living struggle. The prosperous and busy world about him might indeed have saved him much, by stretching forth its helping hand: but it had taught him not little in its lesson of unrequited expectation, and there was nothing now to distract him with delusive hope from meditation of the wisest form of revenge.

The "impatient expectation" of the result of Griffiths's resolutions, ended in a contract to write him a Life of Voltaire for a translation of the *Henriade* he was about to publish: the payment being twenty pounds, and the price of the clothes to be deducted from that sum. His brother Henry wrote to him of the *Polite Learning* scheme, while engaged on this trade task; and the answer he made at its close, written early in February 1759, is in some sort the indication of his altered mind and purpose. There is still evidence of his personal weakness in the idle distrusts and suspicion it charges on himself, and in its false pretences to conceal his rejection and sustain his poor Irish credit: yet the general tone of it marks not the less, a new, a more sincere, and a more active epoch in his life. While the quarrel with Griffiths was still proceeding, he had again written of the *Polite Learning* essay, and had sent some scheme of a new poem to Henry (first fruit of the better uses of his adversity); but absolute silence as to the Coromandel appointment appears to have suggested a doubt in his brother's answer, to which very cursory and slight allusion is made in this reply. The personal portrait, in which the "big "wig" of his Bankside days plays its part, will hardly support his character for personal vanity! Thus the letter ran.*

"Dear Sir, Your punctuality in answering a man, whose trade is writing, is more than I had reason to expect; and yet you see me generally fill a whole sheet, which is all the recompense I can make for being so frequently troublesome. The behaviour of Mr. Mills and Mr. Lawder is a little extraordinary. However, their answering neither you nor me is a sufficient indication of their disliking the employment which I assigned them. As their conduct is different from what I had expected, so I have made an alteration in mine. I shall the beginning of next month send over two hundred and fifty books, which are all that I fancy can be well sold among you, and I would have you make some distinction in the persons who have subscribed. The money, which will amount to sixty pounds, may be left with Mr. Bradley, as soon as possible. I am not certain but I shall quickly have occasion for it. I have met with no disappointment with respect to my East India voyage; nor are my resolutions altered; though, at the same time, I must confess it gives me some pain to think I am almost beginning the world at the age of thirty-one. Though I never had a day's sickness since I saw you, yet I am not that strong and active man you once knew me. You scarcely can conceive how much eight years of disappointment, anguish, and study, have worn me down. If I remember right, you are seven or eight years older than me, yet I dare venture to say, that if a stranger saw us both, he would pay me the honours of seniority. Imagine to yourself a pale melancholy visage, with two great wrinkles between the eyebrows, with an eye disgustingly severe, and a big wig; and you may have a perfect picture of my present appearance. On the other hand, I conceive you as perfectly sleek and healthy, passing many a happy day among your own children, or those who knew you a child. Since I know what it was to be a man, this is a pleasure I have not known. I have passed my days among a parcel of cool designing beings, and have contracted all their suspicious manner in my own behaviour.* I should actually be as unfit for the society of my friends at home, as I detest that which I am obliged to partake of here. I can now neither partake of the pleasure of a revel, nor contribute to raise its jollity. I can neither laugh nor drink, have contracted a hesitating disagreeable manner of speaking, and a visage that looks ill-nature itself; in short, I have thought myself into a settled melancholy, and an utter disgust of all that life brings with it.—Whence this romantic turn, that all our family are possessed with? Whence this love for every place and every country but that in which we reside? for every occupation but our own? this desire of fortune, and yet this eagerness to dissipate? I perceive, my dear sir, that I am at intervals for indulging this splenetic manner, and following my own taste, regardless of yours.

"The reasons you have given me for breeding up your son as a scholar, are judicious and convincing. I should however be glad to know for what particular profession he is designed. If he be assiduous, and divested of strong passions (for passions in youth always lead to pleasure), he may do very well in your college; for it must be owned, that the industrious poor have good encouragement there, perhaps better than in any other in Europe. But if he has ambition,

---

* Percy Memoir, 53-9. It is addressed to "The Rev. Henry Goldsmith, at Low- "field, near Ballymore, in Westmeath, "Ireland."

* "This," observes the Percy Memoir writer, in a note, "is all gratis dictum, "for there never was a character so "unsuspicious and so unguarded as the "writer's." 54.

strong passions, and an exquisite sensibility of contempt, do not send him there, unless you have no other trade for him except your own. It is impossible to conceive how much may be done by a proper education at home. A boy, for instance, who understands perfectly well Latin, French, Arithmetic, and the principles of the civil law, and can write a fine hand, has an education that may qualify him for any undertaking. And these parts of learning should be carefully inculcated, let him be designed for whatever calling he will. Above all things let him never touch a romance or novel; those paint beauty in colours more charming than nature, and describe happiness that man never tastes. How delusive, how destructive are those pictures of consummate bliss. They teach the youthful mind to sigh after beauty and happiness which never existed; to despise the little good which fortune has mixed in our cup, by expecting more than she ever gave; and in general, take the word of a man who has seen the world, and has studied human nature more by experience than precept, take my word for it, I say, that books teach us very little of the world. The greatest merit in a state of poverty would only serve to make the possessor ridiculous; may distress, but cannot relieve him. Frugality, and even avarice, in the lower orders of mankind, are true ambition. These afford the only ladder for the poor to rise to preferment. Teach then, my dear sir, to your son thrift and economy. Let his poor wandering uncle's example be placed before his eyes. I had learned from books to be disinterested and generous, before I was taught from experience the necessity of being prudent. I had contracted the habits and notions of a philosopher, while I was exposing myself to the insidious approaches of cunning; and often by being, even with my narrow finances, charitable to excess, I forgot the rules of justice, and placed myself in the very situation of the wretch who thanked me for my bounty. When I am in the remotest part of the world, tell him this, and perhaps he may improve from my example. But I find myself again falling into my gloomy habits of thinking.

"My mother, I am informed, is almost blind: even though I had the utmost in-

1758.

Æt. 30.

clination to return home, under such circumstances I could not; for to behold her in distress without a capacity of relieving her from it, would add too much to my splenetic habit. Your last letter was much too short, it should have answered some queries I had made in my former. Just sit down as I do, and write forward until you have filled all your paper; it requires no thought, at least from the ease with which my own sentiments rise when they are addressed to you. For, believe me, my head has no share in all I write; my heart dictates the whole. Pray, give my love to Bob Bryanton, and intreat him, from me, not to drink. My dear sir, give me some account about poor Jenny.* Yet her husband loves her; if so, she cannot be unhappy.

"I know not whether I should tell you —yet why should I conceal those trifles, or indeed anything from you?—there is a book of mine will be published in a few days, the life of a very extraordinary man, no less than the great Voltaire. You know already by the title, that it is no more than a catch-penny. However I spent but four weeks on the whole performance, for which I received twenty pounds. When published, I shall take some method of conveying it to you, unless you may think it dear of the postage, which may amount to four or five shillings. However, I fear you will not find an equivalence of amusement. Your last letter, I repeat it, was too short: you should have given me your opinion of the design of the heroicomical poem which I sent you. You remember I intended to introduce the hero of the poem, as lying in a paltry alehouse: you may take the following specimen of the manner, which I flatter myself is quite original. The room in which he lies may be described somewhat this way:

The window, patch'd with paper, lent a ray,
That feebly shew'd the state in which he lay.
The sandy floor, that grits beneath the tread:
The humid wall with paltry pictures spread;

---

* His younger sister, who had married unprosperously.

The game of goose was there expos'd to
  view,
And the twelve rules the royal martyr
  drew;
The seasons fram'd with listing, found a
  place,
And Prussia's monarch shew'd his lamp-
  black face.
The morn was cold; he views with keen
  desire,
A rusty grate unconscious of a fire.
An unpaid reck'ning on the freeze was
  scor'd,
And five crack'd teacups dress'd the
  chimney board.

"And now imagine after his soliloquy,
the landlord to make his appearance, in
order to dun him for the reckoning:

Not with that face, so servile and so gay,
That welcomes every stranger that can
  pay,
With sulky eye he smoak'd the patient
  man,
Then pull'd his breeches tight, and thus
  began, &c.

"All this is taken, you see, from nature. It is a good remark of Montaigne's,
that the wisest men often have friends,
with whom they do not care how much
they play the fool. Take my present
follies as instances of regard. Poetry is
a much easier, and more agreeable
species of composition than prose, and
could a man live by it, it were not unpleasant employment to be a poet. I am resolved to leave no space, though I should
fill it up only by telling you, what you
very well know already, I mean that
I am

"Your most affectionate
"Friend and brother,
"OLIVER GOLDSMITH."

There is a practical condition
of mind in this letter, notwithstanding its self-reproachful pictures, and protestations of sorrowful disgust. It is very clear,
were it only by the alehouse
hero's example, that not all the
miseries which surround him will
again daunt his perseverance,
or tempt him to begin life anew.

If the bowl is now to be broken,
it will be broken at the fountain.
Could a man live by it, it were
not unpleasant employ-
ment to be a poet: but as $\frac{\text{1758.}}{\text{Æt. 30.}}$
he has made up his mind
to live, and on the world's beggarly terms, he will take what
practicable work he can get, and
be content with its fare till the
pleasanter employment comes.
When the man in black describes
the change of good-humour with
which he went to his precarious
meals; how he forbore rants of
spleen at his situation, ceased to
call down heaven and the stars to
behold him dining on a half-
pennyworth of radishes, taught
his very companions to believe
that he liked salad better than
mutton, laughed when he was not
in pain, took the world as it went,
and read his *Tacitus* for want of
more books and company; it
figures some such change as this
which I notice here. Whatever
the work may be, the resolution
to stick to nature is a good and
hopeful one, and will admit of
wise application, with many original results.

The poem seems to have gone
no further: but its cheerful hero
reappeared, after some months,
in a "club of authors;" protested
that the alehouse had been his
own bed-chamber often; reintro-
duced the description with six
new lines;

Where the Red Lion flaring o'er the
  way,
Invites each passing stranger that can
  pay;

Where Calvert's butt, and Parson's black
        champagne,
Regales the drabs and bloods of Drury-
        lane;
        There, in a lonely room, from
1758.   bailiffs snug,
───────
Æt. 30. The   muse   found   Scroggen
         stretch'd beneath a rug . .

flattered himself that his work should not be of the order of your common epic poems, which come from the press like paper kites in the summer; swore that people were sick of your Turnuses and Didos, and wanted an heroical description of nature; offered, for proof of sound and sense and truth and nature, in the trifling compass of ten syllables, the last of two added lines;

A night-cap deck'd his brows instead of
        bay,
A cap by night, a stocking all the day!

and having quoted them, was so much elated and self-delighted that he was quite unable to proceed.

Thus could Goldsmith already turn aside the sharpest edge of poverty; thus wisely consent to be Scroggen till he could be Goldsmith; in the paltry, slovenly pothouse of Drury-lane, give promise of the neat village alehouse of Auburn; and betake himself meanwhile to less agreeable daily duties, in a spirit that would make them, also, the not indifferent source of profit and delight.

CHAPTER VI.

Work and Hope.
1759.

"SPEEDILY will be pub-"lished," said the *Public Advertiser* of the 7th of February 1759, "*Memoirs of the Life of* "*Monsieur de Voltaire*, with critical "observations on the writings of "that celebrated poet, and a "new *Translation of the Henriade.* "Printed for R. Griffiths, in Pa-"ternoster Row." Nevertheless, the publication did not take place. The *Translation* was by an old fellow-student of Dublin, Edward Purdon; the poor uncertain hack whose notoriety rests on Goldsmith's epigram, as his hunger was, even at this early date, supposed to be mainly appeased by a share of Goldsmith's crust; and Purdon's share of the work was probably not completed in time. Some months later, it appeared in a magazine, and the *Life* was given to the public through the same bookselling channel; but it is clear that Goldsmith, when he wrote to his brother, had really performed his portion of the contract. It was but a catchpenny matter, as he called it; yet it included passages of interesting narrative as well as just remark, and was gracefully written. It announces that early admiration of the genius of Voltaire and Rousseau, which he consistently maintained against some celebrated friends of his later life: it contains the best existing notice known to me of Voltaire's residence in England: and for proof of the time at which it was written, passages might be given in exact paraphrase of the argument of his *Polite Learning;* such sayings from the last-quoted letter to his brother, as "frugality "in the lower orders of mankind "may be considered as a sub- "stitute for ambition;" and such apophthegms from his recent sharp experience, as "the school "of misery is the school of wis- "dom."

The *Polite Learning* was now completed, and passing through the press: the Dodsleys of Pall-mall, who gave Johnson ten guineas for the poem of *London,* having taken it under their charge. This too was the time when, being accidentally in company with Grainger at the Temple-exchange coffee-house, he was introduced to Thomas Percy, already busily engaged in collecting the famous *Reliques,* * now chaplain to Lord Sussex, and who

became afterwards Bishop of Dromore. Percy, who had a great love of letters and of literary men, was attracted to this new acquaintance; * for before he returned to his vicarage of Easton Mauduit in Northamptonshire, he discovered Goldsmith's address in Green-arbour-court, and resolved to call upon him. "A friend of his pay- "ing him a visit" (I quote from the Memoir to which the grave church dignitary and descendant of the ancient Earls of Northumberland communicated this and other anecdotes), "at the begin- "ning of March 1759, found him "in lodgings there so poor and "uncomfortable that he should "not think it proper to mention "the circumstance, if he did not "consider it as the highest proof "of the splendour of Doctor "Goldsmith's genius and talents,

1759
Æt. 31.

---

* See a letter of the poet Shenstone (to whose suggestion we owe the *Reliques*) in Nichols's *Illustrations*, VII. 220-3. Shenstone was one of Goldsmith's favourites (see *post*, Book IV. Chap. XIV), and I will here add a sketch of him by Jupiter Carlyle, who visited the Leasowes a few months before the present date (in 1758), and startles one as much by his description of the poet, as the poet seems to have surprised him. "He was a large heavy "fat man, dressed in white clothes and "silver lace, with his grey hairs tied be- "hind and much powdered:" being moreover very "shy, reserved, and me- "lancholy." However this did not pre-vent his becoming at last "very good "company." *Autobiog.* p. 370.

* Percy will frequently appear in these pages; and though, for some unexplained reason, Johnson said harsher things to him as well as *of* him than was ordinarily his habit towards men of Percy's calling and station, he has also in a few lines so happily expressed his literary claims and character, that they will best introduce him here: "He is a "man very willing to learn, and very "able to teach; a man out of whose com- "pany I never go without having learned "something. It is sure that he vexes me "sometimes, but I am afraid it is by "making me feel my own ignorance. So "much extension of mind, and so much "minute accuracy of inquiry, if you "survey your whole circle of acquaint- "ance, you will find so scarce, if you "find it at all, that you will value Percy "by comparison. . . . . Percy's attention "to poetry has given grace and splendour "to his studies of antiquity. A mere "antiquarian is a rugged being." *Boswell,* VII. 117.

"that by the bare exertion of "their powers, under every dis-"advantage of person and for-"tune, he could gradually "emerge from such ob-"scurity to the enjoyment "of all the comforts and even "luxuries of life, and admission "into the best societies of Lon-"don. The Doctor was writing "his *Enquiry* &c. in a wretched "dirty room in which there was "but one chair, and when he, "from civility, offered it to his "visitant, himself was obliged to "sit in the window. While they "were conversing, some one "gently rapped at the door, and "being desired to come in, a "poor ragged little girl of very "decent behaviour entered, who, "dropping a curtsey, said, 'My "'mamma sends her compli-"'ments, and begs the favour of "'you to lend her a chamber-pot "'full of coals.'" *

1759.
Æt. 31.

* *Percy Memoir*, 60-1. "I have him now "in London," writes Campbell to the bishop in 1790 (Nichols's *Illustrations*, VII. 779), when describing his progress in throwing Percy's biographical anecdotes into the form of a memoir, "and am "endeavouring to recollect your first "visit to him, when the loan, or repay-"ment, of the chamber-pot of coals was "asked." To this the bishop answered promptly, by sending the anecdote, which Campbell (*Ibid*, 780) thus acknowledges: "My account of your visit to him there "was almost verbatim, from my recol-"lection of your words, what you have "set down in your last. But could there "be any harm in letting the world know "who the visitant was? without the cir-"cumstance of the dignity of the guest, "the contrast will be in a great mea-"sure lost." In truth, however, the contrast, though amusing enough, was not so very great as Dr. Campbell, pre-

If the February number of the *Critical Review* lay by the reverend, startled, and long-descended visitor, perhaps good-natured Goldsmith, as he scraped together his answer to that humble petition proffered with the respectful "curtsey" which yet had also shown the esteem in which his poor neighbours held him, may have pointed with a smile to his description of the fate of poets just published there. "There is a strong "similitude," he had said, reviewing a new edition of the *Fairy Queen*, "between the lives "of almost all our English "poets. The Ordinary of New-"gate, we are told, has but one "story, which serves for the "life of every hero that happens "to come within the circle of "his pastoral care; and however "unworthy the resemblance ap-"pears, it may be asserted that "the history of one poet might "serve with as little variation "for that of any other. Born "of creditable parents, who gave "him a pious education: how-"ever, in spite of all their en-"deavours, in spite of all the "exhortations of the minister of "the parish on Sundays, he "turned his mind from follow-"ing *good things*, and fell to —— "writing verses! Spenser, in "short, lived poor, was reviled "by the critics of his time, and

maturely transforming the vicar of a small living into a bishop full-blown, appears to have presented to his imagination.

"died at last in the utmost dis-
"tress." *

Oliver was again working for Hamilton. Smollett himself had not seen his new reviewer, but, the success of the Ovid papers having proclaimed the value of such assistance,** he appears to have sent the publisher with renewed offers to Green-arbour-court. Goldsmith had resumed with this notice of Spenser; a discriminating proof of his varied appreciation of true mastery in the divine art. Popular and practical himself, he wonders not the less at the "great magician;" suddenly taken "from the ways "of the present world," and far from Drury-lane alehouses or Auburn villages, in the sequestered remoteness of a gorgeous and luxurious fancy he thinks of Virgil, and even Homer, as moderns in comparison with Elizabeth's Englishman; and when he wakes from this Elysium, and comes back to the ways of the world, his conclusions are, that "no poet enlarges the imagina-
"tion more than Spenser;" that "Cowley was formed into poetry "by reading him;" that "Gray "and Akenside have profited by

* *Critical Review*, vii. 105, February 1759.

** Dr. Aikin (who had the means of knowing) adopts and confirms a statement of Glover's to the effect that "it "was the merit which Goldsmith dis-"covered in criticising a despicable trans-"lation of Ovid's *Fasti* by a pedantic "schoolmaster, and his *Enquiry into* "*Polite Literature*, which first intro-"duced him to the acquaintance of Dr. "Smollett."

"their study of him;" and that "his verses may one day come "to be considered the standard "of English poetry." His next article, which appeared in the following number, was a notice of young Langhorne's translation of Bion's *Elegy of Adonis*; wherein he not unhappily contrasted the false and florid tastes of the day with the pure simplicity of the Greek. "If an hero or a poet happens to "die with us, the whole band of "elegiac poets raise the dismal "chorus, adorn his hearse with "all the paltry escutcheons of "flattery, rise into bombast, and "paint him at the head of his "thundering legions, or reining "Pegasus in his most rapid career. "They are sure to strew cypress "enough upon the bier, to dress "up all the muses in mourning, "and look themselves every whit "as dismal and as sorrowful as "an undertaker's shop. Yet "neither pomp nor flattery agrees "with real affliction. It is not "thus that Marcellus, even that "Marcellus who was adopted by "the emperor of the world, is "bewailed by Propertius; his "beauty, his strength, his milder "virtues, seem to have caught "the poet's affections, and in-"spired his affliction. Were a "person to die in these days, "tho' he was never at a battle in "his life, our elegiac writers "would be sure to make one for "the occasion."* Subsequently, and with as happy and clear a

* *Critical Review*, vii. 263, March 1759.

spirit, he discussed a book on *Oratory* by a Gresham professor of rhetoric: instancing the lawyer who, on "hearing his ad-"versary talk of the war "of Troy, the beauteous "Helena, and the river Sca-"mander, intreated the court to "observe that his client was "christened, not Scamander, but "Simon." *

1759.
Æt. 31.

And here I will sum up briefly as I may, what remain to be noticed of these humble and unacknowledged labours in the *Critical Review.* The tone is more confident than in the days when he wrote under the sign of the Dunciad; but the fair appreciation is the same. Obscure and depressed as the writer was, his free running hand very frankly betrays its work, amid the cramped laborious penmanship with which Smollett's big-wigged friends surrounded it. No man ever put so much of himself into his books as Goldsmith, from the beginning to the very end of his career; and no man wishing to hide under cover of a mean fortune, was ever so easily detected. Favourite expressions, which to the end of his life continued so, are here; thoughts he had turned to happy use in his Irish letters, reappear again and again; and, disguise himself for Scroggen or James Willington as he may, he cannot write from other inspiration, or with a less natural instinctive grace, than his own. The work I now refer

* *Critical Review,* vii. 369, April 1759.

to connects itself, for this reason, with the most brilliant to follow. The foibles and social vanities which his Chinese friend is soon with indulgent humour to correct, are here already clear to him;* the false poetic taste which he will shortly supplant with his natural manly verse, he does his best thus early to weaken and expose; and the do-me-good family romances, with which the moralmongers of the day would make stand against such books as *Roderick Random* and *Tom Jones,* are thrust back from before the *Vicar's* way.

Among his reviews, then, was one of Murphy's *Orphan of China;* containing not only better critical remarks than were usual with him both on Shakespeare and Voltaire, but goodnatured evidence of curiosity as to the Chinese people, and of interest in the plans of his recent reverend visitor (Mr. Percy), at that time preparing a Chinese translation** for the press. Butler's *Remains* furnished him another subject; in which, bewailing the "indigence

* The reader will hardly fail to have observed that he seems already to have had in his mind a forecast of his Chinese Letters when he was writing to Bryanton, *ante,* p. 102, and p. 107.

** *Critical Review,* vii. 434-40, May 1759. Goldsmith put this note to his article: "A specimen of this kind" [Chinese fiction] "will probably appear next season "at Mr. Dodsley's, as we are informed." For the amusing and unsuccessful attempts of Grainger on his friend Percy's behalf, in 1758, to effect a bargain for the publication with Griffiths, see Nichols's *Illustrations,* vii. 219, 250, 259, 261, &c.

"in which the poet lived and "died," he protested with generous horror "at the want of discernment, at the more than "barbarous ingratitude, of his "contemporaries."* A third was Marriott's *Answer to the Critical Review:* containing whimsical and humorous apology for his own satirical comparisons of three months before. And a fourth he found in Dunkins's *Epistle to Lord Chesterfield:* which he closed with humorous application of a Spanish story in exposure of the toadyism prevailing in small literary coteries. A traveller passing through the city of Burgos in Spain, and desirous of knowing their most learned men, applied to one of the inhabitants for information. "What," replied the Spaniard, who happened to be a scholar, "have "you never heard of the ad- "mirable Brandellius, or the "ingenious Mogusius? one the "eye and the other the heart of "our university, known all over "the world." "Never," cries the traveller; "but pray inform me "what Brandellius is particularly "remarkable for." "You must "be very little acquainted in the "republic of letters," says the other, "to ask such a question. "Brandellius has wrote a most "sublime panegyric on Mogu- "sius." "And prithee what has "Mogusius done to deserve so "great a favour?" "He has "written an excellent poem in "praise of Brandellius." "Well! "and what does the public, "I mean those who are out "of the university, say of "those mutual compliments?" "The public are a parcel of "blockheads, and all blockheads "are critics; and all critics are "spiders, and spiders are a set "of reptiles that all the world "despises."*

Noticeable also, in recapitulation of this drudgery, are his papers on President Gouget's *Origin of Laws, Arts, and Sciences,*** and on Formey's *Philosophical Miscellanies,* written with a lively perception of the characters of French and German intellect respectively;*** — on Van Egmont's *Travels in Asia,* wherein a scheme of later life was shadowed forth ("a man shall go a hundred "miles to admire a mountain "only because it was spoken of in "Scripture, yet what information "can be received from hearing "that Ægidius Van Egmont went "up such a hill only in order to "come down again? Could we "see a man set out upon this "journey, not with an intent to "discover rocks and rivers, but "the manners, the mechanic in- "ventions, and the imperfect

1759.
Æt. 31.

---

* *Critical Review,* viii. 1, July 1759. The same subject was resumed in the September number, at page 208 of the same volume.

** *Critical Review,* ix. 235, March 1760.

** *Ibid,* vii. 270, March 1759.

*** *Ibid,* vii. 486, June 1759. In this paper occurs an expression repeated both in his letters and his novel, where he laughs at professors in college with "their "whole lives passed away between the "fireside and the easy-chair."

"learning of the inhabitants; re-
"solved to penetrate into coun-
"tries as yet little known, and

1759.

Æt. 31.

"eager to pry into all their
"secrets, with a heart
"not terrified at trifling
"dangers; if there could be found
"a man who could thus unite
"true courage with sound learn-
"ing, from such a character we
"might expect much informa-
"tion ") *—on Guicciardini's *History of Italy*, showing some knowledge of Italian literature;**—
on Montesquieu's *Miscellaneous
Pieces*, justifying, by many expressions of intelligent interest
in the minor and unacknowledged works of a man of genius,
such rapid indication as I now
am giving of his own earlier
and less known performances
("Cicero observes," he remarks
in it, "that we behold with trans-
"port and enthusiasm the little
"barren spot, or ruins of a house,
"in which a person celebrated
"for his wisdom, his valour, or
"his learning, lived; and when
"he coasted along the shore of
"Greece, all the heroes, states-
"men, orators, philosophers, and
"poets of those famed republics,
"rose in his memory, and were
"present to his sight; but how
"much more would he have been
"delighted with any of their
"posthumous works, however in-
"ferior to what he had before
"seen!");***—and finally, for

* *Critical Review*, VII. 501-12, June 1759.

** *Ibid*, VIII. 85, August 1759.

*** *Ibid*, VII. 535, June 1759.

my summary must be brief, on
the Rev. Mr. Hawkins's *Works*, *
and on the same irritable person's *Impartial Reader's Answer* to
the said review of those works;**
where Goldsmith thus drily, in
the second of his articles, put
the difference between himself
and the reverend writer.*** "He

* *Critical Review*, VII. 85, August 1759.

** *Ibid*, IX. 214, March 1760.

*** Parson Hawkins was an Oxford professor of poetry, and the author not only of the *Thimble*, but of a wretched tragedy called the *Siege of Aleppo*, which Garrick declined to act; and as to which the reader may find it worth while to compare the capital letters in which the judicious manager met the angry professor's outraged vanity, with the confused account of those letters he afterwards gave in conversation when flattered and agitated by Johnson's laughter and sarcasm. See *Garrick Correspondence*, II. 6, and *Boswell*, VII. 91-5. I happen myself to be able to quote a couple of passages from the letter, hitherto unprinted, that accompanied this very tragedy when it first went to Garrick (in the autumn of 1771); which will not only amuse the reader, but show him the preposterous vanities that, under cover of the utmost humility and the most friendly professions of service, were the plague of the Drury-lane manager's life. In the remark about Hawkins and Shakespeare on the same shelf, quoted in my text, Goldsmith had hit the leading weakness of the reverend poet. This letter shows us that he had written his tragedy in express imitation of Shakespeare, that he sent it to Garrick solely because of his admiration for Shakespeare, and that he was willing Garrick should have it for a mere nothing expressly because of the obligations he had conferred on Shakespeare. "I flatter myself this letter when favoured "with your perusal will carry its apology "with it. As a passionate admirer of "Shakespeare it is but natural for me to "wish to be connected with Mr. Garrick, "and I hope I shall be understood to "mean more than a base compliment "when I add that I really desire this from

"is for putting his own works "upon the same shelf with Mil- "ton and Shakespeare, and we "are for allowing him an inferior "situation; he would have the "same reader that commends "Addison's delicacy to talk with "raptures of the purity of Haw- "kins; and he who praises the "*Rape of the Lock* to speak with "equal feelings of that richest "of all poems, Mr. Hawkins's "*Thimble.* But we, alas! cannot "speak of Mr. H. with the same "unrestrained share of panegyric "that he does of himself. Per- "haps our motive to malevolence "might have been, that Mr. "Hawkins stood between us and

"motives rather of an honouring than "lucrative nature. In short (to give your- "self and me as little trouble as may be) "the case is this—I have a Play by me, "written in imitation of Shakespeare in "point of style, but on a plan &c. wholly "new, which I have an ambition to re- "commend to your acceptance." Re- commend it to his acceptance he accord- ingly proceeds to do, by declaring that the Wartons, Tom and Joe, might be asked to give their opinion of it, by which he, Hawkins, would willingly be judged. And then he concludes. "If "you please I will send the performance "in a few weeks to yourself, relying "cheerfully on your candour and im- "partiality. Having only to say farther, "that in case it be honoured with your "acceptance, the copy shall be at your "service upon your own terms of pur- "chase. These I shall leave with the "most implicit confidence to your honor, "as I choose for many reasons to be con- "cerned in this business rather as an "Author than Proprietor; and as (to say "the truth honestly) I have herein prin- "cipally in view the cultivation of a "correspondence, and give me leave to "say and hope a friendship, with a gen- "tleman to whom the Immortal Shake- "speare is confessedly under infinite "obligations."

"a good living; yet we can "solemnly assure him we are "quite contented with our pre- "sent situation in the "church, are quite happy "in a wife and forty pounds "a year, nor have the least ambi- "tion for pluralities." *

1759.
———
Æt. 31.

Nor should I close this rapid account of Goldsmith's labours in the *Critical Review*, without at least referring to the unsparing yet not ill-natured satire with which he laughed at a form of novel which was then beginning to be popular; a foreshadowing of the insipidities of the Minerva Press; a kind of fashionable family novel with which the stately mother, and the board- ing-school miss, were instructed to fortify themselves against the immoralities of Smollett and of Fielding. As with Jonathan Wild in the matter of Cacus, Gold- smith "knew a better way;" and, in his witty exposure of *Jemima and Louisa*, seems to show him- self prepared to make it known. The tale professed to be written by a lady, in a series of letters: and thus he described it.

"The female muse, it must be owned, has of late been tolerably fruitful. Novels written by ladies, poems, morality, es- says, and letters, all written by ladies, show that this beautiful sex are resolved to be, one way or other, the joyful mo- thers of children. Happy it is that the same conveyance which brings an heir to a family, shall at the same time pro- duce a book to mend his manners, or teach him to make love, when ripe for the occasion. Yet let not the ladies carry

* *Critical Review*, ix. 217, March 1760.

off all the glories of the late productions ascribed to them; it is plain by the style, and a nameless somewhat in the manner, that pretty follows, coffee-critics, and dirty shirted dunces, have sometimes a share in the achievement. We have detected so many of these impostors already, that for the future it is resolved to look upon every publication that shall be ascribed to a lady as the work of one of this amphibious fraternity. Thus, by wholesome severity, many a fair creature may be prevented from writing, that cannot spell; and many a blockhead may be deterred from commencing author, that never thought. The plan of the work is as follows:

1759. Æt. 31.

"Two Misses, just taken home from the boarding-school, are *prodigious* great friends, and so they tell each other their secrets by way of letter. In the first letter, Miss Jemima Courtly, or Mima for shortness' sake, lets her old and intimate friend know that her mother died when she was eight years old; that she had one brother and one sister, with several other secrets of this kind, all delivered in the confidence of friendship. In the progress of this correspondence we find she has been taken from home for carrying on an intrigue with Horatio, a gentleman of the neighbourhood, and by means of her sister's insinuations, for she happens to be her enemy, confined to her chamber, her father at the same time making an express prohibition against her writing love-letters for the future. This command Miss Mima breaks, and of consequence is turned out of doors; so up she gets behind a servant without a pillion, and is set down at Mrs. Weller's house, the mother of her friend Miss Fanny. Here, then, we shall leave, or rather forget her, only observing that she is happily married, as we are told in a few words towards the conclusion. We are next served up with the history of Miss Louisa Blyden, a story no way connected with the former. Louisa is going to be married to Mr. Evanlon; the nuptials, however, are interrupted by the death of Louisa's father, and at last broke off by means of a sharper, who pretends to be miss's uncle, and takes her concerns under his direction. What need we tell as *how* the young *lover* runs mad, Miss is spirited away into France, at last returns, the sharper and his accomplices hang or drown themselves, her lover dies, and she, oh tragical! keeps her chamber? However, to console us for this calamity, there are two or three other very good matches struck up; a great deal of money, a great deal of beauty, a world of love, and days and nights as happy as heart could desire; the old butt-end of a modern romance."[*]

That was his last contribution either to Smollett or to Mr. Griffiths. And so Goldsmith's adieu

[*] *Critical Review*, VIII. 165-6, August 1759. Let me here add that our knowledge of Goldsmith's labours in the *Critical Review* is mainly derived from the fact mentioned in a letter by George Stevens (Sept. 3, 1797) giving information about "our little poet's works" to Bishop Percy, then engaged in preparing the edition delayed by so many mischances. After remarking that "several pieces of "the Doctor's are still in MS. in the "hands of various people" (this could hardly be news to the bishop, who had himself more than one unpublished piece, which he lost), he continues: "The late "Mr. Wright, the printer, who had been "either apprentice to or in the service of "Mr. Hamilton, at a time when Gold-"smith composed numerous essays for "Magazines, articles for Reviews, &c. &c. "preserved a list of those fugitive pieces, "which are now reprinting, and will "make their appearance in the course of "next winter. Goldsmith likewise began "a periodical paper, which being unsuc-"cessful, was laid aside, after a few "numbers of it had been issued out." Nichols's *Illustrations*, VII. 25. I cannot help doubting, however, if the true source has been at all times pointed out by Mr. Wright to the editor of these reprinted articles (Mr. Isaac Reed, ed. 1798). Certainly the reviews of Formey's *Philosophical Miscellanies*, Van Egmont's *Travels into Asia*, Murphy's *Orphan of China*, and Marriott's *Female Conduct, or Art of Pleasing*, assigned to numbers of the *Critical Review* for 1759, do not all appear as stated. (The plan since adopted, in Mr. Murray's edition of the *Works*, of printing all the unacknowledged essays in a type distinct from the text, is the only safe one. 1870.)

to both Reviews was said, and he left them to fight out their quarrels with each other. Mr. Griffiths might accuse Smollett of selling his praise for a fat buck, and Smollett might retort upon Mrs. Griffiths that an antiquated Sappho sat ill in the chair of Aristarchus; but this interchange of abuse will in future cease to have a bitterness personal to Goldsmith's fortunes. We are gradually now to follow him, and them, to "a more re-"moved ground." Yet not until the scene of life shall entirely close, will it be permitted him to forget that he once toiled in humiliating bondage at the sign of the Dunciad in Paternoster-row, and was paid retainer and servant to "those significant "emblems, the owl and the long-"ear'd animal, which," to say of them what Smollett said, "Mr. "Griffiths so sagely displays for "the mirth and information of "mankind."*

* *Critical Review*, iv. 471, November 1757. See also viii. 82-3, July 1759. In the latter, the *Monthly Review* is characterised as "that repository of dulness and "malevolence, replenished by the inde-"fatigable care of the industrious night-"man R—h G—s, and his spouse." Smollett, or his writer, is speaking of a translation of Ariosto attacked by the Monthly reviewers, which he had himself praised; and characterises this review as "an instance of presumption in an il-"literate bookseller and his wife, which "can scarcely be paralleled in the annals "of dulness and effrontery .... Ha! ha! "ha! who is this venerable Aristarchus, "who mounts the chair of criticism? No "Aristarchus, but an antiquated Sappho, "a Sibyl, or rather a Pope Joan in taste "and literature, pregnant with abuse

CHAPTER VII.

An Appeal for Authors by Profession.
1759.

MEANWHILE the Dodsleys had issued their advertisements, and the *London Chronicle* of the 3rd of April, 1759, announced the appearance, the day before, of *An Enquiry into the Present State of Polite Learning in Europe*. It was a very respectable, well-printed duodecimo; was without the author's name on the title-page, though Goldsmith was anxious to have the authorship widely known; and had two mottoes in the learned languages. The Greek signified that the writer esteemed philosophers, but was no friend to sophists; and the Latin, that those only should destroy buildings who could themselves build.

The first idea of the work has been seen; as it grew consolingly, like the plant in the *Picciola*, from between the hard and stony environments of a desperate fortune. Some modifications it received, as the prospects of the writer were subjected to

"begot by rancour under the canopy of "ignorance. Purge your choler, goody; "have recourse to your apothecary in "this adust weather, who will keep you "cool and temperate. Meanwhile, you "and your obsequious spouse may confer "together on your vain importance, like "the two owls in the fable,

"Husband, you reason well, replies
 The solemn mate with half-shut eyes:
 My parlour is the seat of learning;
 In choosing authors you're discerning,
 Besides, on saddled ass you sit
 The type and ornament of wit."

1759.
Æt. 31.

change; and its title was much too large for the limited materials, both of reading and ex-perience, brought to its composition. But it was in advance of any similar effort in that day. No one was prepared, in a treatise so grave, for a style so enchantingly graceful. To combine liveliness with even the shows of learning, is thought something of a heresy still.

With any detailed account of this well-known *Enquiry* I do not propose to detain the reader, but for illustration of the course I have taken in this memoir, some striking passages should not be overlooked, and others will throw light forward on new scenes that await us. The contents of the treatise, too, as found in the current collections, are wanting in much that gives interest to the duodecimo now lying before me, the first of the Dodsley editions. For it is not, in these days at least, with any remarkable concern for the state of polite learning in Europe that we turn to its pages. We may feel its title to be so far a misnomer that to substitute, for *Europe*, the more confined area of *Mr. Griffiths's shop*, would more correctly describe its contents; but it is this very fact, and the personal interest derived from it, which constitute now for us the book's principal and great attraction.

Manifest throughout it is one overruling feeling, under various forms; the conviction that, in

1759.
Æt. 31.

bad critics and sordid book-sellers, learning has to contend with her worst enemies. When Goldsmith has described at the outset the wise reverence for letters which prevailed in the old Greek time, when "learning "was encouraged, protected, "honoured, and in its turn "adorned, strengthened, and "harmonised the community," he turns to the sophists and cri-tics for the day of its decline. By them the ancient polite learning was in his view "separated from "common sense, and made the "proper employment of specula-"tive idlers. . . The wiser part of "mankind would not be imposed "upon by unintelligible jargon, "nor, like the knight in Pan-"tagruel, swallow a chimera for a "breakfast, though even cooked "by Aristotle."* In this way he distinguishes three periods in the history of ancient learning: its commencement, or the age of poets; its maturity, or the age of philosophers; and its decline, or the age of critics. *Corruptissima respublica, plurimæ leges.* In like manner, when he turns to the consideration of the decay of modern letters, critics are again brought up for judgment as the principal offenders; and as he too manifestly thinks of the starving scribblers whom Mr. Griffiths had at hand to do his bidding, it is with a melancholy consciousness that he must him-self stand at the same bar. "This decay which criticism pro-

* Chap. II.

"duces may be deplored, but can "scarcely be remedied, as the "man who writes against the "critics is obliged to add himself "to the number."* Neverthe-less, it was with manly self-asser-tion of attainments which raised him above the herd, that he afterwards scornfully disclaimed the viler brotherhood. "I fire "with indignation when I see "persons wholly destitute of edu-"cation and genius indent to the "press, and thus turn book-"makers, adding to the sin of "criticism the sin of ignorance "also; whose trade is a bad one, "and who are bad workmen in "the trade." So much was not to be said of his own workman-ship, by even the deity of the Dunciad, the dictator of books to be made, the master-employer in the miserable craft, Griffiths himself.

But with him there comes upon the scene the other arch-foe, to whom, in modern days, the literary craftsman is only minister and servant. The critic or sophist might have been contriver of all harms, while the field of mis-chief was his own, and limited to a lecture-room of Athens or Alexandria; but he bowed to a more potent spirit of evil when the man of Paternoster-row or the Poultry came up in later days, took literature into chari-table charge, and assumed exclusive direction of laws of taste and men of learn-ing. Drawing on a hard ex-perience, Goldsmith depicted the "precarious" subsistence and daily fate of the bookseller's workman: "coming down at "stated intervals to rummage the "bookseller's counter for mate-"rials to work upon:"* a fate which other neglects now made inevitable. "The author," Gold-smith had previously said, "when "unpatronised by the great, has "naturally recourse to the book-"seller. There cannot perhaps "be imagined a combination "more prejudicial to taste than "this. It is the interest of the "one to allow as little for writ-"ing, and of the other to write as "much, as possible; accord-"ingly tedious compilations and "periodical magazines are the "result of their joint endeavours. "In these circumstances the au-"thor bids adieu to fame, writes "for bread, and for that only "imagination is seldom called in; "he sits down to address the "venal muse with the most "phlegmatic apathy; and, as we "are told of the Russian, courts "his mistress by falling asleep in "her lap. His reputation never "spreads in a wider circle than "that of the trade, who generally "value him, not for the fineness "of his compositions, but the

1759.
Æt. 31.

* Chap. XI. The chapters (x. and XI.) of the _Enquiry into Polite Learning_ here quoted are from Percy's edition of 1801, and do not so stand in the ordinary edi-tions. I should also remark that passages are occasionally quoted from the same edition of 1801; though in the main I have followed the first edition, both here and in the chapter on David Garrick in Book III.

* Chap. XL.

"quantity he works off in a given "time. A long habit of writing "for bread thus turns the ambi- *1759.* "tion of every author at *Æt. 31.* "last into avarice. He "finds that he has written "many years, that the public are "scarcely acquainted even with "his name; he despairs of ap- "plause, and turns to profit which "invites him. He finds that "money procures all those ad- "vantages, that respect, and that "ease which he vainly expected "from fame. Thus the man who "under the protection of the "great might have done honour "to humanity, when only pa- "tronised by the bookseller be- "comes a thing little superior to "the fellow who works at the "press."* In connection with this unpromising picture he then presented "the two literary re- "views in London, with critical "newspapers and magazines with- "out number;" remarking that, "were these Monthly Reviews "and Magazines frothy, pert, or "absurd, they might find some "pardon, but to be dull and "dronish is an encroachment on "the prerogative of a folio;"** and for an example of the evil, instancing, as Fielding had done before him, the power of a single monosyllable in such productions to express the victory over hu- mour amongst us, from which no one in later years was to suffer as much as himself.*** "Does

"the poet paint the absurdities of "the vulgar, then he is *low:* does "he exaggerate the features of "folly to render it more thorough- "ly ridiculous, he is then very "*low.*"* He also laughingly sug- gested (but this joke he con- fined to his first edition) that check might possibly be given to it by some such law "enacted

style, in the same chapter. "It were to "be wished that we no longer found "pleasure with the inflated style that has "for some years been looked upon as fine "writing, and which every young writer "is now obliged to adopt, if he chooses "to be read .. it is not those who make "the greatest noise with their wares in "the streets that have most to sell. Let "us, instead of writing finely, try to "write naturally; not hunt after lofty ex- "pressions to deliver mean ideas, nor be "for ever gaping, when we only mean to "deliver a whisper." Not against John- son was this levelled, however, but at the swarm of empty imitators begotten of Johnson's success. The author of the *Rambler* would think all the more highly of Goldsmith for such remarks. No one better knew his own defects, or made more candid avowal of them. "Sir," he said to Boswell, "if Robertson's style be "faulty, he owes it to me; that is, having "too many words, and those too big "ones." *Life,* VI. 316. So when Langton one day read one of his *Ramblers* to him, and asked him how he liked it, he shook his head, and said, "Too wordy." *Ib.* VII. 353. Langton also tells us that at another time, when a friend was reading his tragedy of *Irene* to a company at a house in the country, he left the room; and somebody having asked him the reason of this, he replied, "Sir, I thought "it had been better." *Ibid.* In these personal matters, as in all others so far as his views and judgment carried him, Johnson was a just and righteous man. Boswell often bored him to say that he thought Goldsmith his imitator; but he would not, nor would he allow others to say it.

* Chap. X.
** Chap. XI.
*** Admirable are his remarks on

* Chap. XI. And see *Tom Jones,* In- troductory chapters to Books V. and VII.

"in the republic of letters as we "find takes effect in the House "of Commons. As no man there "can show his wisdom, unless "qualified by three hundred "pounds a-year, so none here "should possess gravity, unless "his work amounted to three "hundred pages." At the same time, in other parts of the treatise, he guards himself from being supposed to wish that a mere money-service, a system of flattery and beggary, should replace that of the booksellers. He would object, he says, to indigence and effrontery subjecting learning itself to the contempts incurred by its professors; but he would no more have an author draw a quill merely to take a purse, than present a pistol for the same purpose.*

These passages in the *Enquiry* were startling, and not to be protected from notice even by the obscurity of the writer. They struck at a monstrous evil. "We "must observe," said Smollett, noticing the book in the *Critical Review*, "that, against his own "conviction, this author has in"discriminately censured the two "Reviews; confounding a work "undertaken from public spirit "with one supported for the "sordid purposes of a bookseller. "It might not become us to say "more on this subject."** The sordid bookseller was not so delicate, and did say much more; calling in for the purpose the pen of Kenrick, a notorious and convicted libeller. "It requires "a good deal of art and temper," said the *Monthly Review*, after objections to the whole treatise, some just enough on the score of its want of learning and too hasty decision on national literatures, others connected with the subject of patronage very poor and shallow, "for a man to write con"sistently against the dictates of "his own heart. Thus, notwith"standing our author talks so "familiarly of *us*, the great, and "affects to be thought to stand "in the rank of Patrons, we can"not help thinking that in more "places than one he has be"trayed, in himself, the man he "so severely condemns for draw"ing his quill to take a purse. "We are even so firmly con"vinced of this that we dare put "the question home to his con"science, whether he never ex"perienced the unhappy situa"tion he so feelingly describes "in that of a Literary Under"strapper? His remarking him as "coming down from his garret, "to rummage the bookseller's "shop for materials to work "upon, and the knowledge he "displays of his minutest labours, "give great reason to suspect" (generous and forbearing Griffiths!) "he may himself have had "concerns in the *bad trade* of "bookmaking. *Fronti nulla fides.* "We have heard of many a "writer, who, 'patronised only "'by his bookseller,' has never-

1759.
Æt. 31.

<hr>

* Chap. x.
** *Critical Review*, vii. 372, April 1759.

"theless affected the Gentleman "in print, and talked full as "cavalierly as our author himself.

1759. Æt. 31. "We have even known one "hardly enough publicly to "stigmatise men of the "first rank in literature for their "immoralities,* while conscious "himself of labouring under the "infamy of having, by the vilest "and meanest actions, forfeited "all pretensions to honour and "honesty. If such men as these, "boasting a liberal education and "pretending to genius, practise "at the same time those arts "which bring the Sharper," the reader will remember this word in the affecting letter of remonstrance to Griffiths, "to the "cart's-tail or the pillory, need "our author wonder that 'Learn-"'ing partakes the contempt of "'its professors?' If characters "of this stamp are to be found "among the Learned, need any "one be surprised that the Great "prefer the society of fiddlers, "gamesters, and buffoons?"**

The time will come when Mr. Griffiths, with accompaniment such as that of his ancient countryman's friend when the leek was offered, will publicly withdraw these vulgar falsehoods; and meanwhile they are not deserving of remark. Indeed the quarrel, or interchange of foul reproach, as between author and bookseller, may claim at all times the least possible part of attention. It is a third more serious influence to which appeal is made, and on whose right interference the righteous arrangement must at last depend. But at the close of the second epoch, so brief yet so sorrowful, in the life of this genuine man-of-letters, it becomes us at least to understand the appeal he would have entered against the existing control and government of the destinies of literature. It was manifestly premature, and some passages of his after-life will plainly avow as much: but it had

* Kenrick has here the mock decency to subjoin, in a note, exactly that kind of affected disclaimer of any personal allusion to Goldsmith in this particular passage, which fixes the offence charged more expressly upon him. "Even our "author," he says, "seems to have wan-"dered into calumny when he speaks of "the Marquis d'Argens as attempting to "add the character of a philosopher to "the vices of a debauchee." That he was himself intended would require no clearer evidence to Goldsmith's mind than the identity of the subsequent expression — *sharper* — with the "sharper "and villain" of Griffiths's letter *ante*, p. 118.

** *Monthly Review*, xxi. 389, November 1759. Can any one doubt that these

painful passages in Goldsmith's history were vividly present with him two years later, when his man in black, talking of genius and its rewards among the tombs of Westminster Abbey, surprised the Chinese citizen by describing a class of men who "have no other employment "but to cry out Dunce, and Scribbler; to "praise the dead and revile the living; to "grant a man of confessed abilities some "small share of merit; to applaud twenty "blockheads, in order to gain the reputa-"tion of candour; and to revile the "moral character of the man whose writ-"ings they cannot injure? Such wretches "are kept in pay by some mercenary "bookseller, or more frequently *the book-"seller himself* takes this dirty work off "their hands, as all that is required is to "be very abusive and very dull." *Citizen of the World*, xiii.

too sharp an experience in it not to have also much truth, and it would better have become certain bystanders in that age to have gone in and parted the combatants, than, as they did, make a ring around them for enjoyment of the sport, or in philosophic weariness abandon the scene altogether.

"You know," said Walpole to one of his correspondents, "how "I shun authors, and would never "have been one myself, if it "obliged me to keep such bad "company. They are always in "earnest, and think their pro- "fession serious, and dwell upon "trifles, and reverence learning. "I laugh at all these things, and "divert myself." "It is pro- "bable," said David Hume, "that "Paris will be long my home .. "I have even thoughts of settling "in Paris for the rest of my life ".. I have a reluctance to think "of living among the factious "barbarians of London. Letters "are there held in no honour. "The taste for literature is nei- "ther decayed nor depraved "here, as with the barbarians "who inhabit the banks of the "Thames .. Learning and the "learned are on a very different "footing here, from what they "are among the factious bar- "barians." *

Matter of diversion for one, of disgust and avoidance for others, the factious barbarian struggle was left to a man more single-hearted, who thought the business of life a thing *to be* serious about, and who, unlike the Humes and Walpoles, was solely dependent for his bread on the very booksellers of the danger of whose absolute power he desired to give timely warning. This he might do, as it seems to me, without personal injustice, and without pettish spite to the honest craft of bookselling, or to any other respectable trade. So far he had the perfect right to use the bitter experience he had acquired, and to argue from his particular case to the general question before him. He might believe that those trade-indentures would turn out ill for literature; that in enlarging its channels by vulgar means, might be mischief rather than good; that facilities for appeal to a wide circle of uninformed readers, were but facilities for employment to a circle of writers nearly as wide and quite as uninformed; that, in raising up a brood of writers whom any other earthly employment would have better fitted, lay the danger of bringing down the man of genius to their level; and, in short, that literature, properly understood and rightly cherished, had altogether a higher duty and significance than the profit or the loss of a tradesman's counter. In this I hold him to have taken fair ground. The reputations we have lived to see raised on these false foundations, the good clerks and accountants whom magazines

1759.
Æt. 31.

* See various letters, Burton's *Life*, II. 190, 268, 278, 290, 292, &c.

have turned into bad literary men, the readers whose tastes have been pandered to and yet further lowered, the writers whose better talents have been disregarded and wasted, and the venal puffery which has more depressed the modern man-of-letters than ever shameless beggary reduced his predecessors; are evidence on that point quite unanswerable.

But when Goldsmith wrote, there was still a certain recognised work for the bookseller to do. With the aftercourse of my narrative this will more fully appear, even in such assent and adhesion from Goldsmith himself as he certainly did not contemplate when the *Enquiry* was planned, although, at the close of his life's experience, he would almost seem to have silently withdrawn it, by leaving his book revised for a posthumous edition with its protest against booksellers unabated and unmodified. To complete that protest now (a most essential part of this chapter in his fortunes), I will add proof, from other parts of the *Enquiry*, of the manly and unselfish bearing of the appeal that was built upon it. By those who have studied the disclosures made recently by men who take the deepest interest in the welfare of our universities; and who contrast them, as they now are, with the original purpose for which those grand foundations of princely prelates and nobles in advance of their age first arose

1759.
Æt. 31.

in Cambridge and Oxford; there will be found no inconsistency between the opening and closing lines of the sentences subjoined.

"No nation gives greater encouragements to learning than we do; yet none are so injudicious in the application. We seem to confer them with the same view that statesmen have been known to grant employments at Court, rather as bribes to silence than incentives to emulation. All our magnificent endowments of colleges are erroneous;* and at best, more

* A kind of endowment partaking of both pension list and college lectureship, yet free from the vice of both, has been suggested in a generous criticism on the first edition of this biography in the *Edinburgh Review* (LXXXVIII. 218-20). "The "principle of a pension list is not one "that dignifies the community of letters, "nor does it meet the questions at issue. "Even in a pecuniary point of view, a "sum might often be necessary for a "limited period in the production of a "particular work, which it would not be "necessary to continue for life, and "which need not be applied to the mere "relief of positive distress, or the sup-"port of infirmity and age. Schiller was "in the prime of his life, and quite "capable of being a bookseller's drudge, "perhaps of writing Grecian histories "and works on Animated Nature, when "two noblemen, thinking that his genius "was meant for other things, subscribed "to endow him with a pension for three "years to enable him to do that which "he was calculated best to do. It came "to Schiller at the right time of his ex-"istence. It served, we believe, not "only to aid his genius, but to soften his "heart. Some help of a similar nature, "a national fund in connection with the "pension list might not unprofitably be-"stow. Perhaps, in any comprehensive "system of national education which the "conflicting opinions and prejudices of "party may permit the legislature ulti-"mately to accomplish, means may be "taken to render the Mechanics' In-"stitutes (many of which are fast decay-"ing, and cannot, we believe, long exist "upon resources wholly voluntary) per-

frequently enrich the prudent than reward the ingenious. Among the universities abroad I have ever observed their riches and their learning in a reciprocal proportion, their stupidity and pride increasing with their opulence..... Every encouragement given to stupidity, when known to be such, is also a negative insult upon genius. This appears in nothing more evident than the undistinguished success of those who solicit subscriptions. When first brought into fashion, subscriptions were conferred upon the ingenious alone, or those who were reputed such. But at present, we see them made a resource of indigence, and requested not as rewards of merit, but as a relief of distress. If tradesmen happen to want skill in conducting their own business, yet they are able to write a book; if mechanics want money, or ladies shame, they write books and solicit subscriptions. Scarcely a morning passes, that proposals of this nature are not thrust into the half-opening doors of the rich, with perhaps a paltry petition, showing the author's wants, but not his merits. .... What then are the proper encouragements of genius? I answer, subsistence and respect, for these are rewards congenial to its nature."*

This is not the language of one who would have had literature again subsist, as of old, on servile adulation and vulgar charity. Goldsmith indeed seems rather to have thought, with a man of noble genius in our own day, that grants of money and subscriptions are by no means the

"manent and valuable auxiliaries to "popular instruction; and endowed lec-"tureships or professorships, at the more "important of these in our larger towns, "might be devoted to men distinguished "in letters and science, connect them "more with the practical world, occupy "but little of their time, and yield them "emoluments, if modest, still sufficient "to relieve them from actual dependence "on the ordinary public and trading "booksellers." Lord Lytton has since avowed himself the writer.
    * Chap. x.

chief things wanted for proper organisation of the literary class. "To give our men of let-"ters," says Mr. Carlyle, "stipends, endowments, $\frac{1759.}{\text{Æt. 31.}}$ "and all furtherance of "cash, will do little toward the "business. On the whole, one is "weary of hearing about the "omnipotence of money. I will "say rather, that, for a genuine "man, it is no evil to be poor .. "Money, in truth, can do much, "but it cannot do all. We must "know the province of it, and "confine it there; and even spurn "it back, when it wishes to get "farther."*   One of the lively illustrations of the *Enquiry* is not very unlike this.   "The bene-"ficed divine," says Goldsmith, "whose wants are only imagi-"nary, expostulates as bitterly as "the poorest author that ever "snuffed his candle with finger "and thumb. Should interest or "good fortune advance the divine "to a bishopric, or the poor son "of Parnassus into that place "which the other has resigned, "both are authors no longer: the "one goes to prayers once a day, "kneels upon cushions of velvet, "and thanks gracious Heaven for "having made the circumstances "of all mankind so extremely "happy; the other battens on all "the delicacies of life, enjoys his "wife and his easy chair, and "sometimes, for the sake of con-"versation, deplores the luxury "of these degenerate days. All "encouragements to merit are
    * On Heroes, Lecture x.

"therefore misapplied, which "make the author too rich to con- "tinue his profession."*

_1759._
_Æt. 31._ But he would not therefore starve him, or to the mercies of blind chance altogether surrender him. He recalls a time he would wish to see revived; when, with little of wealth or worldly luxury, the writer could yet command esteem for himself and reverence for the claims of his calling (this, and not the vulgar thought of merely feasting with a lord, being what he intends by the allusion to Lord Somers); and he dwells upon the contrast of existing times, in language which will hereafter connect itself with the deliberate dislike of Walpole, and the uneasy jealousy of Garrick.**

"When the link between patronage and learning was entire, then all who deserved fame were in a capacity of attaining it. When the great Somers was at the helm, patronage was fashionable among our nobility. The middle ranks of mankind, who generally imitate the Great, then followed their example, and applauded from fashion if not from feeling. I have heard an old poet" [he alludes to Young] "of that glorious age say, that a dinner with his lordship has procured him invitations for the whole week following; that an airing in his patron's chariot has supplied him with a citizen's coach on every future occasion. For who would not be proud to entertain a man who kept so much good company? But this link now seems entirely broken. Since the days of a certain prime-minister of inglorious memory, the learned have been kept pretty much at a distance.* A jockey, or a laced player, supplies the place of the scholar, the poet, or the man of virtue. ... Wit, when neglected by the Great, is generally despised by the vulgar. Those who are unacquainted with the world, are apt to fancy the man of wit as leading a very agreeable life. They conclude, perhaps, that he is attended to with silent admiration, and dictates to the rest of mankind with all the eloquence of conscious superiority. Very different is his present situation. He is called an author, and all know that an author is a thing only to be laughed at. His person, not his jest, becomes the mirth of the company. At his approach the most fat unthinking face brightens into malicious meaning. Even aldermen laugh, and avenge on him the ridicule which was lavished on their forefathers:

Etiam victis redit in præcordia virtus,
Victoresque cadunt.

.... "The poet's poverty is a standing topic of contempt. His writing for bread is an unpardonable offence. Perhaps of all mankind an author in those times is used most hardly. We keep him poor and yet revile his poverty. Like angry parents, who correct their children till they cry and then correct them for crying, we reproach him for living by his wit and yet allow him no other means to live. His taking refuge in garrets and cellars has of late been violently objected to him, and that by men who I dare hope are more apt to pity than insult his distress. Is poverty the writer's fault? No doubt he knows how to prefer a bottle of champaign to the nectar of the neighbouring alehouse, or a venison pasty to a plate of potatoes. Want of delicacy is not in him but in us, who deny him the opportunity of making an elegant choice. Wit certainly is the property of those who have it, nor should we be displeased if it is the only property a man sometimes has. We must not underrate him who uses it for subsistence, and flies from the ingratitude of the age even to a

---

* Chap. x.
** In Lord Stanhope's _History_ (1853, ii. 223-4) will be found a passage pertinent to the matter under discussion, and very honourable to the writer.

* This allusion to the "inglorious "memory" of Sir Robert Walpole is more than enough to explain the never-ceasing indifference, dislike, or contempt avowed by Horace Walpole for its author.

bookseller for redress. If the profession of an author is to be laughed at by the stupid, it is certainly better to be contemptibly rich than contemptibly poor. For all the wit that ever adorned the human mind will at present no more shield the author's poverty from ridicule, than his high-topped gloves* conceal the unavoidable omissions of his laundress. To be more serious, new fashions, follies, and vices, make new monitors necessary in every age. An author may be considered as a merciful substitute to the legislature; he acts not by punishing crimes but preventing them; however virtuous the present age, there may be still growing employment for ridicule or reproof, for persuasion or satire. If the author be therefore still so necessary among us, let us treat him with proper consideration as a child of the public, not a rent-charge on the community.** And indeed a *child* of the public he is in all respects; for, while so well able to direct others, how incapable is he frequently found of guiding himself! His simplicity exposes him to all the insidious approaches of cunning; his sensibility, to the slightest invasions of contempt. Though possessed of fortitude to stand unmoved the expected bursts of an earthquake, yet of feelings so exquisitely poignant as to agonise under the slightest disappointment. Broken rest, tasteless meals, and causeless anxiety, shorten his life, or render it unfit for active employment; prolonged vigils and intense application still farther contract his span, and make his time glide insensibly away. Let us not then aggravate those natural inconveniences by neglect; we have had sufficient instances of this kind already. Sale and Moore will suffice for one age

------

* "I asked Mr. Gray," says Nicholls, "what sort of a man Dr. Hurd was. He "answered, 'The last person who left "'off stiff-topped gloves.'" *Works,* v. 52. Mr. Rogers has often humorously quoted this as a good trait of character.

** Unprofitably kept at Heaven's expense,
  I live a rent-charge on His providence.
          Dryden to Congreve.
Instinctively on this subject Goldsmith seems always to have thought of Dryden (*ante,* 106).

at least. But they are dead, and their sorrows are over. The neglected author of the Persian *Eclogues* [Collins], which however inaccurate excel any in our language, is still alive. Happy, if *insensible* of our neglect, not *raging* at our ingratitude. It is enough that the age has already produced instances of men pressing foremost in the lists of fame, and worthy of better times, schooled by continued adversity into an hatred of their kind, flying from thought to drunkenness, yielding to the united pressure of labour, penury, and sorrow, sinking unheeded, without one friend to drop a tear on their unattended obsequies, and indebted to charity for a grave."*

1759.
Æt. 31.

These words had been written but a very few years, when the hand that traced them was itself cold; and, yielding to that united pressure of labour, penury, and sorrow, with a frame exhausted by unremitting and ill-rewarded drudgery, Goldsmith was indebted to the forbearance of creditors for a peaceful burial. It is not, then, in the early death of learned Sale, driven mad with those fruitless schemes of a society for encouragement of learning, which he carried, it may be hoped, to a kinder world than this; it is not from the grave of Edward Moore, with melancholy playfulness anticipating, in his last unsuccessful project, the very day on which his death would come; it is not even at the shrieks of poor distracted Collins, heard through the melancholy cathedral-cloister where he had played in childhood: but it is in the life, adventures, and death of Oliver Goldsmith, that

------

* Chap. x.

the mournful moral speaks its warning to us now.

I know of none more deeply impressive, or of wider import and significance. When Collins saw the hopes of his youth in the cold light of the world's indifference, with a mixed impulse of despair and revenge he collected the unsold edition of his hapless *Odes and Eclogues*, and with a savage delight beheld them slowly consume, as, in his own room, he made a bonfire of them. When Goldsmith was visited with a like weakness, something of a like result impended; but the better part was forced upon him in his own despite, and in the present most affecting picture of his patience the hectic agony of Collins is but an idle frenzy. Steadily gazing on the evil destinies of men-of-letters, he no longer desires to avoid his own; conscious of the power of the booksellers, he condemns and denounces it; without direct hope save of some small public favour, he protests against cruelties for which the public are responsible. The protest will accompany us through the remainder of his life: and be remembered as well in its lightest passages, as in those where any greatness of suffering will now be less apparent than a calmness of endurance; a resolute quiet power of persevering exertion, in which, with whatever infirmities of disposition or temper, he will front and foil adversity.

1759.
Æt. 31.

Such, at the worst, is the resource of a healthy genius, working evil into good, because carrying within itself a principle of sustainment and consolation; and very particularly does it become the world to take note of this, as a party far more deeply concerned than either the bookseller or the author. That cry of Goldsmith is little for himself. Who wins his passage to the goal, may care little at the close for a larger suffering or a less: the cry is raised for others, meanwhile perishing by the way. When *Irene* failed, and Johnson was asked how he felt, he answered "like the Monument;"[*] but when he had arrived at comfort and independence, and carelessly taking up one day his own fine satire, opened it at the lines which paint the scholar's fate, and the obstructions, almost insurmountable, in his way to fortune and fame, he burst into a passion of tears.[**] Not for what he had himself endured, whose labour at last was victoriously closed; but for all the disastrous chances that still awaited others. It is the world's concern. There

<hr>

[*] Boswell's *Life*, i. 230.

[**] Mrs. Piozzi's *Anecdotes*, 60. "The "family and Mr. Scott only were present, "who in a jocose way clapped him on the "back, and said, 'What's all this, my "'dear sir? Why you, and I, and *Her-* "'*cules*, you know, were all troubled "'with *melancholy*.' .... He was a very "large man, and made out the triumvirate "with Johnson and Hercules comically "enough. The Doctor was so delighted "at his odd sally, that he suddenly em-"braced him, and the subject was im-"mediately changed."

is a subtle spirit of compensation at work, when men regard it least, which to the spiritual sense accommodates the vilest need, and lightens the weariest burden. Milton talked of the lasting fame and perpetuity of praise, which God and good men have consented should be the reward of those whose published labours have advanced the good of mankind; and it is a set-off, doubtless, in the large account. The "two carriages" and the "style" of Griffiths are long passed away into the rubbish they sprang from, and all of us will be apt enough now to thank heaven that we were not Griffiths. Jacob Tonson's hundred thousand pounds are now of less account than the bad shillings he insinuated into Dryden's payments; and the fame of Secretary Nottingham is much overtopped by the pillory of De Foe. The Italian princes who beggared Dante are still without pity writhing in his deathless poem, while Europe looks to the beggar as to a star in heaven; nor have Italy's greater day, and the magnificence that crowded the court of Augustus, left behind them a name of any earthly interest to compare with his who restored land to Virgil, and who succoured the fugitive Horace. These are results which have obtained in all countries, and been confessed by every age; and it will be well when they win for literature other living regards, and higher present consideration, than it has yet been able to obtain. Men of genius can more easily starve, than the world, with safety to itself, can continue to neglect and starve them. What new arrangement or what kind of consideration may be required, will not be very distant from the simple acknowledgment that greater honour and respect ARE due.

1759.
Æt. 31.

This is what literature has wanted in England, and not the laced coat or powdered wig, the fashionable acceptance or great men's feasts, which have on rare occasions been substituted for it. The most liberal patronage vouchsafed in this country to living men-of-letters, has never been unaccompanied by degrading incidents; nor their claims at any time admitted without discourtesy or contumely. It is a century and a half since an act of parliament was passed to "protect" them, under cover of which their most valuable private rights were confiscated to the public use; and it is not twenty years since another act was passed with a sort of kindly consideration on their behalf, by favour of which the poet and the teacher of writing, the historian and the teacher of dancing, the philosopher and the royal coachman, Sir Christopher Wren's great grand-daughter and the descendant of Charles the Second's French riding-master, are permitted to appear in the same annual charitable list. But though

statesmen have yet to learn what it can do, and in a higher and larger sense than was intended by the minister: but whether society can take care of itself, is also a material question.

the state loses by such unwise scorn of what enlightens and refines it, they cannot remain much longer ignorant to what extent they are themselves enslaved by the power they thus affect to despise, or unacquainted with the functions of government and statesmanship it is gradually assuming to itself. Its progress has been uninterrupted since Johnson's and Goldsmith's time, and cannot for as many more years continue unacknowledged. Pitt sneered when the case of Burns was stated to him, and talked of literature taking care of itself; which indeed

Towards the solution, one sentence of Goldsmith's protest is an offering from his sorrow in these times of authorship by compulsion, not less worthy than his more cheerful offerings in those days of authorship by choice to which the reader is now invited. "An author may "be considered as a merciful "substitute to the legislature. "He acts not by punishing crimes, "but by preventing them."

*1759.
Æt. 31.*

END OF BOOK THE SECOND.

BOOK THE THIRD.

AUTHORSHIP BY CHOICE.

1759 TO 1767.

CHAPTER I.

Writing the Bee.
1759.

THE Booksellers were never more active than at the close of 1759. If literature had anything to hope from such exertions, its halcyon days were come. If it could live on magazines and reviews; if strength, subsistence, and respect, lay in employment of the multitudinous force of Grub-street; if demand and supply were law sufficient for its higher interests; literature was prosperous at last, and might laugh at all Pope's prophecies. Every week had its spawn of periodical publications; feeble, but of desperate fecundity. *Babblers,* and *Schemers; Friends,* and *Advisers; Auditors, Comptrollers,* and *Grumblers; Spendthrifts,* and *Bachelors; Free-Enquirers, Scrutators,* and *Investigators; Englishmen, Freeholders,* and *Moderators; Sylphs,* and *Triflers; Rangers,* and *Collegers; Templars, Gentlemen,* and *Skeptics;* in constant succession rose and fell.* "Sons of a day, "just buoyant on the flood," next day might see them "num- "bered with the puppies "in the mud;" but the parents of the dull blind offspring had meanwhile eaten and drunk, and the owners or masters profited. Of magazines alone, weekly and monthly, I will enumerate the specimens which a very few weeks, between the close of 1759 and the beginning of 1760, added to a multitude already wearing out their brief existence. They were: the *Royal Magazine, or Gentleman's Monthly Companion;* the *Impartial Review, or Literary Journal;* the *Weekly Magazine, or Gentlemen and Ladies' Polite Companion;* the *Ladies' Magazine;* the *Public Magazine;* the *Imperial Magazine;* the *Royal Female Magazine;* the *Universal Review;* the *Lady's Museum;* the *Musical Magazine;* and the *British Maga-*

1759.
Æt. 31.

* See the list in Nichols's *Literary Anecdotes,* iv. 38-97.

10*

sine, *or Monthly Repository for Gentlemen and Ladies.*

See all her progeny. Illustrious sight!
    Behold, and count them, as they
       rise to light.
As Berecynthia, while her off-
    spring vie
In homage to the Mother of the sky,
Surveys around her, in the blest abode,
A hundred sons, and ev'ry son a God:
Not loss with glory mighty Dulness
    crown'd,
Shall take thro' Grub-street her triumph-
    ant round,
And her Parnassus glancing o'er at once,
Behold a hundred sons, and each a
    Dunce.

Whether with equal triumph she beheld the new recruit advance to take his place, may admit of question. But her favourite Purdons, Hills, Willingtons, Kenricks, Shiels, Bakers, Guthries, Wotys, Ryders, Collyers, Joneses, Pilkingtons, Huddlestone Wynnes, and Hiffernans, were always at hand to comfort her: and there was an ill-fashioned, out-of-the-way corner, in even her domain, for temporary reception of the Smolletts and the Johnsons; men who owed her no allegiance, but had not yet deserted Grub-street altogether. "It is a street in Lon-"don," was Johnson's definition, four years before the present, "much inhabited by writers of "small histories, dictionaries, "and temporary poems: whence "any mean production is called "Grub-street." Why, a man might enter even Grub-street, then, with bold and cheerful heart, seeing the author of the *English Dictionary* there. For there, as occasion called, he was

still to be seen: poor, persevering, proud;

"Unplaced, unpension'd, no man's heir
    or slave;"

inviting the world to take heed that indeed he *was* there, "tug-"ging at the oar."

With that great, independent soul of his, Samuel Johnson had no reproach for Fortune: she might come to him now, or stay away for ever. What other kind of man he might have been, if something more than fourpence-halfpenny a day had welcomed him in the outset; or if houseless and homeless street-wanderings with Savage, and resolutions to stand by his country,* had been forestalled by house and home, and resolution of his country to stand by him; is not in his case a matter of much importance. He dealt with life as he found it; toil, envy, want, the patron, and the jail, he grappled with as they came; and he had now quietly, and finally, accepted the profession of literature upon

* Johnson told Murphy that he and Savage, on one occasion, walked round Grosvenor-square till four in the morning; in the course of their conversation not only falling foul of Walpole for laying restraints upon the stage, neglecting the arts, and letting science go unrewarded, but themselves reforming the world generally, dethroning princes, establishing new forms of government, giving laws to different states, and, when at last fatigued with their legislative office, and sorely in need of refreshment and rest, finding themselves both together unable to make up more than the sum of fourpence-halfpenny. *Monthly Review,* LXXVI. 261-262. And see Murphy's *Essay,* 17.

its own terms. Repulsed from the west-end mansion, he turned to the counters of the east; insulted by bookseller Osborne, he knocked him down with one of his own folios;* decently paid by bookseller Millar, he told the world to honour him for raising the rewards of books; and treating authorship, since the world would have it so, as any other trade, and still heartily embracing poverty as a trusted and honourable companion, was content in Grub-street, or any other street, to work out his case as he could. "Seven years, my lord, have "now passed," he wrote to Lord Chesterfield, on appearance of the *Dictionary* four years before, "since I waited in your outward "rooms, or was repulsed from ' your door; during which time I "have been pushing on my work "through difficulties for which it "is useless to complain, and have "brought it, at last, to the verge "of publication, without one act "of assistance, one word of en- "couragement, or one smile of "favour. .... Is not a patron, "my lord, one who looks with "unconcern on a man struggling "for life in the water, and when "he has reached ground, encum- "bers him with help? The "notice which you have — "been pleased to take of "my labours, had it been early, "had been kind: but it has been "delayed till I am indifferent, "and cannot enjoy it; till I am "solitary, and cannot impart it; "till I am known, and do not "want it. I hope it is no very "cynical asperity not to confess "obligations where no benefit "has been received; or to be un- "willing that the public should "consider me as owing that to a "patron, which Providence has "enabled me to do for myself." What! said he to Garrick in more familiar mood, have I sailed a long and difficult voyage round the world of the English language, and does he *now* send out his cock-boat to tow me into har-bour?*

And from this man, even now, there was nothing to separate the humblest of literary work-

* Mrs. Thrale (*Anecdotes*, 232-233) is the best authority for this knocking down of bookseller Osborne. "And how was "that affair, in earnest; now, do tell me, "Mr. Johnson?" "There is nothing to "tell, dearest lady, but that he was in-"solent and I beat him, and that he was "a blockhead and told of it, which I "should never have done; so the blows "have been multiplying, and the wonder "thickening, for all these years, as "Thomas was never a favourite with the "public. I have beat many a fellow, but "the rest had the wit to hold their "tongues."

* His letter to Thomas Warton announcing the near completion of his *Dictionary* is less known; yet I do not know that his manly courage and self-reliance have anywhere found more masterly expression. "I now begin to see land, "after having wandered, according to "Mr. Warburton's phrase, in this vast "sea of words. What reception I shall "meet with on the shore, I know not: "whether the sound of bells, and ac-"clamations of the people, which Ariosto "talks of in his last canto, or a general "murmur of dislike, I know not: whether "I shall find upon the coast a Calypso "that will court, or a Polypheme that will "resist. But if Polypheme comes, *have at* "*his eye*." *Boswell*, II. 28.

men. Here were his words, as a trumpet, to call them to the field; and there he was himself, in person, to animate the struggle. To what then should he first look, who, hitherto a compelled and reluctant dweller on the threshold of literature, was now of his own resolute choice advancing within to try his fortune, if not to this great unyielding figure of Samuel Johnson, for courage and sustainment? There, beyond a doubt, were the thoughts of Oliver Goldsmith now: with poverty, not simply endured, but made a badge of honour; with independence, though indeed but a bookseller's servant; without remonstrance or uneasy resistance, should even the worst attendants of the garret continue to be his lot for ever. "He assured me," says the author of the *Rambler* of his friend Ofellus, "that thirty "pounds a year was enough to "enable a man to live in Lon"don without being contemptible. "He allowed ten pounds for "clothes and linen. He said a "man might live in a garret at "eighteenpence a week; few "people would inquire where he "lodged; and if they did, it was "easy to say, *Sir, I am to be found* "*at such a place.* By spending "threepence in a coffee-house, "he might be for some hours "every day in very good com"pany; he might dine for six"pence, breakfast on bread and "milk for a penny, and do with"out supper. On *clean-shirt day,*

1759.
Æt. 31.

"he could go abroad and pay "visits."* Nor were these the holiday theories of one to whom the practice of poverty was not still familiar. Here lay the singular worth of Johnson's example: that the world of enemies as well as friends were beginning, in a poor man, to recognise an intellectual chief and potentate of literature, a man who had the right to rule them. "He "and I were never cater-cousins," wrote Smollett to Wilkes a month or two before the date to which I have brought this narrative, and in the same letter Smollett calls him the "Great Cham of "literature." Yet the great cham's poverty was obliged in this very year to surrender Gough-square for a humbler lodging in Gray's-inn: that same Gough-square in Fleet-street, where Doctor Burney had found him amid a chaos of Greek folios, and with the moderate accom-

* Comparing this with his actual experience, one feels that Ofellus had decidedly the advantage on the whole. It is true that when Johnson first came to London his dinner cost him twopence more. ("I had a cut of meat for six"pence, and bread for a penny, and "gave the waiter a penny; so that I was "quite well served, nay, better than the "rest, for they gave the waiter nothing." *Boswell,* i. 113.) But then no *fasting days* appear in Ofellus's bill of fare, and at that period of his life, as he surprised the party in the Hebrides by telling them several years later, "*he had fasted for two* "*days at a time,* during which he had "gone about visiting, though not at the "hours of dinner or supper; that he had "drank tea, but eaten no bread; that this "was no intentional fasting, but hap"pened just in the course of a literary "life." *Boswell,* v. 8, 9.

modation of one deal writing-desk and a chair and a half; the entire seat offered to his visitor, and himself tottering on its three-legged and one-armed fellow. Nay, some few brief years before, he had been placed under arrest for five pounds eighteen shillings; though already he had written *London*, the *Vanity of Human Wishes*, and the *Rambler*, and was author of *The English Dictionary*.

Now, week by week, in a paper of Mr. John Newbery's, he sent forth the *Idler*.* What he was, and what with a serious earnestness, be it wrong or right, he had come into the world to say and do, were at last becoming evident to all. Colleges were glad to have him visit them, and a small enthusiastic circle was gradually forming around him. The Reynoldses, Bennet Langtons, and Topham Beauclercs, had thus early given in their allegiance; and Arthur Murphy was full of wonder at his submitting to contradiction, when they dined together this last Christmas day with young Mr. Burke of Wimpole-street. But not more known or conspicuous was the consideration thus exacted, than the poverty which still waited on it, and claimed its share. So might literature avenge herself, in this penniless champion, for the disgrace of the money-bags of Walpole and Pelham. "I have several times "called on Johnson," wrote Grainger to Percy some months before the present date, "to pay "him part of your subscription" (for his edition of Shakespeare). "I say part, because he never "thinks of working if he has "a couple of guineas in his "pocket."** And again, a month later: "As to his Shakespeare, "*movet, sed non promovet*. I shall "feed him occasionally with "guineas."*** It was thus the good Mr. Newbery found it best

* Among the papers of Newbery, in the possession of Mr. Murray, is the account rendered on the collection of the *Idler* into two small volumes, when the arrangement seems to have been that Johnson should receive two-thirds of the profits. It shows the growing popularity of Johnson, and is also worth comparing with similar charges in our own time.

"THE IDLER.

"Dr.	£	s.	d.	"Cr.	£	s.	d.
Paid for Advertising	20	0	6	1500 Sets at 16*l.* per 100	240	0	0
Printing two vols, 1500	41	13	0				
Paper	52	3	0	Dr. Johnson two-thirds	84	2	4
	113	16	6	Mr. Newbery one-third	42	1	2
Profit on the Edition	126	3	6		126	3	6."
	240	0	0				

** Nichols's *Illustrations*, vii. 259.

*** *Ibid*, vii. 261. Letter of 20th July, 1758. Mr. John Nichols communicated to Boswell the subjoined anecdote. "In the year 1763 a young bookseller, who "was an apprentice to Mr. Whiston, waited on him with a subscription to his "*Shakespeare*: and observing that the doctor made no entry in any book of the sub-"scriber's name, ventured diffidently to ask whether he would please to have the

to feed him too; and in that worthy publisher's papers many memoranda of the present year

1759.
Æt. 31.

were found, in record of *Lent Mr. Johnson one pound one.* For, in his worst distress, it was still but of literature Mr. Johnson begged or borrowed: to her he was indebted for his poverty, and to her only would he owe his independence. When his mother was dying, he did not ask his friend Mr. Reynolds, the fashionable painter in receipt of thousands, for the six guineas he sent to comfort her death-bed: it was the advance of a printer.* When, in the present year, she died, he paid the expenses of her funeral with the manuscript of *Rasselas.*

So schooled to regard the struggle of life and literature as one, and in midst of all apparent disadvantage to venerate its worth and sacredness, the author of the *Enquiry into the State of Polite Learning* stepped cheerfully forward into the market of books, and offered his wares for sale.

Bookseller Wilkie, of the Bible in St. Paul's-churchyard, a spirited man in his way and one of the foremost of magazine speculators, proposed a weekly publication of original essays, something in the *Rambler* form, but once instead of twice a week and with greater variety of matter. Goldsmith assented; and on Saturday the 6th of October, 1759, there appeared, price threepence, to be continued every Saturday, *The Bee.*

Floriferis ut apes saltibus omnia libant
Omnia non itidem

was its motto; learned, yet of pleasant promise; taken from Lucretius. It was printed "neat-"ly," as the advertisement in the *London Chronicle* of the 29th September had promised that it should be; "in crown octavo, and "on good paper, containing two "sheets or thirty-two pages, "stitched in blue covers." In other respects also it kept the bookseller's advertised promise; "consisting of a variety of es-"says on the amusements, fol-"lies, and vices in fashion, par-"ticularly the most recent topics "of conversation, remarks on "theatrical exhibitions, memoirs "of modern literature, &c. &c." And on the back of the blue cover, Mr. Wilkie begged leave to inform the public "that every "twelve numbers would make a "handsome pocket volume, at "the end of which should be "given an emblematical fron-"tispiece, title, and table of con-"tents." So there was reason-

---

"gentleman's address, that it might be "properly inserted in the printed list of "subscribers. '*I shall print no list of sub-*"'*scribers,*' said Johnson, with great ab-"ruptness; but almost immediately re-"collecting himself, added, very com-"placently, 'Sir, I have two very cogent "'reasons for not printing any list of "'subscribers: one, that I have lost all "'the names; the other, that I have "'spent all the money!'" *Boswell,* vn. 88.

* "I find in his diary a note of the "payment to Mr. Allen the printer, of six "guineas, which he had borrowed of "him, and sent to his dying mother." *Hawkins,* 366.

able hope at starting; and no doubt a long line of handsome pocket volumes already jostled each other, in Goldsmith's lively brain.

The first number, it must be said, was of good promise. One finds a lack of its wisdom and its lightness in books "stitched "in blue covers" now. The introduction disclaimed relationship to the magazine trade and family; refused to tempt its readers with "three beautiful "prints, curiously coloured from "nature," or to take any kind of merit from "its bulk or its "frontispiece;" and invoked for itself, with mixed mirth and earnestness, a class of readers that should know the distinction between a *bon-mot* for White's, and a jest for the Cat and Bagpipes in St. Giles's. There was a letter on the Poles; a notice of the death of Voltaire's victim, Maupertuis; and, under the title of Alcander and Septimius, a popular version of that beautiful tale of Boccaccio which afterwards suggested to a writer who belonged to Goldsmith's country, took early inspiration from his genius, and bore up uncrushed against as desperate poverty by the force of his example, the manly and earnest tragedy of *Gisippus*.* Nor, since

the delightful gossip of Cibber had raised the curtain on the Mountforts, Nokeses, and Bettertons of a past age, had any such just or lively writing on the theatres been given to the world, as

1759.
Æt. 31.

the age of twenty, eager to make a great dash upon the stage, he came up to London without a friend, but with one tragedy finished in his pocket, and another rapidly forming in his brain. The desperate *craving* of his youth was to force his way into the London theatres, and he seems to have determined very resolutely to use the faculty of which he felt himself possessed to that end, failure or neglect to the contrary notwithstanding. *Aguire*, his first tragedy, making no way towards a hearing, he wrote a second. This was *Gisippus*: and, written as it was in his twentieth year, I do not hesitate to call it one of the marvels of youthful production in literature. The solid grasp of character, the manly depth of thought, the beauties as well as defects of the composition (more than I can here enumerate), wanted only right direction to have given to our English drama another splendid and enduring name. In little London coffee-houses, on little slips of paper, this tragedy was written. But he could get no hearing for it. Still undaunted, he wrote a comedy, he wrote farces,—he tried the stage at every avenue, and it would have none of him. Meanwhile, he had been starving for two miserable years; writing all day within doors, and never venturing out till darkness threw its friendly veil over his threadbare coat; to use the common phrase, *denying himself* (because he could not get them) the common necessaries of life; passing "three days together with-"out tasting food," in a small room in an obscure court near St. Paul's; living for the most part, in short, on such munificent booksellers' rewards as two guineas for the translation of a volume and a half of a French novel. Something better presented itself at last, however; and, emerging from his misery, he became a critic, a reporter, and, stimulated by Banim's success, a writer of Irish tales. His dramatic dream was dreamt, and he

* Gerald Griffin's life was one of those strange, silent romances which pass quite unheeded amid the roar and movement of the busier life around them, yet the reader will find a brief mention of it not at all inappropriate to my present subject. He was a Limerick man, and at

the playhouse criticism of the *Bee*.

The first of his papers on this subject pointed out the superiority of French comic acting over English, with its causes;* and had some happy illustrations from his own experience.* His later remarks, on the want of general stage discipline in England ("dirty-shirted "guards rolling their eyes round "upon the audience, instead of "keeping them fixed upon the

1759.
Æt. 31.

---

never turned to the stage again. But not without ill effects to himself could he hope to keep thus dormant and unused the faculty which, as it seems to me, he had received in greatest abundance. More even than the zeal of God's House in his later years, this *eat him up*. What he wrote thereafter achieved a reasonable success; but, in the character of its pretension or achievement, bore so little proportion to the performances that shed lustre on his boyhood, that a growing sense of the worthlessness of literary pursuit at last led to a desire for the priesthood, and in his thirty-fifth year he entered a convent. He passed the various grades of his novitiate, and after two years of rigorous monastic seclusion, in which the monkish passion became more and more intense, fell into a sudden fever, and died in 1840. Before he entered the convent, he had committed his existing MSS. to the flames. Among them was *Aguire*, but (perhaps in touching memory of his early hopes, and that some record might be left in vindication of them) he saved *Ginippus*. It was produced during Mr. Macready's management of Drury Lane in 1842, nineteen years after its first composition. See Appendix (D) to this volume.

* This essay touches the vital distinction between comic acting as an art, or study, and comic acting as a mere expression of personal humour or enjoyment. I heard my honoured friend Charles Lamb say, shortly before he died, that the difference of the existing race of comedians from those he remembered in early life was that less study is now found necessary than was formerly judged to be requisite. That I believe to be the truth. We do not want capable actors, at least in comedy; but their end is answered with less pains. The modern way, as Lamb too truly objected, is to get a familiarity with the audience, to strike up a kind of personal friendship, or reciprocity of greeting, and be hail-fellow-well-met with them. Thus carelessness of personation at once slips in; such coquetting between the performer and the public, where ladies are in question, is a temptation to alarming excesses; and what used to be a sort of sauce piquant for the pert epilogue is made to give the standing relish to the whole play. "Oh!" exclaimed Charles Lamb, at the conclusion of some such description as this, "when shall we see a "female part acted in the quiet unappeal- "ing manner of Miss Pope's Mrs. Candour? "When shall we get rid of the Dalliahs "of the stage?" It is something of the same tone which Goldsmith adopts in his criticism. "I would particularly recom- "mend our rising actresses never to take "notice of the audience, on any occasion "whatever; let the spectators applaud "never so loudly, their praises should "pass, except at the end of the epilogue, "with seeming inattention."

* Need I quote from his later *Essays* to show what a thorough notion he had of country acting, and, for the matter of that, town acting too? "There is one "rule by which a strolling player may be "ever secure of success; that is, in our "theatrical way of expressing it, to make "a great deal of the character. To speak "and act as in common life, is not play- "ing, nor is 't what people come to see: "natural speaking, like sweet wine, runs "glibly over the palate, and scarcely "leaves any taste behind it; but being "high in a part resembles vinegar, which "grates upon the taste, and one feels it "while he is drinking." *Adventures of a Strolling Player*. And who does not remember Partridge's reason for not thinking Garrick an actor! "*He* the best "player? why I could act as well as he "myself ... The King for my money. "He speaks all his words distinctly, half "as loud again as the other; anybody "may see he is an actor."

"actors"); on skilful manage-ment of gesture (in which he ex-cepts Garrick and Mrs. Clive from his censure, placing them on a level with the French); and in explanation of the ill-success of the English operatic stage, where he touches the springs that operate to this hour; still further demonstrate how com-petent he was to this department of criticism.

But, like Hume's *Epicurist* ef-fort, it was all uphill work: his first *Bee* had an idle time of it, and greater favour was asked for the second in a paid-for news-paper paragraph of particular earnestness. "The public," said this advertisement, which had a pathetic turn in it, "is requested "to compare this with other "periodical performances which "more pompously solicit their "attention. If upon perusal it "be found deficient either in "humour, elegance, or variety, "the author will readily acquiesce "in their censure. It is possible "the reader may sometimes draw "a prize, and even should it turn "up a blank it costs him but "threepence." In number the second, for that small sum, was a most agreeable little lesson on Dress, against fault-finders and dealers in ridicule, proving by example of cousin Hannah that such folks are themselves the most ridiculous; and a much sounder notion of a patriot king than Bolingbroke's, in homely sketches of Charles the Twelfth of Sweden, in remark on the dif-ficulties of so educating princes that "the superior dignity of man "to that of royalty" should be their leading lesson, and in warning against the folly of entrusting a charge so sacred to men "who themselves "have acted in a sphere too high "to know mankind." A delight-ful essay in the same number, with Cardinal de Retz and Dick Wildgoose side by side, to prove that pleasure is in ourselves, not in the objects offered for our amusement, and that philosophy should force the trade of hap-piness when nature has denied the means,* also well deserves mention.

1759.
Ætat. 31.

The third number opened with a paper on the Use of Language: to which the grave philologist resorting found language he was little used to. It was a plea for the poor: an essay to prove that he who best knew how to con-ceal his necessities and desires, was the most likely person to find redress, and that the true use of speech was not to express wants, but conceal them.** All

---

* This latter remark, I should add however, did not appear in the essay until its reprint in 1765.

** I learn from the valuable and well-conducted *Notes and Queries* (I. 83) the curious fact, that four years after this re-mark had thus been made by Goldsmith, it was repeated by Voltaire (from whom, no doubt, Talleyrand afterwards stole it) in his satiric little dialogue of *Le Chapon et la Poularde* (*Œuvres Complètes*, XXIX. 83, 84. Ed. 1822), where the capon, com-plaining of the treachery of men, says, "Ils n'emploient les paroles que pour "déguiser leurs pensées." But see *post*, Book IV, Chap. XIII.

of us have known the Jack Spindle of this exquisite sketch, some perhaps relieved him; and
_1759._
_Æt. 31._
many have undergone the truth of his life's philosophy, that to have much, or to seem to have it, is the only way to have more, since it is the man who has no occasion to borrow that alone finds plenty willing to lend. "You "then, O ye beggars of my ac-"quaintance;" exclaimed Gold-smith, "whether in rags or lace, "whether in Kent-street or the "Mall, whether at Smyrna or St. "Giles's, might I advise you as a "friend, never seem in want of "the favour you solicit. Apply "to every passion but pity for "redress. You may find relief "from vanity, from self-interest, "or from avarice, but seldom "from compassion." Following this were three well-written cha-racters: of Father Feyjoo, whose popular essays against degrading superstitions have since pro-cured him the title of the Spanish Addison; of Alexandrian Hypa-tia, afterwards immortalised by Gibbon; and of Lysippus, an imaginary representative of some peculiarities in the essayist him-self, and timely assertor of the ordinary virtues as opposed to what are commonly mistaken for the great ones.

Still the churlish public would not buy the _Bee;_ and the fourth number's opening article was a good-humoured comment on that fact. Not a newspaper or ma-gazine, he said, that had not left him far behind; they had got to Islington at least, while the sound of Bow-bell still stayed in his ears: nevertheless, "if it were "only to spite all Grub-street," he was resolved to write on; and he made light-hearted announce-ment to the world of what he had written to Bryanton.* "If the "present generation will not hear "my voice, hearken, O Posterity! "to you I call, and from you I "expect redress! What rapture "will it not give, to have the "Scaligers, Daciers, and War-"burtons of future times com-"menting with admiration upon "every line I now write, and "working away those ignorant "creatures who offer to arraign "my merit, with all the virulence "of learned reproach. Ay, my "friends, let them feel it; call "names; never spare them; they "deserve it all, and ten times "more." In a like playful tone are his closing threats, that, if not better supported, he must throw off all connection with taste, and fairly address his countrymen in the engaging style and manner of other periodical pamphlets. He will change his title into the _Royal Bee_, he says, the _Anti-gallican Bee_, or the _Bee's Magazine._ He will lay in a proper stock of popular topics; such as encomiums on the King of Prus-sia, invectives against the Queen of Hungary and the French, the necessity of a militia, our un-doubted sovereignty of the seas, reflections upon the present state

* _Ante,_ p. 102.

of affairs, a dissertation upon liberty, some seasonable thoughts upon the intended bridge of Blackfriars, and an address to Britons;—the history of an old woman whose tooth grew three inches long shall not be omitted, nor an ode upon "our victories," nor a rebus, nor an acrostic upon Miss Peggy P, nor a journal of the weather; —and he will wind up the whole, so that the public shall have no choice but to purchase, with four extraordinary pages of letterpress, a beautiful map of England, and two prints curiously coloured from nature. Such was the booksellers' literature of the day: the profitable contribution of Paternoster-row and Grub-street, to the world's intellectual cultivation.

While he satirised it thus good-naturedly, Goldsmith took care to append also graver remarks on the more serious matter it involved, and which with his own experience lay so near his heart; but in no querulous spirit. He is now content to have found out the reason why mediocrity should have its rewards at once, and excellence be paid in reversion. There is in these earliest essays something more pleasing than even their undoubted elegance and humour, in that condition of mind. If neglects and injuries are still to be his portion, you do not now despair that he will turn them to commodities. It is not by his cries and complainings you shall hereafter trace him to his neglected, ill-furnished, wretched home. As he watches its naked cobwebbed walls, he finds matter for amusement to the readers of the *Bee*, in watching the spiders that have refuge there; and in his fourth number puts forth an instructive paper on the habits and predatory life of that most wary, ingenious, hungry, and persevering insect.

1759.
Æt. 31.

He was not to be daunted now. Looking closely into his life, one finds that other works beside this of the *Bee* were eking out its scanty supplies. He was writing for the *Busy Body*, published thrice a week for twopence by worthy Mr. Pottinger, and brought out but three days after the *Bee*. He was writing for the *Lady's Magazine*, started not many days later by persevering Mr. Wilkie, in the hope of propping up the *Bee*. He had taken his place, and would go to his journey's end. Since the "pleasure stage coach" had not opened its door to him, he had mounted "the waggon of industry;" not yet despairing, it might be, to be overtaken again by his old "vanity whim;" and with such help, even hopeful to come up with the "landau of riches," and find lodgment at last in the "fame machine." We note this pleasant current of his thoughts in the *Bee's* fifth number. There, in that last conveyance he places Addison, Swift, Steele, Pope, and Congreve; and, vainly stretching out a number of his own little blue-backed book to entice the goodly company, resolves to be useful since he may not be ambitious, and to earn by assiduity what merit does not open to him. But not the less cheerfully does he concede to others, what for himself he may not yet command. He shuts fame's door, indeed, on Arthur Murphy, but opens it to Hume and to Johnson: he closes it against Smollett's *History*, but opens it to his *Peregrine Pickle* and his *Roderick Random*. And with this paper, I doubt not, began his first fellowship of letters in a higher than the Grubstreet region. Shortly after this, I trace Smollett to his door; and, for what he had said of the author of the *Rambler*, Johnson soon grasped his hand. "This was a "very grave personage, whom "at some distance I took for one "of the most reserved and even "disagreeable figures I had seen; "but as he approached, his ap- "pearance improved; and when I "could distinguish him thorough- "ly, I perceived that in spite of "the severity of his brow, he "had one of the most good- "natured countenances that could "be imagined." In that sentence lay the germ of one of the pleasantest of literary friendships.

The poor essayist's habits, however, know little change as yet. His single chair and his window-bench have but to accommodate Mr. Wilkie's devil, waiting for proofs; or Mr. Wilkie himself, resolute for arrears of

1759. Æt. 31.

copy. The landlady of Greenarbour-court remembered one festivity there, which seems to have been highly characteristic. A "gentleman" called on a certain evening, and asking to see her lodger, went unannounced up-stairs. She then heard Goldsmith's room door pushed open, closed again sharply from within, and the key turned in the lock; after this, the sound of a somewhat noisy altercation reached her; but it soon subsided; and to her surprise, not unmingled with alarm, the perfect silence that followed continued for more than three hours. It was a great relief to her, she said, when the door was again opened, and the "gentleman," descending more cheerfully than he had entered, sent her out to a neighbouring tavern for some supper.* Mr. Wilkie or Mr. Pottinger had obtained his arrears, and could afford a little comforting reward to the starving author.

Perhaps he carried off with him that mirthful paper on the clubs of London, to which a pleasant imagination most loved to pay festive visits on solitary and supperless days. Perhaps that paper on public rejoicings for a victory which described the writer's lonely wanderings a few nights before, from Ludgate-hill to Charing-cross, through crowded and illuminated streets, past punch-houses and coffee-houses, and where excited shoemakers, think-

* *Prior, i. 328, 329.*

ing wood to be nothing like leather, were asking with frightful oaths what ever would become of religion if the wooden-soled French papishes came over! Perhaps that more affecting lonely journey through the London streets, which the *Bee* soon after published with the title of the City Night Piece,* in which there was so much of the past struggle and the lesson it had left, so much of the grief-taught sympathy, so much of the secret of the genius, of tolerant, gentle-hearted Goldsmith. What he was to the end of his London life, when miserable outcasts had cause with the great and learned to lament him, this paper shows him to have been at its beginning. The kind-hearted man would wander through the streets at night, to console and reassure the misery he could not otherwise give help to. While he thought of the rich and happy who were at rest, while he looked up even to the wretched roof that gave shelter to himself, he could not bear to think of those to whom the streets were the only home. "Strangers, wan-"derers, and orphans," too humble in their circumstances to expect redress, too completely and utterly wretched for pity; "poor shivering girls" who had seen happier days, and been flattered into beauty and into sin, now lying peradventure at the very doors of their betrayers; "poor houseless creatures" to whom the world, responsible for their guilt, gives reproaches, but will not give relief. These were teachers in life's truths, who spoke with a sterner and wiser voice than that of mere personal suffering. "The "slightest misfortunes of the "great, the most imaginary un-"easiness of the rich, are ag-"gravated with all the power of "eloquence, and held up to en-"gage our attention and sym-"pathetic sorrow. The poor weep "unheeded, persecuted by every "subordinate species of tyranny; "and every law which gives "others security, becomes an "enemy to them. Why was this "heart of mine formed with so "much sensibility, or why was "not my fortune adapted to its "impulse?" In thoughts like these, and in confirmed resolution to make the poor his clients and write down those tyrannies of law, the night wanderings of the thoughtful writer not unprofitably ended.*

It was a resolution very manifest in his next literary labour.

* The greater portion of this striking paper was repeated in Letter cxvii. of the *Citizen of the World.*

* Elia's complaint of the Decay of Beggars in the metropolis, as originally published in the *London Magazine*, closed with a characteristic mention of Goldsmith suppressed when the essays were collected, which I am happy to preserve here: "My friend has a curious manu-"script in his possession, the original "draught of the celebrated Beggar's Peti-"tion (who cannot say by heart the Beg-"gar's Petition?), as it was written by "some school usher (as I remember) with "corrections interlined from the pen of "Oliver Goldsmith. As a specimen of the

CHAPTER II.

David Garrick.
1750.

On the 29th of November the *Bee's* brief life closed, with its eighth number; and in the following month its editor, Mr. Oliver Goldsmith, was sought out both by that distinguished author Doctor Smollett, and by Mr. John Newbery the bookseller, of St. Paul's-churchyard. But as he had meanwhile made earnest application to Mr. David Garrick for his interest in an election at the Society of Arts, it will be best to describe at once the circumstances involved in that application, and its result on the poor author's subsequent intercourse with the rich manager and proprietor of the theatre royal in Drury-lane.

Goldsmith was passionately fond of the theatre. In prosperous days, it will ring with his humour and cheerfulness; in these struggling times, it was the help and refuge of his loneliness. We have seen him steal out of his garret to hear Columba sing: and if she fell short of the good old music he had learnt to love at Lissoy, the other admiration he was taught there, of happy human faces, at the theatre was always in his reach. If there is truth in what was said by Sir Richard Steele, that being happy, and seeing others happy, for two hours, is a duration of bliss not at all to be slighted by so short-lived creature as man, it is certain that he who despises the theatre adds short-sightedness to short life.* If he is a rich man, he will be richer for hearing there of what account the poor may be; if he is a poor man, he will not be poorer for the knowledge that those above him have their human sympathies. Sir Thomas Overbury held a somewhat strong opinion as to this; thinking the playhouse more necessary in a well-governed commonwealth than the school, because men were better taught by example than by precept: and, however light the disregard it has fallen into now, it might really seem to be a question not altogether unimportant, whether a high and healthy entertainment, the nature of which, conservative of all kindly relations between man and man, is to encourage, refine, and diffuse humanity, might not claim a kind and degree of support which in England has always been withheld from it.**

"doctor's improvement, I recollect one
"most judicious alteration—

> *A pamper'd menial drove me from the
> door.*

"It stood originally,

> *A livery servant drove me, &c.*

"Here is an instance of poetical or
"artificial language, properly substituted
"for the phrase of common conversa-
"tion; against Wordsworth."

* "At all other assemblies," says Johnson characteristically (in *The Idler*), "he "that comes to receive delight, will be "expected to give it; but in the theatre, "nothing is necessary to the amusement "of two hours, but to sit down and be "willing to be pleased."

** Alas! the three and twenty years that have passed, with their changes,

This remark occurs to me here, because many disappointments in connection with it will occur hereafter; and already even Garrick's fame and strength had been shaken by his difficult relations with men of letters. "I "am as much an admirer of Mr. "Garrick," said Mr. Ralph, in his *Case of Authors by Profession,* published in 1758, "and his ex-"cellences, as I ought to be: and "I envy him no part of his good "fortune. But then, though I "am free to acknowledge he was "made for the stage, I cannot "be brought to think the stage "was made only for him; or that "the fate of every dramatic writer "ought either to be at his mercy, "or that of any other manager "whatever; and the single con-"sideration that there is no alter-"native but to fly from him, in "case of any neglect or con-"tempt, to Mr. Rich, is enough "to deter any man in his senses "from embarking a second time "on such a hopeless voyage." Manifestly, however, this was the fault neither of Rich nor of Garrick, but of the system which left both to shift as they could, and made self-protection the primary law. "The manager," continues Mr. Ralph, admitting the whole question at issue in his complaints, "whether player or "harlequin, must be the sole "pivot on which the whole

"machine is both to move and "rest; there is no drawback on "the profit of the night in old "plays; and any access of "reputation to a dead au-"thor carries no imper-"tinent claims and invidious dis-"tinctions along with it. When "the playhouse is named," he added bitterly, "I make it a point "to pull off my hat, and think "myself obliged to the lowest "implement belonging to it. I "am ready to make my best ac-"knowledgments to a harlequin "who has continence enough to "look upon an author in the "green-room, of what considera-"tion soever, without laughing "at him." Other pamphlets followed in the cry; and Ned Purdon drew up a number of anonymous suggestions as to "how Mr. "Garrick ought to behave."*

It was the employment of this tone that introduced needlessly elements of bitterness, for the charge was a simple one, and might have been stated simply. No doubt Garrick, in common with every manager-actor before or since his time, was fairly exposed to it. I have turned to the play-bills of the season directly preceding the appearance of Mr. Ralph's pamphlet,** and find,

<div style="margin-left:1759.
Æt. 31.">

1759.
Æt. 31.

since this was written, have sufficed entirely to alter, from what they then were, the position and the claims of the theatres. [1870].

* For which he was afterwards obliged to apologise to the people abused, and to promise the public, by advertisement, never again to offend in the like manner. *Monthly Review,* xxi. 368.

** An unpublished letter is before me, written by this same Mr. Ralph to Garrick, the year before his pamphlet, containing a brief summary of his private wrongs, and furnishing so complete an

amidst revivals of Fletcher's *Rule a Wife and Have a Wife* and Shirley's comedy of *The Gamester*, and Shakespeare's *Tempest* as an opera and *Taming of the Shrew* as a farce, but

1750.
Æt. 31.

Illustration of Garrick's case, as well as of that of his opponents, that I am glad to have the opportunity of printing it. The weakness as well as strength of both may be observed in it. The manager's mistake was to encourage hopes up to the point when it no longer seemed unreasonable to the expectant to claim a sort of property in their realisation. The author's mistake was to suppose that any such encouragement could involve the right to force a play upon a theatre irrespective not only of the manager's convenience, but of his final right of judgment and rejection. Let it be observed, too, that Garrick has evidently obliged Mr. Ralph with money, and that the offence which causes the rupture does not appear to have been anything more grave than the suggestion that Mr. Ralph should wait one season more. "Sir," he writes, dating his letter the 17th September 1757, "No long ago as the year 1743, I had "reason to be convinced that the stage "was enchanted ground to me, which I "might see, but was never to take hold "of, and I then resolved to turn my back "on the delusion for good and all. This "resolution I adhered to invariably for "ten years in succession, and you were "the only man that could have induced "me to break it, which you did by put-"ting me on altering some old comedy "under promise that it should be per-"formed when done. In this service I "employed time enough to convince me "that to compose was as easy as to cobble. "I then turned my hand from old to new "things, hoping to be instrumental at "least in preserving a secret which "seemed to be on the point of being lost "to the country; but on this I was again "unlucky, for having submitted to be "judged in part by producing three acts "only out of five, my plan was con-"demned without mercy, and I ac-"quiesced in the sentence almost without "a murmur. I then became humble "enough to think of stooping to a farce, "which it is true I was promised room

one original production: *Lilliput,* played by children. It is not immaterial to the question, how-

"for, by Mr. Lacy in your name: but on "second thoughts chose to avoid the im-"prudence of risking the little character "I had in a way which could add so little "to it, and again applied myself to the "construction of another comedy, on a "plan acknowledged by yourself to be "new and striking, which, having licked "into something like shape, I took care "to tender before your doors were "opened, believing in such case no "danger of a disappointment could be "against me in point of time. But by "some strange fatality, I was never, it "seems, to make a right judgment with "regard to the theatre. Your letter of "the 10th gave me to understand this be-"lief of mine was ill-grounded, and your "other letter of Wednesday the 14th is "full of resentment that a man of the "wrong side of fifty should find out an-"other year of waiting was too large a "tax on a short term for any man of com-"mon sense to pay, which was the "amount of mine to you, expressed in the "most complaisant terms in my power "to use; and if some little impatience "had been visible at bottom, allow me to "ask you, Sir, whether it would not have "been nobler in you to have imputed it "to the peevishness incident to all man-"kind under disappointments and dif-"ficulties, and whether in your happy "situation you could not very well have "afforded to do so. For the rest, Sir, "you must be convinced that I cannot be "so absurd as to put my time into the "scale against yours *or even your very* "*harlequin's*. I was in fact desirous to "avoid a farther éclaircissement which I "foresaw would administer no consola-"tion to me; and as to the favours you "have done me, and the trouble you have "bestowed upon me, nothing that has "happened, or can happen, shall ever "put me on diminishing their value, or "explaining away the duties of acknow-"ledgment incumbent on me for them. "Being still, with truth and sincerity, "Sir, Your most obliged, humble Ser-"vant, J. RALPH." It is characteristic of Mr. Ralph that even in this last appeal for a friendly settlement before open war (for so I apprehend the letter should be

ever, to recount the highest tragic claimants thus affronted by Shakespeare, Fletcher, Shirley, and *Lilliput*. They were Whitehead, Crisp, Francis, Francklin, Glover, Brown, Mallet, Murphy, and Dodsley: for denying whose higher attractiveness to the Shakespeares and Fletchers, nay, for preferring even the comic to that tragic Lilliput,* the public seems a better object of attack than the manager. When, some years afterwards, Horace Walpole joined the cry, this had sarcastic admission. "Garrick is "treating the town as it de- "serves," he said, *"and likes to "be treated:* with scenes, fireworks, "and his own writing. A good "new play I never expect to see "more; nor have seen since the "*Provoked Husband*, which came "out when I was at school."** Was it Garrick's crime, without

good new plays, to make the venture of good old ones?

In truth, looking fairly at his theatrical management, with the light his published *Correspondence* has thrown upon it, it was a great improvement, in all generous and liberal points, on those which preceded it. Booth treated writers of Anne much more scurvily than the writers of George the Second were treated by Garrick. "Booth "often declared," says his biographer, "in public company, "that he and his partners lost "money by new plays; and that, "if he were not obliged to it, he "would seldom give his consent "to perform one of them." Garrick transposed and altered often; but he never forced upon the unhappy author of a tragedy a change in the religion of his hero, nor told a dramatist of good esteem that he had better have turned to an honest and laborious calling, nor complacently prided himself on *choaking singing birds* when his stern negative had silenced a young aspirant. Those were the achievements of manager Cibber. Garrick was at all times fonder than needful of his own importance, it is true: but society has no right to consent to even the nominal depression, in the so-called social scale, of a man whose calling exacts no common accomplishments, and then resent the self-exaggeration unwholesomely begotten on its own injustice. When Junius took offence at the player whom dukes

1759.
Æt. 31.

---

taken), he cannot suppress his joer about the harlequins. For farther very pleasant illustration of the subject of this chapter see Mr. Percy Fitzgerald's *Life of Garrick*, i. 367-89 (1870).

  * Most happily did Goldsmith himself, a few months later, ridicule these tragedies as "good, instructive, moral "sermons enough," which a theatre-goer might turn to much profit. "There," he says, "I learn several great truths: as, "that it is impossible to see into the ways "of futurity; that punishment always at- "tends the villain; that love is the fond "soother of the human breast; that we "should not resist heaven's will, for in "resisting heaven's will, heaven's will is "resisted: with several other sentiments "equally new, delicate, and striking." "*Barbarossa* I have read," says Gray, "but I did not cry; at a modern tragedy, "it is sufficient not to laugh." *Works*, iii. 127.

  ** *Collected Letters*, v. 388.

and duchesses tolerated at their table, it was not a matter to waste wit upon, or sarcasm, or scathing eloquence: he simply told the "*Vagabond*" to stick to his pantomimes. Even men of education were known to have pursued Garrick, when on country visits to noblemen of his acquaintance, with dirty clumsily-folded notes, passed amid the ill-concealed laughter of servants to the great man's guest, with the address of "*Mr. David Garrick, Player.*" It asked for a strength which Garrick did not possess, to disregard this vulgar folly; it wounded him where he was known to be weak; it tempted him to those self-assertions which imply the failure of self-reliance; it poisoned his perfect faith in all who were not solely governed by his will; and it blinded him to the ridicule with which even dependents listened to his public distress on the mornings of crowded rehearsals, that to decline some ambassador's proffered courtesies made him wretched, but prior promises to countess dowagers must be kept.

1759.
Æt. 31.

A satisfaction of this kind was afforded to Mr. Ralph, when, in the season ('57-'58) of this the appearance of his pamphlet, the outraged manager, laughing heartily at all authors' complaints and attacks, and tearing up their rebellious pamphlets with as elaborate carelessness as he would the card of a duke, lord, judge, or bishop, to strike awe and admiration into bystanders, did yet, most laboriously and most clumsily, *bring out* Doctor Smollett, in a piece altogether unworthy of his genius.[*] The concession was appropriately followed by production of the *Agis* of Mr. Home; not without reason, by *Douglas*-loving Gray, cried over for its exclusively modern Greek, and compared to "an antique statue "painted white and red, frizzed "and dressed in a negligée made "by a Yorkshire mantua-ma-"ker."[**]   Then, failure and laughter repaying this pains and warmth, the cold fit came violently back; and in the season of '58 and '59 the wrongs of Robert Dodsley and Arthur Murphy, the bereaved *Cleone* and deserted *Orphan of China*, were the talk of the town.   The topic seemed to force itself on one who was delivering in a protest against the wrongs of men of letters; and with the *Enquiry into Polite Learning* appeared these remarks, in a chapter devoted to the stage.[***]

"Our poet's performance must "undergo a process truly chemi-"cal, before it is presented to "the public.   It must be tried in "the manager's fire, strained "through a licenser, and suffer "from repeated corrections till it

[*] *The Reprisals, or the Tars of Old England,* written and acted to animate the people against the French; a poor comedy, or rather farce, but containing some capital sailor-talk, and inimitable touches of caricature.

[**] Murphy's *Garrick*, I. 317. See also Gray's *Works*, III. 161, 188, &c.

[***] Chap. XII.

"may be a mere *caput mortuum* "when it arrives before the "public. It may be said that we "have a sufficient number of "plays upon our theatres already, "and therefore there is no need "of new ones. But are they suf- "ficiently good? And is the "credit of our age nothing? "Must our present times pass "away unnoticed by posterity? "If these are matters of indif- "ference, it then signifies no- "thing, whether we are to be "entertained with the actor or "the poet, with fine sentiments "or painted canvas; or whether "the dancer or the carpenter be "constituted master of the cere- "monies. How is it at present? "Old pieces are revived, and "scarcely any new ones admitted. "The actor is ever in our eye, "the poet seldom permitted to "appear; and the stage, instead "of serving the people, is made "subservient to the interests of "avarice. Getting a play on "even in three or four years, is a "privilege reserved only for the "happy few who have the arts of "courting the Manager as well as "the Muse: who have adulation "to please his vanity, powerful "patrons to support their merit, "or money to indemnify disap- "pointment. Our Saxon ances- "tors had but one name for a "wit and a witch. I will not dis- "pute the propriety of uniting "those characters then: but the "man who, under the present "discouragements, ventures to "write for the stage, whatever

"claim he may have to the ap- "pellation of a wit, at least has "no right to be called a con- "juror."

It is impossible to think — 1759. Goldsmith wholly justified Æt. 31. in this, and there are passages of sneering and silly objection to Shakespeare in immediate con- nection with it which very pain- fully reveal the temper in which it was written; but it is yet un- questionable that the feeling pervading equally the extract and Mr. Ralph's pamphlet was now becoming general with the literary class, and tended greatly to embitter the successes of Garrick's later life. In connec- tion with it, at the same time, a regret will always arise, remem- bering the differences of a Gold- smith and a Ralph, that the lively irritable actor should have been indiscriminate in the resentments it provoked, and unable, in any instance, to conceive a better ac- tuating motive than the envy his prosperity had excited. Thomas Davies tells us, that when, some- where about the time of his con- nection with the *Bee*, Goldsmith sought to obtain, what a strug- gling man of letters was thought to have some claim to, the vacant secretaryship of the Society of A ts, Garrick made answer to a personal application for his vote that "Mr. Goldsmith having taken "pains to deprive himself of his "assistance by an unprovoked "attack upon his management of "the theatre in his *Present State* "*of Learning*, it was impossible "he could lay claim to any re-"commendation from him."* Davies adds, that "Goldsmith, "instead of making an "apology for his conduct, "either from misinforma-"tion or misconception, bluntly "replied, 'In truth he had spoken "'his mind, and believed what "'he said was very right.' The "manager dismissed him with "civility."

1799.
Æt. 31.

The manager might with wisdom have done more. The blunt reply, in a generous man's interpretation, should at least have blunted the fancied wrong. It is painful to think that neither of these famous men, whose cheerful gaieties of heart were natural bonds for a mutual sympathy and strong alliance, should throughout life have wholly lost the sense of this first unlucky meeting. As Goldsmith himself removed from the second edition of the *Polite Learning* much that had given Garrick most offence and in the ordinary copies it is now no longer found, it may more freely be admitted that the grounds of offence were not altogether imaginary. Indeed, besides what I have quoted, there were incidental expressions yet more likely to breed resentment in a sensitive, quick nature. "I "am not at present writing for a "party," said Goldsmith, "but "above theatrical connections in "every sense of the expression. "I have no particular spleen "against the fellow who sweeps

"the stage with the besom, or "the hero who brushes it with "his train. It were a matter of "indifference to me, whether our "heroines are in keeping, or "our candle-snuffers burn their "fingers, did not such make a "great part of public care and "polite conversation. Our ac-"tors assume all that state off the "stage which they do on it; and, "to use an expression borrowed "from the green-room, every "one is *up* in his part. I am "sorry to say it, they seem to "forget their real characters."* With sorrow is it also to be said, that here the writer was manifestly wrong. Mr. Ralph's "imple-"ments" and "harlequins" were not more tasteful and considerate than this jeering tone.

There is no intellectual art so peculiarly circumstanced as that of the actor. If, in the hurried glare which surrounds him, each vanity and foible that he has comes forth in strong relief, it is hard to grudge him the better incidents to that brilliant lot for which he pays so dearly. His triumphs had need be bright and dazzling, for their fires are spent as soon as kindled; his enjoy-

* Davies's *Life of Garrick*, II. 149.

* The same feeling and spirit are perceptible in Letter LXXXV. of the *Citizen of the World*. "How will your surprise, my "Fum, increase when told that though "the law holds them as vagabonds, many "of them earn more than a thousand a "year! You are amazed! There is "cause for amazement. A vagabond with "a thousand a year is indeed a curiosity "in nature; a wonder far surpassing "the flying-fish, petrified crab, or tra-"velling lobster."

ments intense, for of all mental influences they wither soonest. He may plant in infinite hearts the seeds of goodness, ideal beauty, and practical virtue; but with their fruits his name will not be remembered, or remembered only as a name. And surely, if he devotes a genius that might command success in any profession, to one whose rewards, if they come at all, must be immediate as the pleasure and instruction it diffuses, it is a short-sighted temper that would eclipse the pleasure and deny the rewards.

The point of view at this time taken by Goldsmith was in fact obscured by his own unlucky fortunes; but the injustice he shrunk from committing in the case of the prosperous painter, Mr. Reynolds, he should not thus carelessly have inflicted on the prosperous actor, Mr. Garrick. If to neither artist might be conceded the claim of creative genius, at least the one might have claimed to be a painter of portraits, even as the other was. Uneasy relations, indeed, which only exist between author and actor, have had a manifest tendency at all times unfairly to disparage the actor's intellectual claims, and to set any of the inferior arts above them. Nevertheless, the odds might be made more even. The deepest and rarest beauties of poetry are those which the actor cannot grasp; but, in the actor's startling triumphs, whether of movement,

gesture, look, or tone, the author has no great share. Thus, were accounts fairly struck with the literary class, a Garrick might honestly be left between the gentle and grand superiority of a Shakespeare on the one hand, who, from the heights of his immeasurable genius, smiles down help and fellowship upon him; and the eternal petulance and pretensions of an Arthur Murphy on the other, who, from the round of a ladder to which of himself he never could have mounted, looks down with ludicrous contempt on what Mr. Ralph would call the "imple-"ments" of his elevation.

1759.
Æt. 31.

Let me here add, that since this portion of my book was first written, I have become the possessor of unprinted letters which not only place Garrick in a more favourable light than his biographers generally have shown him in, but suggest a tenderness of consideration for what was defective in his character, even greater than I have ventured to claim for him. In the actual path of life he crossed Goldsmith so often, that perhaps the reader will not think it a censurable digression, if in some few additional pages I give him tidings he has not before seen of a man so famous, and whose gay, bright, glancing little figure, reappears with such frequent and pleasant cheerfulness in every social picture of the time.

David Garrick was, as all of us know, the son of a recruiting captain whose family originally was French (the name was *Garrique*), and from whom he appears to have inherited his little figure, his expressive eye, his happy buoyancy of spirit, and restless vivacity of motion. His biographers describe him acting Serjeant Kite at a private play when he was eleven years old; and the first of these letters I possess, written to his father when he was fifteen, marks exactly that bent of his tastes in describing "a very pretty woman, "only she squints a little, as Cap-"tain Brazen says in the *Recruit-*"*ing Officer.*" His father was then stationed at Gibraltar, having taken the place of an officer who had occasion to return, and whose full pay Captain Garrick's increasing family made it desirable that he should exchange for his own half-pay, even at the sacrifice of a lengthened exile from his home at Lichfield. What Johnson said of his old friend, the year after his death, stands out on the very face of this correspondence. "Garrick, "sir, was a very good man, the "cheerfullest man of his age. He "began the world with a great "hunger for money. The son of "a half-pay officer, he was bred "in a family whose study was to "make fourpence do as much as "others made fourpence half-"penny do. But when he had got, "money he was very liberal."*

1759. Æt. 31.

In no querulous or complaining spirit, the boy's letters yet show us, from year to year, the straitened circumstances of that otherwise happy home. Their "accoutrements," as, in the necessity of describing the family wardrobe to his father, he prefers dramatically to express himself, are shabby. Another year, his mother's health is not strong, and wine has to be purchased for her. Another, and he is himself showing off quite grand at a fine house in the neighbourhood, on the strength of two half-crowns which Mr. Walmsley has given him to bestow on the servants. Then, sisters Lenny and Jenny (Magdalen and Jane) want small sums to buy lace for their head-dresses, or how otherwise distinguish them from the vulgar madams? And at length he has to inform his dear papa that he is himself turned quite philosopher; but yet, to show that he is not vain of it, he protests that he would gladly "get shut" of the philosopher's characteristic, to wit, a ragged pair of breeches (especially as he has lately had a pair of silver breeches-buckles presented to him); wherefore, if the gallant captain would cure his son of philosophic contemplation, the only way will be to send some handsome thing for a waistcoat and breeches as aforesaid. "They tell me velvet "is very cheap at Gibraltar. "Amen, and so be it!"

One fancies the smile and tear together starting to the father's

* *Boswell*, vii. 262.

face as he reads little David's letters; and if, over that last, the tear lingered a little, its successor of a fortnight's later date brought happier thoughts again. Here the young letter-writer broke off into talk about art and painters, saying suddenly, that there existed one piece of Le Grout's (a miniature-painter of that day) which he valued above all the pieces of Zeuxis or Apelles; and it gave him more pleasure, he would affirm, to have one glance of that than to look a whole day at the finest picture in the world; nay, it had this effect upon him, that whenever he looked upon it he fancied himself at Gibraltar, saw the Spaniards, and sometimes mounted garrison. The portrait was then in his hand, he added, yet he could not satisfactorily describe it. "It is the figure of "a gentleman, and I suppose "military by his dress; I think "Le Grout told me his name was "one Captain Peter Garrick; per- "haps as you are in the army "you may know him, he is pretty "jolly, and I believe not very "tall." Is not the letter a bit of comedy in itself, a piece of character and feeling such as Farquhar might have written?

Meanwhile there has been talk of the University for the young letter-writer, which again and again recedes under pressure of wants more craving, but still is not wholly given up, when, on the good Gilbert Walmsley's suggestion, he avails himself of

an advertisement in the *Gentleman's Magazine** for ever memorable to all students of our English tongue, which informs him that "At Edial, near Litch- "field in Staffordshire, "young gentlemen are boarded, "and taught the Latin and Greek "languages, by SAMUEL JOHN- "SON." Here he remains but a very few months; which suffice nevertheless to break up the teacher's establishment, to dissipate the scholar's hopes either of army-chaplaincy or country-rectory, and to bring up both to London in search of other fortune. They separate on arriving there, in what altered circumstances to meet again!

1759.
ÆT. 31.

Another interval of some five years has seen little David a student of Lincoln's-inn, a lounger about the theatres, a mourner within the same year for the deaths of his father and mother, and, on the receipt of a legacy of a thousand pounds from an uncle who had been in the wine trade in Lisbon, a partner with his elder brother Peter as wine merchant of London and Lichfield. Peter, born six years before David, was an honest worthy man, who according to Boswell strongly resembled David in countenance, though of more sedate and placid manners, and of whom Johnson believed that if he had cultivated all the arts of gaiety as much as David he might have been as

* For June and July, 1736.

brisk and lively;* but in reality of very formal cut, anything but brisk or lively, not in the least a cultivator of gaiety, on the contrary methodical and precise in the extreme, and always objecting to his brother's hankering for the stage, even from those youthful days when the sprightly lad of fourteen underwent sharp lectures from his grave senior of twenty, on the impropriety of getting up theatrical squibs, or writing comic verses against the ladies of Lichfield. Davies, Murphy, Galt, and Boaden, all tell us that their altercations became at last so frequent, that in 1740, by the intercession of mutual friends, their partnership was dissolved; but this I can now show to be a mistake. They were partners to the close of that year, though Peter even then had heard painful rumours of the younger member of the firm being frequently seen in company with an actor and playhouse manager, Mr. Giffard of Goodman's-fields. They were in partnership in the summer of the following year, when Peter, on coming to London, found his brother subject to unaccountable fits of depression, abstraction, and lowness of spirits; warned him against play-actors and play-managers (notwithstanding advantages gained to the firm by Mr. Giffard having recommended it to supply the Bedford coffee-house, "one of the best in

1759.
———
Æt. 31.

London"); and, happily for himself, did not know that his associate in a respectable business had already, impelled by a secret passion he dared not openly divulge, gone privately to Ipswich with that very manager Giffard, and under the name of Lyddal had played in *Oronoko* and the *Orphan*, and had performed Sir Harry Wildair and our old friend Captain Brazen. They were partners still, as that year went on, though the business had fallen very low, and Foote always remembered Davy, as he said in his malicious way, living in Durham-yard with three quarts of vinegar in the cellar, calling himself a wine merchant. They continued even to be partners, when at last, on the evening of the 19th October 1741, the curtain rose on the performance of *Richard the Third* in the theatre at Goodman's-fields.

The tragic stage was then sunk very low. Betterton had been dead more than thirty years, Booth had quitted the profession fourteen years before, Wilks was no longer one of its ornaments, and even the traditions of that brilliant time now chiefly lived with Cibber. When that veteran tried his hand at tragedy, he is careful to tell us what pains he took to ground himself on some great actor of the days of his youth, to the minutest copy of look, gesture, gait, speech, and "every motion of him;" nor does it appear that at this time any higher impression of the

* *Boswell*, vi. 95.

tragic art prevailed. In comedy, genius might yet be seen; it was something more than tradition that shone in Mrs. Clive, Mrs. Pritchard, and Mrs. Woffington;[*] Cibber still occasionally (and to good audiences) played one of his comic parts,[**] Quin's Falstaff and Fondlewife were not yet passed away, and originality, by those who had a taste for it in no very tasteful form, might be enjoyed in Harper, Neale, Hippisley, Ben Johnson, Woodward, and Macklin. But the lovers were now bellowed forth by Ryan, Bridgewater and Walker stormed in the tyrants, and the heroes belonged exclusively to Milward and Delane, except when Quin, turning from what he could to what he could not do, mouthed forth Othello, Richard, or Lear. In such a night of tragedy, it was with the sudden effulgence as of new-risen day that Garrick burst upon the scene. It is not for one who can speak but from report of others, to pretend to describe the effect upon those who actually witnessed it. But let me borrow the description of a sixth-form scholar of Westminster-school, who saw Garrick's acting at the age most impressible to all such emotions, and saw it side by side with the style of acting it displaced; who remem- bered it as vividly to the close as at the opening of life; and who recalled it in language which seems to vouch for the truth and exactness of its record.

1759.
Æt. 31.

The scene is Covent-garden, for the time is nearly five years advanced from the first night at Goodman's-fields; and the play, which is Rowe's *Fair Penitent*, is to be played by Quin and Ryan in Horatio and Altamont; by Mrs. Cibber, Mrs. Pritchard, and Garrick, in Calista, Lavinia, and Lothario. The curtain rises, and Quin presents himself. His dress is a green velvet coat, embroidered down the seams, an enormous full-bottomed periwig, rolled stockings, and high-heeled square-toed shoes. He goes through the scene with very little variation of cadence. In a deep full tone, accompanied, by a sawing kind of action which has more of the senate than the stage in it, he rolls out his heroics with an air of dignified indifference that seems to disdain the plaudits bestowed on him. Then enters Mrs. Cibber, and in a key high-pitched, but sweet withal, sings, or rather recitatives, Rowe's lines: but her voice so extremely wants contrast, that though it does not wound the ear it wearies it; when she has once recited two or three speeches, the man-

* Horace Walpole (who however was seldom a just, and never an indulgent critic of theatres) was thus writing to Mann three days (22nd October 1741) after Garrick's first appearance at Goodman's-fields. "I have been two or three "times at the play, very unwillingly; for "nothing was ever so bad as the actors, "except the company. There is much "vogue in a Mrs. Woffington; a bad ac- "tress, but she has life." *Coll. Lett.* I. 84.
** "Old Cibber plays to-night, and all "the world will be there." Walpole to Mann, Dec. 3, 1741. *Coll. Lett.* I. 98.

ner of every succeeding one is known; and the hearer listens as to a long old legendary ballad of innumerable stanzas, every one of which is chanted to the same tune, eternally chiming without variation or relief.   Mrs. Pritchard follows; and something of the habit of nature, caught from comedy, enters the scene with her.   She has more change of tone, more variety both of action and expression; and the comparison is decidedly in her favour. "But when," continues Richard Cumberland, for it is he whom I quote, "after a long and eager "expectation, I first beheld little "Garrick, then young and light "and alive in every muscle and "in every feature, come bound-"ing on the stage and pointing at "the wittol Altamont and heavy-"paced Horatio—Heavens! what "a transition! it seemed as if a "whole century had been stepped "over in the passage of a single "scene; old things were done "away, and a new order at once "brought forward, bright and "luminous, and clearly destined "to dispel the barbarisms of a "tasteless age, too long super-"stitiously devoted to the illu-"sions of imposing declama-"tion."*

Such was the actor whose Richard first blazed forth on the night of the 19th October 1741, to the sudden amazement of all whom sympathy or chance had brought to Goodman's-fields, and

1759.
Æt. 31.

* *Memoirs*, i. 80-1.

the abiding delight of the few who had the taste or powers of appreciation of this Westminster scholar. But if any such were present, they have made no sign for us, and the glories of that night are passed away.   What survives of it, and alone I can exhibit, are the fears that dashed the triumph; the misgivings inseparable from the calling on which little David had entered; the sense as of a shameful forfeiture of station, which had lowered the son of a marching-captain into a mean stage-player; and the trembling deference and deprecation with which tidings had to be conveyed to the sedate and respectable Lichfield wine-merchant, that his younger brother had taken that fatal step in life, which at no distant day was to associate him with whatever the land contained illustrious by birth or genius, to open to him such instant means of giving innocent pleasure to great masses of his fellow-creatures as any other human being has perhaps never enjoyed, to load himself with wealth, to lift above necessity all who were related to him, and to make the name they bore a pleasant and long-remembered word all over England.

One of the audience on that 19th of October was a staid, elderly gentleman of Lichfield, one Mr. Swynfen; and the letter which he wrote on the following day to "Mr. Peter Garwick" lies now before me, with post-mark corresponding to its date of the

20th of October 1741. Many there are, this good old citizen does not question, who, because their fathers were called gentlemen, or themselves the first so called, will think it a disgrace and a scandal that the child of an old friend should endeavour to get an honest livelihood, and is not content to live in a scanty manner all his life because his father was a gentleman. But Mr. Swynfen thinks he knows "Mr. "Garwick" well enough to be convinced that he has not the same sentiments; and he knows better of his friend's judgment than to suppose him partaking of the prejudices of other country friends of theirs, who have been most used to theatrical performances in town-halls &c. by strollers, and will be apt to imagine the highest pitch a man can arrive at on the stage is about that exalted degree of heroism which they two, in old days at Lichfield, used to laugh and cry at in "the Herberts and "the Hallams;" but, as he does not doubt but that Mr. Peter will soon hear "my good friend Da-"vid Garwick performed last "night at Goodman's Fields "theatre," for fear he should hear any false or malicious account that may perhaps be disagreeable to him, "I will give "you the truth," says the good old gentleman plunging into it, "which much pleased me. *I was* "*there*, and was witness to a most "general applause He gain'd in "the character of Richard the

"Third; for I believe their was "not one in the House that was "not in Raptures, and I heard "several Men of Judgment "declare it their Opinion "that nobody ever ex-"celled Him in that Part; and "that they were surprised, with "so peculiar a Genius, how it "was possible for Him to keep "off the Stage so long." It is to be hoped that Mr. Peter was able to read thus far with reasonable patience; but, if he had opened his old friend's letter first (as David, who no doubt suggested it, seems to have reckoned on his doing), one may imagine the nervous haste with which he now took up another letter that had travelled to him by the same post, superscribed in the well-known hand of brother David himself.

1750.
____
Æt. 31.

It began by telling "Dear "Peter" that he had received his shirt safe, and was now to tell him what he supposes he may already have heard; but before he lets him into the affair, it was proper to premise some things that the writer may appear less culpable in his brother's opinion than he might otherwise do. He has made an exact estimate of his stock of wine, and what money he has out at interest; and finds that since he has been a wine-merchant he has run out near four hundred pounds, and, trade not increasing, he became very sensible some way must be thought of to redeem it. Then out ventures a weakness never before confessed. "My mind (as "you must know) has been al-"ways inclined to y° Stage, nay "so strongly so that all "my Illness and lowness "of Spirits was owing to "my want of resolution to tell "you my thoughts when here. "Finding at last both my Inclina-"tion and Interest requir'd some "new way of Life, I have chose "y° most agreeable to myself, "and though I know you will be "much displeas'd at me, yet I "hope when you shall find that I "may have y° genius of an Actor "without y° vices you will think "less severe of me, and not be "asham'd to own me for a Bro-"ther." After this appeal to the fraternal sympathies he falls back on business again. He is willing to agree to anything Peter shall propose about the wine. He will take a thorough survey of the vaults, and making what Peter has at Lichfield part of the stock, will either send him his share, or settle it any other way he shall propose. Then, at last, out comes the awful fact which can no longer be withheld; and then, as suddenly on the heels of it, as if ashamed of the brief show of courage he had made, the wine business again! "Last "night I played Richard y° Third "to y° Surprise of Every Body, "and as I shall make very near "£300 per annum by it, and as it "is really what I doat upon, *I* "*am resolv'd to pursue it.* I believe "I shall have Bower's money, "which when I have it shall go

1759.
Æt. 31.

"towards my part of the wine "you have at Lichfield. Pray "write me an answer imme-"diately. I am, Dr Brother, y^rs "sincerely D. GARRICK. I have "a farce (y° *Lying Valet*) coming "out at Drury Lane."

Ah, poor David! a brother who has the charge of a respectable business, who is the eldest of a family, including two sisters, that have yet to hold up their heads among the gentlefolks at Lich-field, who has to bear the up-braidings of an uncle too pros-perous in trade to have any toleration for those who do *not* prosper, and who has never him-self done anything to discredit your father's memory and red coat, is not propitiated so easily. Peter's reply is now only to be inferred from the prompt re-joinder it wrung from David, bearing date the 27th October, and too plainly revealing to us all that both brother and sisters had suffered from the dreadful news. He begins by assuring his dear brother that the uneasiness he has received at his letter is inexpressible. However, it was a shock he expected, and had guarded himself against as well as he could. Nay, the love he sincerely bore his brother Peter, together with the prevailing ar-guments he had made use of, would have been enough to over-throw his own strongest resolu-tions, did not necessity (a very pressing advocate) on his side convince him that he was not so much to blame as Peter seemed

image

not

available

the Third, which brings crowded audiences every night, and Mr. Giffard returns the service he has done him very amply.

1759.
Æt. 31.

However (as though again in dread that he may be showing too little regard to his objectors), let "dear Peter" send him a letter next post, and he'll give a full answer, not having time enough at present. He has not a debt of twenty shillings upon him; "so in that," he concludes, "be very easy. I am "sorry my sisters are under such "uneasinesses, and, as I really "love both them and you, will "ever make it my study to ap- "pear your affectionate Brother, "D. Garrick."

The post brings back the letter asked for, but as far as ever from the tone desired. Peter still protests, urges, entreats, casts discredit on Giffard, and, while he washes his own hands of the consequences he sees impend-ing, warns David against them with such persevering emphasis, that, but for each day's felt and palpable increase to the actor's unexampled success, it might have gone hard with him in this epistolary war. But how should he now turn back with the in-centives that on the other side urged him on—plebeian Good-man's-fields lighted up with the splendour of Grosvenor-square and St. James's! grand people's coaches jammed up in the nar-row alleys between Temple-bar and Whitechapel! and, though he has not yet been three weeks

on the stage, the very patriots from Whitehall, in the agony of their struggle with Walpole, flocking to that wretched little theatre in the lowest and most vulgar of the suburbs! Has not the Prince's confidant, Mr. Glover, been every night to see him? And, since he wrote last to Lich-field, even grave Mr. Lyttelton has been there, the Prince him-self is daily expected, and he has been praised and encouraged by that fiery young orator Mr. Pitt, who, already reckoned the greatest actor in the House of Commons, has given eager wel-come to an actor reported to be even greater than himself. "Sometimes, at Goodman's-"fields," writes Gray to Chute, "there are a dozen dukes of a "night." *

Shall we wonder, then, that writing again on the 10th of No-vember "to Mr. Garrick at Lich-field Staffordshire," little David, beginning with professions of extreme sorrow that his "Dear "Brother" should still seem so utterly averse to what he was so greatly inclined to, and to what the best judges think he has the greatest genius for, should go on to say that the great, nay, in-credible success and approbation he has met with from the greatest persons in England, had almost made him resolve (though he is

* "Did I tell you about Mr. Gar-"rick, that the town are born-mad after: "there are a dozen dukes of a night at "Goodman's-fields sometimes, and yet "I am still in the opposition." *Works,* II. 185.

sorry to say it, against dear Peter's entreaties) to pursue it, as he shall certainly make a fortune by it if health continues? He then talks of money affairs in the old strain; and as to Giffard, protests that £30 was all he had ever lent that manager in former days, which sum was paid long ago. He adds, that at present he receives from Giffard (though this was a secret) six guineas a week, and was to have a clear benefit, and the benefit was to be very soon, and he had been offered £120 for it, and dear Peter cannot imagine what regard he meets with, and on the occasion of that benefit the pit and boxes are to be put together, and he shall have all his friends (who still continue so though his brother is not to be brought over), and if his brother will only come his lodgings shall cost him nothing. "Mr. Littleton, Mr. Pit, and "Several other Members of Parliament were to see me play "Chamont, in ye *Orphan*, and Mr. "Pit, who is reckon'd ye greatest "Orator in the House of Com-"mons, said I was ye best Actor "ye English Stage had produc'd, "and he sent a Gentleman to me "to let me know he and ye other "Gentlemen would be glad to "see Me. The Prince has heard "so great a Character of me that "we are in daily expectations of "his coming to see me." And so the gossiping, kindly, anxious letter ends, with another entreaty that Peter will let him know what he resolves upon, the writer as-

suring him once more of what the letter very amply exhibits, that it is his greatest desire to continue his "affectionate "Brother, D. Garrick."

But not Pitt, nor Lyttelton, nor Glover, nor the Prince himself, can yet entirely break down the obdurate resolution of Peter, who proves well worthy of his name. There are *some* signs of relenting, nevertheless; as even the rock may yield at last to melting influences. He cannot, of course, save David the pain of feeling that he has inflicted irreparable hurt on the respected mercantile position of Mr. Peter Garrick of Lichfield; but he brings himself to close his letter by saying, that though he never can approve of the stage, yet he will always be David's affectionate brother. Well, for even such scant mercies, the brother is thankful. In the first flush of a success that might well have spurned at every kind of control, the good-hearted little fellow continues as eager to propitiate this formal, unsympathising, intolerant old vendor of claret and sherry, as if he were himself still the hobbledehoy youth of fourteen looking up with timid deference to his revered superior of twenty. Every point of complaint, as if each were the first and not the dozenth time of urging, he meets with respectful argument or loving remonstrance; and, as to the alleged injury to him in his mercantile position, he has now to tell Peter that their uncle, he has it on good authority, will be reconciled to him, "for even the "Merchants say 'tis an "honour to him, not Otherwise. As to hurting you "in yᵉ affairs," he goes on (his letter bears date the 24th Novʳ), "it shall be my constant En-"deavour to promote yʳ welfare "with my all. If you should "want Money, and I have it, you "shall command my whole, and "I know I shall soon be more "able by playing and writing to "do you service than any other "way."

Backed by which honest purposes, may he not again venture to tell his brother that he is very near *quite* resolved to be a player? as he has the best judgment of the best judges, who to a man are of opinion that he shall turn out (nay, they say that already he is) not only the best tragedian but comedian in England. "I would not," he prettily interposes here, "say so much "to any body else; but as this "may somewhat palliate my "folly, you must excuse me. Mr. "Littleton was wᵗʰ Me last Night, "and took me by yᵉ hand and "said, he never saw such play-"ing upon yᵉ English Stage be-"fore." And for other more practical proofs of his success, he tells Peter that he has had great offers from Fleetwood; that they have had finer business than either Drury-lane or Covent-garden; that Mr. Giffard himself had given him yesterday twenty guineas for a ticket; and (for a climax) that next week he designed buying £200 of his stock out of his profits of playing. So, as to the business between them, and the selling off of their joint stock in London, if his brother should want more money than his share comes to he will supply it. In conclusion he admits that the trade is rather better than it was, but, his mind being quite turned another way, he desires to be released from it as soon as possible.

Now, that this was a highly practical, business-like letter, though written by a flighty stage-player, even the obstinately unbelieving Peter appears to have felt. It went, at any rate, straight to the heart of the partnership affairs between them; and, however reluctantly, he would seem to have made up his mind to accept it as the best of a bargain that must be any way a bad one. But one matter he should like to have cleared up. *Had his brother really been playing Harlequin, as reported, before he came out at Goodman's-fields?*

Here was a question to be addressed to a man whom the great and noble were delighting to honour, who was charming the whole town both in comedy and tragedy, nay, who had just come out as an author, and whose farce of the *Lying Valet*, acted (not at Drury-lane, but) at Goodman's-fields six days after the date of his last letter, was taking prodigiously, and was approved of by men of genius, and 'thought the most diverting farce that ever was performed. "I believe you'll "find it read pretty well," he continues, addressing Peter with somewhat more courage than usual, and sending him a copy; "and in performance 'tis a "General Roar from beginning "to end; and I have got as much "Reputation in ye Character of "Sharp, as in any other character "I have perform'd, tho far dif-"ferent from ye others."

Far different, indeed! as different as Romeo from Sir John Brute, as Othello from Fondle-wife, as Richard from Jack Smatter, as Shakespeare's Lear from Colley Cibber's Master Johnny, as eighty-four from fifteen.* Yet even such was the surprising versatility now displayed with consummate ease by this greatest of actors; who alone, of all performers on record, seems to have hit the consummation of the actor's art in being able to drop altogether his own personality. "All the run "is now after Garrick," writes Walpole. "The Duke of Argyll "says he is superior to Better-"ton."*   "We are all wrong, if "this is right," said Quin, decisively. "I' faith, Bra-"cey," said Cibber, taking snuff, and turning to his ancient partner in theatrical glory Mrs. Bracegirdle, "the lad is "clever!"

1741.
Æt. 24.

Justly was Garrick proud of that opinion; for only a year before, the *Apology* had given proof of what a masterly critic Cibber was, and all the old man's prejudices and tastes went strongly counter to the admission thus wrung from him. That it *was* given, however, and in still stronger terms, may fairly be inferred from what Garrick goes on to say to his brother, in this letter dated the 22nd December. "You perhaps would be glad to "know what parts I have play'd. "King Rich^d, Jack Smatter in "*Pamela*, Clody *Fop's Fortune*, "Lothario *Fair Penitent*, Chamont "*Orphan*, Ghost *Hamlet*, and shall "soon be ready in Bays in y^e "*Rehearsal*, and in ye part of "Othello, Both which I believe "will do Me and Giffard great "service. I have had great suc-"cess in all, and 'tis not yet

---

* "For his benefit on the 18th of "March," says Mr. Boaden, "he amazed "the town by repeating" (he had first played it on the preceding 22nd of February) "after his performance of King "Lear, his Master Johnny, a lad of fif-"teen, in the *Schoolboy*. The farce was "written by Colley Cibber, who was still "living; and he might, and very probably "did, see that wonderful junction of "eighty-four and fifteen by the same ac-"tor." *Memoir*, VII—VIII (*Gar. Cor.*) "The "stage," said the play-bills of the night, "will be formed into an amphitheatre, "where servants will be allowed to keep "places." *Account of the Stage*, IV. 34.

* The whole passage is too characteristic not to be given. "All the run is "now after Garrick, a wine-merchant, "who is turned player, at Goodman's-"fields. He plays all parts, and is a very "good mimic. His acting I have seen, "and may say to you, who will not tell it "again here, I see nothing wonderful in "it; but it is heresy to say so: the Duke "of Argyll says he is superior to Better-"ton." *Coll. Lett.* I. 189.

"determin'd whether I play Tra-
"gedy or Comedy best. Old
"Cibber has spoke with y⁰
        "Greatest Commendation
 _1759_ "of my Acting." Of course
Æt. 31. the reader has observed
that the grave question as to
Harlequin has not been answered. But it creeps into the
letter before its close. "As to
"playing a Harlequin, 'tis quite
"false. Yates * last season was
"taken very ill, and was not able
"to begin y⁰ Entertainment; so
"I put on y⁰ Dress, and did two
"or three scenes for him, but
"Nobody knew it but him and
"Giffard. I know it has been
"said I play'd Harlequin at
"Covent Garden, but 'tis quite
"false." With which imperfect
explanation Peter's ruffled dignity had to compose itself, as
best it might.

The anticipation of a triumph
in Bayes proved thoroughly well
founded. After his Bayes there
was no disputing the predominance he had reached. To the
roar of laughter and delight at
its imitations, what still remained
of the old school came tumbling
down irrecoverably. "Heresy,"
growled Quin;* "Reformation,"
cried Garrick; and the smartness
of the retort showed off his
pretensions also as a man of wit.
Noblemen had him to their
houses; Pope came out of his
retirement to see him play; the
great Mr. Murray, leader of the
King's-bench, forgot his briefs
and his politics to entertain him
at supper in Lincoln's-inn-fields;
ladies fell in love with him; he
had to write to Lichfield to protest he was not going to be married; and if, in the last letter I
shall quote from this remarkable
collection, and which is dated
within less than six months from
the first I have quoted, he refers
to some of these distinctions and
compliments with a modest and
manly pride, let us admit that
some such set-off was needed to
all the bitter mortifications his
brother Peter had been heaping
upon him, and that while he re-

---

* Then a brother-actor at Goodman's-
fields, who afterwards married the celebrated actress, his second wife, for whom
Goldsmith, as will hereafter be seen,
had the highest admiration. The occasion was, no doubt, when Yates in
the preceding March had to appear with
Miss Hippsley, a Columbine, in a new
pantomime called "*Harlequin Student;
"or, the Fall of Pantomime with the Restora-
"tion of the Drama*, the whole to con-
"clude with a representation of Shake-
"speare's Monument as lately erected."
Some Account of the English Stage (Bath,
1832), III. 641.

* "Pooh! pooh!" exclaimed that old
stage despot. "This Garrick is a new
"religion. Whitfield was followed for a
"time, but they'll all come to church
"again." It was the "Bayes" which gave
Quin mortal offence. Quin was not himself among the actors who were ridiculed,
but he took to himself the laughter at
others who were in fact *his* imitators and
disciples. "Delane," says Murphy, "was
"at the head of his profession. He was
"tall and comely, had a clear and strong
"voice, but was a mere declaimer. Gar-
"rick began with him. He retired to the
"upper part of the stage, and drawing
"his left arm across his breast, rested his
"right elbow on it, raising a finger to his
"nose; and then came forward in a
"stately gait, nodding his head as he ad-
"vanced, and in the exact tone of Delane,
"spoke," &c. &c. *Life*, I. 53. And see
Davies, *Life*, I. 17-8.

mains victor in the epistolary duel he sings no strained or excessive song of triumph. "The "favor I meet with from yᵉ "Greatest men," he writes to his brother on the 19th of April, "has made me far from repent-"ing of my choice. I am very "intimate with Mr. Glover, who "will bring out a Tragedy next "winter upon my accᵗ. Twice I "have sup'd wᵗʰ yᵉ Great Mr. "Murray, Counsellʳ, and shall "wᵗʰ Mr. Pope, by his Introduc-"tion. I sup'd with yᵉ Mr. Lit-"tleton, yᵉ Prince's Favourite, "last Thursday night, and that "with yᵉ highest Civility and "complaisance. He told me he "never knew what Acting was "till I appeared, and said I was "only born to act wᵗ Shake-"spear writ. These things daily "occurring give me Great Plea-"sure. I din'd with Lᵈ Hallifax "and Lᵈ Sandwich, two very in-"genious Noblemen, yesterday, "and am to dine at Lᵈ Hallifax's "next Sunday with Lᵈ Chester-"field. I have the Pleasure of "being very intimate, too, with "Mr. Hawkins Browne of Bur-"ton.* In short, I believe no-"body (as an Actor) was ever "more caress'd, and my Charac-"ter as a private Man makes 'em "more desirous of my "Company. (All this *entre* "*nous*, as one Brothʳ to an-"other.) I am not fix'd for next "year, but shall certainly be at "yᵉ Other End of yᵉ Town. I "am offered 500 guineas and a "Clear Benefit, or part of yᵉ "Management."

'759.— Æt. 31.

Here, then, I leave him, rapidly on his way to the other end of town, manager in expectancy already, the architect in six months of a fortune which went on increasing for thirty-six years, now as always the darling of the great,* and a taster by anticipation of the bitters as well as the sweets of the cup so plentifully

---

* The author, among other things, of *A Pipe of Tobacco* (the original of the *Rejected Addresses, Odes and Addresses*, &c. &c.), which Goldsmith praises deservedly in his *Beauties of English Poetry*, not on the ground that the parody is ridiculous, but that the imitation is excellent. "I am "told," he remarks, "that he had no "good original manner of his own, yet "we see how well he succeeds when he "turns an Imitator." i. 361. Johnson thought him the best "converser" he had ever met. *Mrs. Piozzi*, 173. A good illustration of Goldsmith's remark is afforded by what Pope so sensibly says (*Spence's Anecdotes*, 157-158): "Browne is "an excellent copyist; and those who "take it ill of him are very much in the "wrong. They are very strongly man-"nered, and perhaps could not write so "well if they were not so; but still 'tis "a fault that deserves the being pointed "out."

* "I dined to-day at Garrick's," writes Horace Walpole to Bentley (August 15, 1755): "there were the Duke of Grafton, "Lord and Lady Rochford, Lady Holder-"ness, the crooked Mostyn, and Dabreu "the Spanish minister; two regents, of "which one is lord chamberlain, the other "groom of the stole; and the wife of a "secretary of state. This is being sur "*un assez bon ton* for a player! Don't "you want to ask me how I like him? "Do want, and I will tell you.—I like "*her* exceedingly; her behaviour is all "sense, and all sweetness too. I don't "know how, he does not improve so fast "upon me: there is a great deal of parts, "and vivacity, and variety, but there is a "great deal too of mimicry and burlesque." *Coll. Lett.* iii. 139.

filled for him. For those re-proaches of his brother's had a sting to be remembered when his brother's outraged dig-nity had been long for-gotten. The latter we have seen sensibly assuaged even in the letters quoted; and its conclusion and moral might be yet more pointedly drawn out of others of later date in the same collection, which show Mr. Peter Garrick solely indebted to the actor for retrieval of his shattered fortune, a successful suppliant for favours over and over again conferred on him, and finally indebted to no less a friend and patron of David's than the Duke of Devonshire for "the finger that lifted" himself "out of those cursed wine-"vaults."   But notwithstanding all this, very correctly did Pe-ter's first shock of horror on learning that David had become a player, reflect a feeling which others used throughout David's life to gall and to humiliate him; which, while it could not shut against him the favours of the great, for that reason more bit-terly exposed him to the malice and insult of the little; which threw him into uneasy relations with men of his own social sta-tion; obscured too often his bet-ter nature; and remains for us the clue by which, if we would judge him favourably, we may unravel what appears least con-sistent in his character. I have had the less scruple in giving at some length, therefore, even to

*1759.
Æt. 31.*

the temporary interruption of my narrative, that critical pas-sage of his life which till now has never been authentically told.

CHAPTER III.

Overtures from Smollett and Mr. Newbery.
1759—1760.

BUT, at the door of Mr. Oliver Goldsmith, Doctor Smollett and Mr. Newbery have been waiting us all this while, and neither of them belonged to that leisurely class which can very well afford to wait. The Doctor was full of energy and movement always, as one of his own headlong heroes; and who remembers not the philanthropic bookseller in the *Vicar of Wakefield*, the good-na-tured man with the red-pimpled face, who had no sooner alighted but he was in haste to be gone, "for he was ever on business of "the utmost importance, and "was at that time actually com-"piling materials for the history "of one Mr. Thomas Trip." But not on Mr. Thomas Trip's affairs had the child-loving publisher* now ventured up Break-neck-steps; and upon other than the old *Critical* business was the au-thor of *Peregrine Pickle* a visitor in Green-arbour-court. Both had new and important schemes in

* "He called himself their friend," says Doctor Primrose, "but he was the "friend of all mankind .... he had pub-"lished for me against the Deuterogamists "of the age, and from him I borrowed a "few pieces." And see Nichols's *Literary Anecdotes*, III. 731-2.

hand, and with both it was an object to secure the alliance and services of Goldsmith. Smollett had at all times not a little of the Fickle in him, and Newbery much of the Mr. Trip; but there was a genial good-heartedness in both, which makes it natural and pleasant to have to single out these two men as the first active friends and patrons of the author of the unsuccessful *Bee*. Their offers were of course accepted; and it seems to imply something, however slight, of a worldly advance in connection with them, that, in the month which followed, the luckless *Bee* was issued in the independent form of a small half-crown volume by Mr. Wilkie, and Kenrick received instructions from Mr. Ralph Griffiths to treat it in the *Monthly Review* "with the greatest candour toward an unsuccessful Author."*

The 1st of January, 1760, saw the first venture launched. It was published for sixpence, "embellished with curious copper-"plates," and entitled "*The* "*British Magazine, or Monthly Re-* "*pository for Gentlemen and* "*Ladies*. By T. Smollett "M.D. and others." It *1759. Æt. 31.* was dedicated with much fervour to Mr. Pitt; and Mr. Pitt's interest (greatly to the spleen of Horace Walpole, who thinks the matter worthy of mention in his *Memoirs of George the Second**) enabled Smollett to put it forth with a royal license, granted in consideration of the fact that Doctor Smollett had "repre-"sented to his Majesty that he "has been at great labour and "expense in writing original "pieces himself, and engaging "other gentlemen to write origi-"nal pieces." The Doctor, in truth, had but lately left the "Bench," at the close of that three months' imprisonment for libel into which his spirited avowal of the authorship of a criticism on Admiral Knowles had betrayed him; and the king's patronage had probably been sought as a counterpoise to the king's prison. But the punishment had not been without its uses. In the nature of Smollett, to the last, there were not a few of the heedless impulses of boyhood; and from this three months' steady gaze on the sadder side of things, he seems to have turned with tempered and gentler

---

* *Monthly Review*, xxii. 42, January 1760. A specimen of the candour is worth quoting. "We do not mean" (after saying that experience had no doubt proved the justice of the author's anticipations of failure, as well as of his belief that nobody but himself would regret it) "to insinuate that his lucubra-"tions are so void of merit as not to de-"serve the public attention. On the con-"trary, we must confess ourselves to "have found no inconsiderable entertain-"ment in their perusal. His stile is not "the worst, and his manner is agreeable "enough, in our opinion, however it may "have failed of exciting universal ad-"miration. The truth is, most of his sub-"jects are already sufficiently worn-out, "and his observations frequently trite "and common."

* iii. 250, 261. It follows an allusion to the abusive portrait of Lord Lyttelton in *Roderick Random*, "a novel of "which sort he published two or "three."

thoughts. In the first number of the *British Magazine* was the opening of the tale which con-tained his most feminine heroine (Aurelia Darnel), and the most amiable and gentlemanly of his heroes (Sir Launcelot Greaves); for, though Sir Launcelot is mad, wise thoughts have made him so; and in the hope to "remedy evils "which the law cannot reach, to "detect fraud and treason, to "abase insolence, to mortify "pride, to discourage slander, to "disgrace immodesty, and to "stigmatise ingratitude," he stumbles through his odd adven-tures. There is a pleasure in connecting this alliance of Smol-lett and Goldsmith, with the first approach of our great humorist to, that milder humanity and more genial wisdom which shed their mellow rays on Matthew Bramble.*

1759. Æt. 31.

1760. Æt. 32.

Nor were the services engaged from Oliver un-worthy of his friend's Sir Launcelot. Side by side with the kindly enthusiast, appeared some of the most agreeable of the *Essays* which were afterwards republished with Goldsmith's name; and many which were never connected with it, until half a century after their writer's death. Here Mr. Rigmarole fell into that Boar's-head reverie in Eastcheap, since so many times dreamt over, and so full of kind-ly rebuke to undiscriminating praisers of the past. Here the shabby man in St. James's-park (Goldsmith, like Justice Wood-cock, loved a vagabond) re-counted his strolling adventures, with a vivacity undisturbed by poverty; and, with his Merry-Andrew, Bajazet, and Wildair, laughed at Garrick in his glory. Here journey was made to the Fountain in whose waters sense and genius mingled, and by whose side the traveller found Johnson and Gray (a pity it did not prove so!) giving and receiv-ing fame.* And here, above all, the poor, hearty, wooden-legged beggar first charmed the world with a philosophy of con-tent and cheerfulness which no misfortune could subdue. This was he who had lost his leg and the use of his hand, and had a wound in his breast which was troublesome, and was obliged to beg, but with these exceptions blessed his stars for knowing no reason to complain: some had lost both legs and an eye, but thank Heaven it was not so bad with him. This was he who re-marked that people might say this and that of being in gaol, but when he was found guilty of being poor, and was sent to Newgate, he found it as agree-

* "Hark yo, Clinker! you are a most "notorious offender! You stand con-"victed of sickness, hunger, wretched-"ness, and want." Matthew Bramble to the outcast parish lad.

* Another proof that Goldsmith had not yet surrendered his own judgment to Johnson's in the matter of Gray. The four papers enumerated will be found in *Miscell. Works*, i. 179, 229, 195, and ii. 461; the last having been transferred to the *Citizen of the World.*

able a place as ever he was in, in all his life:* who fought the French in six pitched battles, and verily believed, that, but for some good reason or other, his captain would have given him promotion and made him a corporal: who was beaten cruelly by a boatswain, but the boatswain did it without considering what he was about: who slept on a bed of boards in a French prison, but with a warm blanket about him, because, as he remarked, he always loved to lie well: and to whom, when he came to sum up and balance his life's adventures, it occurred that had he had the good fortune to have lost his leg and the use of his hand on board a king's ship, and not a privateer, he should have had his sixpence a week for the rest of his days; but that was not his chance; one man was born with a silver spoon in his mouth, and another with a wooden ladle: "however, blessed be God, I "enjoy good health." This was philosophy as wise as *Candide's*, at which Europe was then laughing heartily; and it is worthy of mention that from the countrymen of Voltaire this little essay

* "O liberty! liberty! liberty! that is "the property of every Englishman, and "I will die in its defence; I was afraid, "however, that I should be indicted for a "vagabond once more, so did not much "care to go into the country, but kept "about town, and did little jobs when I "could get them. I was very happy in "this manner for some time; till one "evening, coming home from work, two "men knocked me down, and then de-"sired me to stand still. They belonged "to a press-gang." II. 465.

should have first derived its fame. So popular in France was the "humble optimist," as his translator called him, that he is not unlikely to have visited even the halls of *Les Délices;* to be read there, as everywhere, with mirth upon the face and tenderness at the heart; perhaps to reawaken recollections of the ungainly, wandering scholar.

1760.
————
Æt. 32.

Of upwards of twenty essays thus contributed to Smollett's magazine, few were republished by Goldsmith; but from other causes, certainly, than lack of merit. One was a criticism of two rival singers, two Polly Peachums then dividing Vauxhall, so pleasantly worded that neither could take offence; but of temporary interest chiefly. Another was a caution against violent courtships, from a true story in the family of his uncle Contarine; perhaps thought too private for reappearance in more permanent form. A third (not reproduced, it may be, lest the wooden-legged philosopher should lose in popularity by a companion less popular than himself) described, as a contrast to the happiness of the maimed and luckless soldier, the miseries of a healthy half-pay officer from unexpected good fortune, unable to bear the transition from moderate to extravagant means, and rendered so. insensible by unused indulgences that he had come to see *Falstaff* without a smile and the *Orphan* without emotion. A fourth was a little history of seduction, hasty, abrupt, and not very real; but in which the hero bore such a general though indistinct resemblance to the immortal family of the Primroses, as to have fitly merged and been forgotten in their later glory.*

1760.
Æt. 32

The last of these detached essays which I shall mention for the present, did not appear in the *British Magazine*, but much concerned it; and, though not reckoned worthy of preservation by its writer, is evidence not to be omitted of his hearty feeling to Smollett, and his ready resource to serve a friend. It was in plain words a puff of the *British Magazine* and its projector; and a puff of as witty pretension as ever visited the ingenious brain of the yet unborn friend of Mr. Dangle. It purported to describe a Wow-wow; a kind of newspaper club of a country town, to which the writer amusingly described himself driven, by his unavailing efforts to find anybody anywhere else. All

were at the Wow-wow, from the apothecary to the drawer of the tavern; and there he found, inspired by pipes and newspapers, such a smoke and fire of political discussion, such a setting right of all the mistakes of the generals in the war, such a battle, conducted with chalk, upon the blunders of Finck and Daun, and such quidnunc explosions against the Dutch in Pondicherry, that infallibly the Wow-wow must have come to a war of its own "had not an Oxford Scholar, led "there by curiosity, pulled a new "magazine out of his pocket, in "which he said there were some "pieces extremely curious and "that deserved their attention. "He then read the *Adventures of* "*Sir Launcelot Greaves* to the en- "tire satisfaction of the audience, "which being finished, he threw "the pamphlet upon the table; "'That piece, gentlemen,' says "he, 'is written in the very spirit "'and manner of Cervantes; "'there is great knowledge of "'human nature, and evident "'marks of the master in almost "'every sentence; and from the "'plan, the humour, and the exe- "'cution, I can venture to say "'that it dropped from the pen "'of the ingenious Doctor ——' "Every one was pleased with "the performance, and I was par- "ticularly gratified in hearing all "the sensible part of the com- "pany give orders for the *British* "*Magazine.*"

So said a not less ingenious Doctor ——, in that newspaper-

* The "History of Miss Stanton" is included in the edition of the *Miscellaneous Works*, (i. 214) published with Mr. Prior's name, but in reality (as Mr. Murray's papers show) edited by Mr. Wright: this, with many other pieces not before collected, rendering the book by far the best of the collections that have yet appeared, though it is by no means carefully or accurately edited. The other three papers mentioned above are in i. 201, 205, 224; and for the Wow-wow, see i. 322. Mr. Wright's has since been superseded by a much more careful edition, also published by Mr. Murray (1870).

venture of good Mr. Newbery's which started but twelve days after Smollett's, and in which also had been enlisted the services of the Green-arbour-court lodger. War is the time for newspapers; the inventive head which planned the *Universal Chronicle*, with the good taste that enlisted Johnson in its service, now made a bolder effort in the same direction; and the first number of *The Public Ledger* was published on the 12th of January 1760. Nothing less than a Daily Newspaper had the busy publisher of children's books projected. But a daily newspaper was not an appalling speculation, then. Not then, morning after morning, did it throw its eyes of Argus over all the world. No universal command was needed for it then, over sources of foreign intelligence potent to dispose and to control the money transactions of rival hemispheres. There existed with it, then, no costly arts for making and marring fortunes; cultivated to a perfection high as the pigeon's flight, swift as the courier's horse, or deep as the secret drawer of the diplomatist's bureau. In those days it was no more essential to a paper's existence that countless advertisements should be scattered broadcast through its columns, than to a city's business that puffing-vans should perambulate its highways, and armies of placard-bearing paupers seize upon its pavements. Neither as a perfect spy of the time, nor as a full informer or lofty improver of the time, did a daily journal yet put forth its claims; and neither to prompt or correct intelligence, or to great political or philanthropic aims, did it assume to devote itself. The triumphs or discomfitures of Freedom were not yet its daily, themes: and distant still were the days in which it was to ride on the whirlwind, and direct the storm, of great political passions; to grapple resistlessly with social abuses; or to take broad and philosophic views of the world's contemporaneous history, the history which is a-making from day to day.* It was content with humbler duties. It called itself a daily register of commerce and intelligence, and fell short of even so much modest pretension. The letter of a Probus or a Manlius sufficed for discussion of the war; and a modest rumour in some dozen lines, for what had occupied parliament during as many days. "We are unwilling," said the editor of the *Public Ledger* (Mr. Griffith Jones, who wrote children's books for Mr. Newbery)**

---

* This rather high-flown passage was written at the time of a struggle to establish a new daily paper in London, which Mr. Dickens and myself took part in.

** "It is not perhaps generally known, "that to Mr. Griffith Jones, and a brother "of his, Mr. Giles Jones, in conjunction "with Mr. John Newbery, the public are "indebted for the origin of those numerous and popular little books for the "amusement and instruction of children,

in his first number, "to raise ex-
"pectations which we may per-
"haps find ourselves unable to
"satisfy: and therefore
"have made no mention of
"criticism or literature,
"which yet we do not profess-
"edly exclude; nor shall we re-
"ject any political essays which
"are apparently calculated for
"the public good."· Discreetly
avoiding thus all undue expectation, there quietly came forth
into the world, from Mr. Bristow's
office "next the great toy-shop
"in St. Paul's-churchyard," the
first number of the *Public Ledger*.
It was circulated gratis: with announcement that all future numbers would be sold for twopence
halfpenny each.

The first four numbers were
enlightened by Probus in politics
and Sir Simeon Swift in litera-

ture; the one defending the
war, the other commencing the
"Ranger," and both very mildly
justifying the modest editorial
announcements. The fifth number was not so common-place.
It had a letter (vindicating with
manly assertion the character
and courage of the then horribly
unpopular French, and humorously condemning the national
English habit of abusing rival
nations) which implied a larger
spirit as it showed a livelier pen.
The same hand again appeared
in the next number but one; and
the correspondent of Green-
arbour-court became entitled to
receive two guineas from Mr.
Newbery for his first week's contributions to the *Public Ledger*.
His arrangement was to write
twice in the week, and to be paid
a guinea for each article.

CHAPTER IV.

The *Citizen of the World*.

WITH the second week of his
engagement on the *Public Ledger*,
Goldsmith had taken greater
courage. The letter which appeared on the 24th of January,
though without title or number-
ing to imply intention of continuance, threw out the hint of a
series of letters, and of a kind of
narrative as in the *Lettres Persanes*
or those pages of the *Spectator*
which Swift suggested to Steele.[*]

"the Lilliputian histories of Goody Two-
"shoes, Giles Gingerbread, Tommy
"Trip, &c. &c. which have been ever
"since received with universal approba-
"tion." Nichols's *Literary Anecdotes*, III.
466. Hereafter are given some reasons
for suspecting that Newbery may have
had a more distinguished fellow-labourer
than Mr. Jones; but I think that too
much stress has been laid on them, and I
believe that to Newbery himself the
great merit is due of having first sought
to reform in some material points the
moral of these books. He did not thrust
all naughty boys into the jaws of the
dragon, nor elevate all good boys to ride
in King Pepin's coach. Goldsmith did
undoubtedly say, however, more than
once, that he had a hankering to write
for children; and if he had realised his
intention of composing the fables in
which little fishes and other creatures
should talk, our children's libraries
would have had one rich possession the
more.

[*] "The *Spectator* is written by Steele
"with Addison's help: 'tis often very
"pretty. Yesterday it was made of a

The character assumed was that of a Chinese visitor to London: the writer's old interest in the flowery people having received new strength, of late, from the Chinese novel on which his dignified acquaintance Mr. Percy had been recently engaged.[*] The second letter, still without title, appeared five days after the first; some inquiry seems to have been made for their continuance; and thence uninterruptedly the series went on. Not until somewhat advanced, were they even numbered; they never received a title, until republished; but, they were talked of as the Chinese Letters, assumed the principal place in the paper, and contributed more than any other cause to its successful establishment. Sir Simeon Swift and his "Ranger," Mr. Philanthropy Candid and his "Visitor," struggled and departed as newspaper shadows are wont to do; Lien Chi Altangi became real, and lived. From the ephemeral sprang the immortal. On that column of ungainly-looking, perishable type, depended not alone the paper of the day, but a book to last throughout the year, a continuous pleasure for the age, and one which was for all time. It amused the hour, was wise for the interval beyond it, is still diverting and instructing us, and will delight generations yet unborn. At the close of 1760, ninety-eight of the letters had been published; within the next few months, at less regular intervals, the series was brought to completion; and in the following year, the whole were republished by Mr. Newbery "for the author"[*] in two duodecimo volumes, but without any author's name, as "*The Citizen of the World; or, Letters*

1760.
Æt. 32.

"noble hint I gave him long ago for his "*Tatlers*, about an Indian supposed to "write his travels into England. I repent he ever had it. I intended to have "written a book on that subject. I believe he has spent it all in one paper, "and all the under hints there are mine "too."

   * "I will endeavour," writes Shenstone in the following year (Nichols's *Illustrations*, VII. 222), "to procure and "send you a copy of Percy's translation "of a genuine Chinese novel in four "small volumes, printed months ago, but "not to be published before winter." Percy was the editor, and wrote the preface and notes; but the actual translation of *Han Kiou Choaan* from the Chinese was executed by Mr. Wilkinson, and all that Percy did in this respect was to translate the translator "into good reading Eng-"lish." It may be worth remarking, that, three years before, some noise had been made by a smart political squib of Horace Walpole's, which he protested he had writ in an hour-and-a-half, and which passed through five editions in a fortnight, the *Letter from Xo Ho, a Chinese Philosopher at London, to his friend Lien Chi at Pekin.* See *Coll. Lett.* IV. 289, 290.

   * This specification, which appears upon no other book written by Goldsmith, appears to imply either some reluctance on Newbery's part to undergo the risk of the republication, or some quarrel as to terms; but whichever it may have been, it is clear that a very small payment a few months later put the bookseller in possession of the whole "copy" (copyright) of the book. "Re-"ceiv'd of Mr. Newbery five guineas "which, with what I have receiv'd at dif-"ferent times before is in full for the "copy of the Chinese letters as witness "my hand OLIVER GOLDSMITH. March 5, "1762." Newbery MSS. in Mr. Murray's possession.

"from a Chinese Philosopher in "London, to his Friend in the "East."

1760. "Light, agreeable, sum-
——— "mer reading," observed
Æt. 32. the *British Magazine*, with but dry and laconic return for the Wow-wow. The *Monthly Review* had to make return of a different kind, Mr. Griffiths now decently resolving to swallow his leek; and his obedient Mr. Kenrick, under orders not to bite or even bark, but to profess admiration and supplicate forgiveness, thus, after remarking that the Chinese philosopher had nothing Asiatic about him, did his master's miserable bidding: "The public have been already "made sufficiently acquainted "with the merit of these enter-"taining Letters, which were first "printed in *The Ledger*, and are "supposed to have contributed "not a little towards the success "of that paper. They are said "to be the work of the lively and "ingenious Writer of *An Enquiry* "*into the Present State of Polite* "*Learning in Europe*; a Writer "whom, it seems, we undesigned-"ly offended by some Strictures "on the conduct of many of our "modern Scribblers. As the ob-"servation was entirely general "in its intention, we were sur-"prised to hear that this Gen-"tleman had imagined himself in "any degree pointed at, as we "conceive nothing can be more "illiberal in a Writer, or more "foreign to the character of a "Literary Journal, than to descend

"to the meanness of personal "reflection."* Pity might reasonably be given to men so lowered and self-abased; but Goldsmith withheld forgiveness. Private insults could not thus be retracted; nor could imputations which sink deepest in the simplest and most honourable natures, be so easily purged away. Mr. Griffiths was left to the consolation of reflecting that he had himself eaten the dirt which it would have made him far happier to have flung at the *Citizen of the World.*

In what different language, by what different men, how highly and justly this book has since been praised, for its fresh original perception, its delicate delineation of life and manners, its wit and humour, its playful and diverting satire, its exhilarating gaiety, and its clear and lively style, need not be repeated. What is to be said of it here will have more relation to the character than to the genius of its writer. The steadier direction of his thoughts, and the changing aspect of his fortunes, are what I would now turn back to read in it.

One marked peculiarity its best admirers have failed to observe upon; its detection and exposure, not simply of the foibles and follies which lie upon the surface, but of those more pregnant evils which rankle at the heart, of society. The occasions were frequent in which the

* *Monthly Review*, xxvi. 477, June 1762.

Chinese citizen so lifted his voice that only in a later generation could he find his audience; and they were not few, in which he has failed to find one even yet. He saw in the Russian Empire, what by the best English statesmen since has not been sufficiently guarded against, the natural enemy of the more western parts of Europe, "an "enemy already possessed of "great strength, and, from the "nature of the government, every "day threatening to become more "powerful."* He warned the all-credulous and too-confident English of their insecure tenure of the American colonies; telling them, with a truth as prophetic as Dean Tucker's, and which anticipated his vigorous reasoning, that England would not lose her vigour when those colonies obtained their independence. He unveiled the social pretences, which, under colour of protecting female honour, are made the excuse for its violation. He denounced the evil system which left the magistrate, the country justice, and the 'squire, to punish transgressions in which they had themselves been the guiltiest transgressors. He laughed at the sordidness which makes penny shows of our public temples, turns Deans and Chapters into importunate "beggars," and stoops to pick up half-pence at the tombs of our patriots and poets. He laughed at, even while he gloried in, the national vaunt of superiority to other nations, which gave fancied freedom to the prisoner, riches to the beggar, and enlisted on behalf of church-and-state fellows who had never profited by either.* He protested earnestly against the insufficient pretexts that availed for the spilling of blood, in the contest then raging between France and England. He inveighed against the laws which meted out, in so much gold or silver, the price of a wife's or daughter's honour. He ridiculed the prevailing nostrums current in that age of quacks; doubted the graces of such betailing and bepowdering

1760.
Æt. 32.

* Letter LXXXVII. A remark I should hardly make if writing now. 1870.

* Who does not remember what the astonished traveller had to listen to soon after his arrival, outside a metropolitan gaol; where the talk (upon a threatened French invasion) is carried on between a debtor through the grate of his prison, a porter who had stopped to rest his burthen, and a soldier at the window. "For my part," cries the prisoner, "the "greatest of my apprehensions is for our "freedom; if the French should conquer, "what would become of English liberty?" "Ay, slaves," cries the porter, "they are "all slaves, fit only to carry burthens, "every one of them. Before I would "stoop to slavery, may this be my poison" (holding up his goblet of drink), "may "this be my poison—but I would sooner "list for a soldier." To which the soldier, taking the goblet from his friend, with much awe fervently cries out, "It is "not so much our liberties as our re- "ligion that would suffer by such a "change; ay, our religion, my lads. May "the Devil sink me into flames," such was the solemnity of his adjuration, "if "the French should come over, but our "religion would be utterly undone." *Citizen of the World.* Letter IV. Byron's *Tom the Porter* is now forgotten, but Goldsmith evidently knew those lines.

fashions as then made beauty hideous, and sent even lads cocked-hatted and wigged to school; and had sense and courage to avow his contempt for that prevailing cant of connoisseurship ("your "Raffaelles, Correggios, and "Stuff") at which Reynolds shifted his trumpet. The abuses of church patronage did not escape him; any more than the tendency to "superstition and "imposture" in the "bonzes "and priests of all religions." He thought it a fit theme for mirth, that holy men should be content to receive all the money, and let others do all the good; and that preferment to the most sacred and exalted duties should wait upon the whims of members of parliament, and the wants of younger branches of the nobility.* The incapacities and

1760.
————
Æt. 32.

neglect thus engendered in the upper clergy, he also connected with that disregard of the lower which left a reverend Trulliber undisturbed among his pigs, and a parson Adams to his ale in Lady Booby's kitchen. Yet as little was he disposed to tolerate any false reaction from such indifference; and at the ascetic saints of the new religious sect which had risen to put down cheerfulness, and could find its

* I refer the reader to George Selwyn's *Correspondence* if he should desire to study attentively one of the latest full-blown specimens of the breed of clergymen engendered by this system, and would introduce himself to by no means one of the most objectionable of the smoking, reading, claret-drinking, toadying, gormandising, good-humoured parsons of the time when Goldsmith lived and wrote. He will find Dr. Warner quite an ornament to the Establishment throughout that book, and only cursing, flinging, stamping, or gnashing when anything goes amiss with Selwyn. He will observe that the reverend doctor is ready to wager his best cassock against a dozen of claret any day; and that the holy man would quote you even texts with the most pious of his cloth, "If our "friend the Countess had not blasted "them." In short, at whatever page he opens the *Correspondence*, he will find parson Warner in the highest possible spirits, whether quizzing "canting pot-

"bellied justices," contemplating with equanimity "a fine corpse at Surgeon's-"hall," or looking forward with hopeful vivacity to the time when he shall "be a "fine grey-headed old jollocks of sixty-"five." They who would hastily accuse Fielding of exaggeration in his portraitures taken from the church, should first contemplate this. Goldsmith is less severe in his exposure, but it is efficient, too; and I confess I never read a letter of Doctor Warner's, or think of his guzzling, his telling the same story over and over again, and his indifference to any kind of treatment shown him or service exacted of him so long as his bumper of claret is well filled, without being forcibly reminded of Doctor Marrowfat. "'As good a story,' cries he, bursting "into a violent fit of laughter himself, "'as ever you heard in your lives. There "'was a farmer in my parish who used "'to sup upon wild ducks and flummery; "'so this farmer'—'Doctor Marrowfat,' "cries his lordship, interrupting him, "'give me leave to drink your health'— "'so being fond of wild ducks and flum-"'mery'—'Doctor,' adds a gentleman "who sat next him, 'let me advise you to "'a wing of this turkey;'—'so this "'farmer being fond'—'Hob and nob, "'doctor, which do you choose, white or "'red?'—'so being fond of wild ducks and "'flummery;'—'Take care of your band, "'sir, it may dip in the gravy.' The "doctor, now looking round, found not a "single ear disposed to listen: where-"fore, calling for a glass of wine, he "gulped down the disappointment and "the tale in a bumper." Letter LVIII.

only music in a chorus of sighs and groans, he aimed the shafts of his wit as freely, as at the over-indulging, gormandising priests of the bishop's visitation-dinner, face to face with whom, gorged and groaning with excess, he brought the hungry beggar, faint with want, to ask of them the causes of his utter destitution, body and soul. Nor did he spare that other dignified profession, which, in embarrassing what it professed to make clear, in retarding with cumbrous impediments the steps of justice, in reserving as a luxury for the rich what it pretended to throw open to all, in fencing round property with a multiplicity of laws and exposing poverty, without a guard to whatever threatened or assailed it, countenanced and practised no less a falsehood. *

Almost alone in that age of indifference, the Citizen of the World raised his voice against the penal laws which then, with wanton severity, disgraced the statute book; insisted that the sole means of making death an efficient, was to make it an infrequent, punishment; and warned society of the crime of disregarding human life and the temptations of the miserable, by visiting petty thefts with penalties of blood. *

He who does not read for

1760.
Æt. 32.

---

* The simple notions of the Chinese citizen on this subject appear very alarming to his friend, who uses precisely the defensive argument with which the absurdity has been upheld ever since. " 'I see,' cries my friend, 'that you are for 'a speedy administration of justice; but 'all the world will grant, that the more 'time there is taken up in considering 'any subject, the better it will be 'understood. Besides, it is the boast 'of an Englishman, that his *property is* 'secure, and all the world will grant 'that a deliberate administration of 'justice is the best way to *secure his* '*property?* Why have we so many 'lawyers, but to *secure our property?* 'why so many formalities, but to secure '*our property?* Not less than one hundred thousand families live in opulence, 'elegance, and ease, merely by secur-'ing our property.' .... 'But bless me,' returned I, 'what numbers do I see here '—all in black—how is it possible that 'half this multitude find employment?' '—'Nothing so easily conceived,' re-turned my companion, 'they live by 'watching each other. For instance, 'the catchpole watches the man in debt, 'the attorney watches the catchpole, 'the counsellor watches the attorney, 'the solicitor the counsellor, and all 'find sufficient employment.'—'I con-'ceive you,' interrupted I, 'they watch 'each other: but it is the client that 'pays them all for watching.'" Letter xcviii. The reader is to remember that this was written a hundred years ago, and that we are only at this hour bestirring ourselves to provide something of a remedy. 1858.

* Is there anything better reasoned than this in Romilly or Bentham? "When a "law, enacted to make theft punishable "with death, happens to be equitably "executed, it can at best only guard our "possessions; but when, by favour or "ignorance, justice pronounces a wrong "verdict, it then attacks our lives, since "in such a case the whole community "suffers with the innocent victim: if, "therefore, in order to secure the effects "of one man, I should make a law which "may take away the life of another, in "such a case, to attain a smaller good, I "am guilty of a greater evil; to secure "society in the possession of a bauble, I "render a real and valuable possession "precarious..... Since punishments are "sometimes necessary, let them at least "be rendered terrible, by being executed "but seldom, and let justice lift her "sword rather to terrify than revenge." Letter LXXX.

amusement only, may also find in these delightful letters, thus published from week to week, a comment of special worth on casual incidents of the time. There was in this year a city-campaign of peculiar cruelty. A mob has indiscriminate tastes for blood, and after hunting an Admiral Byng to death will as eagerly run down a dog. On a groundless cry of hydrophobia, dogs were slaughtered wholesale, and their bodies literally blocked up the streets. "The dear, good-natured, honest, "sensible creatures!" exclaimed Horace Walpole. "Christ! How "can anybody hurt them?" But what Horace said only to his friend, Goldsmith said to everybody: publicly denouncing the cruelty, in a series of witty stories ridiculing the motives alleged for it, and pleading with eloquent warmth for the honest associate of man.* Nor was this the only

1760.
Æt. 32.

mad-dog-cry of the year. The yell of a Grub-street mob as fierce, on a false report of the death of Voltaire, brought Goldsmith as warmly to the rescue. With eager admiration, he asserted the claims of the philosopher and wit; told the world it was his lusts of war and sycophancy which unfitted it to receive such a friend; set forth the independence of his life, in a country of Pompadours and an age of venal oppression; declared (this was before the Calas family) the tenderness and humanity of his nature; and claimed freedom of religious thought for him and all men. "I am not displeased "with my brother because he "happens to ask our father for "favours in a different manner "from me." As we read the Chinese Letters with this comment of the time, those actual days come vividly back to us. Earl Ferrers glides through them again, with his horrible passion and yet more ghastly composure. The theatres again contend with their Pollys and Macheaths, and tire the town with perpetual *Beggars' Operas*. Merry and fashionable crowds repeople White-conduit and Vauxhall. We get occasional glimpses of even the stately commoner and his unstately ducal associate. Old George the Second dies, and young George the Third ascends the throne. Churchill makes his hit with the *Rosciad*; and Sterne, having startled the town with the humour and extravagance of his

* It is pleasant to quote his kindly speech. "Of all the beasts that graze the "lawn, or hunt the forest, a dog is the "only animal that, leaving his fellows, "attempts to cultivate the friendship of "man; to man he looks in all his neces- "sities with a speaking eye for as- "sistance; exerts for him all the little "service in his power with cheerfulness "and pleasure; for him bears famine and "fatigue with patience and resignation; "no injuries can abate his fidelity, no "distress induce him to forsake his bene- "factor; studious to please, and fearing "to offend, he is still an humble stedfast "dependant; and in him alone fawning "is not flattery. How unkind, then, to "torture this faithful creature, who has "left the forest to claim the protection "of man! how ungrateful a return to "the trusty animal for all his services!" Letter LXIX.

Tristram Shandy, comes up from country quiet to enjoy popularity.

How sudden and decisive it was, need not be related. No one was so talked of in London this year, and no one so admired, as that tall, thin, hectic-looking Yorkshire parson. He who was to die within eight years, unheeded and untended, in a common lodging-house, was everywhere the honoured guest of the rich and noble. His book had become a fashion, and east and west were moved alike. Mr. Dodsley offered him 650*l.* for a second edition and two more volumes; Lord Falconberg gave him a curacy of 150*l.* a year: Mr. Reynolds painted his portrait; and Warburton, not having yet pronounced him an "irrecover-"able scoundrel," went round to the bishops and told them he was the English Rabelais. "They had "never heard of such a writer," adds the sly narrator of the incident.* "One is invited to din-"ner where he dines," said Gray, "a fortnight beforehand:"** and Sterne was boasting, to friends, of dinner engagements fourteen deep, even while he declared the way to fame to be like that to heaven, through much tribulation, and de- _{1760.} _{Æt. 32.} scribed himself, in the midst of his triumphs, "attacked and "pelted from cellar and garret." Perhaps he referred to Goldsmith, from whose garret in Green-arbour-court the first heavy blow was levelled at him; but there were other assailants, as active though less avowed, in cellars of Arlington-street and garrets of Strawberry-hill. Yet Walpole may more easily be forgiven than Goldsmith in such a case. The attack in the *Citizen of the World* was aimed, it is true, where the work was most vulnerable;* and it was not ill

---

* Walpole's *Coll. Lett.* IV. 39.

** Letter to Wharton, 22nd April 1760. *Works*, III. 241. In another letter to Wharton two months later, he writes, with his usual manly appreciation of all that is good and original, "there is much "good fun in *Tristram*, and humour "sometimes hit, and sometimes missed. "I agree with your opinion of it, and "shall see the two future volumes with "pleasure. Have you read his sermons "(with his own comic figure at the head "of them)? They are in the style, I "think, most proper for the pulpit, and "show a very strong imagination and a "sensible heart. But you see him often

"tottering on the verge of laughter, and "ready to throw his periwig in the face "of his audience." III. 251. For a most masterly criticism of *Tristram Shandy* I refer to a paper on Sterne in the *Quarterly Review*, understood to be by the Rev. Mr. Elwin. It is one of a series which appeared between 1851 and 1859, comprising Johnson, Gray, and other writers; and belonging to a time now nearly extinct, when English literature was really understood by the persons who wrote about it, or had charge of the reviews professing to give account of it. 1870.

* "If a bawdy blockhead thus breaks "in on the community, he sets his whole "fraternity in a roar; nor can he escape, "*even though he should fly to the nobility* "*for shelter.*" *Citizen of the World*, Letter LXXV. The sarcasm of this may be forgiven, since Goldsmith showed always an honest and high-minded dislike of all commoners, all approach to even sensual allusion, in his own writings. But why blockhead? except indeed that the man who resorts to improprieties of that kind may be held so far to open himself to the

done to protest against the indecency and affectation, which doubtless had largely contributed to the so sudden popularity, as they found promptest imitators;—but the humour and wit ought surely to have been admitted; and if the wisdom and charity of an uncle Toby, a Mr. Shandy, or a Corporal Trim, might anywhere have claimed frank and immediate recognition, it should have been in that series of essays which Beau Tibbs and the Man in Black have helped to make immortal.

Most charming are these two characters. Addison would have admired, and Steele delighted in them. Finery and poverty, surliness and goodnature, were never brought together with more playful wit, or a more tender sweetness. Fielding's majestic major who will hear of nothing less than the honour and dignity of a man, and is caught in an old woman's bedgown warming his sick sister's posset, is not a nobler specimen of manhood than the one; Steele's friend at the trumpet club, that very insignificant fellow but exceeding gracious, who has but a bare subsistence, yet is always promising to introduce you into the world, who answers to matters of no consequence with great circumspection, maintains an insolent benevolence to all whom he has to do with, and will desire one of ten times his substance to let him see him sometimes, hinting that he does not forget him, is not more delicious in his vanity than the other. The country ramble of the Man in Black, wherein, to accompaniment of the most angry invective, he performs acts of the most exquisite charity; where with harsh loud voice he denounces the poor, while with wistful compassionate face he relieves them; where, by way of detecting imposture, he domineeringly buys a shilling's worth of matches, receives the astonished beggar's whole bundle and blessing, and, intimating that he has taken in the seller and shall make money of his bargain, bestows them next moment on a tramper with an objurgation; is surely never to be read unmoved. For Beau Tibbs, who has not laughed at and loved him, from the first sorry glimpse of his faded finery?* Who has not felt in the airs of wealth and grandeur with which his amusing impudence puffs up his miserable poverty, that he makes out a title to good natured cheerfulness and thorough enjoyment

Imputation expressed by Roscommon's couplet, so often given to Pope,

> "Immodest words admit of no de-
> fence,
> For want of decency is want of
> sense."

* "His hat was pinched up with peculiar smartness; his looks were pale, thin, and sharp; round his neck he wore a broad black ribbon, and in his bosom a buckle studded with glass; his coat was trimmed with tarnished twist; he wore by his side a sword with a black hilt; and his stockings of silk, though newly washed, were grown yellow by long service." Letter LIV.

which all the real wealth might have purchased cheaply? What would his friends Lords Muddler and Crump, the Duchess of Piccadilly or the Countess of All-night, have given for it? Gladly, for but a tithe of it, might the lords have put up with his two shirts, and uncomplainingly the ladies assisted Mrs. Tibbs, and her sweet pretty daughter Carolina Wilhelmina Amelia, in seeing them through the wash-tub. It is an elegant little dinner he talks of giving his friend, with bumpers of wine, a turbot, an ortolan, and what not: but who would not as soon have had the smart bottled-beer which was all he had to give, with the nice pretty bit of ox-cheek, piping-hot, and dressed with a little of Mrs. Tibbs's own sauce which "his grace" was so fond of? It is supposed that this exquisite sketch had a living original in one of Goldsmith's casual acquaintance; a person named Thornton, once in the army.

This is not improbable, any more than that the beau's two shirts might have been copied from Goldsmith's own; for everywhere throughout the Letters actual incidents appear, and the "fairy tale" of the prince and the white mouse had an origin whimsical as the story itself. Mr. Newbery's two guineas a week would seem to have attracted weekly levies, in a double sense, from Grub-street (when was there ever a goodnatured Irishman with five shillings in his pocket, and any lack of Irish hangers-on to share the spoil?), at which Pilkington, son of the notorious Lætitia, was most assiduous. But with other than his usual begging aspect, he appeared in Green-arbour-court one day; for good luck had dawned on him at last, he said, and his troubles were over. A very small sum (and he ran about the room for joy of the announcement) was all he wanted to make his fortune. There was a great duchess who had the most surprising passion for white mice; two she had procured already, and for years had been looking out for two more, which she was ready to offer the most extravagant price for. Aware of her grace's weakness, he had long ago implored of a friend going out to India to procure him, if possible, two white mice, and here they were actually arrived; they were in the river at that moment, having come by an Indiaman, now in the docks; and the small sum, to which allusion had been made, was all that now stood between Jack Pilkington and independence for life! Yes; all he wanted was two guineas, to buy a cage for the creatures sufficiently handsome to be received by a duchess;—but what was to be done, for Goldsmith had only half a guinea? The anxious client then pointed to a watch, with which his poor patron (indulging in a luxury which Johnson did not possess till he was sixty) had lately

1760.
——
Æt. 32.

enriched himself; deferentially suggested one week's loan as a solution of the difficulty; and

1760.
——
Æt. 32.

carried it off.* And though Goldsmith never again had tidings of either, or of the curious white mice, till a paragraph in the *Public Ledger* informed him of certain equivocal modes whereby "Mr. P—lk—g—on was "endeavouring to raise money," —yet a messenger, not long afterwards, carried to the poor starving creature's death-bed "a "guinea from Mr. Goldsmith."

* Cooke gives the story as one which Goldsmith used himself to tell very humorously; informing us, however, that even Goldsmith's credulity could not at first be imposed upon by so preposterous a flam. But Jack was prepared for the worst, and he instantly produced his friend's letter advising of the shipping of the white mice, their size, qualities, &c. which so entirely convinced the Doctor of the fact, that he wished him joy of it. "'How much will a cage cost?' said "Goldsmith, upon this. "'About two "'guineas,' replied Pilkington. 'In truth, "'Jack, then you're out of luck, for I "'have got but half-a-guinea in the "'world.' 'Ay, but my dear Doctor,' "continues Pilkington, 'you have got a "'watch, and though I would rather die "'than propose such an indelicacy upon "'any other occasion than the present, "'if you could let me have that, I could "'pawn it across the way for two "'guineas, and be able to repay you, "'with heartfelt gratitude, in a few "'days.' This last bait took poor Gold-"smith fully on the hook; he confidently "gave him his watch, which he was some "months after obliged to take up himself, "without hearing anything more of his "friend or the success of his white mice. "The Doctor used to tell this story with "some humour, and never without an "eulogium on the ingenuity of Pilking-"ton, who could take him in after "such experience of his shifts and con-"trivances." *European Magazine*, xxiv. 259-60.

The same journal (by the favour of an old friend, Kenrick) described for the public at the same time an amusing adventure in White-conduit-gardens, of which no other than "Mr. "G— d—th" himself was the hero. Strolling through that scene of humble holiday, he seems to have met the wife and two daughters of an honest tradesman who had done him some service, and invited them to tea; but after much enjoyment of the innocent repast, he discovered a want of money to discharge the bill, and had to undergo some ludicrous annoyances, and entertain his friends at other expense than he had bargained for, before means were found for his release. Another contemporary anecdote reverses this picture a little, and exhibits him reluctant paymaster, at the Chapter-coffee-house, for Churchill's friend Charles Lloyd, who in his careless way, without a shilling to pay for the entertainment, invited him to sup with some friends of Grub-street, and left him to pay the reckoning.*

* Cooke tells this story pleasantly enough, and I think it worth quoting, with some obvious and unimportant corrections rendered necessary by its date. "Goldsmith sitting one morning at the "Chapter-coffee-house, Lloyd came up to "him with great frankness, and asked "him how he did? Goldsmith, who cer-"tainly was a very modest man, seeing a "stranger accost him so intimately, "shrunk back a little, and returned his "inquiries with an air of distant civility. "'Pho! pho!' says Lloyd, 'my name is "'Lloyd, and you are Mr. Goldsmith, "'and, though not formally introduced

A third incident of the same date presents him with a similar party at Blackwall, where so violent a dispute arose about *Tristram Shandy* at the dinner-table, that personalities led to blows, and the feast ended in a fight. "Why, "sir," said Johnson laughing, when Boswell told him some years later of a different kind of fracas in which their friend had been engaged, "I believe it is "the first time he has *beat*; he "may have been *beaten* before.

"This, sir, is a new plume to "him." If the somewhat doubtful surmise of the beating be correct, the scene of it was Blackwall; and if (a surmise still more doubtful) the story Hawkins tells about the trick played off by Roubiliac, which like all such tricks tells against both the parties to it, be also true, this was the time when it happened. The "little" sculptor, as he is called in the Chinese Letters, being a familiar acquaintance and fond of music, Goldsmith would play the flute for him; and to such assumed delight on the part of his listener did he do this one day, that Roubiliac, protesting he must copy the air upon the spot, took up a sheet of paper, scored a few lines and spaces (the form of the notes being all he knew of the matter), and with random blotches pretended to take down the tune as repeated by the good-natured musician; while gravely, and with great attention, Goldsmith, surveying these musical hieroglyphics, "said they "were very correct, and that if "he had not seen him do it, he "never could have believed his "friend capable of writing music "after him." Sir John Hawkins tells the story with much satisfaction. Exposure of an ignorant flute-player, with nothing but vulgar accomplishments of "ear" to bestow upon his friends, yet with an innocent conceit of pretending to the science of music, gives great delight to the pomp-

1760.
———
Æt. 32.

"'to one another, we should be ac-
"'quainted as brother poets and literary
"'men; therefore, without any cere-
"'mony, will you sup with me this even-
"'ing at this house, where you will meet
"'half-a-dozen honest fellows, who, I
"'think, will please you?' Goldsmith,
"who admired the frankness of the in-
"troduction, immediately accepted. The
"party, which principally consisted of
"authors and booksellers, was, as Lloyd
"predicted, quite agreeable to Gold-
"smith, and the glass circulated to a late
"hour in the morning. A little before
"the company broke up, Lloyd went out
"of the room, and, in a few minutes
"afterwards, his voice was heard rather
"loud in the adjoining passage in con-
"versation with the master of the house.
"Goldsmith immediately flew to his new
"friend, to inquire what was the matter;
"when he found Lloyd in vain attempt-
"ing to come to an understanding with
"the landlord, who, protesting that al-
"ready he owed more than 14*l.*, swore
"that nothing should induce him to take
"either his word or his note for the
"reckoning. 'Pho! pho!' says Gold-
"smith, 'my dear boy, let's have no more
"'words about the matter, 'tis not the first
"'time a gentleman wanted cash; will
"'you accept *my* word for the reckon-
"'ing?' The landlord assented. 'Why
"'then,' says Lloyd, whispering to him
"and forgetting all animosities, 'send in
"'another cask of wine, and add it to the
"'bill.' The bill ultimately had to be
"paid by Goldsmith." *European Magazine,* XXIV. 93-4.

ous historian of crotchets and quavers. It seems more than probable, notwithstanding, that there is not a syllable of truth in the story.* So passed the thoughtless life of Goldsmith in his first year of success: if so may be called the scanty pittance which served to expose his foibles, but not to protect him from their consequence. So may his life be read in these Letters to the *Public Ledger;* and still with the comment of pleasure and instruction for others, though at the cost of suffering to himself. His habits as well as thoughts are in them. He is at the theatre, enjoying Garrick's Abel Drugger, and laughing at all who call it

1760.
Æt. 32.

"low;" a little tired of Polly and Macheath;* not at all interested by the famous and fortunate tumbler, who, between the acts of tragedies as well as farces, balances a straw upon his nose;** and zigzagging his way

* I quote an address "to the Philological Society of London," on Sir John Hawkins's *Life of Johnson*, published in May 1787. "The writer of this is acquainted with a gentleman who knew "Goldsmith well, and has often requested "him to play different pieces from music "which he laid before him; and this, "Goldsmith has done with accuracy and "precision, while the gentleman, who is "himself musical, looked over him: a "circumstance utterly impossible, if we "admit the foolish story related by Sir "John Hawkins of Roubiliac's imposition "on Goldsmith." Nor can I help thinking that this explicit contradiction is strongly countenanced by his essay on the different schools of music (written for Smollett's magazine in 1760), and still more by the notes which ("In so much "respect were his talents then held, "though he had not obtained celebrity, "but lived in an obscure lodging in "Green-arbour-court," &c.) Smollett permitted him to append to the remonstrance of a correspondent against that essay. The notes (*Miscell. Works*, I. 176) possess great merit, and show a larger amount of knowledge in ready use than Goldsmith was always able to display.

* The allusion however, implies no envy of the popularity of this piece of genuine wit, as unfriendly critics have implied. The complaint expressly is that singing women, instead of singing for the public, should be allowed to "sing at "each other," and nothing but the same song. "What! Polly and the Pickpocket "to-night, Polly and the Pickpocket to-"morrow night, and Polly and the Pick-"pocket again! I want patience. I will "hear no more." Goldsmith took no part whatever in a graver outcry which was afterwards levelled against Gay's masterpiece, and which at last, the year before his death, took the form of an application from the magistrates of Bow-street to request the managers of Drury-lane and Covent-garden "not to exhibit "this opera, deeming it productive of "mischief to society." (Peake's *Memoirs of the Colmans*, I. 317.) To which, let me add, Colman's reply was very spirited. He declined, on behalf of Covent-garden, to be a party to the consent which Garrick timidly had given for Drury-lane; and "for his own part cannot help differ-"ing in opinion with the magistrates, "thinking that the theatre is one of the "very few houses in the neighbourhood "that does not contribute to increase the "number of thieves." *Post. Let.* 194.

** "A singing-woman," he says, with a sarcastic humour that may be forgiven him in his garret, "shall collect subscrip-"tions in her own coach-and-six; a fellow "shall make a fortune by tossing a straw "from his toe to his nose; one in par-"ticular has found that eating fire was "the most ready way to live; and an-"other who gingles several bells fixed to "his cap, is the only man that I know of "who has received emolument from the "labours of his head." Letter XLV. The chance of encouragement, he had before remarked, lay not in the head, but the heels. "One who jumps up and flourishes "his toes three times before he comes to home, after all is over, through a hundred obstacles from coach-wheels and palanquin-poles, "like "a bird in its flight through the "branches of a forest." He is a visitor at the humble pothouse clubs, whose follies and enjoyments he moralises with touching pleasantry. "Were I to be "angry at men for being fools, I "could here have found ample "room for declamation; but, "alas! I have been a fool myself, "and why should I be angry with "them for being something so "natural to every child of "humanity?" Unsparing historian of this folly of his own, he conceals his imprudence as little as his poverty; and his kind heart he has not the choice to conceal. Everywhere it betrays itself. In hours of depression, recalling the disastrous fate of men of genius, and "mighty "poets in their misery dead;" in imaginary interviews with book-sellers, laughing at their sordid mistakes; in remonstrances with his own class, warning them of the danger of despising each other; and in rarer periods of perfect self-reliance, rising above the accidents around him, asserting the power as well as claims of writers, and denouncing the

"the ground, may have three hundred a "year; he who flourishes them four "times, gets four hundred; but he who "arrives at five is inestimable, and may "demand what salary he think proper. "The female dancers, too, are valued for "this sort of jumping and crossing; and "it is a cant word among them that "she deserves most who shows highest." Letter XII.

short-sightedness of statesmen. "Instead of complaining that "writers are over-paid, when "their works procure them "a bare subsistence, I "should imagine it the "duty of a state, not only to en-"courage their numbers, but "their industry. ... Whatever be "the motives which induce men "to write, whether avarice or "fame, the country becomes "most wise and happy in which "they most serve for instructors. "The countries where sacerdotal "instruction alone is permitted, "remain in ignorance, superstition, and hopeless slavery. In "England, where there are as "many new books published as "in all the rest of Europe toge-"ther, a spirit of freedom and "reason reigns among the people: "they have been often known to "act like fools, they are generally "found to think like men."* The close of the same paper becomes almost pathetic while it pleads for those who have thus served and instructed England; men "whom nature has blest "with talents above the rest of "mankind, men capable of think-"ing with precision and impress-"ing their thoughts with rapidity, "beings who diffuse those re-"gards upon mankind which "others contract and settle upon "themselves. These deserve "every honour from that com-"munity of which they are more "peculiarly the children; to such "I would give my heart, since to

* *Citizen of the World.* Letter LXXV.

1760.
Æt. 32.

"them I am indebted for its hu-"manity!" In another letter the subject is more calmly resumed,

1760.
——
Æt. 32.

with frank admission that old wrongs are at length in the course of coming right. "At present, the few poets "of England no longer depend "on the great for subsistence; "they have now no other patrons "but the public, and the public, "collectively considered, is a "good and a generous master. "It is, indeed, too frequently "mistaken as to the merits of "every candidate for favour; but "to make amends, it is never "mistaken long. .. A man of "letters at present, whose works "are valuable, is perfectly sen-"sible of their value. Every "polite member of the com-"munity, by buying what he "writes, contributes to reward "him. The ridicule therefore of "living in a garret, might have "been wit in the last age, but "continues such no longer, be-"cause no longer true."*

The quiet composure of this passage exhibits the healthiest aspect of his mind. Bookseller and public are confronted calm-ly, and the consequences fairly challenged. It is indeed very obvious, at the close of this first year of the *Public Ledger*, that in-creasing opportunities of em-ployment (to say nothing of the constant robbery of his writings by pirate magazine-men) were really teaching him his value, and suggesting hopes he had not

earlier dared to entertain. He resumed his connection with the *Lady's Magazine*, and became its editor: publishing in it, among other writings known and un-known, what he had written of his Life of Voltaire; and retiring from its editorship at the close of a year, when he had raised its circulation (if Mr. Wilkie's ad-vertisements are to be believed) to three thousand three hundred. He continued his contributions, meanwhile, to the *British Maga-zine*; from which he was not wholly separated till two months before poor Smollett, pining for the loss of his only daughter, went upon the continent (in 1763) never to return to a fixed or settled residence in London. He furnished other booksellers with occasional compilation-pre-faces;* and he gave some papers (among them a *Life of Christ* and *Lives of the Fathers*, republished with his name in shilling pam-phlets a few months after his death) to a so-called *Christian Magazine*, undertaken by New-bery in connection with the

* *Citizen of the World.* Letter LXXXIV.

* Of course these prefaces were al-ways strictly taskwork. To seek to con-nect them in any way with the work pre-faced, would be generally labour in vain. The moral of them is in a remark of Johnson's, when Boswell, admiring great-ly his preface to *Rolt's Dictionary of Trade and Commerce*, asked him whether he knew much of Rolt and of his work. "Sir," said Johnson, "I never saw the "man, and never read the book. The "booksellers wanted a Preface to a Dic-"tionary of Trade and Commerce. I "knew very well what such a Dictionary "should be, and I wrote a Preface ac-"cordingly." *Boswell*, II. 125.

macaroni parson Dodd, and conducted by that villainous pretender as an organ of fashionable divinity.*

It seems to follow as of course upon these engagements, that the room in Green-arbour-court should at last be exchanged for one of greater comfort. He had left that place in the later months of 1760, and gone into what were called respectable lodgings in Wine-office-court, Fleet-street. The house belonged to a relative of Newbery's, and he occupied two rooms in it for nearly two years.

CHAPTER V.

Fellowship with Johnson.
1761—1762.

A CIRCUMSTANCE occurred in the new abode of which Goldsmith had so taken possession in Wine-office-court, which must have endeared it always to his remembrance; but more deeply associated with the wretched habitation he had left behind him in Green-arbour-court, were days of a most forlorn misery as well as of a manly resolution, and, round that beggarly dwelling ("the "shades," as he used to call it in the more prosperous aftertime), and all connected with it, there crowded to the last the kindest memories of his gentle and true nature. Thus, when bookseller Davies tells us, after his death, how tender and compassionate he was; how no unhappy person ever sued to him for relief without obtaining it, if he had anything to give; and how he would borrow, rather than not relieve the distressed, — he adds that "the poor woman with whom "he had lodged during his ob- "scurity several years in Green- "arbour-court, by his death lost "an excellent friend; for the "Doctor often supplied her with "food from his own table, and "visited her frequently, with the "sole purpose to be kind to "her."* As little, in connection with Wine-office-court, was he likely ever to forget that Johnson now first visited him there.

They had probably met before. I have shown how frequently the thoughts of Goldsmith vibrated to that great Grub-street figure of independence and manhood,

* Here I had stated, in my last edition, on the authority of Mr. Crossley (*Notes and Queries*, 1st Series, v. 584), that another of Newbery's compilations issued at this time in four duodecimos, *A Poetical Dictionary; or the Beauties of the English Poets alphabetically displayed*, was also Goldsmith's; but this is a mistake. It was by his friend and countryman, Derrick; though, short of the "evidently by "Goldsmith," both preface and selection deserve all that Mr. Crossley says of them. George Faulkner writes from London on the 14th February, 1761, to Derrick (then on a visit to Dublin): "I sent "over your *Poetical Dictionary*, which I "suppose you have seen before this time, "and assure you it is in good reputation, "as you may judge, Mr. Johnson speak- "ing very well of it." I quote from Derrick's unpublished correspondence, formerly belonging to Mr. Croker and now in my possession, which further shows that he was at this time collecting materials for Lives of the Poets, placed afterwards in Johnson's hands.

* *Life of Garrick*, II. 169.

which, in an age not remarkable for either, was undoubtedly presented in the person of the author of the *English Dictionary.* One of the last Chinese Letters had again alluded to the "Johnsons and Smolletts" as veritable poets, though they might never have made a verse in their whole lives; and among the earliest greetings of the new essay-writer, I suspect that Johnson's would be found. The opinion expressed in his generous question of a few years later ("Is there a man, sir, now, who "can pen an essay with such ease "and elegance as Goldsmith?"*) he was not the man to wait for the world to help him to. Himself connected with Newbery, and engaged in like occupation, the new adventurer wanted his helping word, and would be therefore sure to have it; nor, if it had not been a hearty one, is Mr. Percy likely to have busied himself to bring about the present meeting. It was arranged by that learned divine; and this was the first time, he says, he had seen them together. The day fixed was the 31st of May 1761, and Goldsmith gave a supper in Wine-office-court in honour of his visitor.

Percy called to take up Johnson at Inner-Temple-lane, and found him, to his great astonishment, in a marked condition of studied neatness; without his rusty brown suit or his soiled shirt, his loose knee-breeches, his unbuckled shoes, or his old little shrivelled unpowdered wig; and not at all likely, as Miss Reynolds tells us his fashion in these days was, to be mistaken for a beggarman. He had been seen in no such respectable garb since he appeared behind Garrick's scenes on the first of the nine nights of *Irene*, in a scarlet gold-laced waistcoat, and rich gold-laced hat. In fact, says Percy, "he had on a new suit "of clothes, a new wig nicely "powdered, and everything about "him so perfectly dissimilar "from his usual habits and ap- "pearance, that his companion "could not help enquiring the "cause of this singular trans- "formation. 'Why, sir,' said "Johnson, 'I hear that Gold- "'smith, who is a very great "'sloven, justifies his disregard "'of cleanliness and decency by "'quoting my practice; and I "'am desirous this night to show "'him a better example.'"* The example was not lost, as extracts from tailors' bills will shortly show; and the anecdote, which offers pleasant proof of the interest already felt by Johnson for his new acquaintance, is our only record connected with that memorable supper. It had no Boswell-historian, and is gone

* Doctor Farr was dining with Reynolds the year before Goldsmith's death, when, in answer to a sneer which had fallen from Mr. (afterwards Lord) Eliot, he heard Johnson fire up in defence of his absent friend, and use, among others, the expression in the text. *Prior,* i. 367.

* *Percy Memoir,* 62, 63.

into oblivion. But the friendship which dates from it will never pass away.

Writing to Percy about that supper while the Memoir was in progress, Doctor Campbell says: "The anecdote of Johnson I had "recollected, but had forgot that "it was at Goldsmith's you were "to sup. The story of the *Valet* "*de Chambre* will, as Lord Bristol "says, fill the basket of his ab- "surdities; and really we may "have a hamper full of them." * Unfortunately the anecdote of the *Valet de Chambre* has not emerged; and to another anecdote, also unluckily lost, Campbell refers in a previous letter to Percy. "One thing, however, I "could wish, if it met your ap- "probation, that I had before me "some hints respecting the affair "of Goldsmith and Perrot: it "may, without giving offence, be "related; at least so as to em- "bellish the work, by showing "more of Goldsmith's character, "which he himself has fairly "drawn: fond of enjoying the "present, careless of the future, "his sentiments those of a man "of sense, his actions those of a "fool; of fortitude able to stand "unmoved at the bursting of an "earthquake, yet of sensibility "to be affected by the breaking "of a tea-cup." ** To which, in a later letter, this is added: "Your sketch of Sir Richard "Perrot will come in as an "episode towards the conclusion,

"with good effect; but there, "neither that nor anything that "can sully shall appear as com- "ing from you." * So the Perrot anecdote is also lost, and the basket of absurdities by no means full!

1761.
———
Æt. 33.

"Farewell," says Milton, at the close of one of his early letters to his friend Gill, "and on Tues- "day next expect me in London "among the booksellers." ** The booksellers were of little mark in Milton's days; but the presence of such men among them began a social change important to both, and not ill expressed in an incident of the days I am describing, when Horace Walpole met the wealthy representative of the profits of *Paradise Lost* at a great party at the Speaker's, while Johnson was appealing to public charity for the last destitute descendant of Milton. But from the now existing compact between trade and letters, the popular element could not wholly be excluded; and, to even the weariest drudge, hope was a part of it. From the loopholes of Paternoster-row, he could catch glimpses of the world. Churchill had emerged, and Sterne, for a few brief years; and but that Johnson had sunk into idleness, he might have been reaping a harvest more continuous than theirs, and yet less dependent

---

* Nichols's *Illustrations*, vii. 780.
** Ibid, 779.

* Nichols's *Illustrations*, vii. 781.
** Todd's *Milton*, vii. 176-7. See also Aubrey's *Letters and Lives*, ii. 285, 440; and my *Life of Eliot*, ii. 175, Second Edition.

on the trade. Drudgery is not good, but flattery and falsehood are worse; and it had become plain to Goldsmith, even since the days of the *Enquiry*, how much better it was for men of letters to live by the labour of their hands till more original labour became popular with trading patrons, than to wait with their hands across, as Johnson contemptuously described it, till great men came to feed them.* Whatever the call that Newbery or any other bookseller made, then, he was there to answer it. He had the comfort of remembering that the patron had himself patrons; that something of their higher influence had been attracted to his Chinese Letters; and that he was not slaving altogether without hope.

1761.
Æt. 33.

His first undertaking in 1762 was a pamphlet on the Cock-lane Ghost, for which Newbery paid him three guineas:** but whether, with Johnson, he thought the impudent imposture worth grave inquiry; or, with Hogarth, turned it to

1762.
Æt. 34.

wise purposes of satire; or only laughed at it, as Churchill did; it is not quite certain that the pamphlet has survived to inform us. But if, as appears probable, a tract on the *Mystery Reveal'd*, published by Newbery's neighbour Bristow,* be Goldsmith's three-guinea contribution, the last is the most correct surmise. It is, however, a poor production.** His next labour, which has been attributed to him on the authority of "several personal acquaintances,"*** was the revision of a *History of Mecklenburgh from the first settlement of the Vandals in that country*, which the settlement of the young Queen Charlotte in this country was expected to make popular; and for which, according to his ordinary rates of payment, he would have received £20. This

---

* Occasions for observing with what cheerful acquiescence Goldsmith hereafter accepted these relations of author and bookseller, will frequently occur. According to his friend Cooke, indeed, it seems to have been a favourite topic with him to "tell pleasant stories of Mr. New-"bery, who, he said, was the patron of "more distressed authors than any man "of his time." *Europ. Mag.* xxiv. 92.

** "Received from Mr. Newbery three "guineas for a pamphlet respecting the "Cock Lane Ghost. OLIVER GOLD-"SMITH, March 5th, 1762." Newbery MSS. in Mr. Murray's possession.

* Newbery certainly had occasional business connection with Bristow; and Mr. Crossley, who possesses a copy of Bristow's pamphlet, says (*Notes and Queries*, v. 77) that he thinks the beginning and conclusion, "though evidently "written in haste, are not without marks "of Goldsmith's serious and playful man-"ner." Of course all this can only be conjecture, but it is at the least very unlikely that Newbery should have declined to issue what he had consented to pay Goldsmith for writing; and that Bristow published for him is certain, for at his shop the *Public Ledger* was first sold.

** With one or two lively passages, notwithstanding, which may be seen in an account given of it by Mr. Rimbault in *Notes and Queries* (3rd Series, vii. 371). A particular passage, there quoted, satisfactorily shows that our modern spirit-rapping impostures are merely a reproduction of the Ghost of Cock-lane.

*** *Prior*, i. 388.

may have been that first great advance "in a lump," which seemed to his moneyed inexperience a sum so enormous as to require the grandest schemes for disposing of it.* For a subsequent payment of £10, he assisted Newbery with an *Art of Poetry on a New Plan*, or in other words, a compilation of poetical extracts;** and concurrently with this, Mr. Newbery begged leave to offer to the young gentlemen and ladies of these kingdoms a *Compendium of Biography*, or an history of the lives of those great personages, both ancient and modern, who are most worthy of their esteem and imitation, and most likely to inspire their minds with a love of virtue; for which offering to the juvenile mind, beginning with an abridgment of Plutarch,* he was to pay Goldsmith at the rate of about eight pounds a volume. The volumes were brief, published monthly, and meant to have gone through many months if the scheme had thriven; but it fell before Dilly's *British Plutarch*, and perished with the seventh volume.

Nor did it run without danger even this ignoble career. Illness fell upon the compiler in the middle of the fifth volume. "D[r] "Sir," he wrote to Newbery, "As I have been out of order for "some time past and am still "not quite recovered, the fifth "volume of Plutarch's lives re- "mains unfinished. I fear I shall "not be able to do it, unless "there be an actual necessity "and that none else can be "found. If therefore you would "send it to Mr. Collier I should "esteem it a kindness, and will "pay for whatever it may come "to. N.B. I received twelve "guineas for the two Volumes. "I am Sir Your obliged humble "serv[t], OLIVER GOLDSMITH. Pray "let me have an answer." The

---

* *Europ. Mag.* xxiv. 92.

** Goldsmith confessed to Percy that he had helped Newbery with this book, which was the bookseller's own design and selection; and an ingenious writer, Mr. Yeowell, has gone far to show in *Notes and Queries* (3rd Series, iv. 61), that a four-line paraphrase of a couplet in *Hudibras*, still often quoted instead of the original, and which has baffled many a seeker for it in the pages of Butler, is an insertion by Goldsmith while engaged in the revision of this *Art of Poetry*. If that be so, it would seem, that, in midst of a long extract among Newbery's selections, coming upon the couplet,

> For those who fly may fight again,
> Which he can never do that's slain,

Goldsmith found it to be an irresistible temptation to expand it thus:

> For he who fights and runs away
> May live to fight another day;
> But he who is in battle slain,
> Can never rise and fight again.

Which accordingly he did, leaving all the rest of the original untouched, much to the confusion of many later learned inquirers. Even so, however, Goldsmith had but imitated the parody of a magazine of six-and-twenty years' earlier date, which was probably known to him. (*Grub Street Journal*, May 1736.)

> "The coiner that extends a rope,
> To coin again can never hope;
> But he that coins and gets away,
> May live to coin another day."

---

* "Received from Mr. Newbery eleven "guineas and a half for an abridgment "of Plutarch's Lives, March 5th, 1762. "OLIVER GOLDSMITH." Newbery MSS. in Mr. Murray's possession.

answer was not favourable. Twelve guineas had been advanced, the two volumes were due, and Mr. Collier, *1762.* though an ingenious man, *Æt. 34.* was not Mr. Goldsmith. "Sir," rejoined the latter coldly, on a scrap of paper not even wafered like the last, "One "Volume *is* done, namely the "fourth. When I said I should "be glad Mr. Collier would do "the fifth for me, I only de-"manded it as a favour, but if "he cannot conveniently do it, "tho' I have kept my chamber "these three weeks and am not "yet quite recovered yet I will "do it. I send it per bearer, "and if the affair puts you to "the least inconvenience return "it, and it shall be done im-"mediately. I am, &c. O. G. "The Printer has the Copy of "the rest." To this, his good-nature having returned, Newbery acceded; and the book was finished by Mr. Collier, to whom a share of the pittance advanced had of course to be returned.*

These paltry advances are a hopeless entanglement. They bar freedom of judgment on anything proposed, and escape is felt to be impossible. Some days, some weeks perhaps, have been lost in idleness or illness, and the future becomes a mortgage to the past; every hour has its want forestalled upon the labour of the succeeding hour, and Gulliver lies bound in Lilliput. "Sir," said Johnson, who had excellent experience on this head, "You "may escape a heavy debt, but "not a small one. Small debts "are like small shot; they are "rattling on every side, and can "scarcely be escaped without a "wound. Great debts are like "cannon, of loud noise but little "danger."*

Mention of Goldsmith's illness now frequently recurs. It originated in the habits of his London life, contrasting with the activity and movement they had replaced; and the remedy prescribed was change of scene, if change of life was impossible. He is to be traced in this year to Tunbridge and Bath; to the latter place he seems to have been a frequent visitor,** and I find him known to Mr. Wood, whose solid and tasteful architecture was then ennobling the city; one of Mr. Newbery's pithy acknowledgments being connected with those brief residences, where the *improbus labor* had not failed to follow him. "March 5, 1762. Receiv'd from "Mr. Newbery at different times "and for which I gave receipts

---

* Newbery MSS. In Mr. Murray's possession. Mr. Newbery's grandson appears to have collected all such papers as he could find of his grandfather's, throwing light on Goldsmith's connection with him; and to these, which are the property of Mr. Murray and have been placed at my disposal for the purposes of this work, I shall have frequent occasion to refer as the Newbery MSS.

* From a letter written in 1759, to the son of an old Lichfield friend.

** For an interesting recollection of visits made by him to Bath in later days see Mr. Mangin's letter to the author (Appendix A).

"fourteen guineas which is in "full for the Copy of the life "of Mr. Nash. OLIVER GOLD- "SMITH."* The recent death of the celebrated Beau had suggested a subject, which, with incidents in its comedy of manners that recommended it to a man of wit in our own day, had some to recommend it to Goldsmith.** The king of fashion had at least the oddity of a hero; and sufficient harmlessness, not to say usefulness, to make him original among heroes and kings. It is a clever book; and as one examines the original edition with its 234 goodly pages, still not uncommon on the bookstalls, it appears quite a surprising performance for fourteen guineas. Nor was anything added to this munificent payment on the book reaching a second impression, though it then received curious and important additions, dictated doubtless by a real love of the subject. No name was on the title-page; but the writer, whose powers were so various and performance so felicitous "that he "always seemed to do best that

"which he was doing," finds it difficult not to reveal his name. The preface was discerningly written. That a man who had diffused society and made manners more cheerful and refined, should have claims to attention from his own age, while his pains in pursuing pleasure and his solemnity in adjusting trifles were a claim to even a smile from posterity, was so set forth as to reassure the stateliest reader; and if somewhat thrown back by the biographer's bolder announcement, in the opening of his book, that a page of Montaigne or Colley Cibber was worth more than the most grandiose memoirs of "im- "mortal statesmen already for- "gotten," he had but to remember after how many years of uninterrupted power the old Duke of Newcastle had just resigned, to suspect that as worthy a lesson might really await him in the reign of an old minister of fashion.

In truth the book is neither uninstructive nor unamusing; and it is difficult not to connect some points of the biographer's own history with its oddly-mixed anecdotes of silliness and shrewdness, taste and tawdriness, blossom-coloured coats and gambling debts, vanity, carelessness, and good-heartedness. The latter quality in its hero was foiled by a want of prudence which deprived it of half its value: and the extenuation is so frequently and so earnestly set forth in

1762.
Æt. 34.

* Newbery MSS.

** Davies and others speak of the book as Goldsmith's, which it was generally known to be at the time; Percy of course assigns it to him in the *Memoir* (63); and the cleverness of its treatment, with its touches of "knavish subtleties and "compunctious visitings" in the letter of the highway rogue, Poulter *alias* Baxter, suggested Mr. Jerrold's pleasant comedy of *The King of Bath*. It contains also (149-154) some specimens of Nash's stories, and of his manner of telling them, given in the very best manner of Goldsmith himself.

connection with the fault, as, with what we now know of the writer, to convey an uneasy personal reference. Remembering, indeed, that what *1762.* *Æt. 34.* now is known to us was at this date not only unknown, but waiting for what remained of Goldsmith's life fully to develop and call it forth, this *Life of Beau Nash* is in some respects a curious, and was probably an unconscious, revelation of character. As yet restricted in his wardrobe, and unknown to the sartorial books of Mr. William Filby, he gravely discusses the mechanical and moral influence of dress, in the exaction of respect and esteem. Quite ignorant, as yet, of his own position among the remarkable men of his time, he dwells strongly on that class of impulsive virtues, which, in a man otherwise distinguished, are more adapted to win friends than admirers, and more capable of raising love than esteem. A stranger still to the London whist-table, even to the moderate extent in which he subsequently sought its excitements, he sets forth with singular pains the temptation of a man who has "led a life of expedients, "and thanked chance for his "support," to become a stranger to prudence, and fly back to chance for those "vicissitudes of "rapture and anguish" in which his character had been formed. * With light and shade that might seem of any choosing but his,

he exhibits the moral qualities of Nash, as of one whose virtues, in almost every instance, received some tincture from the follies most nearly neighbouring them; who, though very poor, was very fine, and spread out the little gold he had as thinly and far as it would go,* but whose poverty was the more to be regretted, that it denied him the indulgence not only of his favourite follies, but of his favourite virtues; who had pity for every creature's distress, but wanted prudence in the application of his benefits, and in whom this ill-controlled sensibility was so strong, that, unable to witness the misfortunes of the miserable, he was always borrowing money to relieve them; who had notwithstanding done a thousand good things, and whose greatest vice was vanity.** The self-painted picture will appear more striking as this narrative proceeds; and it would seem to have the same sort of unconscious relation to the future, that one of Nash's friends should be mentioned in the book as having gone by the name of The Good-natured Man. Nor must I omit the casual evidence of acquaintanceship between its hero and his biographer that occurs in a lively notice of the three periods of amatory usage which the beau's long life had witnessed, and in which not only

* *Life*, 20—22, aud see 50—64.

* *Life*, 9, 14. The passage suggests the original of Beau Tibbs.
** *Life*, 104—119.

had flaxen bobs been succeeded by majors, and negligents been routed by bags and ramilies, but the modes of making love had varied as much as the periwigs. "The only way to make love "*now*, I have heard Mr. Nash say, "was to take no manner of notice "of the lady."*

Johnson's purchase of this book, which is charged to him in one of Newbery's accounts, shows his interest in whatever affected Goldsmith at this opening of their friendship. His book-purchases were never abundant; though better able to afford them now than at any previous time, for the May of this year had seen a change in his fortunes. Bute's pensions to his Scottish crew showing meaner than ever in Churchill's daring verse, it oc-

curred to the shrewd and wary Wedderburne (whose sister had married the favourite's most intimate friend) to advise, for a set-off, that Samuel Johnson should be pensioned. 1762.
Æt. 34. Of all the wits at the Grecian or the Bedford, Arthur Murphy, who had been some months fighting the *North Briton* with the *Auditor*, and was now watching the Courts at Westminster preparatory to his first circuit in the following year, was best known to Bute's rising lawyer; and Arthur was sent to Johnson. It was an "abode of "wretchedness," said this messenger of glad tidings, describing on his return those rooms of Inner-Temple-lane where a visitor of some months before had found the author of the *Rambler* and *Rasselas*, now fifty-three years old, without pen, ink, or paper, "in poverty, total idleness, and "the pride of literature." Yet great as was the poverty, and glad the tidings, a shade passed over Johnson's face. After a long pause, "he asked if it was "seriously intended." Undoubtedly. His majesty, to reward literary merit, and with no desire that the author of the *English Dictionary* should "dip his pen in "faction" (these were Bute's own words), had signified through the premier his pleasure to grant to Samuel Johnson three hundred pounds a year. "He fell into a "profound meditation, and his "own definition of a pensioner "occurred to him." He was told

* *Life*, 75. "*I have known him*," he remarks in another passage, "on a ball-"night strip even the dutchess of Q——, "and throw her apron at one of the "hinder benches among the ladies' "women; observing that none but Abi-"gails appeared in white aprons ... and "the good-natured dutchess acquiesced "in his censure." 36. I cannot help adding one more passage of very unconscious and most amusing self-revelation. "The business of love somewhat re-"sembles the business of physic; no "matter for qualifications, he that makes "vigorous pretensions to either is surest "of success. Nature had by no means "favoured Mr. Nash for a beau garçon; "his person was clumsy, too large, and "awkward, and his features harsh, strong, "and peculiarly irregular; yet, even "with these disadvantages, he made love, "became an universal admirer, and was "universally admired. He was possessed, "at least, of some requisites of a lover. "He had assiduity, flattery, fine cloaths, "and as much wit as the ladies he ad-"dressed." 74.

that "he, at least, did not come "within the definition;" but it was not until after dinner with Murphy at the Mitre on the following day that he consented to wait on Bute and accept the proffered bounty.* To be pensioned with the fraudulent and contemptible Shebbeare, so lately pilloried for a Jacobite libel on the Revolution of '88; to find himself in the same Bute-list with a Scotch court-architect, with a Scotch court-painter, with the infamous David Mallet, and with Johnny Home, must have chafed Sam Johnson's pride a little; and when, in a few more months, as author of "another" *English Dictionary*, old Sheridan the actor received two hundred a year (because his theatre had suffered in the Dublin riots, pleaded Wedderburne; because he had gone to Edinburgh to teach Bute's friend to talk English, said Wilkes), it had become very plain to him that Lord Bute knew nothing of literature. But he had compromised no independence in the course he took, and might afford to laugh at the outcry which followed. "I wish "my pension were twice as large, "sir," he said afterwards at Davies's, "that they might make "twice as much noise."**

But Davies was now grown into so much importance, and his shop was a place so often

memorable for the persons who met there, that more must be said of both in a new chapter.

CHAPTER VI.

Introductions at Tom Davies's.
1762.

THOMAS DAVIES, ex-performer of Drury-lane, and present publisher and bookseller of Russell-street, Covent-garden, had now (with his "very pretty wife") left the stage and taken wholly to bookselling, which he had recently, and for the second time, attempted to combine with acting. The *Rosciad* put a final extinguisher on his theatrical existence.* He never afterwards mouthed a sentence in one of the kingly and heavy parts he was in the habit of playing, that Churchill's image of his "gnaw-"ing a sentence as a cur a bone" did not confuse the sentence that followed; and his eye never fell upon any prominent figure in the front row of the pit, that he did not tremble to fancy it the brawny person of Churchill. What he thus lost in self-possession, Garrick meanwhile lost in temper; and matters came to a breach, in which Johnson, being appealed to, took part against Garrick, as he was seldom dis-

---

* See Murphy's account in his *Essay* prefixed to Johnson's works, 51. Ed. 1825.
** *Boswell*, ii. 254, *note*.

* The Rev. Mr. Granger mentions the most interesting fact in it. "In 1736, he "acted at the theatre in the Haymarket, "where he was the first person who per-"formed Young Wilmot in Lillo's tra-"gedy of the *Fatal Curiosity*, under the "management of the celebrated Henry "Fielding." *Letters*, 69.

inclined to do. Pretty Mrs. Davies may have helped his inclination here; for when seized with his old moody abstraction, as was not unusual, in the bookseller's parlour, and he began to blow, and *too-too*, and mutter prayers to be delivered from temptation, Davies would whisper his wife with waggish humour, "You, my dear, are the cause of "this." But be the cause what it might, the pompous little bibliopole never afterwards lost favour; and it became as natural for men interested in Johnson, or those who clustered round him, to repair to Davies's the bookseller in Russell-street, as for those who wanted to hear of George Selwyn, Lord March, or Lord Carlisle, to call at Betty's the fruiterer in St. James's-street.

A frequent visitor was Goldsmith; his thick, short, clumsy figure, and his awkward though genial manners, oddly contrasting with Mr. Percy's, precise, reserved, and stately. The high-bred and courtly Beauclerc might deign to saunter in. Often would be seen there the broad fat face of Foote, with wicked humour flashing from the eye; and sometimes the mild long face of Bennet Langton, filled with humanity and gentleness. There had Goldsmith met a rarer visitor, the bland and gracious Reynolds, soon after his first introduction to him, a few months back, in Johnson's chambers;[*]

and there would even Warburton drive on some proud business of his own, in his equipage "be-"sprinkled with mitres," after calling on Garrick in Southampton-street.[*] For Garrick himself, it was perhaps the only place of meeting he cared to avoid, in that neighbourhood which had so profited and been gladdened by his genius; in which his name was oftener resounded than that of any other human being; and throughout which, we are told, there was a fondness for him, that, as his sprightly figure passed along, "darted electri-"cally from shop to shop." What the great actor indeed said some years later, he already seems to have fancied: that "he believed "most authors who frequented "Mr. Davies's shop met merely "to abuse him." Encouraged, meanwhile, by the authors, Davies grew in amusing importance; set up for quite a patron of the players;[**] affected the insides as well as outsides of books; became a critic, pronounced upon plays and actors,[***] and discussed themes

1762.
————
Æt. 34.

* In Reynolds's note-books there is an entry of a dinner at Tom Davies's on the 27th March, 1762, where Goldsmith also dined.

* Granger's *Letters*, 25.

** Granger's *Letters*, 26. Beauclerc, on being told by Boswell that Davies had clapped Moody the player on the back to encourage him, remarked that "he could "not conceive a more humiliating situa-"tion than to be clapped on the back by "Tom Davies." Boswell, *Life*, v. 257.

*** "Pray, when you see Davies, the "bookseller," writes Garrick to Colman from Bath (April 12, 1766), "assure hi

of scholarship; inflicted upon every one his experiences of the Edinburgh university, which he had attended as a youth; and when George Steevens called one day to buy the *Oxford Homer*, which he had seen tossing about upon his shelves, was told by the modest bookseller that he had but one, and kept it for his own reading.*

1762.
Æt. 34.

"that I bear him not the least malice, "which he is told I do, for having men- "tioned the vulgarisms in *The Clandestine* "*Marriage*; and, that I may convince him "that all is well between us, let him "know that I was well assured that he "wrote his criticism before he had seen "the play. *Quod erat demum.*" *Memoirs of the Colmans*, i. 181.

* Steevens to Garrick, *Correspondence*, i. 598. In another letter (i. 597-8) Steevens protests to Garrick that the mighty Tom continues "to the full as "much a king in his own shop as ever he "was on your stage. When he was on "the point of leaving the theatre he most "certainly stole some copper diadem "from a shelf and put it in his pocket. "He has worn it ever since." So too Johnson, in a passage well worth quoting, when Boswell mentioned to him the fact of Davies having protested he could not sleep for thinking of a certain sad affair: "'As to his sleeping, sir, Tom "'Davies is a very great man; Tom has "'been upon the stage and knows how "'to do those things; I have not been "'upon the stage, and cannot do those "'things.' BOSWELL: 'I have often "'blamed myself, sir, for not feeling for "'others as sensibly as many say they "'do.' JOHNSON: 'Sir, don't be duped "'by them any more. You will find "'these very feeling people are not very "'ready to do you good. They *pay* you "'by *feeling*.'" *Life*, III. 95-6. Worthy of that last admirable saying is what Swift says in the Journal to Stella. "There is something of farce in all those "mournings, let them be ever so serious. "People will pretend to grieve more than "they really do, and that takes off from "their true grief." *Works*, III. 196.

Poor Goldsmith's pretensions, as yet, were small in the scale of such conceit; he being but the best of the essay writers, not the less bound on that account to unrepining drudgery, somewhat awkward in his manners, and laughed at for a careless simplicity. Such was the character he was first seen in here, and he found its impressions always oddly mingled with whatever respect or consideration he challenged in later life. Only Johnson saw into that life as yet, or could measure what the past had been to him; and few so well as Goldsmith had reason to know the great heart which beat so gently under those harsh manners. The friendship of Johnson was his first relish of fame; he repaid it with affection and deference of no ordinary kind; and so commonly were they seen together, now that Johnson's change of fortune brought him more into the world, that when a puppet-caricature of the Idler was threatened this summer by the Haymarket Aristophanes, the Citizen of the World was to be a puppet too. "What is the com- "mon price of an oak stick, sir?" asked Johnson, when he heard of it. "Sixpence," answered Davies. "Why then, sir, give "me leave to send your ser- "vant to purchase me a shil- "ling one. I'll have a double "quantity; for I am told Foote "means to *take me off*, as he calls "it, and I am determined the "fellow shall not do it with impunity."* The *Orators* came out without the attraction promised: attacking instead a celebrated Dublin printer, George Faulkner, who consoled himself (pending his prosecution of the libeller) by pirating the libel and selling it most extensively; —— while the satirist had the [1762. Æt. 34.] more doubtful consolation of reflecting, three years later, that his "taking off" of Faulkner's one leg* would have been much more perfect, if he could have waited till the surgeon had taken off his own. It was the first dramatic piece, I may add, in which actors were stationed among the audience, and spoke from the public boxes.

It had been suggested by a debating society called the Robin Hood, somewhat famous in those days, which used to meet near Temple-bar; with which the connection of Burke's earliest eloquence may serve to keep it famous still, since it had num-

---

* *Boswell*, v. 232-3. Johnson's offence to Foote was reported from Garrick's dinner-table, at which, on the occasion of a Christmas party (1760) with Burke, the Wartons, Murphy, and others, after hearing that somebody in Dublin had thought it worth while to horsewhip the modern Aristophanes, he had said he was glad "the man was rising in the world." Foote in return gave out that he would in a short time produce the Caliban of literature on the stage. Being informed of this design, Johnson sent word to Foote, that, the theatre being intended for the reformation of vice, he would go from the boxes on the stage, and correct him before the audience. "Foote aban-"doned the design. No ill-will ensued. "Johnson used to say that for broad-"faced mirth, Foote had not his equal." See an article in the *Monthly Review* (LXXVI. 374), one of a series admirably written, I suspect by Murphy. Since I threw out this suggestion, I have found several passages from these reviews reproduced in Murphy's *Essay* on Johnson, and among them the notice of the Christmas-day dinner at Garrick's (55). Let me not here omit what Johnson so admirably said of Foote, in talking of him to Boswell a few years later. BOSWELL: "Foote has a great deal of humour." JOHNSON: "Yes, sir." BOSWELL: "He "has a singular talent of exhibiting char-"acter." JOHNSON: "Sir, it is not a "talent, it is a vice; it is what others ab-"stain from. It is not comedy, which ex-"hibits the character of a species, as that "of a miser gathered from many misers: "it is farce, which exhibits individuals." BOSWELL: "Did not he think of ex-"hibiting you, sir?" JOHNSON: "Sir, "fear restrained him; he knew I would "have broken his bones. I would have "saved him the trouble of cutting off a "leg; I would not have left him a leg to "cut off." *Boswell*, iii. 95-6. No man, at the same time, was less sore than Johnson at more ordinary personal abuse. On some one reporting to him that Gilbert Cooper had invented for him the name, which Foote applies to him above, of the Caliban of literature, he merely smiled and said, "Well, then, I must dub him "the Punchinello." *Ib.* iii. 143-4. I will close this note with Johnson's not unkindly comment to Mrs. Thrale on Foote's death, when he heard of it in 1776. "Did you see Foote at Brightelm-"stone? Did you think he would so soon "be gone? Life, says Falstaff, is a "shuttle. He was a fine fellow in his "way; and the world is really im-"poverished by his sinking glories. "Murphy ought to write his life, at least "to give the world a *Footeana*. Now, will "any of his contemporaries bewail him? "Will Genius change *his sex* to weep? I "would really have his life written with "diligence." *Piozzi Letters*, i. 396. Failing that *Life*, I have myself endeavoured to contribute something towards the better knowledge of the better part of Foote's genius for comedy, which has fallen into undeserved though unavoidable neglect. See my *Biog. Essays*, pp. 329-462. Third Edition, 1860.

* See *Boswell*, iii. 181-2.

bered among its members that eager Temple student, whose public life was now at last beginning with under-secretary Hamilton in Dublin; and to which Goldsmith was introduced by Samuel Derrick, his countryman, and a fellow-worker for Newbery.* Struck by the eloquence and imposing aspect of the president, who sat in a large gilt chair, he thought nature had meant him for a lord chancellor. "No, no," whispered Derrick, who knew him to be a wealthy baker from the city, "only for a master of the rolls." Goldsmith was not much of an orator; Doctor Kippis remembered him making an attempt at a speech in the Society of Arts on one occasion, and obliged to sit down in confusion;* but, until

1762.

Æt. 34.

* Derrick had strange experiences to relate, by which doubtless Goldsmith profited. "Sir," said Johnson to Boswell, "I honour Derrick for his presence "of mind. One night, when Floyd, an- "other poor author, was wandering "about the streets in the night, he found "Derrick fast asleep upon a bulk: upon "being suddenly waked, Derrick started "up, 'My dear Floyd, I am sorry to see "'you in this destitute state: will you go "'home with me to *my lodgings?*'" *Life,* II. 244. Derrick had also something to say to Goldsmith of the old savage persecutor of his college days (*ante,* p. 22), to which he would be likely to listen with a strange interest. A fellow of Trinity, Dr. Wilson, was his frequent correspondent, and his letters contain allusions to Dr. Theaker Wilder, all characteristic of the brutality of the man. One is in a letter of the 26th September, 1762. "*Wilder got a monstrous beating from* "*Rogers*—the particulars in my next." Unfortunately "my next" has not been preserved; but in a letter of congratulation (18th March, 1763) on Derrick's appointment to be master of the ceremonies at Bath, the same names reappear in ominous conjunction. "The happiest "circumstance in your affairs is to be re- "lieved from the vile drudgery of au- "thorship, from subjection to the clamor- "ous demands of devils and booksellers. "Are you acquainted with the Bishop of "Gloucester? I take him to be a man "of great genius, and an admirable "reasoner. Give me an account of Quin, "and if you can learn anything about "Gray. Does Warburton know him? "*Rogers is in London, on the road to the* "*East Indies. Dr. Wilder is not yet hang'd.* "I'm heartily tired of the college." Derrick MSS.

* "The great room of the society now "mentioned," says Doctor Kippis at the close of his memoir of Mr. Gilbert Cooper, and referring to the Society of Arts, "was for several years the place "where many persons chose to try, or to "display, their oratorical abilities. Dr. "Goldsmith, I remember, made an at- "tempt at a speech, but was obliged to "sit down in confusion. I once heard "Doctor Johnson speak there, upon a "subject relating to mechanics, with a "propriety, perspicuity, and energy which "excited general admiration." *Biog. Brit.* (new edit.) IV. 286. Against this, however, in so far as Johnson is concerned, we have to set off the express and very interesting statement in Boswell's *Life,* III. 157-8. "I remember it was observed "by Mr. Flood, that Johnson, having "been long used to sententious brevity, "and the short flights of conversation, "might have failed in that continued and "expanded kind of argument which is "requisite in stating complicated matters "in public speaking; and, as a proof "of this, he mentioned the supposed "speeches in parliament written by him "for the magazine, none of which, in his "opinion, were at all like real debates. "The opinion of one who was himself so "eminent an orator, must be allowed to "have great weight. It was confirmed "by Sir William Scott (Lord Stowell), "who mentioned, that Johnson had told "him that he had several times tried to "speak in the Society of Arts and "Sciences, but had found he could not "get on. From Mr. William Gerard "Hamilton I have heard, that Johnson,

Derrick went away to succeed Beau Nash at Bath, he seems to have continued his visits, and even spoken occasionally; for he figures in a flattering account of the members published at about this time, as "a good orator and "candid disputant, with a clear "head and an honest heart, "though coming but seldom to the "society." The honest heart was worn upon his sleeve, whatever his society might be. He could not even visit the three Cherokees, whom all the world were at this time visiting, without leaving the savage chiefs a trace of it. He gave them some "trifle" they did not look for; and so did the gift, or the manner of it, please them, that with a sudden embrace they covered his cheeks with the oil and ochre that plentifully bedaubed their own, and left him to discover, by the laughter which greeted him in the street, the extent and fervour of their gratitude. *

Not always such ready recipients, however, did Goldsmith find in the objects of his always ready kindness. One of the members of this Robin Hood was Peter Annet, a man who, though ingenious and deserving in other respects, became unhappily notorious by a fanatic crusade against the Bible, for which (publishing weekly papers against the Book of Genesis) he stood twice this year in the pillory, and was now undergoing imprisonment in the King's bench. To Annet's rooms in St. George's-fields we trace Goldsmith. He had brought Newbery with him to conclude the purchase of a child's book on grammar by the prisoner, hoping so to relieve his distress; but, on the prudent book-

1762.
——
Æt. 34.

"when observing to him that it was "prudent for a man who had not been "accustomed to speak in public to begin "his speech in as simple a manner as "possible, acknowledged that he rose in "that society to deliver a speech which he "had prepared; 'but,' said he, 'all my "'flowers of oratory forsook me.'"

* "We have a very wrong idea of "savage finery, and are apt to suppose "that like the beasts of the forest, they "rise, and are dressed with a shake; but "the reverse is true: for no birth-night "beauty takes more time or pains in the "adorning her person than they. I re"member, when the Cherokee kings "were over here, that I have waited for "three hours during the time they were "dressing . . . they had their boxes of "oil and ochre, their fat and their per-

"fumes." *Animated Nature*, i. 420. A mention of Foote's visit to the Cherokees, in a letter of Mrs. Thrale's to Johnson in 1781, may be added, because it shows also the impression that remained among the set as to Goldsmith's philosophy about rich and poor, luxury and simplicity, seven years after he had passed away. "It has been thought by many "wise folks," she writes to Johnson, "that we fritter our pleasures all away "by refinement, and when one reads "Goldsmith's works, either verse or "prose, one fancies that in corrupt life "there is more enjoyment: yet *we* should "find little solace from ale-house merri"ment or cottage carousals, whatever *the* "*best wrestler on the green* might do, I "suppose; more brandy and brown sugar "*liqueur*, like that which Foote presented "the Cherokee kings with, and won their "hearts from our fine ladies who treated "them with sponge biscuits and fron"tiniac." *Letters*, ii. 216. She was writing in the same strain to Sir James Fellowes nearly half a century after Goldsmith's death. See *Hayward*, ii. 148-9.

seller objecting to its publication with the author's name, Annet accused him of cowardice, rejected his assistance with contempt, and in a furious rage bade him and his introducer good evening. Yet the amount of Newbery's intended assistance was so liberal as to have startled both Goldsmith and Annet, no less a sum than ten guineas being offered for the child's grammar,* though for the "completion of a history of "England" he had just given Goldsmith himself only two guineas.* Which latter munificent payment was exactly contemporaneous with the completion of another kind of history, on more expensive terms, by paymaster Henry Fox; from whom twenty-five thousand pounds had gone in one morning, at the formal rate of £200 a vote, to patriotic voters for the Peace.

There is reason to believe (from another of the bookseller's memoranda) that the two guineas was for "seventy-nine leaves" of addition to a school-history comprising the reign of George the Second, and paid at the rate of eight shillings a sheet. This payment, with what has before been mentioned, and an addition of five guineas for the assignment and republication of the Chinese Letters (to which Newbery, as we have seen, appears to have assented reluctantly, and only because Goldsmith would else have printed them on his own account), are all the profits of his drudgery which can be traced to him in the present year. He needed to have a cheerful dis-

1762.
———
Æt. 34.

* It was the magnificence of the offer which brought about the catastrophe, such a fervour of gratitude being excited in Annet that he suddenly protested he would add a dedication and append his name, and Newbery should have the benefit of both. I derive the anecdote from Cooke, who says it was one of those stories which he had heard Goldsmith "relate with much colloquial humour;" and he gives a portion of the dialogue in which, as Goldsmith repeated it, the contrast of Newbery's slow gravity, with Annet's impatience, rising at last into fury, had a most amusing effect. "But, "Mr. Annet," says Newbery, in his grave manner, "would putting your name to "it, do you think, increase the value of "your book?" ANNET. "Why not, sir?" NEWB. "Consider a bit, Mr. Annet." ANNET. "Well, sir, I do: what then?" NEWB. "Why, then, sir, you must re- "collect that you have been *pilloried*, and "that can be no recommendation to any "man's book." ANNET. "I grant I have "been pilloried, but I am not the first "man that has had this accident; be- "sides, sir, the public very often support "a man the more for those unavoidable "misfortunes." NEWB. "*Unavoidable*, Mr. "Annet! Why, sir, you brought it on "yourself by writing against the estab- "lished religion of your country; and let "me tell you, Mr. Annet, a man who is "supposed to have forfeited his ears on "such an account, stands but a poor can- "didate for public favour." ANNET. "Well, well, Mr. Newbery, it does not "signify talking; you either suffer me to "put my name to it, or by G—I you.

"publish no book of mine." And so, in a quite unexpected catastrophe of flaming wrath, the visitors vanish, and the *Child's Grammar* is heard of no more. See *Europ. Mag.* xxiv. 92. For a further account of Annet, see Hawkins's *Life of Johnson*, 566.

* I quote from an autograph of Goldsmith in the possession of Mr. Rogers: "Received of Mr. Newbery the sum of "two guineas for the completion of the "*English History*. July 27, 1762."

position to bear him through; nor was nature chary to him now of that choicest of her gifts. He had some bow of promise shining through his dullest weather. It is supposed that he memorialised Lord Bute, soon after Johnson's pension, with the scheme we have seen him throw out hints of in his review of Van Egmont's *Asia;** and, though no such memorial has been found, nothing is more probable than that such a notion might have revived with him, on hearing Johnson's remark to Langton in connection with his pension. "Had "this happened twenty years "ago, I should have gone to Con- "stantinople to learn Arabic, as "Pocock did." But what with Samuel Johnson might be a noble ambition, with little Goldy was but theme for a jest; and nothing so raised the laugh against him, a few years later, as

Johnson's notice of the old favourite project he was still at that time clinging to, that some time or other, "when his "circumstances should be "easier," he would like to go to Aleppo, and bring home such arts peculiar to the East as he might be able to find there. "Of all men Goldsmith is the "most unfit to go out upon such "an inquiry; for he is utterly "ignorant of such arts as we al- "ready possess, and consequent- "ly could not know what would "be accessories to our present "stock of mechanical knowledge. "Sir, he would bring home a "grinding-barrow, which you see "in every street in London, and "think that he had furnished a "wonderful improvement."*

1762.
—
Æt. 34.

But brighter than these visionary fancies were shining for him now. There is little doubt, from allusions which would most naturally have arisen at the close of the present year, that, in moments snatched from his thankless and ill-rewarded toil for Newbery, he was at last secretly indulging in a labour, which, whatever its effect might be upon his fortunes, was its own thanks and its own reward. He had begun the *Vicar of Wakefield*. Without encouragement or favour in its progress, and with

---

* See *ante*, 129. The same subject is pursued in Letter CVIII. of the *Citizen of the World*. "To Lord Bute Goldsmith "made an application to be allowed a "salary to enable him to execute his "favourite plan .. but poor Goldsmith, "who had not then published his *Tra- "eller*, or distinguished his name by any "popular display of genius, being obscure "and unfriended, was not successful. "His petition or memorial was unnoticed "and neglected." *Percy Memoir*, 65. With the hope of discovering some possible trace of the application which there is no reason to doubt was really made by Goldsmith to the first minister, Lord Dudley Stuart was so kind, at my request, as to cause strict search to be made through the voluminous and very interesting unpublished correspondence of Lord Bute. But nothing was discovered of it, or in any way bearing upon it.

* *Boswell*, VII. 370. Yet that Goldsmith took no mean view of the objects to be aimed at in such an enterprise, and felt that its successful accomplishment would task a higher and hardier spirit than his own, appears from the Chinese Letter named in the previous note.

little hope of welcome at the close of it; earning meanwhile, apart from it, his bread for the day by a full day's labour at the desk; it is his "shame in crowds, his "solitary pride," to seize and give shape to its fancies of happiness and home, before they pass for ever. Most affecting, yet also most cheering! With everything before him in his hard life that the poet has placed at the Gates of Hell,* he is content for himself to undergo the chances of them all, that for others he may open the neighbouring Elysian Gate. Nor could the effort fail to bring strength of its own, and self-sustained resource. In all else he might be weak and helpless, dependent on others' judgment and doubtful of his own; but, there, it was not so. He took his own course in that. It was not for Mr. Newbery he was writing then. Even the poetical fragments which began in Switzerland are lying still in his desk untouched. *They* are not to tell for so many pitiful items in the drudgery for existence. They are to "catch the heart, "and strike for honest fame."

He thought poorly, with exceptions already named in this narrative, of the poetry of the day. He regarded Churchill's astonishing success as a mere proof of the rage of faction; and did not hesitate to call his satires lampoons, and his force turbulence. Fawkes and Woty were now compiling their *Poetical Calendar*, and through Johnson, who contributed, they asked if he would contribute; but he declined. Between himself and Fawkes, who was rector of a small Kentish village he had occasionally visited, civilities had passed; but he shrunk from the poetical school of Fawkes and Woty, and did not hesitate to say so. He dined at the close of the year at Davies's, in company with Robert Dodsley, where the matter came into discussion. "This is not a poetical age," said Goldsmith; "there is no "poetry produced in it." "Nay," returned Dodsley, "have you "seen my *Collection?* You may "not be able to find palaces in "it, like Dryden's *Ode*, but you "have villages composed of very "pretty houses, such as the "*Spleen.*" Johnson was not present; but when the conversation was afterwards reported to him by Boswell, he remarked that Dodsley had said the same thing as Goldsmith, only in a softer manner. *

---

* Johnson told Boswell that, in his opinion, Virgil's description of the entrance into hell applied equally to an author's entrance into literature. "All "those," he said, gloomily repeating the terrible phrases of the poet, "are the "concomitants of a printing-house." *Life,* v. 43. I have since found that Burton had made the same comparison, and quoted those very lines before him. *Anatomie of Melancholy,* (ed. XVI. 1838), 203.

* *Life*, VI. 156-7. Yet Dodsley was quite right in his praise of the *Spleen,* which was especially liked by Gray, as it has been by all men of taste. "The *Spleen,*

Another guest, besides Dodsley, was present at Davies's dinner-table that day. A youth of two-and-twenty, the son of a Scottish judge and respectable old whig laird, urged to enter the law but eager to bestow himself on the army, had come up at the end of the year from Edinburgh to see Johnson and the London wits, and not a little anxious that Johnson and the London wits should see him. Attending Sheridan's summer lectures in the northern city, he had heard wonderful things from the lecturer about the solemn and ponderous lexicographer; what he said, and what he did, and how he would talk over his port wine and his tea until three or four o'clock in the morning. It was in the nature of this new admirer that port wine and late hours should throw a brighter halo over any object of his admiration; and it was with desperate resolve to accomplish an introduction which he had tried and failed in two years before, that he was now again in London. But he had again been baffled. Johnson's sneer at Sheridan's pension* having brought coolness between the old friends, that way there was no access; and though Davies had arranged this dinner with the hope of getting his great friend to come, his great friend had found other matters to attend to. James Boswell was not yet to see Samuel Johnson. He saw only

1762.
———
Æt. 34.

"a poem in Dodsley's *Collection*, by Mr.
"Green of the custom-house, was a great
"favourite with him for its wit and
"originality." Nicholls's Reminiscences
of Gray, *Works*, v. 36-7. It is in Green's
poem the neat line occurs, by way of recommending exercise as a cure for the
malady,

Fling but a stone, the giant dies!

In a letter to Walpole, I may add, written
many years before he expressed that
opinion to Nicholls, and which is interesting to me for its mention of Johnson, Gray had pleasantly criticised Dodsley's book on its first appearance (the
letter is undated, but was written at the
close of 1751). In it he says that he had
always thought Tickell's *Colin and Lucy*
the prettiest ballad in the world (one of
the prettiest it surely is, notwithstanding
Southey's depreciation of it); he then
says of Green, after praising his "pro-
"fusion of wit," that reading would have
formed his judgment and harmonised his
verse, for even his wood-notes often
break out into strains of real poetry and
music; and afterwards he continues,
"The *Schoolmistress* is excellent in its
"kind, and masterly; and (I am sorry to
"differ from you, but) *London* is to me
"one of those few imitations that have all
"the ease and all the spirit of an original.
"The same man's verses on the Opening
"of Garrick's Theatre are far from bad."
Works, III. 89-90. A pity that Johnson
had not known of this letter; it might
have mitigated his strange and unaccountable dislike of the writer. *His* criticism of the *Collection* which thus elicited Gray's praise of himself is chiefly
remarkable for its savage scorn of Gray.
Boswell, VI. 157.

* The pension following the *Dictionary*
was not to be forgiven. "He laughed
"heartily," says Boswell, a few days
after their first acquaintance, "when I
"mentioned to him a saying of his concerning Mr. Thomas Sheridan, which
"Foote took a wicked pleasure to circulate. 'Why, sir, Sherry is dull, na-
"'turally dull; but it must have taken
"'him a great deal of pains to become
"'what we now see him. Such an ac-
"'cess of stupidity, sir, is not in nature.'
"'So,' said he, 'I allowed him all his
"'own merit.'" *Life*, II. 240.

Oliver Goldsmith, and was doubtless much disappointed.

Perhaps the feeling was mutual, if Oliver gave a thought to this new acquaintance; and strange enough the dinner must have been. As Goldsmith discussed poetry with Dodsley, Davies, mouthing his words and rolling his head at Boswell, delighted that eager and social gentleman with imitations of Johnson; while, as the bottle emptied itself more freely, sudden loquacity, conceited coxcombry, and officious airs of consequence, came as freely pouring forth from the youthful Scot. He had to tell them all he had seen in London, and all that had seen him. How Wilkes had said "how "d'ye do" to him, and Churchill had shaken hands with him, Scotchman though he was; how he had been to the Bedford to see that comical fellow Foote, and heard him dashing away at everybody and everything ("Have you had good success in "Dublin, Mr. Foote?" "Poh! "damn 'em! There was not a "shilling in the country, except "what the Duke of Bedford, and "I, and Mr. Rigby have brought "away"*); how he had seen Garrick in the new farce of the *Farmer's Return*, and gone and peeped over Hogarth's shoulder as he sketched little David in the Farmer, hitting off in half a dozen minutes, with magical facility of pencil, a likeness that

* *Garrick Correspondence*, i. 116.

was held to be marvellous; and how, above all, he had on another night attracted general attention and given prodigious entertainment in the Drury-lane pit, by extempore imitations of the lowing of a cow. "The "universal cry of the galleries," said he, gravely describing the incident some few years afterwards, "was, encore the cow, "encore the cow! In the pride "of my heart I attempted imita- "tions of some other animals, "but with very inferior effect." A Scotch friend was with him, and gave sensible advice. "My "dear sir," said Doctor Blair, earnestly, "I would confine my- "self to the cow!" or, as Walter Scott tells the anecdote in purer vernacular, "Stick to the cow, "mon."* Nor was the advice lost altogether; for Boswell stuck afterwards to his cow, in other words to what he could best achieve, pretty closely: though Goldsmith, among others, had no small reason to regret, that he should also, doing the cow so well, still "with very inferior "effect" attempt imitations of other animals.

But little does Goldsmith or any other man suspect as yet, that within this wine-bibbing

* Boswell, *Life*, v. 148-9, and *note*. The story was incautiously told to Johnson; and afterwards, on Boswell's talking, as he himself tells us, "too con- "fidently upon some point, which I now "forget, he did not spare me. 'Nay, " 'sir,' said he, 'If you cannot talk better " 'as a man, I'd have you bellow like a " 'cow.' "

tavern-babbler, this meddling, conceited, inquisitive, loquacious lion-hunter, this bloated and vain young Scot, lie qualities of reverence, real insight, quick observation, and marvellous memory, which, strangely assorted as they are with those other meaner habits and parasitical self-complacent absurdities, will one day connect his name eternally with the men of genius of his time, and enable him to influence posterity in its judgments on them. They seem to have met occasionally before Boswell returned to Edinburgh; but only two of Goldsmith's answers to the other's perpetual and restless questionings remain to indicate the nature of their intercourse. There lived at this time with Johnson a strange, silent, grotesque companion, whom he had supported for many years, and continued to keep with him till death; and Boswell could not possibly conceive what the claim of that insignificant Robert Levett could be, on the grand object of his own veneration. "He is poor and honest," was Goldsmith's answer, "which is "recommendation enough for "Johnson."* Discovery of an-

other object of the great man's charity, however, seemed difficult to be reconciled with this; for here was a man of whom Mr. James Boswell had heard a very bad and shameful character,* and, in almost the same breath, that Johnson had been kind to him also. "He is now become miserable," was Goldsmith's quiet explanation, "and that en-

1762.
Æt. 34.

patients could afford him; and his popularity in this was so great that "his walk "was from Houndsditch to Marylebone." He began life as a waiter in a coffee-house in Paris frequented by medical men, whose attention he attracted, and thus qualified himself ultimately. George Steevens, who relates this (*Gentleman's Magazine*, Feb. 1785), describes also the other great event of his life. When past middle life, he married a woman of the town, who had persuaded him (notwithstanding their place of congress was a small coal-shed in Fetter-lane) that she was nearly related to a man of fortune, but was kept by him out of large possessions. Johnson used to say, that, compared with the marvels of this transaction, the stories of the Arabian Nights were familiar occurrences. He had not been married four months before a writ was taken out against him, for debts contracted by his wife. Afterwards she ran away from him, and was tried for picking pockets at the Old Bailey. She pleaded her own cause, and was acquitted; a separation took place; and Johnson then took Levett home, where he continued till his death. His name will always be remembered in connection with Johnson's noble verse:

> "In Misery's darkest caverns known,
> "His useful care was ever nigh,
> "Where hopeless Anguish pour'd his
> "groan,
> "And lonely Want retir'd to
> "die."

* It has been supposed that this was the wretched Bickerstaff, but it was not till ten years later that *his* shame came upon him.

---

* II. 194. See notices of him in Boswell, *Life*, I. 289-90; II. 138-9; VII. 45; VIII. 121, &c. Johnson's letters on the death of his thirty years' companion are most affecting. "He was not unprepared, "*for he was very good to the poor.* How "much soever I valued him, I now wish "I had valued him more." Boswell describes him as an obscure practiser of physic among the lower people, his fees being sometimes such provisions as his

"sures the protection of John-
"son."*

CHAPTER VII.

Hogarth and Reynolds.
1762—1763.

1762.
Æt. 34. NEWBERY'S account-books and memoranda carry us, at the close of 1762, to a country lodging in Islington, kept by a stout and elderly lady named Mrs. Elizabeth Fleming, and inhabited by Oliver Goldsmith. He is said to have moved here to be near Newbery, who had chambers at the time in Canonbury-house or tower; and that the publisher had looked out the lodgings for him, may be inferred from the fact that Mrs. Fleming was a friend of Mr. Newbery's, and, when he afterwards held the lease of Canonbury-house, seems to have rented or occupied part of it. But Goldsmith had doubtless also a stronger inducement in thus escaping, for weeks together, from the crowded noise of Wine-office-court (where he retained a lodging for town uses) to comparative quiet and healthy air. There were still green fields and lanes in Islington. Glimpses were discernible yet, even of the old time when the tower was Elizabeth's hunting seat, and the country all about was woodland.

There were walks where houses were not; where terraces and taverns were still unbuilt; and where stolen hours might be given to precious thought, in the intervals of toilsome labour.

That he had come here with designs of labour, more constant and unremitting than ever, new and closer arrangements with Newbery would appear to indicate. The publisher made himself, with certain prudent limitations, Mrs. Fleming's paymaster; board and lodging were to be charged £50 a year (the reader has to keep in mind that this would be now nearly double that amount), and, when the state of their accounts permitted it, to be paid each quarter by Mr. Newbery; the publisher taking credit for these payments in his literary settlements with Goldsmith. The first quarterly payment had become due on the 24th of March, 1763; and on that day the landlady's claim of £12 *1763.* 10s. made up to £14 by *Æt. 35.* "incidental expenses," was discharged by Newbery. It stands as one item in an account of his cash advances for the first nine months of 1763, which characteristically exhibits the relations of bookwriter and bookseller. Mrs. Fleming's bills recur at their stated intervals; and on the 8th of September there is a payment of £15 to William Filby the tailor. The highest advance in money is one (which is not repeated) of three guineas; the rest vary, with intervals of a week or so

* Ibid, n. 194. "Levett had admired
"Johnson because others admired him;
"Johnson in pity loved Levett, because
"few others could find anything in him
"to love." *Hawkins,* 404. The malicious
knight may here perhaps be believed.

between each, from two guineas to one guinea and half a guinea. The whole amount, from January to October 1763, is little more than £96; upwards of £60 of which Goldsmith had meanwhile satisfied by "copies of different "kinds," when on settlement day he gave his note for the balance.*

What these "copies" in every case were, it is not so easy to discover. From a list of books**

lent to him by Newbery, a 'compilation on popular philosophy seems to have been contemplated; he was certainly engaged in the revision of what was meant to be a humorous recommendation of female government entitled *Description of Millenium Hall*, as well as in making additions to four juvenile volumes of *Wonders of Nature and Art;* and he had yet more to do with another book,

1763.
Æt. 35.

---

* "Doctor Goldsmith   Dr. to John Newbery.

			£	s	d
1761. Oct. 14.	1 set of the *Idler*		0	5	0
1762. Nov. 9.	To cash		10	10	0
Dec. 22.	To ditto		3	3	0
29.	To ditto		1	1	0
1763. Jan. 22.	To ditto		1	1	0
25.	To ditto		1	1	0
Feb. 14.	To ditto		1	1	0
March 11.	To ditto		2	2	0
12.	To Do.		1	1	0
24.	To Cash paid Mrs. Fleming		14	0	0
30.	To Cash		0	10	6
May 4.	To Do.		2	2	0
21.	To Do.		3	3	0
June 3.	To Cash paid Mrs. Fleming		14	11	0
25.	To Cash		2	2	0
July 1.	To Do.		2	2	0
20.	To Cash paid Mrs. Fleming		14	14	0
Sept. 2.	To Cash		1	1	0
8.	To Do. paid your Draft to Wm. Filby		15	2	0
10.	To Cash		0	10	0
19.	To Do.		1	1	0
24.	To Do.		2	3	0
Oct. 8.	To Do.		2	2	0
10.	To Cash paid your Bill to Mrs. Fleming		14	13	0
			£111	1	6
	By Copy of different kinds		63	0	0
Oct. 11.	By note of hand reed.		£48	1	6
	and delivered up the Vouchers."				

A promissory note "on demand," written at the top of a blank page of the account, was given by Goldsmith for the balance. Newbery MSS. In Mr. Murray's possession.

** "Nov. 25, 1762. Lent Dr. Goldsmith. *Martin's Philosophy,* 3 vols 8vo; " *Kiel's Introduction; Machaire's Chemistry,* 3 vols, French; *Encyclopedia* (sic), "8 vols folio, French; *Chinese Letters,* French; *Persian* Do; *Pemberton's View of* " *Newton's Philosophy; Hale's Vegetable Statics,* 2 vols 8vo; *Ferguson's Astronomy,* "4to; *Buffon's Natural History,* 9 vols 4to; *The Origin of Laws, Arts, and Sciences,* "3 vols 8vo, Edinburgh." Newbery MSS. In Mr. Murray's possession.

the *System of Natural History* by Dr. Brookes (the author of the *Gazetteer*), which he thoroughly revised, and to which he not only contributed a graceful preface, but several introductions to the various sections, full of picturesque animation. He was to have received for this labour "eleven "guineas in full," but it was increased to nearly thirty. He had also a large share in the *Martial Review or General History of the late War*, the profits of which Newbery had set apart for his luckless son-in-law, Kit Smart.* In a memorandum furnished by himself to the publisher, he claims three guineas for *Preface to Universal History* (a rival to the existing publication of that name, set on foot by Newbery and edited by Guthrie); two guineas for *Preface to Rhetoric*, and one for *Preface to Chronicle*, neither of these last now traceable; three guineas for *Critical and Monthly*, presumed to be contributions to Newbery's magazines; and twenty-one pounds on account of a *History of England*. A subsequent receipt acknowledges another twenty-one pounds, "which, "with what I received before, is "in full for the copy of the "*History of England* in a series "of Letters, two volumes in "12mo."**

1763.
——
Æt. 35.

This latter book, which was not published till the following year, claims a word of description. Such of the labours of 1763 as had yet seen the light were not of a kind to attract much notice. "Whenever I write "anything," said Goldsmith, "I "think the public *make a point* to "know nothing about it."* So, remembering what Pope had said of the lucky lines that had a lord to own them, the present book was issued, doubtless with Newbery's glad concurrence, as a *History of England in a series of Letters from a Nobleman to his Son.*

from a copy in Goldsmith's own handwriting: "Brookes' History, 11*l* 11*s*; Pre- "face to Universal History, 3*l* 3*s*; Pre- "face to Rhetoric, 2*l* 2*s*; Preface to "Chronicle, 1*l* 1*s*; History of England, "21*l*; The life of Christ, 10*l* 10*s*; The life "(*sic*) of the Fathers, 10*l* 10*s*; Critical "and Monthly, 3*l* 3*s*.—Total, 63*l*. Re- "ceived, October 11, 1763, the contents, "of Mr. Newbery. OLIVER GOLDSMITH." But besides this general receipt the cautious Mr. Newbery seems also to have required specific additional acknowledgments. Thus on one sheet, among the papers in Mr. Murray's possession, I find the following: "October 11, 1763. Re- "ceivd of Mr. John Newbery eleven "guineas in full for writing the introduc- "tion and preface to Dr. Brookes' Na- "tural History. OLIVER GOLDSMITH."— "Oct. 11, 1763. Received of Mr. John "Newbery three guineas for a Preface to "the History of the World. OLIVER "GOLDSMITH."—"Oct. 11, 1763. Receivd "of Mr. John Newbery twenty-one "pounds, which, with what I received "before, is in full for the copy of the "history of England, in a series of let- "ters, two volumes in 12mo. OLIVER "GOLDSMITH."—"Oct. 11, 1763. Receivd "of Mr. John Newbery twenty-one "pounds for translating the Life of Christ, "and the Lives of the Fathers. OLIVER "GOLDSMITH."

* *Boswell*, vii. 81.

---

* This compilation by Goldsmith about the war had been printed from week to week in a newspaper of which Newbery was principal proprietor, and published in his native town of Reading.

** Newbery MSS. The subjoined is

It had a great success in that character; passed through many editions; and was afterwards translated into French by the wife of Brissot, with notes by the revolutionary leader himself. The nobleman was supposed to be Lord Chesterfield, so refined was the style; Lord Orrery had also the credit of it; but the persuasion at last became general that the author was Lord Lyttelton,* and the name of that grave good lord is occasionally still seen affixed to it on the bookstalls. The mistake was never formally corrected:** it being

* As late as 1793, it became matter of discussion in the *Gentleman's Magazine* (LXIII. 799, &c.) which of these three noblemen had written the letters; whereupon a better informed correspondent told Mr. Urban the real name of the writer, and added: "Goldsmith was much "gratified to find the assumed character "so well sustained, as to pass upon the "world for real; and was often diverted "with the contending opinions of such as "ascribed it to one or other of the above "noblemen. This information comes "from one who had a copy given him "by the real author when it first came "from the press, and who had often "laughed with him at the success of his "fiction." *Gent. Mag.* LXIII. 1189.

** It may have been in consequence of its success in this instance that the reckless author of *Dr. Syntax*, Combe, placed the name of the second or "wicked" lord to his wonderfully clever collection of letters. In the course of a recent attempt in the *Quarterly Review* (xc. 91-163) to identify this second lord with *Junius*, which I cannot but regard as altogether unsound though in parts ingenious, a wholly unwarranted assumption is made of the genuineness of these letters in the main. There cannot be a doubt that they are spurious, and all written by Combe. One of them, I may take this opportunity of saying, is a sort of homily on the moral of Goldsmith's life and

the bookseller's interest to continue it, and not less the author's as well, when in his own name he subsequently went over the same ground. But it was not concealed from his friends; copies of the second edition of the book were sent with his autograph to both Percy and Johnson; and his friend Cooke tells us, not only that he had really written it in his lodgings at Islington, but how and in what way he did so. In the morning, says this authority, he would study, in *Rapin*, *Carte*, Kennett's *Complete History*, and the recent volumes of Hume, as much of what related to the period on which he was engaged as he designed for one letter, putting down the passages referred to on a sheet of paper, with remarks. He then walked out with a companion, certain of his friends at this time being in the habit of constantly calling upon him; and if, on returning to dinner, his friend returned with him, he spent the evening convivially, but without much drinking ("which he was never in the "habit of"); finally taking up with him to his bed-room the books and papers prepared in the morning, and there writing the chapter, or the best part of

death, wherein the writer is as severely critical, in regard to the vices of improvidence and extravagance, as it behoved a man to be who ran through more than one fortune, and closed a career of riotous vicissitude by extremely assiduous literary labours in the king's bench prison.

1763.
Æt. 35.

15*

it, before he went to rest. This latter exercise cost him very little trouble, he said; for, having all his materials ready, he wrote it with as much facility as a common letter.[*]

One may clearly trace these very moderate "convivialities," I think, in occasional entries of Mrs. Fleming's incidental expenses. The good lady was not loath to be generous at times, but is careful to give herself the full credit of it; and a not infrequent item in her bill is "*A* "*gentleman's dinner, Nothing.*" Four gentlemen have tea for eighteen-pence; "wine and cakes" are supplied for the same sum; bottles of port are charged two shillings each; and such special favourites are "Mr. Baggott" and one "Doctor Reman," that three elaborate ciphers (*£o. os. od.*) follow their teas as well as their dinners.[**] Redmond was the latter's real name. He was a young Irish physician who had lived some years in France, and was now disputing with the Society of Arts on some alleged discoveries in the properties of antimony. Among Mrs. Fleming's anonymous entries, however, were some that must have related to more distinguished visitors.

The greatest of these I would introduce as he was seen one day in the present year by a young and eager admirer, passing quickly through Cranbourn-alley.

He might have been on his way to Goldsmith. He was a bustling, active, stout little man, dressed in a sky-blue coat. His admirer saw him at a distance, turning the corner; and, running with all expedition to have a nearer view, came up with him in Castle-street, as he stood patting one of two quarrelling boys on the back, and, looking steadfastly at the expression in the coward's face, was saying in very audible voice, "Damn him, if I would take it of "him! at him again!" Enemy or admirer could not in circumstances more appropriate have seen William Hogarth. He might, in that little incident, see his interest in homely life, his preference of the real in art, and his quick apprehension of character; his love of hard hitting, and his indomitable English spirit. The admirer, who, at the close of his own chequered life, thus remembered and related it, was James Barry of Cork; who had followed Mr. Edmund Burke to London with letters from Doctor Sleigh, and whose birth, genius, and poverty soon made him known to Goldsmith.

Between Goldsmith and Hogarth existed many reasons for sympathy. Few so sure as the great, self-taught, philosophic artist, to penetrate at once, through any outer husk of disadvantage, to discernment of an honest and loving soul. Genius, in both, took side with the homely and the poor; and they had personal foibles in common. No

[*] *Europ. Mag.* xxiv. 94.
[**] See *post,* chapter ix. of this Book III.

man can be supposed to have read the letters in the *Public Ledger* with heartier agreement than Hogarth; no man so little likely as Goldsmith to suffer a sky-blue coat, or conceited, strutting, consequential airs, to weigh against the claims of the painter of *Mariage à la Mode*. How they first met has not been related, but they met frequently; and two portrait-memorials from the old artist's pencil, one to be mentioned presently and the other to be referred to on a later page,* remain to show his kindly interest in the clever young Irishman. In these last two years of Hogarth's life, admiration had become precious to him; and Goldsmith was ready with his tribute. Besides, there was Wilkes to rail against and Churchill to condemn, as well as Johnson to praise and love. "I'll "tell you what," Hogarth would say: "Sam Johnson's conversation "is to the talk of other men like "Titian's painting compared to "Hudson's: but don't you tell "people, now, that I say so; for "the connoisseurs and I are at "war, you know; and because I "hate *them*, they think I hate "Titian—and let them!" **

Goldsmith and the connoisseurs were at war, too; and this would help to make more agreeable the intercourse which Hogarth has more particularly associated with these Islington lodgings by both the memorials to which reference has been made. One of them* shows Goldsmith very hard at work, not without satiric indication of the habits that made such drudgery now more than ever needful; while the other, also a portrait in oil, representing an elderly lady in satin with an open book before her and exhibited in London several years back ** as "Goldsmith's Hostess," connects itself not less with the present time, and the difficulties consequent on the habits in question. It involves no great stretch of fancy to suppose it painted in the Islington lodgings, at some crisis of domestic pressure. Newbery's accounts reveal to us how often it was needful to mitigate Mrs. Fleming's impatience, to moderate her wrath, and, when money was not immediately at hand, to minister to her vanities. For Newbery was

1763.
Æt. 35.

---

* See *post*, chap. xiv. of this Book III.

** Mrs. Piozzi's *Anecdotes*, 136. "Many "were the lectures," adds the lively little lady, "I used to have in my very early "days from dear Mr. Hogarth, whose re-"gard for my father induced him per-"haps to take notice of his little girl, and "give her some odd particular directions "about dress, dancing, and many other "matters, interesting now only because "they were his. As he made all his "talents, however, subservient to the "great purposes of morality, and the "earnest desire he had to mend man-"kind, his discourse commonly ended in "an ethical dissertation, and a serious "charge to me never to forget his picture "of the *Lady's last Stake*."

* An engraving from it will be mentioned shortly.

** In the 1832 exhibition of the works of deceased British artists. It then belonged to Mr. Graves, in whose family it had been for many years, always bearing the name of Goldsmith's Hostess.

a strict accountant, and kept sharply within the terms of his bargains; exacting notes of hand at each quarterly settlement for whatever the balance might be, and objecting to add to it by new payments when it happened to be large. It is but to imagine a visit from Hogarth at such time. If his goodnature wanted any stimulus, the thought of Newbery would give it. He had himself an old grudge against the booksellers. He charges them in his autobiography with "cruel "treatment" of his father, and dilates on the bitterness they add to the hard necessity of earning bread by the pen. But, though the copyrights of his prints were a source of certain and not inconsiderable income, his money at command was scanty; and it would better suit his generous good-humour, as well as better serve his friend, to bring his easel in his coach some day, and enthrone Mrs. Fleming by the side of it. So may the portrait have been painted; and much laughter there would be in its progress, I do not doubt, at the very different sort of sitters and subjects whose coroneted coaches were crowding the west side of Leicester-square.

The good-humour of Reynolds was a different thing from that of Hogarth. It had no antagonism about it. Ill-humour with any other part of the world had nothing to do with it. It was gracious and diffused; singling out some, it might be, for special warmth, but smiling blandly upon all. He was eminently the gentleman of his time; and if there is a hidden charm in his portraits, it is that. His own nature pervades them, and shines out from them still. He was now forty years old, being younger than Hogarth by a quarter of a century; was already in the receipt of nearly six thousand pounds a year; and had known nothing but uninterrupted prosperity. He had moved from St. Martin's-lane into Newport-street, and from Newport-street into Leicester-square; he had raised his prices from five, ten, and twenty guineas (his earliest charge for the three sizes of portraits), successively to ten, twenty, and forty, to twelve, twenty-four, and forty-eight, to fifteen, thirty, and sixty, to twenty, forty, and eighty, and to twenty-five, fifty, and a hundred, the sums he now charged; he had lately built a gallery for his works; and he had set up a gay gilt coach, with the four seasons painted on its panels.* Yet, of

* See Farington's *Memoirs* in the *Works*, i. CLXII, and the *Life* by Beechey, i. 121-5, 139-40. He greatly advanced his prices in later days. Mr. Croker states, in a note to his last edition of *Boswell*, (113): "I have been informed by Sir "Thomas Lawrence, his admirer and "rival (!), that in 1787 his prices were "two hundred guineas for the *whole-* "*length*, one hundred for the *half-length*, "seventy for the *kit-cat*, and fifty for "what is called the *three-quarters*. But "even on these prices some increase "must have been made, as Horace Wal- "pole said, 'Sir Joshua, in his old age,

those to whom the man was really known, it may be doubted if there was one who grudged him a good fortune, which was worn with generosity and grace, and justified by noble qualities; while few indeed should have been the exceptions, whether among those who knew or those who knew him not, to the feeling of pride that an Englishman had at last arisen who could measure himself successfully with the Dutch and the Italian.*

This was what Reynolds had striven for; and what common men might suppose to be his envy or self-sufficiency. Not with any sense of triumph over living competitors did he listen to the praise he loved; not of being better than Hogarth, or than Gainsborough, or than his old master Hudson, was he thinking continually, but of the glory of being one day placed by the side of Titian, Rubens, and Vandyke. Undoubtedly he must be said to have overrated the effects of education, study, and the practice of schools; and it is matter of much regret that he should never have thought of $\frac{1763.}{\text{Æt. 35.}}$ Hogarth but as a moral satirist and man of wit, or sought for his favourite art the dignity of a closer alliance with such philosophy and genius. But the difficult temper of Hogarth himself cannot be kept out of view. His very virtues had a stubbornness and a dogmatism that repelled. What Reynolds most desired, –to bring men of their common calling together, and, by consent and union, by study and co-operation, establish claims to respect and continuance, – Hogarth had been all his life opposing; and was now, at the close of life, standing of his own free choice apart and alone. Study the great works of the great masters for ever, said Reynolds.* There is only one school, cried Hogarth, and that is kept by Nature. What was uttered on the one side of Leicester-square was pretty sure to be contradicted on the other; and neither would make the advance which might have reconciled the views of both. Be it remembered, at the same time, that Hogarth, in the daring confidence of his more astonishing genius, kept himself at the farthest extreme. "Talk of sense, "and study, and all that," he said to Walpole, "why, it is

---

" 'becomes avaricious. He had one thou-
" 'sand guineas for my picture of the
" 'three ladies Waldegrave.' *Walpoliana.*"
This latter picture contained half-lengths
of the three ladies on one canvas. For
curious lists of his prices, see Malone's
Account of Reynolds in the *Works*, i.
LXII-LXXI, and *Northcote*, ii. 317-58.

* "I remember once going through a
"suite of rooms where they were show-
"ing me several fine Vandykes; and we
"came to one where there were some
"children, by Sir Joshua, seen through a
"door: it was like looking at the reality.
"they were so full of life; the branches
"of the trees waved over their heads,
"and the fresh air seemed to play on
"their cheeks—I soon forgot Vandyke!"
Conversations of Northcote, 163, 164. This
must have been at Wilton.

* Close of the Sixth Discourse, *Works*,
i. 186.

"owing to the good sense of "the English that they have not "painted better. The people "who have studied paint-"ing least are the best "judges of it. There's "Reynolds, who certainly has "genius; why but t'other day "he offered a hundred pounds "for a picture that I would not "hang in my cellar."* Reynolds might have some excuse if he turned from this with a smile, and a supposed confirmation of his error that the critic was himself no painter. Thus these great men lived separate to the last. The only feeling they shared in common may have been that kindness to Oliver Goldsmith, which, after their respective fashion, each manifested well. The one, with his ready help and robust example, would have strengthened him for life, as for a solitary warfare which awaited every man of genius; the other, more gently, would have drawn him from contests and solitude, from discontents and low esteem, to the sense that worldly consideration and social respect might gladden even literary toil. While Hogarth was propitiating and painting Mrs. Fleming, Reynolds was founding the Literary Club.

1763.
Æt. 35.

* The whole dialogue from which these expressions are taken will be found in the *Coll. Lett.* iv. 141.

CHAPTER VIII.

The Club and its First Members.
1763.

THE association of celebrated men of this period known as the Literary Club did not receive that name till many years after it came into existence: but that Reynolds was its Romulus (so Mrs. Thrale said Johnson called him),* and this year of 1763 the year of its foundation, is unquestionable, though the meetings did not begin till winter. Johnson caught at the notion eagerly; suggested as its model a club he had himself founded in Ivy-lane some fourteen years before, and which the deaths or dispersion of its members had now interrupted for nearly seven years; and on this suggestion being adopted, the members, as in the earlier club, were limited to nine, and Mr. Hawkins, as an original member of the Ivy-lane, was invited to join. Topham Beauclerc and Bennet Langton were also asked, and welcomed earnestly; and, of course, Mr. Edmund Burke. He had lately left Dublin and politics for a time, and returned to literature in Queen-

* *Anecdotes*, 122. "Or said somebody "else of the company called him so, "which was more likely." It has been alleged that Reynolds, in making the proposal to Johnson, acted on a hint from Lord Charlemont; but I find no good authority for this, which the absence of Charlemont from the club until 1773, when he was elected on Beauclerc's nomination, renders otherwise very unlikely.

Anne-street; where a solid mark of his patron Hamilton's satisfaction had accompanied him, in shape of a pension on the Irish Establishment of £300 a year. Perhaps it was ominous of the mischances attending this pension, that it was entered in the name of "William Birt:" the name which was soon to be so famous, having little familiarity or fame as yet. The notion of the club delighted Burke; and he asked admission for his father-in-law, Doctor Nugent, an accomplished roman-catholic physician, who lived with him. Beauclerc in like manner suggested his friend Chamier, then secretary in the war-office.* Oliver Goldsmith completed the number. But another member of the original Ivy-lane society, Samuel Dyer,** making unexpected appearance from abroad in the following year, was joyfully admitted; and though it was resolved to make election difficult, and only for special reasons permit addition to their number,***

the limitation at first proposed was thus of course done away with. A second limitation, however, to the number of twelve, was definitively made on the occasion of the second balloting, and will be duly described. The place of meeting was the Turk's-head tavern in Gerrard-street, Soho,*

1763.
Æt. 35.

each other sufficiently, without wishing for more company with whom to pass an evening. "This," writes Percy to Boswell (Nichols's *Illustrations*, VII. 311), "I "have heard Johnson mention as the "principal or avowed reason for the "small number of members to which for "many years it was limited." And so far Johnson was right in holding that the club's adversity did not arrive till the numbers were large, and the members not very select; nor is it easy to imagine that Lord Liverpool, in comparatively recent days, when he found himself on one occasion *solus* at the dinner, was able to entertain himself sufficiently without wishing for more company. The men are few who can afford to have "nobody with them at sea but" themselves.

* Here the club remained as long as Goldsmith lived, and until 1783, when the landlord died, and the hotel became a private house. Meanwhile the predominance of whig politics in it, in consequence of the remarkable prominence in its conversations of Burke, Fox, Lord Spencer, Sheridan, Dunning, and others ("the Fox star and the Irish constella-"tion," as Johnson phrased it, when he complained of Reynolds being "too "much under" those planets, *Bos.* VII. 96), had so thoroughly disgusted Johnson, that he almost wholly withdrew himself in the latter years of his life. "He "then," says Mrs. Piozzi, "loudly pro-"claimed his carelessness *who might be* "admitted, when it was become a more "dinner-club." (*Anecdotes*, 122.) After 1783 it removed to Prince's, in Sackville-street; and on his house being soon afterwards shut up, it removed to Baxter's, which subsequently became Thomas's, in Dover-street. In January 1792

---

* Chamier was not appointed under-secretary of state till 1775. In the account of the club there may still be one or two slight inaccuracies, though I have been at some pains to obtain correct information since my last edition. Obvious errors, indeed, exist in every description of this celebrated society, from the first supplied by Malone to the last furnished by Mr. Hatchett.

** For an interesting account of this remarkable man, see Malone's *Life of Dryden*, 181-5 (*note*).

*** It was intended, according to Malone (*Account of Reynolds*, LXXXIII), that the club should consist of such men as that, if only two of them chanced to meet, they should be able to entertain

where, the chair being taken every Monday night at seven o'clock by a member in rotation, 1763. all were expected to attend and sup together. In Æt. 35. about the ninth year of their existence, December 1772, they changed their day of meeting to Friday; and, some years later (Percy and Malone say in 1775),* in place of their weekly supper they resolved to dine together once a fortnight during the meeting of parliament. Each member present was to bear his share of the reckoning; and conversation, from which politics only were excluded, was kept up always to a late hour.

So originated and was formed that famous club, which had made itself a name in literary history long before it received, at Garrick's funeral, the name of The Literary Club by which it is now known. Its meetings were noised abroad; the fame of its conversations received eager addition from the difficulty of obtaining admission to it; and it came to be as generally understood that literature had fixed her social head-quarters here, as

that politics reigned supreme at Wildman's or the Cocoa-tree. Not without advantage, let me add, to the dignity and worldly consideration of men-of-letters themselves. "I believe Mr. Fox "will allow me say," wrote the Bishop of St. Asaph to Mr. William Jones, when the society was not more than fifteen years old, "that the honour of being elected "into the Turk's-head Club is "not inferior to that of being the "representative of Westminster "or Surrey. The electors are "certainly more disinterested; "and I should say they were "much better judges of merit, if "they had not rejected Lord "Camden and chosen me."* Yet in those later days, when, on the same night of that election of the Bishop of St. Asaph, Lord Camden and the Bishop of Chester were black-balled,** the society had begun to lose the high literary tone which made its earlier days yet more remarkable.*** Shall we wonder if distinction in such a society should open a new life to Goldsmith?

It removed to Parsloe's, in St. James's-street; and on February 26, 1799, to the Thatched-house in the same street, where it remained till the tavern was pulled down, shortly after my last edition was published. Such as it now is, "a more "miscellaneous collection of conspicuous "men, without any determinate charac-"ter," it meets at the Clarendon; and, appropriately enough, has for some time dropt its prefix of "Literary" and again calls itself The Club.

* *Percy Memoir*, 73, and Malone's Account *of Reynolds*, LXXXIV.

* Teignmouth's *Life and Correspondence of Sir William Jones*, 1. 317.

** "When bishops and chancellors," says Jones, commenting on this fact, "honour us with offering to dine at a "tavern, it seems very extraordinary "that we should ever reject such an "offer; but there is no reasoning on the "caprice of men. Of our club I will only "say that there is no branch of human "knowledge on which some of our mem-"bers are not capable of giving informa-"tion." Teignmouth's *Life*, 1. 315.

*** See on the other hand what is said, *post*, Book IV. Chap. IV.

His claim to enter it would seem to have been somewhat canvassed, at first, by at least one of the members. "As he "wrote for the booksellers," says Hawkins, "we at the club "looked on him as a mere "literary drudge, equal to the "task of compiling and translat-"ing, but little capable of original "and still less of poetical com-"position: he had, nevertheless, "unknown to us"* .... I need not anticipate what it was that so startled Hawkins with its unknown progress: the reader has already intimation of it. It is, however, more than probable, whatever may have been thought of Goldsmith's drudgery, that this extremely low estimate of his capacity was limited to Mr. Hawkins, whose opinions were seldom popular with the other members of the club. Early associations clung hard to Johnson, and, for the sake of these, Hawkins was borne with to the last; but, in the newly-formed society, even Johnson admitted him to be out of place. Neither in habits nor opinions did he harmonise with the rest. He had been an attorney for many years, affecting literary tastes, and dabbling in music at the Madrigal-club; but, four years before the present, so large a fortune had fallen to him in right of his wife, that he withdrew from the law, and lived and judged with severe propriety as a Middlesex magistrate. Within two years he will be elected chairman of the sessions; after seven years more, will be made a knight: and, in four years after that, will deliver himself of five quarto volumes of a history of music, in the slow and laborious conception of which he is already painfully engaged.*   Altogether, his existence was a kind of pompous, parsimonious, insignificant drawl, cleverly ridiculed by one of the wits in an absurd epitaph: "Here "lies Sir John Hawkins, Without "his shoes and stauckins."   To him belonged the original merit, in that age of penal barbarity and perpetual executions, of lamenting that in no less than fourteen cases it was still possible to cheat the gallows.   Another of his favourite themes was the improvidence of what he called sentimental writers, at the head of whom he placed the author of *Tom Jones;* a book which he charged with having "corrupted the rising genera-"tion," and sapped "the founda-"tion of that morality which it is

1763.
————
Æt. 35.

* *Life of Johnson*, 420.

* *Gent. Mag.* LIX. 473.   A lucky pun condemned Sir John Hawkins's sixteen years' labour to long obscurity and oblivion.   Some wag in the interest of Dr. Burney's rival publication wrote the following catch, which Dr. Calcott set to music:

"Have you read Sir John Hawkins's
    "History?
"Some folks think it quite a mystery;
"Both I have, and I aver
"That Burney's History I prefer."

Burn his History was straightway in every one's mouth; and the bookseller practically took the advice by "wasting" the greater part of the edition.

"the duty of parents and all "public instructors to inculcate "in the minds of young people."*

1763.
ÆT 35.
This was his common style of talk. He would speak contemptuously of Hogarth as a man who knew nothing out of Covent-garden. Richardson, Fielding, Smollett, and Sterne, he looked upon as "stuff;" and for the last three, as men "whose *necessities* and "abilities were nearly commensurate," he had a special contempt. As chairman of quarter-sessions, what other judgment could he be expected to have of them? Being men of loose principles, he would say, bad economists, and living without foresight, "it is their endeavour to "commute for their failings by "professions of greater love to "mankind, more tender affec-"tions and finer feelings than "they will allow men of more "regular lives, whom they deem "formalists, to possess."** With a man of such regular life, denouncing woe to loose characters that should endeavour to commute for their failings, poor Goldsmith had naturally little chance; and it fared as ill with the rest of the club when questions of "economy" or "fore-"sight" came up. Mr. Hawkins, after the first four meetings, begged to be excused his share of the reckoning, on the ground that he did not partake of the supper. "And was he ex-"cused?" asked Doctor Burney, when Johnson told him of the incident many years after. "Oh "yes, sir," was the reply; "and "very readily. No man is angry "at another for being inferior to "himself. We all admitted his "plea publicly, for the gratifica-"tion of scorning him privately. "Sir John, sir, is a very unclub-"bable man. Yet I really be-"lieve him," pursued Johnson on the same occasion, very characteristically, "to be an honest "man at the bottom; though "to be sure he is rather penu-"rious, and he is somewhat "mean, and it must be owned he "has some degree of brutality, "and is not without a tendency "to savageness that cannot well "be defended."* It was this latter tendency which caused his early secession from the club. He was not a member for more than two or three years. His own account is that he withdrew because its late hours were inconsistent with his domestic arrangements:** but the fact was,

* *Life of Johnson*, 211, 215.
** *Ibid*, 218.

* Madame d'Arblay is the authority for this, which she relates with but slight variation both in her *Memoirs* of her father (ii. 164), and in her own *Diary*. See also *Boswell*, ii. 273, and ix. 287-8.

** "We seldom got together till nine; "the enquiry into the contents of the "larder, and preparing supper, took up "till ten; and by the time that the table "was cleared, it was near eleven, at "which hour my servants were ordered "to come for me; and, as I could not "enjoy the pleasure of these meetings "without disturbing the economy of my "family, I chose to forego it." *Life of Johnson*, 125. Their evening toast, he tells us in the same passage, was the motto of Padre Paolo, "Esto perpetua."

says Boswell, that he one evening attacked Mr. Burke in so rude a manner,[*] that all the company testified their displeasure; and at their next meeting his reception was such that he never came again.

Letitia Matilda Hawkins herself, proposing to defend her father, corroborates this statement. "*The Burkes*," she says, describing the impressions of her childhood, "as the men of "that family were called, were not "then what they were afterwards "considered, nor what the head "of them deserved to be con- "sidered for his splendid talents: "they were, as my father termed "them, *Irish Adventurers*; and "came into this country with no "good auguries, nor any very "decided principles of action. "They had to talk their way in "the world that was to furnish "their means of living."[**]

An Irish adventurer who had to talk his way in the world is much what Burke was considered by the great as well as little vulgar, for several more years to come. He was now thirty-three, and yet had not achieved his great want, "ground to stand "upon."[***] Until the present year he had derived his principal help from the booksellers, for whom he had some time written, and continued still to write, the historical portion of $\frac{1763.}{\text{Æt. 35.}}$ the *Annual Register*. He had been but a few months in enjoyment of Hamilton's pension, and was already extremely uneasy as to the conditions on which he began to suspect it had been granted, his patron not seeming to have relished his proposed return to London society. "I know your business "ought on all occasions to have "the preference," wrote Burke in deprecation; "to be the first, "and the last, and indeed in all "respects the main concern. All "I contend for is, that I may not

"time I should say who my friend is. "His name is Edmond Burke. As a "literary man he may possibly be not "quite unknown to you. He is the author "of a piece which imposed on the world "as Lord Bolingbroke's, called the *Ad- "vantages of Natural Society*, and of a very "ingenious book published last year, "called a *Treatise on the Sublime and the "Beautiful*. I must farther say of him, "that his chief application has been to "the knowledge of public business, and "our commercial interests; that he "seems to have a most extensive know- "ledge, with extraordinary talents for "business, and to want nothing but "ground to stand upon to do his country "very important services." *Chatham Cor- respondence*, I. 432. Burke's first piece was the *Vindication* (not the Advantages) *of Natural Society*, which up to 1763 John- son seems to have thought a serious and "imprudent" assertion of the opinions of Bolingbroke. It was not till two years later (1765) that the irony was explicitly laid aside in a preface to the edition then published, and meanwhile both Bishop Warburton and Lord Chesterfield are said to have been deceived. And see *post*, Book, IV. Chap. XI.

[*] *Life*, II. 273. See also the *Percy Memoir*, 72. Burke was attacked in good company, let me subjoin; for on the same authority Lord Chatham was "a "pertinacious yelper," and (for a com- parison quite original) Lord Chesterfield "a bear."

[**] *Memoirs*, I. 98-101.

[***] Doctor Markham thus introduces him to the famous Duchess of Queens- berry, as a candidate for office: "It is

"be considered as absolutely ex-
"cluded from all other thoughts,
"in their proper time and due
"subordination." *   The
whole truth was not made
obvious to him till two
years later. He then found, and
on finding it flung up the pension, that Hamilton had thought
him placed by it in "a sort of
"domestic situation." It was the
consideration of a bargain for
sale of independence. It was a
claim for absolute servitude.
"Not to value myself as a gen-
"tleman," remonstrated Burke,
"a freeman, a man of education,
"and one pretending to litera-
"ture, is there any situation in
"life so low, or even so criminal,
"that can subject a man to the
"possibility of such an engage-
"ment? Would you dare at-
"tempt to bind your footman to
"such terms?" **   Mr. Hawkins,
it is clear, would have thought
the terms suitable enough to the
situation in life of an Irish adventurer; and the incident may
illustrate his vulgar and insolent
phrase.

Let it always be remembered,
in connection with Burke's vehemence of will and sharp im-
petuosity of temper. These were
less his natural defects than his
painful sense of what he wanted
in the eyes of others. When, in
later years, he proudly reviewed
the exertions that had been the
soul of the then revived whig
party, which had re-established

their strength, consolidated their
influence, and been rewarded by
insignificant office and uniform
exclusion from the cabinet, he
had to reflect that every step in
his life had thus been obstructed,
and that in the very teeth of
prejudice and dislike he had
forced every inch of his way.
"The narrowness of his for-
"tune," says Walpole, "kept him
"down." * At every turnpike he
met, he had been called to show
his passport; otherwise no admission, no toleration for him.
Improved by this, his manners
could hardly be; the more other
spheres of consideration were
closed to him, the more he would
be driven to dominate in his
own; and I have little doubt that
he somewhat painfully at times,
in the first few years of the club,
impressed others as well as
Hawkins with a sense of his predominance. He had to "talk his
"way in the world that was to
"furnish his means of living,"
and this was the only theatre
open to him yet. Here only
could he as yet pour forth, to an
audience worth exciting, the
stores of argument and eloquence he was thirsting to employ upon a wider stage; the
variety of knowledge and its
practical application, the fund of
astonishing imagery, the ease of
philosophic illustration, the over-
powering copiousness of words,
in which he has never had a
rival. A civil guest, says Her-
bert, will no more talk all, than

* *Correspondence*, 1. 49-50.
** *Ibid*, 1. 73.

* *Memoirs of George III.* 11. 273-4.

eat all, the feast; and perhaps this might be forgotten now and then. "In my own mind I am "convinced," says Miss Hawkins, "however he might persuade "himself, that my father *was* "disgusted with the overpower-"ing deportment of Burke and "his monopoly of the conversa-"tion, which made all the other "members, excepting his an-"tagonist Johnson, merely his "auditors." Something of the same sort was said by that antagonist ten years after the present date, though in a more generous way. "What I most "envy Burke for," said John-son, after admitting the astonish-ing range of his resources but denying him the faculty of wit, "is, his being constantly the "same. He is never what we "call hum-drum; never unwilling "to begin to talk, nor in haste "to leave off. Take up what-"ever topic you please, he is "ready to meet you. . . His "stream of mind is perpetual. "I cannot say he is good at "listening. So desirous is he to "talk, that if one is speaking "at this end of the table, he'll "speak to somebody at the "other end. Burke, sir, is such "a man, that if you met him "for the first time in the street, "where you were stopped by a "drove of oxen, and you and he "stepped aside to take shelter "but for five minutes, he'd "talk to you in such a manner, "that, when you parted, you "would say, This is an extra-

"ordinary man.* Now, you may "be long enough with me with-"out finding anything extraor-"dinary."**

This was modest in John-son, but there was more truth than he perhaps intended in it. In general, Burke's views were certainly the subtler and more able. He penetrated deeper into the principles of things, be-low common life and what is called good sense, than John-son could. "Is he like Burke," asked Goldsmith, when Boswell seemed to exalt Johnson's talk too highly, "who winds into a "subject like a serpent?"*** A faculty of sudden and striking illustration, too, often highly imaginative, he eminently pos-sessed; and of this, which must have given such a power as well as charm to his familiar conver-

<table><tr><td>1763.</td></tr><tr><td>Æt. 35.</td></tr></table>

* Over and over again Johnson repeated this illustration. BOSWELL: "Mr. Burke "has a constant stream of conversation." JOHNSON: "Yes, sir; if a man were to "go by chance at the same time with "Burke under a shed, to shun a shower, "he would say, This is an extraordinary "man! If Burke should go into a stable "to see his horse dressed, the ostler "would say, We have had an extra-"ordinary man here!" *Life*, iv. 301. He goes on to say, "When Burke does not "descend to be merry, his conversation "is very superior indeed. There is no "proportion between the powers which "he shows in serious talk and in jocu-"larity. When he lets himself down to "that, he is in the kennel." (Mrs. Piozzi's *Anecdotes*, 209.) Not quite; as the reader perhaps will also think, who reads a note which he will find in Book IV. Chap. vi.

** Boswell, *Life*, viii. 273, and see iv. 23, vii. 306-7, viii. 155.

*** Boswell, iii. 301.

sation, what more exquisite ex-ample, or more characteristic both of Johnson and himself, could be named, than the vehement denial he gave to Boswell's mention of Croft's *Life of Young* as a pretty successful imitation of Johnson's style? "No, no, it is *not* a good "imitation of Johnson. It has all "his pomp, without his force. "It has all the nodosities of "the oak without its strength." Then, after a pause, "It has all "the contortions of the Sibyl, "without the inspiration." In the conversational expression of Johnson, on the other hand, there was a strength and clearness which was all his own, and which originated Percy's likening of it, as contrasted with ordinary conversation, to an antique statue with every vein and muscle distinct and bold, by the side of an inferior cast.* Johnson had also wit, often an incomparable humour, and a hundred other interesting qualities, which Burke had not; while his rough dictatorial manner, his loud voice, and slow deliberate utterance, so much oftener suggested an objection than gave help to what he said, that one may doubt the truth of Lord Pembroke's pleasantry to Boswell, that "his say-"ings would not appear so ex-"traordinary, were it not for his "bow-wow way."** Of the ordinary listener, at any rate, the bow-wow way exacted something too much; and was quite as likely to stun as to strike him. "He's a tremendous companion," said poor George Garrick, when urged to confess of him what he really thought.* He brought, into common talk, too plain an anticipation of victory and triumph. He wore his determination not to be thrown or beaten, whatever side he might please to take, somewhat defiantly upon his sleeve; and startled peaceful society a little too much with his uncle Andrew's habits in the ring at Smithfield.** It was a sense, on his own part, of this eagerness to make every subject a battle-ground, which made him say, at a moment of illness and exhaustion, that if he were to see Burke then, it would kill him.***

* Murphy's *Essay*, 77.

** Mrs. Piozzi's *Anecdotes*, 5-6. Sir James Mackintosh remembered that while spending the Christmas of 1793 at Beaconsfield, Burke said to him that Johnson showed more powers of mind in company than in his writings; but he argued only for victory; and when he had neither a paradox to defend, nor an antagonist to crush, he would preface his *assent* with "*Why no, sir!*" *Croker*, 768. Boswell mentions the same peculiarity, and tells us that he used to consider the *Why no, sir!* as a kind of flag of defiance; as if he had said, "Any argument you may offer "against this is not just. No, sir, it is "not." It was like Falstaff's "I deny "your major." VIII. 318.

*** "*That fellow calls forth all my* "*powers. Were I to see Burke now, it would* "*kill me.* So much was he accustomed to "consider conversation as a contest, and "such was his notion of Burke as an "opponent." *Boswell*, VI. 80. On the other hand, with what complacency, in his better health, he writes to Mrs. Thrale (*Letters*, II. 127). "But [Mrs. Mon-"tagu] and you have had, with all your

* *Boswell*, VII. 169.

** *Ibid*, IV. 8.

From the first day of their meeting, now some years ago, at Garrick's dinner-table, his desire had been to measure himself with Burke on all occasions. "I "suppose, Murphy," he said to Arthur as they came away from that dinner, "you are proud of "your countryman. *Cum talis* "*sit, utinam noster esset.*"* The club was an opportunity for both, and promptly seized; to the occasional overshadowing, no doubt, of the comforts and opportunities of other members. Yet for the most part their wit-combats seem not only to have interested the rest, but to have improved the temper of the combatants themselves, and made them more generous to each other. "How very great Johnson has been to-night," said Burke to Langton, as they left the club together. Langton assented, but could have wished to hear more from another person. "Oh, no!" replied Burke, "it is enough for me to have "rung the bell to him."**

"adulation, nothing finer said of you "than was said last Saturday night of "Burke and me. We were at the Bishop "of [St. Asaph's], a bishop little better "than *your* bishop [Hinchliffe]; and to- "wards twelve we fell into talk, to which "the ladies listened, just as they do to "you; and said, as I heard, *There is no* "*rising unless somebody will cry Fire!*"

   * Murphy's *Essay*, 53.

   ** Langton's collectanea, in *Boswell*, vii. 374. It must surely have been only for the purpose of ringing the bell to him that he took the particular part in the argument described to Boswell. "My "excellent friend, Dr. Langton, told me, "he was once present at a dispute be- "tween Dr. Johnson and Mr. Burke, on

Bennet Langton was, in his own person, an eminent example of the high and humane class who are content to ring the bell to their friends. Admiration of the *Rambler* made him seek admittance to its author, when he was himself,

1763.
Æt. 35.

"the comparative merits of Homer and "Virgil, which was carried on with ex- "traordinary abilities on both sides. Dr. "Johnson maintained the superiority of "Homer." *Life*, iv. 78. Another argument one would like to have heard, on those frequent occasions when Johnson would quote Dryden's lines (of which he was so fond) about living past years again, and for his part protest that he never lived that week in his life which he would wish to repeat were an angel to make the proposal to him (*Boswell*, iii. 130); to which Burke would reply (Boswell does not represent it as addressed to Johnson, but it obviously must have been), that for his part he believed that every man "would lead his life over "again; for every man is willing to go on "and take an addition to his life, which, "as he grows older, he has no reason to "think will be better, or even so good as "what has preceded." viii. 304. A subtle remark, which Johnson might nevertheless have met by simply again repeating the masterly lines of the old poet, which hit the truth so finely in marking as an inconsistency, a self-cozenage, what the argument of Burke would bring within the control of consistency and reason. "Strange cozen-"age!" cries the poet,

   " When I consider life, 'tis all a cheat,
   " Yet, fool'd with hope, men favour the
         "deceit;
   "Trust on, and think to-morrow will
         "repay:
   "To-morrow's falser than the former
         "day . . . .
   "Strange cozenage! None would live
         "past years again,
   "Yet all hope pleasure in what yet
         "remain;
   "And from the dregs of life think to
         "receive
   " What the first sprightly running could
         "not give.

some eight years back, but a lad of eighteen; and his ingenuous manners and mild enthusiasm at once won Johnson's love. That he represented a great Lincolnshire family, still living at their ancient seat of Langton, had not abridged his merits in the philosopher's regard;* and upon his going up to Trinity-college, Oxford, Johnson took occasion to visit him there, and there made the acquaintance of his college-chum, and junior by two years, Topham Beauclerc, grandson of the first Duke of St. Albans.** These two young men had several qualities in common,—ready intellect, perfect manners, great love of literature, and a thorough admiration of Johnson; but, with these, such striking points of difference also,

1763.
Æt. 35.

that Johnson could not comprehend their intimacy when first he saw them together. It was not till he discovered what a scorn of fools Beauclerc blended with his love of folly, what virtues of the mind were to be set off against his vices of the body, and with how much gaiety and wit he carried off his licentiousness, that the sage became as fond of the laughing rake as of his quiet contemplative companion. "I shall have my old "friend to bail out of the round-"house," exclaimed Garrick, when he heard of it; and of an incident in connection with it, that occurred in the next Oxford vacation. His old friend had turned out of his chambers, at three o'clock in the morning, to have a "frisk" with the young "dogs;"* had gone to a tavern in Covent-garden, and roared out Lord Lansdowne's drinking song over a bowl of bishop; had taken a boat with them and rowed to Billingsgate; and (ac-

---

"I'm tired with waiting for this chemic
   "gold,
"Which fools us young, and beggars
   "as when old."

To which let me add, if Burke wished to make poetical rejoinder, he had but to quote the lines of Nourmahal from the same tragedy (*Aureng-Zebe*),

""Tis not for nothing that we life
   "pursue,
"It pays our hopes with something
   "still that's new!"
                    Scott's *Dryden*, v. 211.

It is extraordinary how little of Burke's conversation Boswell has attempted to report. It is chiefly confined to his *puns*, one or two specimens of which I shall give hereafter.

* "I have heard him say, with plea-"sure, 'Langton, sir, has a grant of free-"'warren from Henry II; and Cardinal "'Stephen Langton, in King John's "'reign, was of this family.'" *Boswell*, i. 295.

** *Ibid*, i. 295-298.

---

* One night when Beauclerc and Langton had supped at a tavern in London, and sat till about three in the morning, it came into their heads to go and knock up Johnson, and see if they could prevail on him to join them in a ramble. They rapped violently at the door of his chambers in the Temple, till at last he appeared in his shirt, with his little black wig on the top of his head instead of a nightcap, and a poker in his hand, imagining probably that some ruffians were coming to attack him. "When "he discovered who they were, and "was told their errand, he smiled, and "with great good-humour agreed to their "proposal: 'What, is it you, you dogs! "'I'll have a frisk with you.'" *Boswell*, i. 298.

cording to Boswell) had resolved, with Beauclerc, "to persevere in "dissipation for the rest of the "day," when Langton pleaded an engagement to breakfast with some young ladies, and was scolded by Johnson for leaving social friends to go and sit with a set of wretched *un-idea'd* girls. "And as for Garrick, sir," said the sage, when his fright was reported to him, "he durst not do "such a thing. His *wife* would "not *let* him!"* It was on hearing of similar proposed extravagances, soon after, that Beauclerc's mother angrily rebuked Johnson himself, and told him an old man should not put such things in young people's heads; but the frisking philosopher had as little respect for Lady Sydney's anger as for Garrick's decorous alarm. "She had no no-"tion of a joke, sir," he said; "had come late into life, and had "a mighty unpliable understand-"ing!"**

The taste for *un-idea'd girls* was not laughed out of Langton, nevertheless; and to none did his gentle domesticities become dearer than to Johnson. He left Oxford with a first-rate knowledge of Greek, and, what then was of rarer growth at Oxford, with untiring and all-embracing tolerance. His manners endeared him to men from whom he differed most; he listened even better than he talked; and there is no figure at this memor-

able club more pleasing, none that takes kinder or vivider shape in the fancy, than Bennet Langton's. He was six feet six inches high, very meagre, stooped very much, pulled out an oblong gold snuff-box whenever he began to talk, and had a habit of sitting with one leg twisted round the other and his hands locked together on his knee, as if fearing to occupy more space than was equitable.* Beauclerc said he was like the stork standing on one leg in Raffaelle's cartoon;**

1763.
Æt. 35.

* Boswell, i. 299.
** Ibid, v. 24.

* Miss Hawkins's *Memoirs*, ii. 280.
** Mr. Best (*Personal and Literary Memorials*, 62) gives another authority for this saying. "In early youth I knew "Bennet Langton .. he was a very tall, "meagre, long-visaged man, much re-"sembling, according to Richard Pagot, "a stork standing on one leg near the "shore, in Raphael's cartoon of the "miraculous draught of fishes. His "manners were, in the highest de-"gree, polished; his conversation mild, "equable, and always pleasing. He had "the uncommon faculty ('tis strange it "should be an uncommon faculty) of "being a good reader; and read Shak-"speare with such animation, such just "intonation and inflexion of the voice. "that they who heard him declared "themselves more delighted with his re-"citation than with an exhibition of the "same dramatic piece on the stage." It may be worth mention that Langton succeeded Johnson as professor of ancient literature in the Royal Academy; and as I cannot always praise Miss Hawkins, I may as well add that her sketch of Langton is very agreeable. Not that even her *liking* for him, however, is free from uncomfortable touches; "for," she says, "wo "females of the family might get through "much occupation of the after-breakfast "description, drive out for two or three "hours, return and dress, and my mother "might turn in her mind the postpone-"ment of dinner, all within the compass

16*

but goodnaturedly; for the still surviving affection of their college-days checked even Beauclerc's propensity to satire, and as freely still, as in those college-days, Johnson frisked and philosophised with his Lanky and his Beau. The man of fashion had changed as little as the easy, kindly scholar. Alternating, as in his Oxford career, pleasure and literature, the tavern and the court, books and the gaming-table,* he had but widened the scene of his wit and folly, his reasoning and 'merriment, his polished manners and well-bred contempt, his acuteness and maliciousness. Between the men of letters at the Turk's-head, and the glittering loungers in St. James's-street, he was the solitary link of connection; and with George Selwyn at White's, or at Strawberry-hill

1763.
Æt. 35.

with Walpole, was as much at home as with Johnson in Gerrard-street. It gave him an influence, a sort of secret charm, among these lettered companions, which Johnson himself very frankly confessed to. "Beauclerc could take more liberty "with him," says Boswell, "than "anybody with whom I ever saw "him;" and when his friends were studying stately congratulations on his pension, and Beau simply hoped, with Falstaff, that he'd in future purge and live cleanly like a gentleman, he laughed at the advice and took it.* Such, indeed, was the effect upon him of that kind of accomplishment in which he felt himself deficient, that he more than once instanced Beauclerc's talents as those which he was more disposed to envy than those of any whom he had known.** "Sir," he said to Boswell, "everything "comes from him so easily. It "appears to me that I labour "when I say a good thing."***

This peculiarity in Beauclerc's conversation seems undoubtedly,

---

" of a morning visit from Bennet Lang-"ton. But I never saw my father weary "of his conversation, or knew any body "complain of him as a visitor." *Memoirs*, I. 233, 234.

* He wasted a fortune in pleasure and at the gaming-table, yet at his death his library was sold by auction for upwards of 6,000*l.* With it was sold, let me add, a portrait of Johnson, which now became Langton's property, and on the frame of which had been inscribed by Beauclerc, "Ingenium ingens inculto latet hoc sub "corpore;" which inscription Langton caused to be defaced. "It was kind in "you to take it off," said Johnson to him, complacently; and then, after a short pause, with a manly kindness and delicacy of feeling he added, "and not "unkind in him to put it on." He was much affected by Beauclerc's direction in his will, that he should be buried by the side of his mother. *Boswell*, VII. 310-11.

* *Boswell*, I. 298. Johnson was some time with Beauclerc at his house at Windsor, where he was entertained with experiments in natural philosophy. One Sunday, when the weather was very fine, Beauclerc enticed him, insensibly, to saunter about all the morning. They went into a churchyard, in the time of divine service, and Johnson laid himself down at his ease upon one of the tombstones. "Now, sir (said Beauclerc), you "are like Hogarth's Idle Apprentice."
** *Ibid*, VII. 321.
*** *Ibid*, IV. 76. "You are loud, sir," interposed Boswell, "but it is not an "effort of mind."

and half unconsciously, to have impressed every one. Boswell tries to describe it by assigning to it "that *air of the world* which "has I know not what impressive "effect, as if there were some- "thing more than is expressed, "or than perhaps we could per- "fectly understand."   Arthur Murphy calls it a humour which pleased the more for seeming undesigned.*   It might more briefly have been defined, I imagine, as the feeling of a superiority to his subject. No man was ever so free, Johnson said very happily, when he was going to say a good thing, from a look which expressed that it was coming; or, when he had said it, from a look that ex- pressed that it had come.**

This was a sense of the same superiority; and it gave Beau- clerc a predominance of a certain sort over his company, little likely to be always pleasant, and least so when it pointed shafts of sarcasm against his friends. Fond of him as he was, even Johnson some- times lost his patience and tolerance, though he only made matters worse by pushing rudely at his friend. "Sir," he said to him after one of his malicious sallies, "you never open your "mouth but with intention to "give pain; and you have often "given me pain, not from the "power of what you said, but "from seeing your intention."* The habit was doubtless an evil one, and few suffered from it so much as Goldsmith.

His position in the club will be better understood from this sketch of its leading members. He found himself, of course, at a great disadvantage. The lead- ing traits of character which this narrative has exhibited, here, for the most part, told against him. If, on entering it, his rank and claims in letters had been better

* *Essay*, 28. *Boswell*, VII. 265. "As "Johnson and I," Boswell adds, "accom- "panied Sir Joshua Reynolds in his "coach, Johnson said, 'There is in Beau- "'clerk a predominance over his com- "'pany, that one does not like. But he "'is a man who has lived so much in the "'world, that he has a short story on "'every occasion: he is always ready to "'talk, and is never exhausted.'"

** *Boswell*, VII. 321. Mrs. Piozzi, de- scribing (*Anecdotes*, 184) Johnson's fre- quently expressed dislike of what he called "effort" in conversation, adds that his encomiums on Beauclerc's manner always ended in the special phrase that "it was without effort." I could give many examples of this exquisite ease of Beauclerc's talk, but one perhaps will be enough. During one of the frequent dis- putes when the whigs, "the cursed "whigs," "the bottomless whigs," as Johnson called them, had become pre- dominant in the club, and when, in the course of repelling a bitter attack on Fox and Burke, Beauclerc had fallen foul of George Steevens, Boswell interposed: "The gentleman, Mr. Beauclerc, against

"whom you are so violent, is, I know, a "man of good principles." BEAUCLERC: "Then he does not wear them out in "practice." *Boswell*, VII. 123.

* Lord Charlemont, who loved him thoroughly, has not omitted to observe this. "He was eccentric, often querulous, "entertaining a contempt for the gener- "ality of the world, which the politeness "of his manners could not always con- "ceal; but to those whom he liked, most "generous and friendly." Hardy's *Life*, I. 344. And see *Boswell*, VII. 256-60.

ascertained, more allowance would have then been made, not alone by the Hawkinses, but by the Beauclercs and Burkes, for awkwardness of manners and ungainliness of aspect, for that ready credulity which is said to be the only disadvantage of an honest man, for a simplicity of nature that should have disarmed instead of inviting ridicule, and for the too sensitive spirit which small annoyances overthrew. They who have no other means of acquiring respect than by insisting on it, will commonly succeed; but Goldsmith had too many of those other means unrecognised, and was too constantly contending for them, to have energy to spare for the simpler method. If he could only have arrived, where Steele was brought by the witty yet gentle ridicule of Dick Eastcourt, at the happiness of thinking nothing a diminution to him but what argued a depravity of his will, then might anything Beauclerc or Hawkins could have said, of his shape, his air, his manner, his speech, or his address, have but led to a manly enforcement of more real claims.*

But there was nothing in this respect so trifling that he did not think a diminution to him, exacting effort and failure anew. It was now, more than ever, he called William Filby to his aid, and appeared in tailor's finery which made plainer the defects it was meant to hide. It was now he resented non-acceptance of himself by affecting careless judgments of others. It was now that his very avarice of social

* The reader who is not already familiar with this wise and exquisite paper will thank me for referring him to it in the 468th number of the *Spectator*. How beautiful are the subjoined passages in thought as well as style! "It is an In-"solence natural to the Wealthy, to affix, "as much as in them lies, the Character "of a Man to his Circumstances. Thus "it is ordinary with them to praise "faintly the good Qualities of those be-"low them, and say, It is very extra-"ordinary in such a Man as he is, or the "like, when they are forced to acknow-"ledge the Value of him whose Lowness "upbraids their Exaltation. It is to this "Humour only, that it is to be ascribed, "that a quick Wit in Conversation, a "nice Judgment upon any Emergency "that could arise, and a most blameless "inoffensive Behaviour, could not raise "this Man above being received only "upon the Foot of contributing to Mirth "and Diversion. . . . . It is certainly as "great an Instance of Self-love to a "Weakness, to be impatient of being "mimick'd, as any can be imagined. "There were none but the Vain, the "Formal, the Proud, or those who were "incapable of amending their Faults, "that dreaded him; to others he was in "the highest Degree pleasing; and I do "not know any Satisfaction of any in-"different kind I ever tasted so much, as "having got over an Impatience of my "seeing myself in the Air he could put "me when I have displeased him. It is "indeed to his exquisite Talent this way, "more than any Philosophy I could read "on the Subject, that my Person is very "little of my Care; and it is indifferent "to me what is said of my Shape, my "Air, my Manner, my Speech, or my "Address. It is to poor *Eastcourt* I "chiefly owe that I am arrived at the "Happiness of thinking nothing a Diminu-"tion to me, but what argues a De-"pravity of my Will." This pleasant person appears from time to time in the Journal to Stella. "Dined with Con-"greve and Eastcourt and laughed till "six," says Swift. *Works*, II. 63, 182, &c.

pleasure made him fretful of the restraints of Gerrard-street; and all he had suffered or enjoyed of old, in the college class-room, at the inn of Ballymahon, among the Axe-lane beggars, or in the garret of Griffiths, reacted on his cordial but fitful nature,—never seriously to spoil, but very often to obscure it. Too little self-confidence begets the forms of vanity, and self-love will exaggerate faults as well as virtues. If Goldsmith had been more thoroughly assured of his own fine genius, the slow social recognition of it would have made him less uneasy; but he was thrust suddenly into this society, with little beyond a vague sense of other claims than it was disposed to concede to him, however little it might sympathise with the special contempts of Hawkins; and what argued a doubt in others, seems to have become one to himself, which he took as doubtful means of reinforcing. If they could talk, why so could he; but unhappily he did not talk, as in festive evenings at Islington or the White-conduit, to please himself, but to force others to be pleased. Tom Davies was no very acute observer; yet even he has noted of him, that, so far from desiring to appear to the best advantage, he took more pains to be esteemed worse than he was, than others do to appear better than they are:* which was but saying, awkwardly enough, that

* *Life of Garrick,* II. 168.

he failed to make himself understood. How time will modify all this; how far the acquisition of his fame, and its effects upon himself, will _{1763.} strengthen, with respect, _{Æt. 35.} the love which even they who most laughed at already bore him; and in how much this laughing *habit* will nevertheless still beset his friends, surviving its excuses and occasion; the course of this narrative must show. That his future would more than redeem his past, Johnson was the first to maintain; for his own experience of hardship had helped his affection to discern it, and he was never, at any period of their intercourse, so forbearing as at this. Goldsmith's position in these days should nevertheless be well understood, if we would read aright the ampler chronicle which later years obtained.

He who was to be the chronicler had arrived again in London. "Look, my lord!" exclaimed Tom Davies with the voice and attitude of Horatio, addressing a young gentleman who was sitting at tea with himself and Mrs. Davies in their little back-parlour, on the evening of Monday the 16th of May, and pointing to an uncouth figure advancing towards the glass door by which the parlour opened to the shop, "*It comes!*" The hope of the young gentleman's life was at last arrived. "Don't tell where "I come from," he whispered, as Johnson entered with Arthur

Murphy.* "This is Mr. Bos-"well, sir," said Davies; adding waggishly, "from Scotland, sir!"

1763. "Mr. Johnson," said poor Boswell in a flutter (for Æt. 35. the town was now ringing with *Number Forty-five*, Bute had just retired before the anti-Scottish storm, and Johnson's antipathies were notorious), "I do "indeed come from Scotland, but "I cannot help it." "That, sir, "I find," said the remorseless wit, "is what a very great many "of your countrymen cannot "help. Now," he added, turning to Davies as he sat down, regardless of the stunned young gentleman, "what do you think "of Garrick? He has refused "me an order to the play for "Miss Williams, because he "knows the house will be full, "and that an order would be "worth three shillings." Boswell roused himself at this, for what he thought would be a flattering thing to say. He knew that Garrick had, but a few years before, assisted this very Miss Williams by a free benefit at his theatre; but he did not yet know how little Johnson meant by such a sally, or that he claimed to himself a kind of exclusive property in Garrick, for abuse as well as praise. "O, sir," he exclaimed, "I cannot think Mr. "Garrick would grudge such a "trifle to *you*." "Sir!" rejoined the other, with a look and tone that shut up his luckless admirer for the rest of the evening, "I "have known David Garrick "longer than you have done; "and I know no right you have "to talk to me on the subject."* A characteristic commencement of a friendship very interesting to all men. The self-complacent young Scot could hardly have opened it better than by showing how much his coolness and self-complacency could bear. He rallied from the shock; and, though he did not open his mouth again, very widely opened his ears, and showed eagerness and admiration unabated.

"Don't be uneasy," said Davies, following him to the door as he went away: "I can see he likes "you very well."** So emboldened, the "giant's den" itself was daringly invaded after a few days; and the giant, among other unusual ways of showing his benevolence, took to praising Garrick this time. After that, the fat little pompous figure, now eager to make itself the giant's shadow, might be seen commonly on the wait for him at his various haunts: in ordinaries at the social dinner hour, or by Temple-bar in the jovial midnight watches (Johnson's present habit, as he tells us himself, was to leave his chambers at four in the afternoon, and seldom to return till two in the morning) to tempt him to the Mitre. They

* Arthur has also described the scene; but with small difference from Boswell, and certainly not better. *Essay on Johnson*, 58.

* *Boswell*, ii. 163-165.
** *Ibid*, ii. 163.

supped at that tavern for the first time on the 25th of June; but Boswell, who tells us what passed, has failed to tell us at what particular dish it was of their "good supper," or at what glass of the "two bottles" of port they disposed of, that Johnson suddenly roared across the table, "Give me your hand; I "have taken a liking to you." They talked of Goldsmith. He was a somewhat uneasy subject to Boswell, who could not comprehend how he had managed to become so great a favourite with so great a man. For he had published absolutely nothing with his name (Boswell himself had just published "*Newmarket, a* "*Tale*"); he was a man that as yet you never heard of, but as "one Dr. Goldsmith;" and all who knew him seemed to know that he had passed a very loose, odd, scrambling kind of life. "Sir," said Johnson, "Gold-"smith is one of the first men "we now have as an author, and "he is a very worthy man too. "He *has* been loose in his prin-"ciples, but he is coming "right." *

A first supper so successful would of course be soon repeated, but few could have guessed how often. They supped again at the Mitre on the 1st of July; they were together in Inner-temple-lane on the 5th; they supped a third time at the Mitre on the 6th; they met once more on the 9th; the Mitre again received them on the 14th;* on the 19th they were talking again; they supped at Boswell's chambers on the 20th; they passed the 21st together, and supped at the Turk's-head in the Strand; they were discussing the weather and other themes on the 26th; they had another supper at the Turk's-head on the 28th, and were walking from it, arm in arm down the Strand, when Johnson gently put aside the enticing solicitations of wretchedness with *No, no, my Girl, it won't do;** they sculled down to Greenwich, read verses on the river, and closed the day once more with supper at the Turk's-head, on the 30th; on the 31st they again saw each other; they took tea together, after a morning in Boswell's rooms, on the 2nd of August; on the 3rd they had their last supper at the Turk's-head (Johnson encouraged the house because the mistress of it was a good civil woman, and had not much business) before Boswell's reluctant depar-

1763.
Æt. 35.

* *Boswell*, ii. 181.

* That supper on the 11th might be memorable if only for the immortal thing Johnson said when told of "an impudent "follow from Scotland," who maintained that there was no distinction between virtue and vice. "Why, sir, if the fel-"low does not think as he speaks, he is "lying; and I see not what honour he "can propose to himself from having the "character of a liar. But if he does "really think that there is no distinction "between virtue and vice, why, sir, "when he leaves our houses let us count "the spoons." *Boswell*, ii. 217.

** "He, however, did not treat her "with harshness; and we talked of the "wretched life of such women." *Boswell*, ii. 244.

ture for Utrecht, where the old judge-laird was sending him to study the law;—and so many of Johnson's sympathies had thus early been awakened by the untiring social enjoyment, the eagerness for talk, the unbounded reverence for himself, exhibited by Boswell, strengthened doubtless by his youth and idleness (of themselves enough to make any man acceptable to him), by his condition in life, by a sort of romance in the lairdship of Auchinleck which he was one day to inherit, and not a little, it may be, by even his jabbering conceits and inexpressible absurdities, that on the 5th of August the sage took a place beside him in the Harwich coach, accompanied him to the port he was to sail from, and as they parted on the beach enjoined him to keep a journal, and himself promised to write to him. "Who "*is* this Scotch cur at Johnson's "heels?" asked some one, amazed at the sudden intimacy. "He is "not a cur," answered Goldsmith; "you are too severe. He "is only a bur. Tom Davies "flung him at Johnson in sport, "and he has the faculty of stick-"ing."*

Boswell has retorted this respectful contempt; and in him it is excessively ludicrous. "It has "been generally circulated and "believed," he says, "that the "Doctor was a mere fool in con-"versation; but in truth this has

"been greatly exaggerated." Goldsmith had supped with them at the Mitre on the 1st of July, and flung a paradox at both their heads. He maintained that knowledge was not desirable on its own account, for it often was a source of unhappiness.* He supped with them again at the Mitre five days later, as Boswell's guest, when Tom Davies and others were present; and again was paradoxical. He disputed very warmly with Johnson, it seems, against the sacred maxim of the British Constitution that the king can do no wrong: affirming his belief that what was morally false could not be politically true; and that, as the king might, in the exercise of his regal power, command and cause the doing of what was wrong, it certainly might be said, in sense and in reason, that he could *do* wrong: all which appeared to Boswell sensible or reasonable proof of nothing but the speaker's vanity, and eager desire to be conspicuous wherever he was. Among the guests on this occasion was a presbyterian doctor and small poet, who was unlucky enough to hit upon praise of Scotland for a subject. He began by modestly remarking that there was very rich land around Edinburgh, upon which, says Boswell, "Gold-"smith, who had studied physic "there, contradicted this, very "untruly, with a sneering laugh. "Disconcerted a little by this,

* *Prior*, I. 436.* *Boswell*, II. 191.

1763.
—————
Æt. 35.

"Mr. Ogilvie then took new "grounds, where, I suppose, he "thought himself perfectly safe; "for he observed that Scotland "had a great many noble wild "prospects." "I believe, sir," said Johnson upon this, "you "have a great many. Norway, "too, has noble wild prospects; "and Lapland is remarkable for "prodigious noble wild prospects. "But, sir, let me tell you, the "noblest prospect which a Scotch-"man ever sees is the high road "that leads him to England."* This unexpected and pointed sally produced what Boswell calls "a roar" of applause; and even at all this distance of time one seems to hear the hearty roar—Goldsmith contributing to it not the least. But much to his host's discomposure; to whom the very loudness of his laugh was nothing but the desire to make himself in all ways as prominent as might be. "As "usual, he endeavoured, with too "much eagerness, to shine."** It is added, indeed, that his re-spectful attachment to Johnson was now at its height; but no better reason is given for it than that his own literary reputation had not yet distinguished him so much "as to excite a vain desire "of competition with his great "master."*** In short, it is im-possible not to perceive that, from the first hour of their ac-quaintance, Boswell is impatient of Goldsmith, who appears to him very much what the French call *un lourdi*, a giddy pate: Mr. Boswell, no doubt, feeling quite shocked by the contrast of such levity to his own steady gravity and good sense. Also, he is par-ticular to inform us, he finds Goldsmith's person short, his countenance coarse and vulgar, and his deportment that of a scholar awkwardly affecting the easy gentleman: much of all this being perhaps explainable by one of the later passages in his famous book. "It may also "be observed, that Goldsmith "was sometimes content to be "treated with an easy famili-"arity, but upon occasions "would be consequential and im-"portant."* We have but to imagine Boswell suddenly dis-covering that Goldsmith might be treated with an easy famili-arity, to be quite certain that the familiarity would be carried to an extent which in mere self-defence must have rendered necessary a resort to the con-sequential and important. And *hinc illæ lachrymæ*, hence the re-grets and surprises. How such a man could be thought by John-son one of the first men of letters of the day, was hard to be under-stood; and harder yet to be borne, that such a man should be a privileged man. "Doctor "Goldsmith being a privileged "man, went with him this night" (the first supper at the Mitre)

1763.
——
Æt. 35.

* *Boswell*, ii. 208, 209.
** *Ibid*, ii. 206.
*** *Ibid*, ii. 194.

* *Boswell*, iii. 301.

"strutting away, and calling to "me with an air of superiority, "like that of an esoteric over an "exoteric disciple of a "sage of antiquity, *I go to* "*Miss Williams*."*

1763.
Æt. 35.

To be allowed to go to Miss Williams was decisive of Johnson's favour. She was one of his pensioners,** blind and old; was now living in a lodging in Bolt-court, provided by him till he should have a room in a house to offer her, as in former days; was familiar with his earlier life and its privations, was always making and drinking tea,* knew

---

* *Boswell*, ii. 199.

** Others will appear in the course of this narrative, nor can I ever think of Johnson without thinking of the wise kind words with which Mrs. Thrale tells us he outraged all the laws of political economy in regard to the poor. "He "loved the poor," she says, "as I never "yet saw any one else do, with an "earnest desire to make them happy. "What signifies, says some one, giving "halfpence to common beggars? they "only lay it out in gin or tobacco. And "why should they be denied such "sweeteners of their existence? says "Johnson: It is surely very savage to re-"fuse them every possible avenue to "pleasure, reckoned too coarse for our "own acceptance. Life is a pill which "none of us can bear to swallow without "gilding; yet for the poor we delight in "stripping it still barer, and are not "ashamed to show even visible displea-"sure, if ever the bitter taste is taken "from their mouths." After telling us this, the lively little lady adds, that in consequence of these principles he nursed "whole nests" of people in his house, where the lame, the blind, the sick, and the sorrowful found a sure retreat from all the evils whence his little income could secure them. *Anecdotes*, 84, 85. Mr. Maxwell tells us also, in his collectanea, "that he frequently gave all "the silver in his pocket to the poor, who "watched him between his house and "the tavern where he dined." *Boswell*, iii. 133. We learn, too, from another authority, Mr. Harwood, that when visiting Lichfield, towards the latter part of his life, he was accustomed, on his arrival, to deposit with Miss Porter as much cash as would pay his expenses back to London. He could not trust himself with his own money, as he felt himself unable to resist the importunity of the numerous claimants on his benevolence. *Ibid*, ii. 146. Hawkins notes the same peculiarity. "He now practised a rule which he often "recommended to his friends, always to "go abroad with a quantity of loose "money to give to beggars, imitating "therein, though certainly without in-"tending it, that good but weak man, old "Mr. Whiston, whom I have seen dis-"tributing, in the streets of London, "money to beggars on each hand of him, "till his pocket was nearly exhausted." *Life of Johnson*, 395. Good, but weak Whiston: good, but weak Johnson. Well, Hawkins at any rate is not weak on these points, and, whatever else he may have been, there can be no doubt he was perfectly unexceptionable as a poor-law guardian. "I shall never forget," says Miss Reynolds, "the impression I "felt in Dr. Johnson's favour, the first "time I was in his company, on his say-"ing, that as he returned to his lodgings, "at one or two o'clock in the morning, "he often saw poor children asleep on "thresholds and stalls, and that he used "to put pennies into their hands to buy "them a breakfast." Croker's *Boswell*, 834. "I have heard Gray say that John-"son would go out in London with his "pockets full of silver, and give it all "away in the streets before he returned "home." Nicholls, in the *Works*, v. 33. Let me add that Burke, though no mean political economist, had the same habit, and justified it on similar grounds. But it is also to be remarked that society has during the last century contributed so much more largely towards proper provision for the poor, that it would be difficult to justify the practice now so easily as Burke and Johnson did.

* "Mrs. Williams made it," says Boswell, "with sufficient dexterity, notwith-"standing her blindness, though her "manner of satisfying herself that the

intimately all his ways, and talked well; and he never went home at night, however late, supperless or after supper, without calling to have tea with Miss Williams. "Why *do* you keep "that old blind woman "in your house?" asked Beauclerc. "Why, sir," answered Johnson, "she was a "friend to my poor wife, and "was in the house with her when "she died. She has remained in "it ever since, sir."

Beauclerc's friendships with women were not of the kind to help his appreciation of such gallantry as this; though he seems to have known none so distinguished, in even the circles of fashion, that he did not take a pride in showing them his rusty-coated philosopher-friend. The then reader of the Temple, Mr. Maxwell, has described the levees at Inner-temple-lane. He seldom called at twelve o'clock in the day, he says, without finding Johnson in bed, or declaiming over his tea to a party of morning visitors, chiefly men of letters, among whom Goldsmith, Murphy, Hawkesworth (an old

---

"cups were full enough, appeared to me "a little awkward: for I fancied she put "her finger down a certain way, till she "felt the tea touch it." III. 102. On the other hand, Percy, whose vicarage she visited in Johnson's company during the year following this, says, in a communication to Dr. Robert Anderson: "When she made tea for Johnson and "his friends, she conducted it with so "much delicacy, by gently touching the "outside of the cup, to feel, by the heat, "the tea as it ascended within, that it "was rather matter of admiration than "of dislike." And see Hawkins's *Life of Johnson*, 321-5, &c: "I see her now," says Miss Hawkins, in one of the pleasantest passages of her *Memoirs*, I. 152, "a pale, shrunken old lady, dressed in "scarlet, made in the handsome French "fashion of the time, with a lace cap, "with two stiffened projecting wings on "the temples, and a black lace hood over "it. .. Her temper has been recorded as "marked with the Welsh fire, and this "might be excited by some of the meaner "inmates of the upper floors" (of Dr. Johnson's house); "but her gentle kind- "ness to me I never shall forget, or "think consistent with a bad temper." The bad temper seems nevertheless indisputable. "Age, and sickness, and "pride," Johnson himself writes a few years later, "have made her so peevish, "that I was forced to bribe the maid to "stay with her by a secret stipulation of "half-a-crown a week over her wages." *Boswell*, VI. 283. In another letter he writes to Mrs. Thrale: "Williams hates "every body. Levett hates Desmoulins, "and does not love Williams. Des- "moulins hates them both. Poll loves "none of them." *Piozzi Letters*, (1788), II. 38; and see 28-9. See also II. 66, 80, 171, 175-6, 311, &c. &c. Poll was a Miss Carmichael, who, with Mrs. Desmoulins and her daughter, Miss Williams and Mr. Levett, formed what Miss Hawkins calls the "inmates of the upper floors," and Mrs. Thrale the "whole nests" of people, who were indebted for their only home to the charity of Johnson. "He used to "lament pathetically to me," adds the little lady, in one of the most delightful of her *Anecdotes* (213), "that they made "his life miserable from the impossi- "bility he found of making theirs "happy. . . . If, however, I ventured to "blame their ingratitude and condemn "their conduct, he would instantly set "about softening the one and justifying "the other; and finished commonly by "telling me that I knew not how to "make allowances for situations I never "experienced." Such was his humanity, and such his generosity, exclaims Boswell, "that Mrs. Desmoulins herself told "me he allowed her half-a-guinea a "week. Let it be remembered that this "was above a twelfth part of his pen- "sion." *Life*, VII. 50.

friend and fellow-worker under Cave), and Langton, are named as least often absent. Some-times learned ladies were there, too; and particularly did he remember a French lady of wit and fashion doing him the honour of a visit. It was in the summer of this year: and the lady was no other than the famous Countess de Boufflers, acknowledged leader of French society, mistress of the Prince of Conti, aspiring to be his wife, and of course, in the then uni-versal fashion of the savantes, philosophers, and beaux esprits of Paris, an *Anglomane*. She had even written a tragedy in English prose, on a subject from the *Spectator;* and was now on a round of visitings, reading her tragedy, breakfasting with Wal-pole, dining with the Duke of Grafton, supping at Beauclerc's, out of patience with everybody's ridiculous abuse of everybody that meddled in politics, and out of breath with her own social exertions. "Dans ce pays-ci," she exclaimed, "c'est un effort "perpétuel pour se divertir;" and, exhausted with it herself, she did not seem to think that any one else succeeded any bet-ter. It was a few days after Horace Walpole's great break-fast at Strawberry-hill, where he describes her with her eyes a foot deep in her head, her hands dangling and scarce able to sup-port her knitting-bag, that Beau-clerc took her to see Johnson. They sat and talked with him

1763.
Æt. 35.

some time; and were retracing their way up Inner-temple-lane to the carriage, when all at once they heard a voice like thunder, and became conscious of John-son hurrying after them. On nothing priding himself more than on his politeness, he had taken it into his head, after a little reflection, that he ought to have done the honours of his literary residence to a foreign lady of quality; and, eager to show himself a man of gallantry, was now hurrying down the staircase in violent agitation. He overtook them before they reached the Temple-gate, and, brushing in between Beauclerc and the Countess, seized her hand, and conducted her to her coach.* His dress was a rusty brown morning suit, a pair of old shoes by way of slippers, a little shrivelled wig sticking on the top of his head, and the sleeves of his shirt and the knees of his breeches hanging loose. "A considerable crowd of people "gathered round," says Beau-

* *Boswell*, vi. 25-6. "When our visit "was ended," says Hannah More, de-scribing herself and her sister calling on Johnson in the year of Goldsmith's death, "he called for his hat, as it rained, to at-"tend us down a very long entry to our "coach." *Memoirs*, i. 49. And Miss Rey-nolds expressly tells us (*Croker*, 832) that he never suffered any lady to walk from his house to her carriage, through Bolt-court, unattended by himself to hand her into it; and if any obstacle pre-vented it from driving off, "there he "would stand by the door of it, and "gather a mob around him; indeed they "would begin to gather the moment he "appeared handing the lady down the "steps into Fleet-street."

clerc, "and were not a little "struck by this singular ap-"pearance." The hero of the incident would be the last person to be moved by it. The more the state of his toilet dawned upon him, the less likely would he be to notice it. There was no more remarkable trait in Johnson, and certainly none in which he more contrasted with the subject of this narrative, than that, as Miss Reynolds was always surprised to remark, no circumstances external to himself ever prompted him to make the least apology for them, or to seem even sensible of their existence.

It was not many months after this that he went to see Goldsmith at a new lodging in the locality which not Johnson alone, but its association with a line of the greatest names of English literature, the Dorsets, Raleighs, Seldens, Clarendons, Beaumonts, Fords, Marstons, Wycherleys, and Congreves, has rendered illustrious. He had taken rooms on the then library staircase of the Temple. They were a humble set of chambers enough (one Jeffs, the butler of the society, shared them with him); and, on Johnson's prying and peering about in them, after his short-sighted fashion, flattening his face against every object he looked at, Goldsmith's uneasy sense of their deficiencies broke out. "I shall soon be in better "chambers, sir, than these," he said. "Nay, sir," answered John-son, "never mind that. *Nil te "quæsiveris extra.*" Invaluable advice! if Goldsmith, blotting out remembrance of his childhood and youth, and looking solely and steadily on the present and the future, could but have dared to act upon it.

1763.
Æt. 35.

CHAPTER IX.

The Arrest and what preceded it.
1763—1764.

OLIVER'S removal from the apartments of Newbery's relative in Wine-office-court, to his new lodging on the library staircase of the Temple, took place in an early month of 1764, and seems to connect itself with circumstances at the close of 1763 which indicate a less cordial understanding between himself and Newbery. He had ceased writing for the *British Magazine;* was contemplating an extensive engagement with James Dodsley; and had attempted to open a connection with Tonson of the Strand. The engagement with Dodsley went as far as a formal signed agreement (for a *Chronological History of the Lives of Eminent Persons of Great Britain and Ireland*), in which the initials of medical bachelor are first assumed by him; and at the close of which another intimation of his growing importance appears, in the stipulation that "Oliver "Goldsmith shall print his name "to the said work." It was to be in two volumes, octavo, of the size and type of the *Universal*

History; each volume was to contain thirty-five sheets; Goldsmith was to be paid at the rate of three guineas a sheet; and the whole was to be delivered in the space of two years at farthest. But nothing came of it. Dodsley had inserted a cautious proviso that he was not to be required to advance anything till the book should be completed; and hence, in all probability, the book was never begun.* The overture to

Tonson had not even so much success. It was a proposition from Goldsmith for a new edition of Pope, which Tonson was so little disposed to entertain that he did not condescend to write his refusal. He sent a printer with a message declining it; delivered with so much insolence, that the messenger received a caning for his pains.

The desire to connect himself with Pope seems to point in the direction of those secret labours which are to prove such wonderment to Hawkins. He was busy at this time with his poem and his novel; and, if there be any truth in what great fat Doctor Cheyne of Bath told Thomson, that, as you put a bird's eyes out to make it sing the sweeter, you should keep poets poor to animate their genius, he was in excellent condition for such labour. But what alone seems certain as to that matter is, that be it light or dark, the song, if a true song, will make itself audible; and for the rest, one is better pleased to think that Goldsmith's philosophy was opposed to fat Doctor Cheyne's, and that he preferred to believe, with Thomson, both the birds and the poets happier in the

---

* As an example of such agreements, and the first formal evidence of Goldsmith's growing importance with the booksellers, I subjoin this with Dodsley. The original is now in the British Museum, Mr. Rogers having lately placed it with the more interesting agreements, also his gift to the nation, of Milton for *Paradise Lost* and Dryden for the *Fables*. "It is agreed between Oliver Goldsmith "M.B. on one hand, and James Dodsley "on the other, that Oliver Goldsmith "shall write [for James Dodsley a book "called a Chronological History of the "Lives of Eminent Persons of Great "Britain and Ireland, or to that effect, "consisting of about two volumes 8vo "about the same size and letter with the "Universal History published in 8vo; for "the writing of which and compiling the "same, James Dodsley shall pay Oliver "Goldsmith three guineas for every "printed sheet, so that the whole shall "be delivered complete in the space of "two years at farthest; James Dodsley, "however, shall print the above work in "whatever manner or size he shall think "fit, only the Universal History above "mentioned shall be the standard by "which Oliver Goldsmith shall expect to "be paid. Oliver Goldsmith shall be "paid one moiety upon delivery of the "whole copy complete, and the other "moiety, one half of it at the conclusion "of six months, and the other half at the "expiration of the twelve months next "after the publication of the work, James "Dodsley giving, however, upon the de- "livery of the whole copy, two notes for "the money left unpaid. Each volume "of the above intended work shall not "contain more than five-and-thirty "sheets, and if they should contain more, "the surplus shall not be paid for by "James Dodsley. Oliver Goldsmith shall "print his name to the said work.

"OLIVER GOLDSMITH.
"JAMES DODSLEY.

" *March 31st*, 1763."

light, and singing sweetest amid luxuriant woods with the full spring blooming around them. He has expressed this in a passage of his *Animated Nature* so charming, yet so little known, that I shall be thanked for here subjoining it. "The music "of every bird in captivity pro-"duces no very pleasing sensa-"tions: it is but the mirth of a "little animal insensible of its "unfortunate situation. It is the "landscape, the grove, the golden "break of day, the contest upon "the hawthorn, the fluttering from "branch to branch, the soaring "in the air, and the answering of "its young, that gives the bird's "song its true relish. These "united, improve each other, "and raise the mind to a state of "the highest, yet most harmless "exultation. Nothing can in this "situation of mind be more "pleasing than to see the lark "warbling on the wing; raising "its note as it soars, until it "seems lost in the immense "heights above us; the note con-"tinuing, the bird itself unseen; "to see it then descending with "a swell as it comes from the "clouds, yet sinking by degrees "as it approaches its nest; the "spot where all its affections are "centred, the spot that has "prompted all this joy."* These

sentences, exquisite in feeling, emulate in expression the music they describe.

There is a note among Newbery's papers with the date of the 17th of December, 1763, which states Goldsmith to have received twenty-five guineas from the publisher, for which he promises to account.* At this time, too, he disappears from his usual haunts, and is supposed to have been in concealment somewhere. Certainly he was in distress, and on a less secure footing with Newbery than at the commencement of the year.

My narrative had been thus far printed in my first edition when this statement received corroboration from discovery of a brief note of Goldsmith's. It would seem that between the date of his leaving Wine-office-court in "an early month of "1764," and his return to Islington at "the beginning of April" in that year,** he had occupied,

1763.
———
Æt. 35.

---

* *Animated Nature*, IV. 261-2. In the same chapter Goldsmith incidentally contributes his experience to what Charles Fox, Coleridge, and other famous men have since written on the song of the nightingale. "For weeks together, if "undisturbed, they sit upon the same "tree; and Shakespeare rightly describes "the nightingale sitting nightly in the "same place, which I have frequently "observed she seldom departs from. . . "Her note is soft, various, and inter-"rupted; she seldom holds it without a "pause above the time that one can "count twenty. The nightingale's paus-"ing song would be the proper epithet "for this bird's music with us, which is "more pleasing than the warbling of any "other bird, because it is heard at a "time when all the rest are silent." IV. 256-7.

* "Received from Mr. Newbery "twenty-five guineas. For which I "promise to account. OLIVER GOLD-"SMITH. Decemb. 17th, 1763."
** See *ante*, 255; and *post*, 259.

while his attic in the library staircase of the Temple was preparing, a temporary lodging in Gray's-inn; and that the engagement with Dodsley which I have described as opened at this time had actually proceeded as far as the preparation of copy, and the claim for advance of money. This, as well as the sharp poverty he was suffering, appears from the note in question, which is addressed to the bookseller. "Sir," it runs, being dated from Gray's-inn, and directed "to Mr. James Dodesley "in Pall Mall," on the 10th of March, 1764, "I shall take it as a "favour if you can let me have "ten guineas per bearer, for "which I promise to account. I "am, sir, your humble servant, "OLIVER GOLDSMITH. P.S. I "shall call to see you on Wednes- "day next with copy, &c." Whether the money was advanced, or the copy supplied, does not appear.

Yet it was at this time of his own dire necessities we find him also busied with others' distresses, and helping to relieve them. Among his papers at his death was found the copy of an appeal to the public for poor Kit Smart,* who had married New-

1763.
_____
ÆL. 35.

bery's step-daughter ten years before, and had since, with his eccentricities and imprudences, wearied out all his friends but Goldsmith and Johnson. Very recently, as a last resource, he had been taken to a madhouse; and it was under this restraint, while pens and ink were denied to him, that he indented on the walls of his cell, with a key, his *Song to David.** His friends accounted for the excellence of the composition by asserting that he was most religious when most mad; but Goldsmith and Johnson were nevertheless now exerting themselves for his release. "Sir," said the latter to Boswell at one of their recent interviews, "my poor friend Smart showed "the disturbance of his mind, by "falling upon his knees and say- "ing his prayers in the street, or

"says, is inimitable, true sterling wit, "and humour by God; and he can't hear "the Prologue without being ready to "die with laughter. He acts five parts "himself, and is only sorry he can't do "all the rest. ... All this, you see, must "come to a Jayl, or Bedlam, and that "without any help, almost without pity." See also *Correspondence of Gray and Mason*, 169, 175; and Mrs. Piozzi's *Anecdotes*, 260.

* Boswell did great wrong to Smart by making him the hero of the ever famous comparison with Derrick. (*Life*, VIII. 182-3). It was of *Boyce* and Derrick that Johnson was asked at Lord Shelburne's which he thought the best poet. "Sir, there is no settling the point of "precedency between a louse and a flea!" The question was put by Morgann (who wrote the admirable *Essay on Falstaff*), expressly to provoke Johnson out of an argument he had taken up, "from the "spirit of contradiction," to prove the merits of Derrick as a writer. See *Europ. Mag.* XXX. 160 (Sept. 1796).

* Percy calls it (Letter to Malone, Oct. 17, 1786) "a paper which he wrote to "set about a subscription for poor "Smart, the mad poet." For a very whimsical account of Smart's vagaries, while yet a resident fellow of Pembroke in Cambridge, written in Gray's quaint, thoughtful way, see *Works*, III. 42. He describes him amusing himself with a comedy of his own writing, which, "he

"in any other unusual place. "Now although, rationally speak- "ing, it is greater madness not "to pray at all than to pray as "Smart did, I am afraid there "are so many who do not pray "that their understanding is not "called in question." "I did not "think," he remarked to Burney, "he ought to be shut up. His "infirmities were not noxious "to society. He insisted on "people praying with him; and "I'd as lief pray with Kit Smart "as any one else. Another "charge was, that he did not "love clean linen; and, sir, I "have no passion for it."*

Their exertions were successful. Smart was again at large at the close of the year, and on the 3rd of the following April *1764. Æt. 36.* (1764) a sacred composition named *Hannah*, with his name as its author, and music by Mr. Worgan, was produced at the king's theatre. The effort connects itself with a similar one by Goldsmith, made at the same time. He wrote the words of an Oratorio in three acts, on the subject of the Captivity in Babylon. But it is easier to help a friend than oneself; and his own Oratorio lay unrepresented in his desk. All he received for it was ten guineas, paid by Dodsley for his right to publish it, in which Newbery was to share;* and all of it that *1764. Æt. 36.* escaped to the public while he lived were two songs, in which his own sorrows and hope seemed as legibly written as those of the Israelitish women.

"To the last moment of his breath
    On Hope the wretch relies,
And even the pang preceding death
    Bids Expectation rise.

"Hope, like the gleaming taper's light,
    Adorns and cheers our way,
And still as darker grows the night
    Emits a brighter ray."**

The night was very dark round Goldsmith just now, yet the ray was shining steadily too. In few of the years of his life have we more decisive evidence of struggles and distress than in this of 1764; but in none did he accomplish so much for an enduring fame. It is a year very difficult to describe, however, with any accuracy of detail. We have little to guide us beyond the occasional memoranda of publishers and the accounts of Mrs. Elizabeth Fleming. To the Islington lodging he returned at the beginning of April (having

* *Life*, II. 170-71. Johnson said another whimsical thing to Burney, when, having observed that poor Kit was getting fat in the madhouse, the latter suggested want of exercise as the probable cause: "No, sir; he has partly as much exercise "as he used to have, for he digs in the "garden. Indeed, before his confine- "ment, he used for exercise to walk to "the ale-house; but he was *carried* back "again."

* "Received from Mr. Dodsley ten "guineas for an Oratorio which Mr. New- "bery and he are to share. OLIVER "GOLDSMITH. Oct. 31st 1764." Mr. Murray's Newbery MSS.

** See Nichols's *Illustrations*, VII. 24-5, and *post*, Book IV. chap. XIII. The verses above quoted are from the original manuscript of the Oratorio. The song as appended to *The Haunch of Venison* &c (1776) will be found in *Miscell. Works*, IV. 120-1.

OLIVER GOLDSMITH'S LIFE AND TIMES.

paid rent for the retention of "the room," meanwhile, at the rate of about three shillings a week); and his expenses to the end of June are contained in his landlady's bill. They seem to argue fewer enjoyments, and less credit with Mrs. Fleming. No dinners or teas are thrown into the bargain. The sixpence for "sasafras" (a humble decoction which the poet does not seem to have despised, now dealt in by apothecaries chiefly) is always carefully charged. The loans are only four, and of moderate amount; a shilling to "pay the laundress," and tenpence, one and twopence, and sixpence "in cash." There are none of the old entries for

1764. Æt. 36.

port wine. Twopence, twice, for a pint of ale, and twopence for "opodildock," express his very humble "extras." But as these curious documents are now before me, and have never been very correctly or at all completely printed, it will be well to subjoin a literal transcript of the two principal accounts, for 1763 and 1764, from the original manuscripts in Mr. Murray's possession. They certainly throw curious light upon the domestic economics of poor Goldsmith; whose fate it has been after death, even as it was during life, to be pursued by unsettled accounts scored up against him by tailors and laundresses.

"1763.   Doctr. Goldsmith*   Dr. to Eliz. Fleming.

Date	Item	£	s.	d.
Aug. 22.	A Pint of Mountain	0	1	0
	A Gentleman's Dinner	0	0	0
24.	A bottle of Port	0	2	0
	4 Gentlemen Tea	0	1	6
25.	Doctr. Roman Dinner and Tea	0	0	0
Sept. 5.	Doctr. Roman Dinner	0	0	0
7.	Sasafras	0	0	6
11.	Doctr. Roman Dinner	0	0	0
29.	A bottle Port	0	2	0
	Mr. Baggott Dinner	0	0	0
Oct. 8.	Sasafras	0	0	3
10.	Mr. Baggott Tea	0	0	0
14.	Paper	0	1	0
24.	Sasafras	0	0	3
25.	Paid the Newes Man	0	16	10¼
30.	Wine and Cakes	0	1	6
31.	To the Rev. Mr. Tyrrell	0	2	6
	Mr. Baggott Dinner	0	0	0
	Sasafras	0	0	6
Nov. 5.	Sasafras	0	0	6
	10 sheets of paper	0	0	5
8.	Penns	0	0	2¼
	Paper	0	1	0
	Sasafras	0	0	6
	Carried forward	£1	12	0¼

* Endorsed by Newbery "Dr. G.'s acct, &c. settled. 1763."

		Brought forward . .	£1	12	6¼
Nov. 8.	To 3 Months' Board	12	10	0
	To Shoes cleaning	0	2	6
	To washing	0	18	0¼
		£15	3	0¼

"Recd., Dec. 9, 1763, by the hands of
"Mr. Newbery, the Contents in full.   "ELIZ. FLEMING."

1764.
Æt. 36.

"1763.   Doctr. Goldsmith Dr. to Washing.

Aug. 14.	8 Shirts 2 plain	0	2	6
	6 Neckcloths 1 Cap	0	0	3¼
	4 pr Silk Stockings	0	0	8
	2 pr worsted Do	0	0	2
30.	7 Shirts 1 plain	0	2	3
	5 Neckcloths 1 Cap	0	0	3
	2 pr Silk Stockings 1 pr worsted	0	0	5
Sept. 14.	6 Shirts 1 plain	0	1	11
	5 Neckcloths 1 Cap	0	0	3
	3 pr Silk Stockings 1 pr worsted	0	0	7
27.	7 Shirts 1 plain	0	2	3
	4 pr Silk Stockings 1 pr worsted	0	0	9
	6 Neckcloths 1 Cap	0	0	3½
Oct. 3.	1 Shirt	0	0	4
	4 pr Silk Stockings 2 pr worsted	0	0	10
	4 Neckcloths 1 Cap	0	0	2¼
24.	8 Shirts 2 plain	0	2	6
	5 Neckcloths 1 Cap	0	0	3
	3 pr Silk Stockings 1 pr worsted	0	0	7
Nov. 8.	2 Shirts 1 plain	0	0	7
	2 Neckcloths 1 pr Stockings	0	0	2
		£0	18	0¼ "

"1764.   Doctr. Goldsmith Dr. to Eliz. Fleming.

To the Rent of the Room from Dec. 25 to March 29. .	£1	17	6
April 2. A Post Letter	0	0	1
3. The Stage Coach to London	0	0	6
7. Lent to pay the Laundress	0	1	0
11. A Post Letter	0	0	1
15. A Parcell by the Coach	0	0	2
18. A Post Letter	0	0	1
19. Sasafras	0	0	6
25. Sasafras	0	0	6
May 2. Sasafras	0	0	6
3. A Post Letter	0	0	1
7. A Post Letter	0	0	1
Sasafras	0	0	6
Gave the boy for carrying the Parcell to			
Pall Mall	0	0	8
12. Sasafras	0	0	6
16. A Post Letter	0	0	4
17. Pens and Paper	0	1	3
21. Sasafras	0	0	6
23. A Post Letter	0	0	1
Carried forward. . .	£2	4	11

				£	s.	d.
		Brought forward . .		£2	4	11
May 24.	Lent in Cash			0	0	10
	A Pint of Ale			0	0	2
25.	Paper			0	1	0
	Sasafras			0	0	6
1764.	Opodildock			0	0	2
Æt. 36. June 8.	A letter to the Post			0	0	1
9.	Lent in Cash			0	1	2
	Sasafras			0	0	6
21.	Lent in Cash			0	0	6
27.	A Post Letter			0	0	1
28.	A Post Letter			0	0	1
30.	Sasafras			0	0	6
	To cleaning shoes			0	2	6
	Washing and Mending.					
April 17.	3 Shirts, 3 Neckcloths, 4 pr. Stockings . .			0	1	6½
May 3.	2 Shirts, 2 Neckcloths, 1 Cap			0	0	9¼
12.	4 Shirts, 4 Neckcloths, 3 pr. Stockings . .			0	1	9
	To mending 3 pr. Stockings			0	0	3
26.	3 Shirts, 3 Neckcloths, 1 pr. Stockings . .			0	1	2½
June 8.	4 Shirts, 4 Neckcloths, 1 pr. Stockings, 1 Cap			0	1	7½
	1 Pr. Stockings, mending			0	0	1
22.	4 Shirts, 4 Neckcloths, 4 pr. Stockings . .			0	1	10
	3 Pr. Stockings mending			0	0	3
	For Cloth and wristing a Shirt			0	0	6
	To 3 months' Board, &c., from March 29 to June 29			12	10	0
				15	12	9

"OLIVER GOLDSMITH."

The impression left by the second of these bills is borne out by Newbery's concurrent memoranda of money advanced; in sums ridiculously small, and for such work as the revision of short translations, and papers for the *Christian Magazine*.* What were not unusual in the previous year, as cash advances of one, two, and even four and five guineas, from the publisher, have now dwindled down to "shillings" and "half-crowns;" and the question has been raised whether Newbery, to satisfy outstanding claims, may not have engaged him for some part of the time in work for his juvenile library. The author of *Caleb Williams*, who had been a child's publisher himself, had always a strong persuasion that Goldsmith wrote *Goody Two Shoes* (Mr. Thackeray has claimed *Tom Hickathrift* for Fielding),* and if

---

* For this, the *Life of Christ and Lives of the Fathers*, before referred to, appear to have been translated; Goldsmith receiving 21l. for the task work.

* Yet (such are the differences of taste) Mr. G. S. Carey, author of *Chrononhotonthologos*, thus writes to Garrick three years after the present date. "I had "rather they had laid the History of "Tom Hickathrift to my charge, than to "say I was the author of *The Theatrical* "*Monitor*; for, in my opinion, there was "never published anything more puerile, "invidious, and exceptionable." *Garrick*

so, the effort belongs to the present year; for Mrs. Margery, radiant with gold and gingerbread, and rich in pictures as extravagantly ill drawn as they are dear and well remembered, made her appearance at Christmas. Other aid was also sought to eke out that of Newbery; and a sum of thirteen guineas is acknowledged from Mr. Griffin (the publisher of the *Essays* in the following year), but without mention of the labours it rewarded.

That, in all these memoranda, the entire labours of the year cannot yet be accounted for, it is hardly necessary to add. We are left to guess what other work was in progress, for which advances were not available; and in this an anecdote told by Reynolds to a member of the Horneck family will offer some assistance. He went out to call upon Goldsmith, he says, not having seen him for some time; and no one answering at his door, he opened it without announcement, and walked in. His friend was at his desk, but with hand uplifted, and a look directed to another part of the room; where a little dog sat with difficulty on his haunches, looking imploringly at his teacher, whose rebuke for toppling over he had evidently just received. Reynolds advanced, and looked past Goldsmith's shoulder at the writing on his desk. It seemed to be some portions of a poem; and looking more closely, he was able to read a couplet which had been that instant written. The ink of the second line was wet.

1764.
Æt. 36.

"By sports like these are all their cares
    beguil'd;
The sports of children satisfy the
    child."*

* *Europ. Mag.* Prior has also told it (II. 33) on the relation of Mrs. Gwyn. The authority for the succeeding anecdote is an odd little book called *Axiomata Pacis*, from which I quote: "A venerable "friend who lies buried in Horfield "churchyard, once related to me an "anecdote which seemed to bring me "into contact for a moment with one of "the sweetest minstrels that ever warbled "his native woodnotes wild. The relater "chanced to be at a London tavern one "evening when a gentleman present

Correspondence, I. 270. It may not be out of place to add, that Johnson thought the Tommy Prudent and Goody Two Shoes class of children's books too childish. "Babies do not want," he said to Mrs. Thrale when he saw these books of Newbery's in her nursery, "to hear about "babies. They like to be told of giants "and castles, and of somewhat which "can stretch and stimulate their little "minds." (Mrs. Piozzi's *Anecdotes*, 16.) He would therefore have been more disposed to agree with Mr. Thackeray than with Mr. Carey on the merits of Tom Hickathrift, that redoubtable giant; and such, I must confess, is also my inclining. As to Goldsmith's work for the nursery, which since I made the remark in the text has been insisted on in various quarters (see *Notes and Queries*, 2nd Series, XII. 41), it rests upon authority, I am obliged to say, quite unreliable. A friend suggests even as a strong argument for Goldsmith's authorship of Goody Two Shoes that a medicine is praised in it for which he is known to have had a predilection (the father of Goody dying of some fever, owing to his living unfortunately in a remote village "where the fame of Dr. James's excellent "powders had not reached"); the truth being that Newbery was the proprietor of the powders, which were accordingly puffed in his books on all practicable occasions.

This visit of Reynolds is one of the few direct evidences which the year affords of his usual intercourse with his more distinguished friends; and there is a story, also of this time, told by a humble friend of Reynolds who engraved many of his works in mezzotint, of his having been present in a tavern when he heard Goldsmith read out portions of a manuscript poem that soon after appeared as *The Traveller*, which would show that the society of humbler listeners and admirers had as yet lost none of its charms for him. There is no reason to doubt, however, that he had been pretty constant in his attendance at the club during the past winter; he was a member of the Society of Arts, and had been often at their meetings, of which the only trace now left is the record of loans of money begged from Newbery there (in which, as I find from inspection of the originals, the prudent publisher was careful to note whenever the loan, though but of five shillings and three-pence, was "without receipts");*

and his miseries and necessities must have been great indeed, that would have kept him long a stranger to the theatre.

The last season had been one of peculiar interest. The year 1763 had opened with evil omen to Garrick. For the first time since the memorable night at which I left him in my narrative of his triumph at Goodman's-fields, when, in the midst of un-exampled enthusiasm, his eye fell upon a little deformed figure in a side box, was met by the approving glance of an eye as bright as his own, and in the ad-miration of Alexander Pope his heart swelled with the sense of fame,* Garrick, at the com-

---

"drew a manuscript poem from his "pocket, and requested permission to "read it to the company. The company "assented. My friend (happy listener) "was William Pether the well-known "mezzotinto engraver. The poem was "*The Traveller*, and the reader was Oliver "Goldsmith."

* Several of the entries in the memo-randum subjoined·are entered in pencil. "Lent Dr. Goldsmith for his instrument "(*in pencil*) 10s. 6d. Doctor Goldsmith, "Dr. Money lent at the Society of Arts "(*in pencil*), 3l. 3s. Feb. 14, Lent Dr. "Goldsmith (*in pencil*) 1l. 1s. March 5,

"Dr. Goldsmith, 15l. 15s. May 1, Lent "Dr. Goldsmith, 10s. 6d. Ditto, 2s. 6d. "July 14, Dr. Goldsmith, 29l. 8s. Aug. 15, "Ditto, 4l. 4s. Sept. 1, Ditto, 5l. 5s. "Nov. 17, Lent Dr. Goldsmith, 5s. 3d. "July 7, 1764, Lent Dr. Goldsmith (*in* "*pencil*), 2s. Lent before (*in pencil*), 2s. 6d. "April 30, 1765, Lent Dr. Goldsmith at "the Society (*in pencil*), 3l. 3s." Mr. Murray's Newbery MSS.

* "As I opened the part I saw our "little poetical hero, dressed in black, "seated in a side box near the stage, and "viewing me with a serious and earnest "attention. His look shot and thrilled "like lightning through my frame, and I "had some hesitation in proceeding, "from anxiety and from joy. As Richard "gradually blazed forth, the house was "in a roar of applause, and the conspir-"ing *hand* of Pope shadowed me with "laurels." Percival Stockdale's *Memoirs*, 11. 152-4. Such was Garrick's own ac-count of the greatest triumph of the opening of his career; and, at the close of it, after an interval of six-and-thirty years of uninterrupted success, he told a friend with what emotion he had seen Charles Fox in one of the side boxes, as he rushed off the stage at the close of the second act of *Lear*, holding up his hands

mencement of that year, felt his influence shaken and his ground insecure. On a question of prices, the Fribble whom Churchill has gibbeted in the *Rosciad* led a riotous opposition in his theatre, to which he was compelled to offer a modified submission; and not many weeks

later, after appearing in a comedy by Mrs. Sheridan and giving it out to be his last appearance in any new play (the character was a solemn old coxcomb, and one of his happiest performances),* he announced his determination to go abroad for two years. The pretence was health; but the real cause (resentment of what he thought the public indifference, and a resolve that they should feel his absence) is surmised in a note of Lord Bath's which lies before me, addressed to his nephew Colman, the *ad interim* manager of the theatre.

Garrick left London in the autumn; and his first letter to Colman from Paris describes the honours which were showering upon him, the plays revived to please him, and the veteran actors recalled to act before him. He had supped with Marmontel and d'Alembert; "the Clairon" was at the supper, and recited them a charming scene from *Athalie;* and he had himself given the dagger scene in *Macbeth,* the curse in *Lear,* and the falling asleep of Sir John Brute, with such extraordinary effect, that "the most wonderful wonder of "wonders" was nothing to it. Yet on the very day that letter was written (the 8th of October, 1763), a more wonderful wonder was enacting on the boards of his own theatre. A young bankers' clerk named Powell, to

1764.
———
Æt. 36.

with animated gesture expressive of the wonder of his admiration. It is very pleasing, let me add, to discover repeated evidences, in this not very reverential age, of the deep respect, the feeling akin to awe, with which Pope was regarded towards the close of his life. Even Johnson has his personal pride connected with him, and often "told us with high "satisfaction, the anecdote of Pope's in-"quiring who was the author of his *Lon-*"*don,* and saying he will be soon *de-*"*terré.*" (*Boswell,* III. 86.) Reynolds too, like Johnson and Garrick, had *his* story to tell of the great little monarch, the supreme despot, of the age of literature just passed away. He was in a crowded auction-room on his first arrival in London, watching a sale of pictures for his master Hudson, when, as he stood near the auctioneer at the upper end of the room, he became aware of an extraordinary bustle among the crowd at the other extremity near the door, which he could only account for at the moment by supposing that some one had fainted from the effect of the heat. But he soon heard the name of Mr. Pope whispered from every mouth, and became conscious that the poet was just entering. Every person forming that crowd then drew back and divided to make way for him up the centre of the room, and all present, on either side of the passage which was formed, held out their hands that he might touch them as he passed. Reynolds occupied a modest position behind the front rank, but he put out his hand under the arm of the person who stood before him, and Pope took it as he did those of others in advancing. Reynolds, when his own fame was at its height, never forgot the exquisite pride of that moment. See *Northcote,* i. 19; and *Beechey,* i. 41-5.

* Sir Anthony Branville in the *Discovery.*

whom, on hearing him rehearse, he had given an engagement before he left London of three pounds a week for three years, appeared on that day in Beaumont and Fletcher's *Philaster*, and took the audience by storm. Foote is described to have been the only unmoved spectator.[*] The rest of the audience were not content with clapping; "they stood up "and shouted," says Walpole; and Foote's jeering went for nothing. Walpole describes the scene with what seems to be a satisfied secret persuasion (in which Goldsmith certainly shared) that Garrick had at last met a dangerous rival. He calls the new actor "what Mr. Pitt "called my Lord Clive," a heaven-born hero;[**] says the heads of the whole town are turned; and describes all the boxes taken for a month. Powell's salary was at once raised to ten pounds a week, George Garrick consenting on the part of his brother; and such was the anxiety of the town to see him in new characters, and the readiness of the management in giving way to it, that in this his first season, from October '63 to May '64, he appeared in seventeen different plays, to a profit on the receipts of nearly seven thousand pounds.[***] His most successful efforts indicate the attractive

1764.
Æt. 36.

points of his style. In Philaster he appeared sixteen times, in Posthumus eleven, seven times in Jaffier, six in Castalio, and five in Alexander. Garrick himself had meanwhile written to him from Italy to warn him against such characters as the latter, and restrain him from attempting too much.[*] The advice was admirably written, and gratefully acknowledged; nor is there any reason to doubt its sincerity. Remoteness of place has in some respects the effect of distance of time; and the great actor, doubtless not sorry to be absent till the novelty should abate, was less likely to be jealous in Piedmont or the Savoy than in the green-room of Drury-lane. He knew himself yet unassailed in what he had always felt to be his main strength, his versatility and variety of power.[**] Three men were now

[*] "I am very angry with Powell," he writes to Colman, "for playing that "detestable part of Alexander. Every "genius must despise it, because that, "and such fustian-like stuff, is the bane "of true merit. If a man can act it well, "I mean to please the people, he has "something in him that a good actor "should not have. He might have served "Mrs. Pritchard, and himself too, in "some good natural character. I hate "your roarers." Rome, April 11, 1764. *Memoirs of the Colmans*, I. 111, 112. And see an excellent letter to Powell himself, written from Paris in December 1764, *Garrick Correspondence*, I. 177-8.

[**] The earliest of Garrick's critics was one of the most discriminating, and is entitled on other grounds to be listened to with respect, for he became a bishop, and, even after he had published his book on the *Prophecies*, continued to think Shakespeare and Garrick not un-

<hr>

[*] Davies's *Life of Garrick*, II. 71.
[**] *Letters to Mann*, I. 167.
[***] See Boaden's prefatory memoir to *Gar. Corr.* I. XLII.

dividing his laurels; and till Powell could double Richard and Sir John Brute, till O'Brien could alternate Ranger with Macbeth, and till Weston could exhibit Lear by the side of Abel Drugger, Garrick had no call to be seriously alarmed.

Be that as it might, however, Powell's success was a great thing for the authors. He came to occupy for them, opportunely, a field which the other had avowedly abandoned; and Goldsmith, always earnest for the claims of writers, sympathised strongly in his success. Another incident of the theatrical season made hardly less noise. O'Brien's charms in Ranger and Lovemore proved too much for Lady Susan Fox-Strangways, *

1764.

Æt. 36.

worthy of his regard. Newton lived with Lord Carpenter in Grosvenor-square, as tutor to his son, when the Goodman's-fields prodigy began to be talked about; took additional interest in him as a fellow-townsman of Lichfield; and not only used to travel every week that distance of six or seven miles to see the new actor, but, sending servants beforehand to keep places (necessary then) that nothing of eye or gesture might be lost, carried to Goodman's-fields with him all the great people he could induce to accompany him, and wrote excellent letters of encouragement and advice to the object of his admiration. I quote from one which is dated exactly six months from the day of Garrick's first appearance. After telling him that one of the masters of Westminster school who remembered Booth and Betterton was of opinion that in Lear he had far excelled the first and even equalled the last, "The thing," he continues, "that strikes me above all "others, is that variety in your acting. "and your being so totally a different "man in Lear from what you are in "Richard. There is a sameness in every "other actor. Cibber is something of a "coxcomb in everything; and Wolsey, "and Syphax, and Iago, all smell strong "of the essence of Lord Foppington. "Booth was a philosopher in Cato, and "was a philosopher in everything else. "His passion in Hotspur and Lear was "much of the same nature, whereas "your's was an old man's passion, and "an old man's voice and action; and in "the four parts wherein I have seen you, "Richard, Chamont, Bayes, and Lear, I "never saw four actors more different "from one another, than you are from "yourself." *Garrick Correspondence*, i. 7. This letter (written, be it remembered, when Garrick was only twenty-five) helps to explain what was meant by the celebrated prompter of Drury-lane, Waldron, a man of discernment and even taste in poetry, when he frankly made answer, on a question of comparison between his early master Garrick, and a later ornament of the stage, "No man admires Mr. "Kemble, sir, more than I do. He is a "great man! a very great man! but Mr.

"Garrick, sir, bless my soul! It was quite "a different sort of thing." Even Horace Walpole, in one of his most elaborate depreciations of Garrick (*Coll. Lett.* v. 11, 12), is unconsciously betrayed into an admission of his unrivalled variety and versatility when he summons back two of the Betterton race, lays under contribution the French stage, and has to pick and choose from among the living English actors, before he can establish the fact of his having had equals or superiors in the art. So when Johnson talked of the old actors during the tour to the Hebrides (*Boswell*, iv. 132): "You "compare them with Garrick and see "the deficiency. Garrick's great dis-"tinction is his universality."

* "A very pleasing girl, though not "handsome. ... Lord Ilchester doated "on her." *Letters to Mann*, i. 195. The branch of the Fox family to which Lady Susan belonged took the name of Strangways on her father's marriage with an heiress so called. "The king," writes her uncle Lord Holland to Mr. Grenville, asking him for a place in the New York Customs to banish O'Brien to, "has "shown so much compassion on this un-"happy occasion, that," &c. *Grenville Correspondence*, ii. 447. "O'Brien and "Lady Susan," says Walpole to Lord

and she ran away with him. It cured Walpole for a time of his theatre-going. He had a few days before been protest-ing to Lord Hertford that he had the republican spirit of an old Roman, and that his name was thoroughly Hora-tius;* but a homely-looking earl's daughter running away with a handsome young player, ran away with all his philosophy. He thought a footman would have been preferable,** and

1764.
—————
Æt. 36.

Hertford, "are to be transported to the "Ohio and have a grant of 40,000 acres." *Coll. Lett.* IV. 404. In Taylor's *Records* of his life (I. 177) it is said of O'Brien "that "he was a fencing-master in Dublin, or "the son of a fencing-master, but with "manners so easy and so sprightly that "he was admitted into the best company, "and was a member of several of the "most fashionable clubs at the west end "of the town."

  * *Coll. Lett.* IV. 336.

  ** *Coll. Lett.* IV. 405. Within a very few months his preference was gratified by another of his lady friends, Lord Rockingham's youngest sister, actually marrying her Irish footman, Mr. William Sturgeon. *Coll. Lett.* IV. 460. ("A sen-"sible, well-educated woman," says Gray, "27 years old indeed, and homely "enough." *Correspondence* with Mason, 335.) Yet, such are the strange incon-sistencies of character, this same Horace Walpole could thus write to Mann eight years later: "We have an instance in our "family of real dignity of mind, and I "set it down as the most honourable "alliance in the pedigree. The dowager "Lady Walpole" (his aunt), "you know, "was a French staymaker's daughter. "When ambassadress in France, the "queen expressed surprise at her speak-"ing so good French. Lady Walpole said "she was a Frenchwoman. 'Français!' "replied the queen. 'Vous Français, "'madame! et de quelle famille?' "'D'aucune, madame,' answered my "aunt. Don't you think that *aucune* "sounded greater than Montmorency

could not have believed that Lady Susan would have stooped so low. On the other hand, Goldsmith speaks of O'Brien's elegance and accomplishments ("by nature formed to please," said Churchill), and seems to think them not unfairly matched.*

"would have done? One must have a "great soul, to be of the *aucune* family; "which is not necessary, to be a "Howard." *Lett. to Mann.* II. 221. But then she had become a Walpole.

  * A clever little piece called *Cross Pur-poses*, written by O'Brien, was played after his return from America; and he afterwards less successfully borrowed from the French a comedy called the *Duel*. O'Brien lived to a very great age, and is remembered living "on his farm" in one of the midland counties during the first quarter of the present century; while his wife, Lady Susan, did not die till 1827, at the ripe age of 84. I am happy to be able to quote a hitherto un-published letter of his to George Garrick, which pleasantly exhibits the social na-ture of the man, the regret with which he entered the temporary exile to which the pride of his wife's grand relations had sentenced him, and the wondrous changes which a century has made in the scene of his exile. The letter was probably one of his first from New York, and its date shows with what a horrible haste ("O'Brien and his lady big with child," writes Gray to the master of Pembroke, Oct. 29, 1764, "are embarked for America "to cultivate their 40,000 acres of wood-"land") the fashionable folk had packed them off. "NEW YORK, *Nov.* 10th, 1764. "DEAR GEORGE, Though I think you "don't deserve it at my hands, yet I must "write to you, and beg you will take the "first opportunity to let me hear from "you, how you do, and how every thing "goes on among you at old Drury, where "I often wish myself, just to take a peep "thro' the curtain and have a frisk in the "green-room. . . . I suppose you long to "have an account of our passage, and "this place. As to the first, it was a "very remarkable one for the time of "year, they say, being only 34 days—but "between you and I, the tempest we have

But much depends on whether these things are viewed from a luxurious seat in the private boxes, or from a hard bench in the upper gallery.

Poverty pressed heavily just now upon Goldsmith, as I have said. His old friend Grainger came over on leave from his West India station, to bring out his poem of the *Sugar Cane;* and found him in little better plight than in his garret days. "When "I taxed little Goldsmith "for not writing," he says to Percy, "as he promised "me, his answer was, that he "never wrote a letter in his life; "and 'faith I believe him, unless "to a bookseller for money."*

1764.
——
Æt. 36.

"been used to see on dry land before a "crowded house, is far pleasanter than "some we met with on the American "coast. I assure you I thought it a "serious affair, and began to say my "short prayers. Lady Susan was vastly "ill the whole way, but is now quite well "again and sends you her compliments. "New York is not equal to London, but "we shall be very comfortable I make no "doubt—every one here seems extremely "disposed to make it as agreeable as "possible to us. Everything appears just "in the bud, a world in its infancy, "which to folks used to the conveniences "and luxuries of London is at the first "rather awkward—time makes every- "thing feel less so. Whenever I meet "with anything I think worth your while "accepting, you may be sure I won't "forget you. In the mean time I beg "you'll do me the favor to desire Mr. "Woodfall will send me the Public Ad- "vertisers that I may see the progress of "Politics and Plays at one view. He may "send them regularly by the packets as "they come; and if possible let me have "them from the first day the house opened, "and so on day by day; I'll have them "all the while I continue in this coun- "try. ... Hearing from England will be "my greatest pleasure, therefore I hope "you among the rest won't forget me. "East, West, North, or South, I am over, "Dear George, Yours most sincerely "Wm. O'Brien." After his return to England, O'Brien got the place of re-ceiver-general of the county of Dorset, and you see him in the peerages as Wm. O'Brien, of Stinsford Co. Dorset, Esq (where he died in 1815). See note to *Garrick Correspondence*, I. 170. See also Taylor's *Records of his own Life*, I. 176, and *Selwyn Correspondence*, I. 273.

* Letter to Percy, dated March 24, 1764, in Nichols's *Illustrations*, VII. 286. In the same letter he describes himself to have been robbed, "about three o'clock "of the day we parted, about three miles "on this [London] side of St. Albans. "Luckily he did not ask for my watch, "and went off by telling me he was sorry "to be obliged to take our money. So "civil are our highwaymen. In France "or Spain our death would have pre- "ceded the robbery." Mrs. Thrale writes to Johnson (October 1773), "Mr. M— was "robbed going home two nights ago, "and had a comical conversation with "the highwayman about behaving like a "gentleman. He paid four guineas for "it." *Piozzi Letters*, I. 185. I may here take the opportunity of saying that in the fifty-first volume of the *Gentleman's Maga-zine*, 39, there is given an "Epitaph in "Jamaica. By Dr. Goldsmith. Not "printed in his works;" and it is quite possible that this may in some way be connected with Grainger, whether as written by his request, or at the solicita-tion of some friend introduced by him to Goldsmith. The epitaph itself is worth subjoining as a well-balanced specimen of tombstone-literature, richly merited if true. It is "On Zachary Bayly, Esq. "He was a man, to whom the endow- "ments of Nature rendered those of Art "superfluous. He was wise, without the "assistance of recorded Wisdom; and "eloquent, beyond the precepts of "scholastic Rhetoric. His study was of "Men, and not of Books; and he drank "of Knowledge, not from the Stream, but "from the Source. To Genius, which "might have been fortunate without "Diligence, he added a Diligence, which, "without Genius, might have com- "manded Fortune. He gathered riches

In the present year, it would seem, he had more experience than success in applications of that kind. Yet he was also himself in communication with Grainger's correspondent. Percy was still, as he had long been, busy with his *Reliques;* and in the collection and arrangement of that work, which more than any other in its age contributed to bring back to the study and appreciation of poetry a natural, healthy, and passionate tone, took frequent counsel with Goldsmith. To their intercourse respecting it, we owe the charming ballad with the prettiest of opening lines, "Turn, gentle hermit of the "dale;" and Percy admitted many obligations of knowledge and advice, in which no other man of letters in that day could so well have assisted him. The foremost of them, Johnson himself, was indifferent enough to the whole scheme; though at this time a visitor, with Miss Williams, in Percy's vicarage-house.

Little else than a round of visitings, indeed, does the present year seem to have been to Johnson; though the call for his

Shakespeare (on which he had so long been engaged) was never so urgent as now.* He passed part of the spring with his friend Langton in Lincolnshire, where it was long remembered how suddenly, and to what amazement of the elders of the family, he had laid himself down on the edge of a steep hill behind the house, and rolled over and over to the bottom;** he had stayed the summer months and part of August with Percy, at Easton-Mauduit vicarage in Northamptonshire;*** and on his return to town had formed an acquaintance with the Thrales. Is it necessary to describe the tall, stately, well-informed, worthy brewer, and tory member for

* "Will Mr. Johnson's *Shakespeare* "EVER appear?" had been Dr. Wilson's question to Derrick more than a year before, in a letter in my possession otherwise noticeable for a mention of the Gentleman in Black; whom, says the worthy Doctor, "I should like to have had the "honour to know." To whom he was indebted for what he *did* know, he had as little suspicion as his fellow Doctor in Divinity, Wilder himself.

** "Poor, dear Dr. Johnson," said Langton to Mr. Best, some years after Johnson's death, "when he came to this "spot, turned back to look down the hill, "and said he was determined 'to take a "'roll down.' When we understood "what he meant to do, we endeavoured "to dissuade him; but he was resolute, "saying, 'he had not had a roll for a "'long time;' and taking out of his "lesser pockets whatever might be in "them—keys, pencil, purse, or penknife, "and laying himself parallel with the "edge of the hill, he actually descended, "turning himself over and over, till he "came to the bottom." Best's *Memorials,* 65.

*** *Boswell,* ii. 269, and 282.

"with honour, and seemed to possess "them only to be liberal. His private "virtues were not less conspicuous than "his public benevolence. He considered "Individuals as Brethren, and his Coun-"try as a Parent. May his Talents be "remembered with respect, his Virtues "with emulation!" In a later number of the same magazine, I should add, the authorship is given to Hawkesworth, whom it is said that Goldsmith had assisted in it.

Southwark; or his brisk, vivacious, half-learned, plump little wife? Is not their friendship known as the solace of Johnson's later life, and remembered whenever he is named? Thrale was fond of the society of men of letters and celebrity; and Arthur Murphy, who had for some years acted as provider in that sort to the weekly dinners* at Southwark and Streatham, had the honour of introducing Johnson. Mrs. Thrale was at this time as pretty as she was lively, garrulous, and young;** to more than a woman's quickness of observation, added all a woman's gentleness and kindness of heart; indulged in literary airs and judgments, which she put on with an audacity as *1764. Æt. 36.* full of charms as of blunders; and beyond measure captivated Johnson. She was his *Madam*, *My Mistress*, his *Dearest of all Dear Ladies*, whom he lectured only because he loved, for where she came, she brought him sunshine. Like some "gay creature of the "element" she flitted past the gloomy scholar, still over-toiled and weary, though resting at last. "You little creatures," he exclaimed, on her appearing before him one day in a dark-coloured dress, "you should never wear "those sort of clothes; they are "unsuitable in every way. What! "have not all insects gay "colours?"* The house of the

---

* It was through him "the set" were introduced. He had done the same office in Garrick's case four years earlier. "You stand engaged," he writes to him in May 1760, "to Mr. Thrale for Wednes"day se'enight. You need not apprehend "drinking; it is a very easy house, and "the scheme of going to Ranelagh will "be agreeable to him. I am to dine "with him to-morrow, in order to ad"journ in the evening to Ranelagh, so "fond is he of that place." *Gar. Cor.* i. 116.

** Mr. Croker is the only infallible authority I know on the question of a lady's age, and he has settled Mrs. Thrale's, though not without great difficulty. In his last edition of *Boswell* (170) he says, "She was about twenty"four or twenty-five years of age, when "this acquaintance commenced. At the "time of my first edition I was unable to "ascertain precisely Mrs. Piozzi's age— "but a subsequent publication, named "*Piozziana*, fixes her birth on her own "authority to the 16th January, 1740; yet "even that is not quite conclusive, for "she calls it 1740 *old style*, that is, 1741. "I must now of course adopt, though not "without some doubt, the lady's reckon"ing." Happily this doubt was solved before the completion of his labour, though not in the lady's favour, for in a subsequent note (650) he says, "I have "found evidence under her own hand "that my suspicion was just, and that she

"was born in 1740, new style." In another note to the same edition, Mr. Croker has the satisfaction of settling the late Lady Cork's age, long held to be insoluble. "I found by the register of St. "James's parish that she had understated "her age by one year. She died on the "30th of May, 1840, aged 95." (616). I need hardly add that the same ruthless authority discovered, at the cost of a journey to a much more distant parish-register, that poor Fanny Burney had understated her age by no less than ten years; and that instead of being a girl of seventeen, hardly out of the nursery, when she surprised the world by *Evelina*, she was in truth a mature young lady of twenty-seven! Nevertheless this was a fact in literary history worth setting right, and gratitude is due to Mr. Croker accordingly.

* *Anecdotes*, 279. Her greatest fault was a kind of saucy carelessness of speech, which showed itself sometimes in "little

hospitable brewer became to him a second home, where unaccustomed comforts awaited him, _1764._ and his most familiar _Æt. 36._ friends were invited to please him; immediately after his first visit, the Thursdays in every week were set apart for dinner with the Thrales; and before long there was a "Mr. John-"son's room" both in the Southwark mansion and the Streatham villa. Very obvious was the effect upon him. His melancholy was diverted, and his irregular habits lessened, all said who observed him closely; but not the less active were his sympathies still, in the direction of that Grub-street world of struggle and disaster, of cock-loft lodgings and penny-ordinaries, from which he had at last effected his own escape.

An illustration of this, at the commencement of their intercourse, much impressed Mrs. Thrale. One day, she says, he was called abruptly from their house after dinner, and returning in about three hours, said he had been with an enraged author, whose landlady pressed him for payment within doors, while the bailiffs beset him without; that he was drinking himself drunk with madeira to drown care, and fretting over a novel which when finished was to be his whole fortune; but he could not get it done for distraction, nor could he step out of doors to offer it to sale. Mr. Johnson, therefore, she continues, set away the bottle, and went to the bookseller, recommending the performance, and desiring some immediate relief; which when he brought back to the writer, the latter called the woman of the house directly to partake of punch, and pass their time in merriment. "It was not," she concludes, "till ten years after, I "dare say, that something in "Doctor Goldsmith's behaviour "struck me with an idea that he "was the very man, and then "Johnson confessed that he was "so; the novel was the charming "_Vicar of Wakefield._"*

A more scrupulous and patient writer corrects some inaccuracies of the lively little lady, and professes to give the anecdote authentically from Johnson's own exact narration. "I received one "morning," Boswell represents Johnson to have said, '"a mes-"sage from poor Goldsmith that "he was in great distress, and, "as it was not in his power to "come to me, begging that I

"variations in narrative," never deliberate, and which she would have excused on the score that one cannot be perpetually watching. "Nay, then," wisely observed Johnson, "you _ought_ to be "perpetually watching. It is more from "carelessness about truth, than from in-"tentional lying, that there is so much "falsehood in the world." _Boswell,_ VII. 57.

* _Anecdotes,_ 119-20. Mrs. Thrale fixes the date of the incident as not later than 1765 or 6; but it is to be kept in mind that her little volume of _Anecdotes_ was written and printed while she was in Italy (it appeared in 1786), without the means of correcting any such slip of memory.

"would come to him as soon as "possible. I sent him a guinea, "and promised to come to him "directly. I accordingly went as "soon as I was dressed, and "found that his landlady had ar- "rested him for his rent, at "which he was in a violent pas- "sion. I perceived that he had "already changed my guinea, "and had got a bottle of madeira "and a glass before him. I put "the cork into the bottle, de- "sired he would be calm, and "began to talk to him of the "means by which he might be "extricated.* He then told me "that he had a novel ready for "the press, which he produced "to me. I looked into it, and "saw its merit; told the landlady "I should soon return; and, hav- "ing gone to a bookseller, sold it "for sixty pounds. I brought "Goldsmith the money, and he "discharged his rent, not with- "out rating his landlady in a "high tone for having used him "so ill."**

Nor does the rating seem altogether undeserved, since there are certainly considerable grounds for suspecting that Mrs. Fleming was the land- lady. The attempt to clear her appears to me to fail in many essential points. Tracing the previous incidents minutely, it is almost impossible to discon- nect her from this consummation of them, with which, at the same time, every trace of Goldsmith's residence in her house is brought to a close. As for the incident itself, it has nothing startling for the reader who is familiar with what has gone before it. It is the old story of distress, with the addition of a right to resent it which poor Goldsmith had not felt till now; and in the violent passion, the tone of indignant reproach, and the bottle of madeira, one may see that recent gleams of success and of worldly consideration have not strengthened the old habits of endurance. The arrest is plainly connected with Newbery's re- luctance to make further ad- vances; of all Mrs. Fleming's ac- counts found among his papers, the only one unsettled is that for

1764.
Æt. 36.

---

* Mr. Croker has pointed out that George Steevens (in the *London Magazine*, LV. 253) tells, curiously enough, a not dissimilar story of Johnson himself, who very frankly confessed to have been sometimes in the power of bailiffs, and that Richardson, the author of *Clarissa*, was his constant friend on such occa- sions. "I remember writing to him," said Johnson, "from a sponging house; "and was so sure of my deliverance "through his kindness and liberality, "that, before his reply was brought, I "knew I could afford to joke with the "rascal who had me in custody, and did "so, over a pint of adulterated wine, for "which, at that instant, I had no money "to pay." Croker's *Boswell*, 141.

** *Boswell*, II. 193. For a third and ridiculously inventive account of the in- cident, in which Goldsmith figures as at his wits' end how to wipe off his land- lady's score and keep a roof over his head, "except by closing with a very "staggering proposal on her part, and "taking his creditor for wife, whose "charms were very far from alluring, "whilst her demands were extremely "urgent," and which contains a mass of other preposterous statements, see Cum- berland's *Memoirs*, I. 372-3.

the summer months preceding the arrest;* nor can I even resist altogether the suspicion, considering the intimacy between the families of the Newberys and the Flemings which Newbery's bequests in his will show to have existed,** that the publisher himself, for an obvious convenience of his own, may have suggested, or at least sanctioned, the harsh proceeding. The manuscript of the novel (of which more hereafter) seems by both statements, in which the discrepancies are not so great but that Johnson himself may be held accountable for them, to have been produced reluctantly, as a last resource; and it is possible, as Mrs. Thrale intimates, that it was still regarded as "un-"finished;" but if strong adverse reasons had not existed, Johnson would surely have carried it to Newbery. He did not do this. He went with it to Francis Newbery the nephew; does not seem to have given any very brilliant account of the "merit" he had perceived in it (four years after its author's death he told Reynolds that he did not think it would have had much success*);

_{1764.}
_{Æt. 36.}

[* A fourth version, that of Sir John Hawkins (quoted by Mr. Mitford in his *Life*, p. CLXXVIII), and strongly smacking of the knight's usual vein, appears to me to point to Islington as the locality of the arrest, though it does not directly confirm that suggestion. "Of the book-"sellers whom he styled his friends, Mr. "Newbery was one. This person had "apartments in Canonbury-house, where "Goldsmith often lay concealed from his "creditors. Under a pressing necessity, "he there wrote his *Vicar of Wakefield*, "and for it received of Newbery forty "pounds." It does not detract from the value of this evidence, such as it is, that Sir John gives afterwards (*Life*, 420-1 his own blundering account of the attempted arrest, and Johnson's relief, in apparent ignorance that the piece of writing was the *Vicar of Wakefield*. See the story as discussed in Croker's *Boswell*, 141.

** My friend Mr. Peter Cunningham was so kind as to examine Newbery's will for me, and found in it two bequests. of fifty guineas each, to Mrs. Elizabeth Fleming and Mr. Thomas Fleming. Among the Newbery papers, I should here remark, there is one in the handwriting of Mrs. Fleming, endorsed by Newbery "Dr. Goldsmith's acc.;" and hitherto unprinted, to the following effect: "Feb. 1763. Doctr Goldsmith, To a "Bill paid by the hands of Mr. Newbery, "14*l*; May, ditto, 14*l* 11s; Oct. 10, ditto, "14*l* 13s 6*d*; Nov. 10, ditto, 15*l* 3s. 1764. "Aug. 6, ditto, 16*l* 6s." From this it would appear that the last of Mrs. Fleming's accounts was ultimately settled by Newbery; but, though this might in itself go far to clear her from the imputation of the arrest, the suspicion above expressed in connection with Newbery himself leaves the matter still in doubt,

and the Newbery payments strengthen the belief of a private understanding existing between her and the bookseller.

* The passage is worth quoting from *Boswell*, VII. 172-3. It occurs in an argument which arose at Reynolds's dinnertable, as to whether a man who had been asked his opinion by another whether or not his manuscript were worth publication, is justified in giving such opinion, or under an obligation to speak the truth, on being so put to the torture. In any case, argued Johnson, "I should scruple "much to give a suppressive vote. Both "Goldsmith's comedies were once re-"fused; his first by Garrick, his second "by Colman, who was prevailed on at "last by much solicitation, nay, a kind "of force, to bring it on. His *Vicar of* "*Wakefield* I myself did not think would "have had much success. It was written "and sold to a bookseller before his "*Traveller*, but published after; so little

and, rather with regard to Goldsmith's immediate want than to any confident sense of the value of the copy, asked and obtained the sixty pounds. "And sir," he said to Boswell afterwards, "a sufficient price too, when it "was sold; for then the fame "of Goldsmith had not been "elevated, as it afterwards was, "by his *Traveller;* and the book-"seller had such faint hopes of "profit by his bargain that he "kept the manuscript by him a "long time, and did not publish "it till after the *Traveller* had ap-"peared. Then, to be sure, it "was accidently worth more "money."*

On the poem, meanwhile, which Reynolds had found him busy at, the elder Newbery *had* consented to speculate; and this circumstance may have made it hopeless to appeal to him with a second work of fancy. For, on that very day of the arrest, the *Traveller* lay completed in the poet's desk. The dream of eight years, the solace and sustain-ment of his exile and poverty, verged at last to fulfilment or extinction; and the hopes and fears which centred in it, mingled doubtless on that miserable day with the fumes of the madeira! In the excitement of putting it to press, which followed immediately after, the nameless novel recedes altogether from the view; but will reappear in due time. Johnson approved the verses more than the novel; read the proof-sheets for his friend; substituted here and there, in more emphatic testimony of general approval, a line of his own; prepared a brief but hearty notice for the *Critical Review*, which was to appear simultaneously with the poem; and, as the day of publication approached, bade Goldsmith be of good cheer.

1764.
Æt. 36.

CHAPTER X.

The *Traveller* and what followed it.
1764—1765.

"THIS day is published," said the *Public Advertiser* of the 19th of December, 1764, "price one "shilling and sixpence, *The Tra-*"*veller;* or, a Prospect of Society, "a Poem. By Oliver Goldsmith, "M.B. Printed for J. Newbery "in St. Paul's Church Yard." It was the first time that Goldsmith had announced his name in connection with anything he had written; and with it he had resolved to associate his brother Henry's name. To him he dedicated the poem. From the

---

"expectation had the bookseller from it. "Had it been sold after *The Traveller*, he "might have had twice as much money "for it, though sixty guineas was no "mean price. The bookseller had the ad-"vantage of Goldsmith's reputation from "*The Traveller* in the sale, though Gold-"smith had it not in selling the copy." Sir Joshua Reynolds: "The *Beggars'* "*Opera* affords a proof how strangely "people will differ in opinion about a "literary performance. Burke thinks it "has no merit." All this should be remembered before harsh judgments are passed on the occasional querulous complaints that broke from Goldsmith as to the reception given to his writings.

* *Boswell*, ii. 193.

midst of the poverty which Henry could least alleviate, and turning from the celebrated men with whose favour his own fortunes were bound up, he addressed the friend and companion of his infancy, to whom, in all his sufferings and wanderings, his heart, untravelled and unsullied, had still lovingly gone back. "The friend-"ship between us can acquire no "new force from the ceremonies "of a Dedication," he said; "but "as a part of this poem was "formerly written to you from "Switzerland, the whole can now, "with propriety, be only in-"scribed to you. It will also "throw light upon many parts of "it, when the reader under-"stands that it is addressed to a "man, who, despising fame and "fortune, has retired early to "happiness and obscurity with "an income of forty pounds a "year. I now perceive, my dear "brother," continued Goldsmith, with affecting significance, "the "wisdom of your humble choice. "You have entered upon a sacred "office, where the harvest is "great, and the labourers are "but few; while you have left "the field of ambition, where the "labourers are many, and the "harvest not worth carrying "away." Such as the harvest was, however, he was at last himself about to gather it in. He proceeded to describe to his brother the object of his poem, as an attempt to show that there may be equal happiness in states that are differently governed from our own, that every state has a particular principle of happiness, and that this principle in each may be carried to a mischievous excess: but he expressed a strong doubt, since he had not taken a political "side," whether its freedom from individual and party abuse would not wholly bar its success.

While he wrote, he might have quieted that fear. As the poem was passing through the press, Churchill died. It was he who had pressed poetry into the service of party, and for the last three years, to apparent exclusion of every nobler theme, made harsh political satire the favoured utterance of the Muse. But his rude strong spirit had suddenly given way. Those unsubdued passions; those principles, unfettered rather than depraved; that real manliness of soul, scorn of convention, and unquestioned courage; that open heart and liberal hand; that eager readiness to love or to hate, to strike or to embrace; had passed away for ever. Nine days earlier, his antagonist Hogarth had gone the same dark journey; and the reconciliation that would, surely, even here, have sooner or later vindicated their common genius, the hearty English feeling which they shared, and their common cordial hatred of the false pretences of the world, was left to be accomplished in the grave.*

* In a paper on Churchill in the *Edinburgh Review* (LXXXI. 16-88), printed in my

Be it not the least shame of the profligate politics of these three disgraceful years, that, arraying in bitter hostility one section of the kingdom against the other, they turned into unscrupulous personal enemies such men as these; made a patriot of Wilkes; statesmen of Sir Francis Dashwood, Lord Sandwich, and Bubb Dodington; and, of the free and vigorous verse of Churchill, a mere instrument of perishable faction. Not without reason on that ground did Goldsmith condemn and scorn it. It was that which had made it the rare mixture it so frequently is, of the artificial with the natural and impulsive; which so fitfully blended in its author the wholly and the partly true; which impaired his force of style with prosaical weakness; and controlled, by the necessities of partisan satire, his feeling for nature and truth. Yet should his critic and fellow-poet have paused before, in this dedication to the *Traveller*, he branded him as a writer of lampoons. To Charles Hanbury Williams, but not to Charles Churchill, such epithets belong. The senators who met to decide the fate of turbots were not worthier of the scourge of Juvenal, than the men who, reeking from the gross indulgences of Medmenham-abbey, drove out William Pitt from the cabinet, sat down by the side of Bute,

denounced in the person of Wilkes their own old profligate associate, and took the public morality into keeping. Never, that he might merely fawn upon power or trample upon weakness, had Churchill let loose his pen. There was not a form of mean pretence or servile assumption which he did not use it to denounce. Low, pimping politics he abhorred; and that their worthless abettors, to whose exposure his works are so incessantly devoted, have not carried him into oblivion with themselves, argues something for the sound morality and permanent truth expressed in his manly verse. By these the new poet was to profit, as much as by the faults which perished with the satirist, and left the lesson of avoidance to his successors. In the interval since Pope's and Thomson's death, since Collins's faint sweet song, since the silence of Young, of Akenside, and of Gray, no such easy, familiar, and vigorous verse as Churchill's had dwelt in the public ear. The less likely was it now to turn away, impatient or intolerant of the *Traveller*.

1764.
Æt. 36.

Johnson pronounced it a poem to which it would not be easy to find anything equal since the death of Pope. Though covering but the space of twenty years (Pope died in 1744), this was praise worth coveting, and was honestly deserved. The elaborate skill of the verse, the ex-

<hr>

Biographical Essays (Third Edition, pp. 255-326), I have expressed this view in more detail.

quisite selectness of the diction, at once recalled to others, as to Johnson, the master so lately absolute in the realms of verse; and with these there was a harmony of tone, a softness of touch, a playful tenderness, which belonged peculiarly to the later poet. With a less pointed and practised force of understanding than Pope's, and altogether less refined and subtle, the appeal to the heart in Goldsmith is more gentle, direct, and pure. The predominant impression received from the *Traveller* is of its naturalness and ease. The surpassing charm with which its every-day genial fancies encircle high thoughts of human happiness, arrests the attention later. The serene graces of its style, and the mellow flow of its verse, take us captive, before we feel the enchantment of its lovely images of various life reflected from its calm still depths of philosophic contemplation. Above all, however, we perceive that it is a poem built upon nature; that it rests upon honest truth; not crying to either moon or stars for impossible sympathy, and not dealing with other worlds, in fact or imagination, than the writer has himself lived in and known. Wisely had Goldsmith avoided, what in the false-heroic versifiers of his day he had wittily condemned, the practice, even commoner since, of building up poetry on fantastic unreality, clothing it in harsh in-

1764.
Æt. 36.

versions of language, and patching it out with affectations of bygone vivacity: "as if the more "it was unlike prose, the more "it would resemble poetry." Making allowance for a brief expletive rarely scattered here and there, his poetical language is unadorned yet rich, select yet exquisitely plain, condensed yet home-felt and familiar. He has considered, as he says himself of Parnell, "the language of poetry "as the language of life, and "conveys the warmest thoughts "in the simplest expression."*

In what way the *Traveller* originated, the reader has seen. It does not seem necessary to discuss in what precise proportions its plan may have risen out of Addison's *Letter from Italy.* Shaped in any respect by Thomson's remark, in one of his letters to Bubb Dodington, "that a "poetical landscape of countries, "mixed with moral observations "on their characters and people, "would not be an ill-judged "undertaking," it certainly could not have been;** for that letter was not made public till many years after Goldsmith's death, when it appeared in Seward's *Anecdotes.* The poem had been, eminently and in a peculiar de-

* *Miscell. Works,* III. 374.
** Sir Egerton Brydges has pointed out some resemblance of topics, and a similar union of contemplation and description, in a now forgotten poem of the hardly-treated Blackmore; but there is nothing in the latter (the *Nature of Man*) to suggest anything like imitation. The only couplet quoted, having any resemblance to the turns of Gold-

gree, written from personal feeling and observation; and the course of its composition has been traced with the course of its author's life.* When Boswell came back to London some year or so after its appearance, he tells us with what amazement he had heard Johnson say that "there had not been so fine a "poem since Pope's time;"** and then amusingly explains the phenomenon by remarking, that "much, no doubt, both of the "sentiments and expression were "derived from conversation" with the great lexicographer. What the great lexicographer really suggested was a title, *The Philosophic Wanderer*, rejected for something simpler; as, if offered, the Johnsonian sentiment and expression would, I suspect, have been. But "Garth did not write "his own *Dispensary*," and Goldsmith had still less chance of obtaining credit for his. The rumour that Johnson had given great assistance is nevertheless contradicted by even Hawkins; where he professes to relate the extreme astonishment of the club, that a newspaper essayist and bookseller's drudge should have written such a poem. Undoubtedly that was his own feeling; and others of the members shared it, though it is to be hoped in a less degree. "Well," exclaimed Chamier, "I do believe he wrote "this poem himself; and let me "tell you, that is believing a "great deal." Goldsmith had left the club early that night, after "rattling away as usual." He took in truth little pains himself, in the thoughtless simplicity of those social hours, to fence round his own property and claim. "Mr. Goldsmith," asked Chamier, at the next meeting of the club, "what do you mean by "the last word in the first line of "your *Traveller?*

'Remote, unfriended, melancholy, slow.'

"Do you mean tardiness of loco-"motion?" Johnson, who was near them, took part in what followed, and has related it. "Goldsmith, who would say "something without considera-"tion, answered 'Yes.' I was "sitting by, and said, 'No, sir, "'you did not mean tardiness of "'locomotion: you mean that

1764. Æt. 36.

smith's verse is where Blackmore says of the French,

"Still in extremes their passions they employ,
Abject their grief, and insolent their joy."

But this was not peculiar to Blackmore. See Mitford's *Life of Goldsmith*, LXI.

* I have spoken in a former passage of the plan of the poem, to which Macaulay has since paid splendid tribute. "No "philosophical poem, ancient or modern, "has a plan so noble, and at the same "time so simple. An English wanderer, "seated on a crag among the Alps, near "the point where three great countries "meet, looks down on the boundless pro-"spect, reviews his long pilgrimage, re-"calls the varieties of scenery, of climate, "of government, of religion, of national "character, which he has observed, and "comes to the conclusion, just or unjust, "that our happiness depends little on "political institutions, and much on the "temper and regulation of our own "minds." *Biog. Ess.* 61-2.

** *Life*, ii. 308.

"'sluggishness of mind which 'comes upon a man in solitude.' "'Ah!' exclaimed Goldsmith, "'*that* was what I meant.' "Chamier," Johnson adds, "believed then that I had "written the line, as much as if he "had seen me write it." Yet it might be, if Burke had happened to be present, that Johnson would not have been permitted, so obviously to the satisfaction of every one in the room, dictatorially to lay down thus expressly what the poet meant. For who can doubt that he also meant slowness of motion? The first point of the picture is *that*. The poet is moving slowly, his tardiness of gait measuring the heaviness of heart, the pensive spirit, the melancholy of which it is the outward expression and sign. Goldsmith ought to have added to Johnson's remark that he meant all it said, and the other too; but no doubt he fell into one of his old flurries when he heard the general aye! aye! that saluted the great cham's authoritative version. While he saw that superficially he had been wrong, he must have felt that properly explained his answer was substantially right; but he had no address to say so, the pen not being in his hand.

The lines which Johnson really contributed he pointed out himself to Boswell, when laughing at the notion that he had taken any more important part in it. They were the line which now stands 420th in the poem; and, omitting the last couplet but one, the eight concluding lines. The couplet so grafted on his friend's insertion by Goldsmith himself, is worth all that Johnson added, though its historical allusion was somewhat obscure.

"The lifted axe, the agonising wheel,
  Luke's iron crown, and Damien's bed of
      steel."

Who was Luke, and what was his iron crown? is a question Tom Davies tells us he had often to answer; being a great resource in difficulties of that kind. "The "Doctor referred me," he says, in a letter to the Reverend Mr. Granger, who was compiling his *Biographical History* and wished to be exact, "to a book called "*Géographie Curieuse*, for an ex-"planation of Luke's iron crown." The explanation, besides being in itself incorrect, did not mend matters much. "Luke" had been taken simply for the euphony of the line. He was one of two brothers Dosa, who had headed a revolt against the Hungarian nobles at the opening of the sixteenth century; but, though both were tortured, the special horror of the red-hot crown was inflicted upon George.* "Doctor

* In a note to this passage in my former edition, I explained that this *Géographie Curieuse*, which appeared to have been Goldsmith's authority, was nevertheless itself incorrect in the family name of the brothers, which it reports to have been Zeck. They were George and Luke, as stated, and George underwent the punishment of the "iron crown;" but the family name was Dosa. For this I referred to the *Biographie Universelle*, xi. 604. The origin of the mistake is curious,

"Goldsmith says," adds Davies, "he meant by Damien's iron the "rack; *but I believe* the news-"papers informed us that he was "confined in a high tower, and "actually obliged to lie upon an "iron bed."* So little was Davies, any more than Chamier, Johnson, or any one else, disposed to take the poet's meaning on the authority of his own explanation of it.

"Nay, sir," said Johnson very candidly, when it was suggested, some years afterwards, that the partiality of its author's friends might have weighed too much in their judgment of this poem, "the partiality of his friends was "always *against* him. It was with "difficulty we could give him a "hearing." Explanation of much that receives too sharp a judgment in ordinary estimates of his character, seems to be found, as I have said, in this. When partiality takes the shape of pity, we must not wonder if it should be met by the vanities, the conceits, the half shame and half bravado, of that kind of self-assertion which is but self-distrust disguised. Very difficult did Goldsmith find it to force his

way, with even the *Traveller* in his hand, against these patronising airs and charitable allowances. "But he imitates you, sir," said Mr. Boswell, when, on return from his Dutch studies, he found the poem had really gone far to make its writer for the time more interesting than even Johnson himself. "Why no, sir," Johnson answered. "Jack Hawkesworth is "one of my imitators; but not "Goldsmith. Goldy, sir, has "great merit." "But, sir," persisted the staunch disciple, "he is "much indebted to you for his "getting so high in the public "estimation." "Why, sir," complacently responded the sage, "he has perhaps got *sooner* to it "by his intimacy with me."*

Without the reserves, the merit might sometimes be allowed; but seldom without something of a sting. "Well, I never "more shall think Doctor Gold-"smith ugly," was the frank tribute of the sister of Reynolds, after hearing Johnson read the *Traveller* aloud "from the begin-"ning to the end of it," a few days after it was published.** Here was another point of friendly and most general agreement. "Renny dear," now a mature

1764. —— Æt. 36.

and has since been explained to me by the courtesy of a correspondent who writes from America. The two brothers belonged to one of the native races of Transylvania called Szeklers or Zeeklers, which descriptive addition follows their names in the German biographical authorities; and this, through abridgment and misapprehension, in subsequent books came at last to be substituted for the family name.

* Granger's *Letters*, 52-3. Jan. 26, 1771.

* *Boswell*, III. 253.

** See Miss Reynolds's recollections printed in the appendix to Croker's *Boswell*. Of these I ought to remark, however, that several of them (as Mr. Croker himself admits of one) are manifestly fabricated out of imperfect or confused recollections of anecdotes elsewhere existing, an example of which I give in my next note.

and very fidgety little dame of seven-and-thirty, never was noted for her beauty, and few would associate such a thing with the seamed, scarred face of Johnson; but the preponderating ugliness of Goldsmith was a thing admitted and allowed for all to fling a stone at, however brittle their own habitations. Miss Reynolds founded her admiring promise about the *Traveller* on what she had herself said at a party in her brother's house some days before. It was suddenly proposed, as a social game after supper, to toast ordinary women, and have them matched by ordinary men; whereupon one of the gentlemen having given Miss Williams, Johnson's blind old pensioner, Miss Reynolds instantly matched her with Goldsmith; and this whimsical union so enchanted Mrs. Cholmondeley (Peg Woffington's sister, who had married an honourable and reverend gentleman well known to the set), that, though she had at the time some pique with Renny dear, she ran round the table, kissed her, and said she forgave her everything for her last toast. "Thus," exclaimed Johnson, who was present, and whose wit at his friend's expense was rewarded with a roar, "thus the "ancients, on the making-up of "their quarrels, used to sacrifice "a beast betwixt them."* Poor

1764
——
Æt. 36.

Goldsmith! It was not until the sacrifice was more complete, and the grave had closed over it, that the "partiality" of his friends ceased to take these equivocal shapes. "There is not "a bad line in that poem of the "*Traveller*," said Langton, as they sat talking together at Reynolds's, four years after the poet's death; "not one of Dry-"den's careless verses." "I was "glad," interposed Reynolds, "to hear Charles Fox say it was "one of the finest poems in the "English language." "Why were "you glad?" rejoined Langton. "You surely had no doubt of "this before?" "No," exclaimed Johnson, decisively: "the merit "of the *Traveller* is so well estab-"lished, that Mr. Fox's praise "cannot augment it, nor his cen-"sure diminish it."*

831), hitherto supposed to be the only authority for it, is a writer in the *Gentleman's Magazine* for July 1797. No sacrifice was called for at the commencement of a friendship; it was the cessation or reconciliation of strife that olicited gratitude to the gods. Mrs. Cholmondeley, according to Johnson, was "a very airy "lady." *Boswell*, IV. 272. And see Hunt's *Men and Books*, II. 182-3. Fanny Reynolds, Johnson's "dearest dear," was eighty when she died, in November 1807.

* Reynolds continued: "But his "friends may suspect they had too great "a partiality for him." JOHNSON: "Nay, "sir, the partiality of his friends was al-"ways against him. It was with dif-"ficulty we could give him a hearing. "Goldsmith had no settled notions upon "any subject; so he talked always at "random. It seemed to be his intention "to blurt out whatever was in his mind, "and see what would become of it. He "was angry, too, when catched in an ab-"surdity; but it did not prevent him

* My authority for this anecdote, the point of which is missed in Miss Reynolds's recollections (Croker's *Boswell*,

Not very obvious at the first, however, was its progress to this decisive eminence. From the first it had its select admirers, and, as we now know from his letters, one of the earliest was Charles Fox, though then only a lad of seventeen; but their circle somewhat slowly widened. "The beauties "of this poem," observed the principal literary newspaper of the day, the *St. James's Chronicle*, two months after its publication, "are so great and various, that "we cannot but be surprised they "have not been able to recom- "mend it more to general notice." Goldsmith began to think, as he afterwards remarked to Boswell, that he had come too late into the world for any share of its poetical distinctions; that Pope and others had taken up the places in the temple of fame; and that as but few at any one period can possess poetical reputation, "a "man of genius can now hardly "acquire it."* "That," said Johnson, when this saying was related to him, "is one of the "most sensible things I have "ever heard of Goldsmith. "It is difficult to get liter- "ary fame, and it is every "day getting more difficult." Nevertheless, though slowly, the poem seems to have advanced steadily; and, in due course, translations of it appeared in more than one continental language. A month after the notice in the *St. James's Chronicle*, a second edition was published; a third was more quickly called for; a fourth was issued in August; and the ninth had appeared in the year when the poet died. That anything more substantial than fame arose to him out of these editions is, however, very questionable. The only payment that can with certainty be traced in

1765.
Æt. 37.

---

* "from falling into another the next "minute." *Boswell*, vii. 84-5. A little later, when Johnson was complaining of Langton being too silent at the club, and letting the whigs have it all their own way, "Sir," said Boswell, "you will re- "collect that he very properly took up "Sir Joshua for being glad that Charles "Fox had praised Goldsmith's *Traveller*, "and you joined him." JOHNSON: "Yes, "sir, I knocked Fox on the head without "ceremony." For Fox's earlier opinion, see *post*, chap. xv.

* *Life*, v. 303-4. What on earth can Mr. Croker mean by the subjoined note on that saying of Goldsmith? "Gold- "smith, who read a great deal of light "French literature, probably borrowed "this from La Bruyère. 'Les anciens

"'ont tout dit: en vient aujourd'hui trop "'tard pour dire des choses nouvelles. "*Vigneul-Marvilliana*, i. 336." Where is the resemblance?—Lord Lyttelton replied to this question in a letter to the author. "If Goldsmith had restricted "himself to saying that he had come too "late into the world for any share of "poetical distinction, the resemblance to "La Bruyère would have been obvious. "The general sense of the two is the "same: an exaggerated complaint as if "the stock of possible good things was a "limited one, so that, the more good "things *have* been said, the more difficult "it is for each generation to add to "them. It is true, Goldsmith's following "words rather obscure the point, about "few 'at any one period' being able to "acquire poetical reputation: but the "point itself seems plain." I ought perhaps to have admitted a resemblance, though it is very certain that Goldsmith neither copied La Bruyère nor was in any degree indebted to him in the matter.

Newbery's papers as for "*Copy* "*of the Traveller a Poem*," leaves it in no degree doubtful that for twenty guineas Goldsmith had surrendered all his interest in it, except that which, with each successive issue, still prompted the lime labor.* Between the first and last, thirty-six new lines had been added, and fourteen of the old cancelled. Some of the erasures would now, perhaps, raise a smile. No honest thought disappeared, and no manly word for the oppressed. The "wanton "judge" and his "penal statutes" remained; indignant denunciations of the tyrannies of wealth, sorrowful and angry protestings that

"Laws grind the poor and rich men rule the law,"

were still undisturbed. But words quietly vanished, here and there, that had spoken too plainly of the sordid past; and no longer did the poet proclaim, in speaking of the great, that, "inly "satisfied," above their pomps he held his "ragged" pride. The rags went the way of the confession of poverty in the *Polite Learning;** and of those hints of humble habits which were common in the *Busy Body* and the *British Magazine*, but are found no longer in *Essays by Mr. Goldsmith*.

With that title, and the motto "Collecta revirescunt," a three-shilling duodecimo volume of those re-published essays was now issued by Mr. Griffin for himself and Mr. Newbery, who each paid Oliver ten guineas for liberty to offer this tribute to the growing reputation of the *Traveller*. He corrected expressions, as I have said; lifted Islington tea-gardens into supper at Vauxhall; exalted the stroll in White-conduit-garden to a walk in the

_____

1765.
—————
Æt. 37.

* I subjoin from the Newbery MSS. the account in which this payment for the *Traveller* makes its appearance. Other items in it refer to matters already described. "Settle Dr. Goldsmith's account, "and give him credit for the following "copies: 1. The Preface to the History "of the World, and charge it to the "Partners, 3*l*. 3*s*. 3 Prefaces to the Na- "tural History, 6*l*. 6*s*. Translation of the "Life of Christ. Ditto, the Lives of the "Fathers. Ditto, the Lives of the Philo- "sophers. Correcting 4 vols. Brookes' "Nat. History. 79 Leaves of the History "of England. *Copy of the Traveller a* "*Poem*, 21*l*. Lent in Fleet Street at Mr. "Adams's to pay for the instrument, "15*s*. 6*d*. Lent him without receipts at "the Society of Art, and to pay arrears, "3*l*. 3*s*. Get the Copy of Essays for "which I paid 10*l*. 10*s*. as half, and Mr. "Griffin to have the other." This ac- count is written at the back of a more elaborate memorandum headed, "Settle "the following accounts," of which the sixteenth item runs thus: "Mr. Brookes's, "and charge for alterations made in the "Plates, and the printed copy yt was "obliged to be cancelled, 2*l*, and to Dr. "Goldsmith writing Prefaces and cor- "recting the work, 30*l*, in all 50*l*." I need not remind the reader that the suc- cess of his "prefaces" to this dull book led to his engagement to write the *Animated Nature*. See *Percy Memoir*, 83.

* The lines

"Perish the wish; for inly satisfied, Above their pomps I hold my ragged pride,"

were replaced in the second edition by

"Ye powers of truth that bid my soul aspire, Far from my bosom drive the low de- sire," &c.

park; and, in an amusing preface, disclaimed any more ambitious motive than one of self-preservation in collecting such fragments. As many entertainers of the public, he said, had been partly living upon him for some years, he was now resolved to try if he could not live a little upon himself; and he compared his case to that of the fat man he had heard of in a shipwreck, who, when the sailors, pressed by famine, were taking slices off him to satisfy their hunger, insisted with great justice on having the first cut for himself. "Most of these essays," continued Goldsmith, "have been "regularly reprinted twice or "thrice a year, and conveyed to "the public through the kennel "of some engaging compilation. "If there be a pride in multiplied "editions, I have seen some of "my labours sixteen times re-"printed, and claimed by dif-"ferent parents as their own. I "have seen them flourished at "the beginning with praise, and "signed at the end with the "names of Philautos, Phila-"lethes, Philaleutheros, and Phil-"anthropos."* Names that al-ready figured, as the reader will hardly need to be reminded, in those adventures of a philosophic vagabond which formed part of the little manuscript novel* now lying, apparently little cared for, on the dusty shelves of Mr. Francis Newbery.

Another piece of writing which belongs to this period, and which did not find its way to the public till the appearance of the novel to whose pages it had been transferred, was the ballad of *Edwin and Angelina.* It was suggested, as I have said, in the course of the ballad-discussions with Percy in preparation of the

1765.
Æt. 37.

---

* Even the *Monthly Review*, cannot but admit (xxxiii. 82, July 1765) that "Mr. Goldsmith hath here published a "collection of Essays, which have been "so often printed in the newspapers, "magazines, and other periodical pro-"ductions, that we despair of selecting a "specimen from any one that will not "be previously known to our readers. "But notwithstanding their being so "well calculated for cursory inspection, "and notwithstanding their transient

"success among the duller topics of the "day, we apprehend, &c. &c. &c," and then follows the usual depreciation; as for instance, "It is easy to collect from "books and conversation, a sufficiency "of superficial knowledge to enable a "writer to *flourish away with tolerable* "*propriety through a news-paper essay;* but "when these his lucubrations assume "the form of a book, it is, &c. &c. &c. "The author tells us, in his preface, that "he could have made these Essays more "metaphysical, had he thought fit; for "our part, we do not find any of them "with which metaphysics have much to "do; but be this as it may, we look upon "it as a great mark of Mr. Goldsmith's "prudence, that he did neither meddle "nor make with them." Considerate Mr. Griffiths!

* See chapter xx. of the *Vicar of Wakefield*, one of the evidences which Goldsmith so frequently tenders us of the identity of his own experiences with those narrated in his books. In the same portion of George Primrose's narrative he does not scruple to hint at a weakness of his profession. "I found that no genius "in another could please me. .. I could "neither read nor write with satisfac-"tion; for excellence in another was my "aversion, and writing was my trade."

Reliques, and was written before the *Traveller* appeared. "With-"out informing any of us," says Hawkins, again referring to the club, "he wrote and "addressed to the Coun-"tess, afterwards Duchess of "Northumberland, one of the "first poems of the lyric kind "that our language has to boast "of."* A charming poem un-doubtedly it is, if not quite this; delightful for its simple and mingled flow of incident and imagery, for the pathetic softness and sweetness of its tone, and for its easy, artless grace. He had taken pains with it, and he set more than common store by it himself; so that when, some two years hence, his old enemy Kenrick, taking advantage of its appearance in the novel, as-sumed the character of "Detec-"tor" in the public prints, de-nounced it as a plagiarism from the *Reliques*, and entreated the public to compare the insipidity of Doctor Goldsmith's negus with the genuine flavour of Mr. Percy's champagne, he thought it worth while, even against that as-sailant, to defend his own originality.** The poem he was charged to have copied it from, was a composition by Percy of stanzas old and new (much modern writing, I need hardly remark, entered into the "an-"cient" reliques;* the editor publishing among them, for ex-ample, his friend Grainger's en-tirely modern and exquisite *Bryan and Pereene*): and Gold-smith's answer was to the effect that he did not think there was any great resemblance between the two pieces in question; but that if any existed, Mr. Percy's ballad was the imitation, inasmuch as the *Edwin and Angelina* had been read to him two years be-fore (in the present year), and at their next meeting he had ob-served, "with his usual good-"humour," that he had taken the plan of it to form the fragments of Shakespeare into a ballad of his own. "He then," added

---

* *Life of Johnson*, 420. Mr. Mitford (in the anecdotes appended to his *Life*, CLXXVII.) quotes Hawkins for another statement, which I do not find in his biography, to the effect that this beauti-ful poem was saved from destruction by Dr. Chapman of Sudbury, for that, soon after he wrote it, Goldsmith showed it to the Doctor, and was by him with dif-ficulty dissuaded from throwing it into the fire.

** Another attempt was made, more than twenty years after Goldsmith's death (in an unsuccessful periodical called *The Quiz*), to prove this poem a plagiary from an old French novel; but the attempt at once called forth an expostulatory com-ment from a correspondent, known to be Bishop Percy, in the *Monthly Review* for Oct. 1797. It was afterwards, by another correspondent, elaborately exposed and ridiculed in the same *Review* for July 1798; and by the same writer, on its sub-sequent revival, in the *European Magazine* for May 1812. I mention it here only to guard against any future revival of the slander.

* Since this was written, a valuable contribution has been made to poetical literature by the publication of the origi-nal Folio Manuscript from which Percy's work was taken, under the careful editor-ship of Mr. Hales and Mr. Furnivall. Few more curious or interesting addi-tions to English poetical literature have been made in our time.

Goldsmith, "read me his little "cento, if I may so call it, and I "highly approved it."*

Out of these circumstances it of course arose that Goldsmith's ballad was shown to the wife of Percy's patron, who had some taste for literature, and affected a little notice of its followers. The countess admired it so much that she had a few copies privately printed. I have seen the late Mr. Heber's,

1765.
ÆT. 37.

---

* I subjoin the letter, from the *St. James's Chronicle* (July 23-25, 1767), at the commencement of which is an allusion to another ill-natured comment, of which he had been the subject in the same journal. "Sir, As there is nothing I dislike so "much as newspaper controversy, par- "ticularly upon trifles, permit me to be "as concise as possible in informing a "correspondent of yours, that I recom- "mended Blainville's travels because I "thought the book was a good one; and I "think so still. I said I was told by the "bookseller that it was then first pub- "lished, but in that it seems I was mis- "informed, and my reading was not ex- "tensive enough to set me right. An- "other correspondent of yours accuses "me of having taken a ballad I published "some time ago from one by the in- "genious Mr. Percy. I do not think there "is any great resemblance between the "two pieces in question. If there be any, "his ballad was taken from mine. I read "it to Mr. Percy some years ago; and he, "as we both considered these things as "trifles at best, told me with his usual "good-humour the next time I saw him, "that he had taken my plan to form the "fragments of Shakespeare into a ballad "of his own. He then read me his little "cento, if I may so call it, and I highly "approved it. Such petty anecdotes as "these are scarcely worth printing; and "were it not for the busy disposition of "some of your correspondents, the public "should never have known that he owes "me the hint of his ballad, or that I am "obliged to his friendship and learning "for communications of a much more "important nature. I am, Sir, yours, &c. "OLIVER GOLDSMITH." To this should be added Percy's comment (*Memoir*, 74-5). "He justly vindicated the priority "of his own poem; but in asserting that "the plan of the other was taken from "his (in nothing else have they the most "distant resemblance), and in reporting "the conversation on this subject, his "memory must have failed him; for the "story in them both was evidently taken "from a very ancient ballad in that "collection beginning 'Gentle herds- "'man,' &c." I happen to have before me a copy, now rarely met with, of the original "proposals" for publishing Blain- ville's travels, to which this letter refers; and as it marks the new estimation in which the *Traveller's* success placed its author, and the uses which the book- sellers hastened to make of it, it may be worth description. It is the first but by no means the last instance of such employment of his name. After an elaborate description of the book, great prominence is given to the intimation that it is "Recommended by Doctor "Goldsmith, Author of *The Traveller*, a "poem, &c;" and on the same full title- page which precedes the conditions of subscription and sale, immediately be- low the announcement that the work will be "printed for J. Johnson and H. Daven- "port in Paternoster-row and sold by all "Booksellers and News-carriers in Great "Britain and Ireland," follows the "Re- "COMMENDATION. I have read the "Travels of Monsieur *De Blainville* with "the highest Pleasure. As far as I am "capable of judging, they are at once ac- "curate, copious, and entertaining. I "am told, they are now first translated "from the Author's Manuscript in the "*French* Language, which has never been "published; and if so, they are a valuable "Acquisition to ours. The Translation, "as I am informed, has been made by "Men of Eminence, and is not unworthy "of the Original. All I have to add is, "that, to the best of my opinion, *Blain- "ville's Travels* is the most valuable work "of this kind hitherto published: Con- "taining the most judicious Instructions "to those who read for Amusement, and "being the surest Guide to those who in- "tend to undertake the same Journey. "OLIVER GOLDSMITH, "*Temple*, March 2, 1767."

with the title-page of "*Edwin "and Angelina*, a ballad; by Mr. Goldsmith. "Printed for the amusement of the Countess of Northumberland." It is now rare; and has a value independent of its rarity, in its illustration of Goldsmith's habit of elaboration and painstaking in the correction of his verse. By comparing it with what was afterwards published, we perceive that even the gentle opening line has been an afterthought; that four stanzas have been re-written; and that the two which originally stood last have been removed altogether. These, for their simple beauty of expression, it is worth while here to preserve. The action of the poem having closed without them, they were on better consideration rejected; and young writers should study and make profit of such lessons. Posterity has always too much upon its hands to attend to what is irrelevant or needless; and no one so well as Goldsmith seems to have known that the writer who would hope to live, must live by the perfection of his style, and by the cherished and careful beauty of unsuperfluous writing.

1765.
Æt. 37.

"Here amidst sylvan bowers we'll rove,
    From lawn to woodland stray;
Blest as the songsters of the grove,
    And innocent as they.

"To all that want, and all that wail,
    Our pity shall be given;
And when this life of love shall fail,
    We'll love again in heaven."

Intercourse with Northumberland-house, except when Mr. Percy's library was open to him during his chaplaincy there, began and ended with this poem. Its author is only afterwards to be traced there on one occasion, characteristically described by Hawkins. "Having one day," he says, "a call to wait on the "late Duke, then Earl, of "Northumberland, I found Gold- "smith waiting for an audience "in an outer room; I asked him "what had brought him there: "he told me, an invitation from "his lordship. I made my busi- "ness as short as I could, and, "as a reason, mentioned that "Doctor Goldsmith was waiting "without. The Earl asked me if "I was acquainted with him: I "told him I was, adding what I "thought likely to recommend "him. I retired, and staid in the "outer room to take him home. "Upon his coming out, I asked "him the result of his conversa- "tion. 'His lordship,' says he, "'told me he had red [*sic*] my "'poem,' meaning the *Traveller*, "'and was much delighted with "'it; that he was going lord-lieu- "'tenant of Ireland, and that, "'hearing that I was a native of "'that country, he should be "'glad to do me any kindness.' "And what did you answer, asked "I, to this gracious offer? 'Why,' "said he, 'I could say nothing "'but that I had a brother there, "'a clergyman, that stood in "'need of help:* as for myself'"

* The earl was already lord-lieutenant, holding that office till Grenville's ministry went out; and what sort of

(this was added for the benefit of Hawkins) "'I have no de-"'pendence on the promises of "'great men: I look to the "'booksellers for support; they "'are my best friends, and I am "'not inclined to forsake them "'for others.' Thus," adds the teller of the anecdote, "did this "idiot in the affairs of the world "trifle with his fortunes, and put "back the hand that was held "out to assist him! Other offers "of a like kind he either rejected "or failed to improve, contenting "himself with the patronage of "one nobleman, whose mansion "afforded him the delights of a "splendid table, and a retreat "for a few days from the metro-"polis."*

The incident related may excuse the comment attached to it. Indeed, the charge of idiotcy in the affairs of the Hawkins-world may even add to the pleasure with which we contemplate that older-world picture beside it, of frank simplicity and brotherly affection. This poor poet, who, incomprehensibly to the Middlesex magistrate, would thus gently have turned aside to the assistance of his poorer brother the hand held out to assist himself, had only a few days before been obliged to borrow fifteen shillings and six-pence "in Fleet-street," of one of those "best friends" with whose support he is now fain to be contented. But the reader has already seen that since the essay on *Polite Learning* was written, its author's personal experience had sufficed to alter his view as to the terms and relations on which literature could hereafter hope to stand with the great; and the precise value of Lord Northumberland's offer seems in itself somewhat doubtful. Percy indeed took a subsequent opportunity of stating that he had discussed the subject with the earl, and had received an assurance that if the latter could have known how to serve Goldsmith (it does not seem to have occurred to Percy that one mode had already been suggested without any effect), if he had been made aware, for example, that he wished to travel, "he would have procured him a "sufficient salary on the Irish "establishment, and have had it "continued to him during his "travels."* But this was not said till after Goldsmith's death: when many ways of serving him,

1765.
_____
Æt. 37.

authority a viceroy could then exercise over the benefices of the Irish Church receives vivid illustration from a passage in an unpublished letter written to Derrick a year and a half before the present date by his friend Dr. Wilson of Trinity College. "In the late Duke of Devon-"shire's time there was an ancient "dancing-master, a family piece, who "came over with his grace in order to "be provided for. Various kinds of pro-"vision were proposed for the poor "Frenchman, but all clogged with in-"superable objections and unsurmount-"able difficulties. At last the Church "was thought of, and, though he could "not read a word of English, he was "thrust into orders, and was inducted "into the living of Navan."

   * *Life of Johnson*, 419.

   * *Percy Memoir*, 66.

Oliver Goldsmith's Life and Times. I.   19

meanwhile, had been suffered to pass by unheeded; and when his poor struggling brother, for whom he begged thus explicitly the earl's patronage, had also sunk unnoticed to the grave. The booksellers, on the other hand, were patrons with whom success at once established independent and incontrovertible claims; and the *Traveller*, to a less sanguine heart than its writer's, already seemed to separate with a broad white line the past from that which was to come. No Griffiths bondage could await him again. He had no longer any personal bitterness, therefore, to oppose to Johnson's general allegiance to the "trade;" though, at the same time, with Johnson, he made special and large reservations. For instance, there was old Gardener the bookseller. Even Griffiths, by the side of Gardener, looked less ill-favoured. This was he who had gone to Kit Smart in the depths of his poverty, and drawn him into the most astounding agreement on record. It was not discovered till poor Kit Smart went mad; and Goldsmith had but to remember *how* it was discovered, to forgive all the huffing speeches that Johnson might ever make to him! "I wrote, sir," said the latter, "for some months in the "*Universal Visitor* for poor Smart, "not then knowing the terms on "which he was engaged to write, "and thinking I was doing him "good. I hoped his wits would

"soon return to him. Mine returned to me, and I wrote in the "*Universal Visitor* no longer."[*] It was a sixpenny weekly pamphlet; the agreement was for ninety-nine years; and the terms were that Smart was to write nothing else, and be rewarded with one-sixth of the profits! It was undoubtedly a thing to remember, this agreement of old Gardener's. The most thriving subject in the kingdom of the booksellers could hardly fail to recall it now and then; and the very man to remind Goldsmith of it, in goodnatured contrast to the opportunity he had lost, was the companion with whom he left Northumberland-house that day. Nevertheless he left with greater cheerfulness, and a better-founded sense of independence, than if he had consented to substitute for his present choice a reliance on "the "promises of great men."

CHAPTER XI.

Goldsmith in Practice and Burke in Office.

1765.

THE "nobleman" to whom Sir John Hawkins refers, at the close of his anecdote last related, as having vouchsafed to be Oliver Goldsmith's solitary patron, was not yet ennobled; nor could the relation he had opened with the poet on the appearance of the *Traveller* be properly described as one of "patronage," though it

* *Boswell*, v. 288.

doubtless at times afforded him the delights of a splendid table and a retreat for a few days from the metropolis. Mr. Robert Nugent, the younger son of an old and wealthy Westmeath family, was a jovial Irishman and man of wit who proffered hearty and "unsolicited" friendship to Goldsmith at this time as a fellow patriot and poet,* and maintained ever after an easy intercourse with him. In early life he had written an ode to Pulteney,** which contains the masterly verse introduced by Gibbon in his character of Brutus;

("What though the good, the brave, the wise,
  With adverse force undaunted rise,
    To break the eternal doom!
  Though Cato lived, though Tully spoke,
  Though Brutus dealt the god-like stroke,
    Yet perished fated Rome!")

and had attached himself to the party of the Prince of Wales, whom he largely assisted with money. In the imaginary Leicester-house administrations commemorated by Bubb Dodington he was always appointed to office; and had held appointments more substantial as comptroller of the prince's household, a lord of the treasury, and vice-treasurer of Ireland. He talked well, though coarsely, "with a "vivacity of expression often "bordering on the Irish bull,"

and was a great favourite with women. "Some who knew him "well," said the late Lord Lansdowne to the present writer, "told me he was a "person of singular hu- "mour and talent for conver- "sation," and the portrait that used to be at Stowe shows this. His first wife, Lord Fingal's * daughter, brought him a good fortune, and bore him a son; by his second wife, to whom he was the third husband, the sister and heiress of Secretary Craggs (Pope's friend), and described as "a good-humoured, pleasant, fat "woman,"** he had no issue, but obtained large landed estates, a domain in Essex, and that mansion of Gosfield Hall in which the exiled prince of France found afterwards a refuge;*** and from a third less lucky marriage,

1765.
Æt. 37.

* Plunket the attainted earl.
** *Gent. Mag.* LIX. 406.
*** In his *Historical Memoirs*, (i. 126), Sir Nathaniel Wraxall, who visited Lord Nugent two years after Goldsmith's death. calls the "house and estate" at Gosfield "one of the finest domains in "Essex;" though the present condition of the inclosure or paddock before the mansion would rather seem to confirm the origin of the name (Goosofield). Wraxall's sketch is characteristic, but I can only give one of his anecdotes. "When a bill was introduced into the "House of Commons for better watching "the metropolis, in order to contribute "towards effecting which object one of "the clauses went to propose that watch- "men should be *compelled* to sleep during "the day-time, Lord Nugent, with ad- "mirable humour, got up and desired "that he might be personally included in "the provisions of the bill, being fre- "quently so tormented with the gout, as "to be unable to sleep either by day or "by night." i. 131-135.

* *Percy Memoir,* 66.
** So good in Gray's opinion, that "Mr. Nugent sure did not write his "own *Ode*," he says to Walpole. *Works,* III. 90.

with Elizabeth Drax the Countess Dowager of Berkeley, sprang the daughter (its only issue he consented to recognise) who continued after the separation to live with her father and her aunt, Mrs. Peg Nugent, until she married the Marquis of Buckingham in 1775, and united the names of Nugent and Grenville. Richard Glover, the epic and dramatic poet of Leicester-house, characterises him briefly as a jovial voluptuous Irishman who had left popery for the protestant religion, money, and widows: but Glover lived to see him surrender these favourites, and, not far from his eightieth year, go back to popery again. When his friendship with Goldsmith began, he was a tall, stout, vigorous man of nearly sixty, with a remarkably loud voice and a broad Irish brogue; whose strong and ready wit, careless decision of manner, and reckless audacity of expression, obtained him always a hearing from the House of Commons, in which he had sat for four-and-twenty years. He was now watching, with more than ordinary personal interest, the turn of the political wheel. So, for the interest *they* took in the opening of Burke's great political life, were his new friend Goldsmith and every member of the Gerrard-street club.

The ministry which succeeded Bute's (that of George Grenville and the Bedfords, or, as they were called, the Bloomsbury

1765.
Æt. 37.

gang)* was coming to a close at last, after a series of impolitic blunders without parallel in the annals of statesmen. Early in March of the previous year ('64), after convulsing England from end to end with the question of general warrants and the ignoble persecution of Wilkes, the first attempt was made upon America which roused her to rebellion. In the autumn of that year, all her towns and cities were in loud and vehement protest; and before the year closed, Benjamin Franklin had placed in Grenville's hands a solemn protest of resistance on the part of his fellow-colonists to any proposition to tax them without their consent. But as yet, this met with little sympathy in England; and to Grenville's stubborn nature fear was as strange as wisdom. With only one division in the Commons when the attendance was paltry, and without a single negative in the Lords, he passed, at the opening of the present year, the act which created the Republic of America. Burke was in the gallery of the house during its progress (it had been his habit for some months to attend almost every discussion), and said, nine years afterwards, that, far from anything inflammatory, he had never in his life heard so languid a de-

* So called because Bedford-house stood in Bloomsbury-square. Walpole's *George III.* II. 441. The Pitt and Temple party were styled, happily enough, the whole cousin-[cozen]-hood. Waldegrave's *Memoirs,* 56.

bate. * Horace Walpole described it to Lord Hertford as a "slight day on the America "taxes." Barré, who had served in America and knew the temper of the people, was the only man whose language approached to the occasion; and as he had lately lost his regiment for his vote against general warrants, it was laughed at as the language of a disappointed man. Pitt, on occasions less momentous, had come to the house on crutches, swathed in flannel; yet now he was absent. He afterwards prayed that some friendly hand could have laid him prostrate on the floor of the house to bear his testimony against the bill; but it is doubtful if the desire to see Grenville more completely prostrate had not had more to do with his non-appearance than either gout or fever.

The minister's triumph in his Stamp Act, however, was brief. The King had hardly given it his glad assent, when the first slight seizure of the terrible malady which in later days more sorely afflicted him, necessitated an act of regency; and the mismanagement of the provisions of that act hopelessly embroiled the minister with his master. Then came the clash and confusion of the parties into which the once predominant old whig party had been lately rent asunder, and which the present strange and sullen seclusion of Pitt aggravated and seemed to make hopeless. In vain he was appealed to; in vain the poor King made piteous submissions to him. Fortunate in legacies, a Somersetshire baronet whom he had never seen had just left him three thousand a year; and it was whispered about that he would never take office again. The opposition lost ground, which the ministry did not gain; the coercion of the King became notorious; the city was shaken with riots, which in the general disorganisation rose almost to rebellion; and while, on the one hand, a new administration seemed impossible without Pitt, on the other it was plain that Grenville and the Bedfords were tottering to their final fall. The King was intensely grateful for their invasion of the public liberties, and had joyfully co-operated in their taxation of America: but he hated them for hating Bute, who had placed them in power, and for insulting his mother the Princess Dowager, whose intrigues had sustained them in power; while they had preferred to allow his own Buckingham-gardens to be overlooked, rather than vote him a somewhat paltry grant which would have secured to the crown a property now of almost incredible value. * It was his own

1765.
Æt. 37.

---

* Works, (ed. 1845), i. 477. In the same speech Grenville made his ill-considered attack on Dean Tucker, the only man of that day who thoroughly anticipated the judgment and experience of our own on the great question of the American Colonies.

* Walpole's George III. ii. 100.

chosen system of government to rule without party, and solely by the favour of the crown; and here were its four years' fruits. Ministers had become his tyrants, and statesmen held aloof from his service. When his uncle Cumberland came back from Hayes with Pitt's formal refusal, he thought in his despair of even the old Duke of Newcastle; began to make atonement for recent insults to the house of Devonshire; and threw out baits for those old pure whigs up to this time the objects of his most concentrated hatred. Doubts and distrust shook the Princess Dowager's friends, in which Nugent of course largely shared; and expectation stood on tip-toe in Gerrard-street, where his friends of the club could hardly avoid taking interest in what affected the fortunes of Edmund Burke.

For Burke, not unreasonably, looked to obtain employment in the scramble. Hawkins said he had always meant to offer himself to the highest bidder;* but the calumny is hardly worth refuting. He had honourably disengaged himself from Hamilton, and scornfully given back his pension; nor were his friends kept in ignorance that he had since attached himself to the party of whigs the most pure and least powerful in the state. Lord Rockingham was at their head:**

a young nobleman of princely fortune and fascinating manners, who made up for powers of oratory, in which he was wholly deficient, by an inestimable art of attracting and securing friends; whose character was unstained by any of the recent intrigues; and who had selected for his associates men like himself, less noted for brilliant talents than for sense and honour. The great landed influence of the old Yorkshire family of Savile was worthily represented in their ranks by the present county member, Sir George: and with him were associated the financial ability of Dowdeswell, a country gentleman of Worcestershire, and the many rare virtues of the Duke of Devonshire's youngest uncle, Lord John Cavendish, who, not more remarkable for his fair little clownish person than for his princely soul, carried out in politics the principles of private honour with what Walpole sneeringly calls "the tyranny of a "moral philosopher."*   With

Lord Albemarle has published, as *Memoirs of the Marquis of Rockingham and his Contemporaries*, a series of letters relating chiefly to the public affairs of this period, from the collections of his family, with an intelligent and well-informed comment. At the close of the book (II. 485-8) the reader will find Burke's celebrated character of Lord Rockingham, written for the mausoleum in Wentworth-park, printed more correctly than he will find it in any other place.

* *Memoirs of George III.* II. 25. George Selwyn called him, says Walpole, as well for his small stature and light complexion as for the quaintness with which he untreasured, as by rote, the stores of his memory, "the learned canary bird."

---

* Miss Hawkins's *Memoirs*, I. 101.

** Since my first edition appeared,

the extremer opinions of Lord Temple, these men had little in common. Though staunch against general warrants and invasions of liberty, they were as far from being Wilkite as the reckless demagogue himself; and they had obtained the general repute of a kind of middle constitutional party. Little compatible was this with present popularity, Burke well knew; but he saw beyond the present. To the last he hoped that Pitt might be moved; and in the May of this year so expressed himself to his friend Flood, in a letter which is curious evidence of his possession of the political secrets of the day.* But, though believing that without the splendid talents and boundless popularity of the great commoner, "an ad-"mirable and lasting system" could not then be formed, Burke also believed that the only substitute for Pitt's genius was Rockingham's sense and good faith, and that on this plain foundation might be gradually raised a party that should revive whig purity and honour, and last when Pitt should be no more. Somewhat thus, too, the honest and brave Duke of Cumberland may have reasoned, when to his hapless nephew the King, again crying out to him in utter despair, and imploring him, with or

Gray calls him "the best of all Johns." See *Correspondence of Gray and Mason*, 78. Mason was his tutor at Cambridge. For Burke's opinion of him, see *Corresp.* iv. 526-31, and Addenda, 649-52.

* Burke's *Correspondence*, I. 80.

without Pitt, to save him from George Grenville and the Duke of Bedford, he gave his final counsel. Lord Rockingham was summoned; consented, with his party, to take office; and was sworn in First Lord on the 8th of July. Lord Shelburne would not join without Pitt: but a young whig duke (Grafton), of whom much was at that time expected, gave in his adhesion; and General (afterwards Marshal) Conway, Cumberland's personal friend and the cousin and favourite of Horace Walpole,* a braver sol-

1765.
———
Æt. 37.

* There is no pleasanter trait in Horace Walpole than his affection for Conway, which continued steady and unalterable to the last, and was manifested in many generous disinterested ways. See letters lately published in the *Grenville Correspondence*, II. 296-9, 320-7, 335-44, &c. The brave quiet soldier had hardly seemed to me the man to have inspired so strong a feeling, till I read some fragments of his early correspondence with Walpole lately published by Lord Albemarle from the originals in Sir Denis le Marchant's possession. I subjoin one or two passages which show Conway in a character that but for these letters I should have hesitated (with all my admiration for his sterling sense and manliness) to ascribe to him. The date is at the close of Sir Robert Walpole's ministry, more than twenty years before that to which I have brought my text. "Would you believe "it, Horry," writes Conway in the autumn of 1740, "I have been hitherto in this "dreary city all this live-long summer? "But I can't bear summer people, and so "I live a good deal alone ... Service to "Gray .... Look here, Horry, here is "just such a bit of paper as you wrote to "me upon, and if I can help it I won't "write a word more upon it.. but you know "I am soon appeased. Indeed, Horry, "if one did not love you better than any-"body, and you did not write better than "other people, one could never forgive

dier than politician, but a persuasive speaker, and an honourable as well as very popular man, gave his help as secretary of state: William Burke, Edmund's distant relative and dear friend, being appointed his under-secretary. Upon this the old meddling "fizzling"* Duke of Newcastle went and warned Conway's chief against these Burkes. Edmund's real name, he said, was *O'Bourke*; and he was not only an Irish adventurer, a jacobite, and a papist, but he had shrewd reasons for believing him a concealed jesuit to boot. Nevertheless, seven days after the administration was formed, the jesuit and jacobite, introduced by their common friend Fitzherbert (who had been named to the Board of Trade), was appointed private secretary to the Marquis of Rockingham; and Burke's great political life began.

The first letter of the newly-appointed Secretary to the new Premier, written from Queen-Anne-street the day after his appointment, was to David Garrick; and is the first pleasant evidence we receive, that whatever may be the success of his adventure in politics, there is small chance of its weaning him from the society of wits and men of letters to which this narrative belongs. Burke cheerfully invokes his "little Horace," "lepidissime "homuncio," to call and see his "Mæcenas atavis," and "praise "this administration of Caven- "dishes and Rockinghams in "ode, and abuse their enemies in "epigram."*   Garrick had ar-

1765 — Æt. 37.

"you; but I forgot, those are the very
"reasons why I should be the most angry
"with you. So, know that nothing but a
"vehement long letter can ever make it
"up betwixt us .... So you cannot bear
"Mrs. Woffington? yet all the town is in
"love with her. To say the truth, I am
"glad to find somebody to keep me in
"countenance, for I think she is an im-
"pudent, Irish-faced girl .... Poor Sir
"Robert is to lose his head immediately
"as they say, about which he seems to
"trouble his head very little; but I must
"tell you a good thing of Lady Thanet's
"before I go any further. Lord Bateman
"told her at the Bath that he had Sir
"Robert's head in his pocket. 'Are you
"'sure of it?' says she. 'Nothing surer.'
"'Why then,' says she, 'you cannot pos-
"'sibly do so well as to put it on your
"'shoulders.'"   I close with a pleasant
passage of banter on a love affair of
Horace Walpole's, from a letter of two
years' later date, written from Ghent.
"Dear Horry, I delight in your disown-
"ing your amourette twelve miles out of
"London. Do you forgot all that passed
"in Chelsea summer-house on that head,
"and in Chelsea parlour too? .... Yes,
"twelve miles out of London, Horry; and
"yet you are in the right to commend
"London too. I know your beauty was
"little out of it at that time, gone to shine
"and do mischief in some country vil-
"lage: but its satellites accompanied it
"too, for I remember you made frequent
"excursions about that time, spite of all
"the dust and heat in the world. I am
"not simple; I know the people *like* Lon-
"don, as Dr. Bentley said of apple-pie:
"but nobody *loves* London for London's
"sake, but green girls and quadrille ma-
"trons." *Rockingham Memoirs*, i. 373-381.
  * The epithet is Gray's, who never

cares to conceal his contempt for "Old
"Fobus."
  * *Garrick Correspondence*, i. 189. "My
"dear Garrick," he said in the same
"letter, "you have made me perfectly happy
"by the friendly and obliging satisfac-
"tion you are so good to express on this
"little gleam of prosperity, which has at

rived in England, from his foreign tour, three months before; his old weaknesses coming back as he verged nearer and nearer home, and, for his last few days in Paris, disturbing him with visions of Powell. "I'll answer for nothing and "nobody in a playhouse," he wrote to Colman; "the devil has "put his hoof into it, and he "was a deceiver from the begin- "ning of the world. Tell me "really what you think of Powell. "I am told by several that he "*will* bawl and roar. Ross, I "hear, has got reputation in "*Lear*. I don't doubt it. The "Town is a facetious gen- "tleman."* A few days later, Sterne wrote to him from Bath "strange" things of Powell;** and when himself on the point of starting from Paris for Lon- don, he met Beauclerc, who reported of the new tragedian not less strangely. "What, 'all "'my children!' I fear he has "taken a wrong turn. Have you "advised him?" he wrote again to Colman. "Do you see him? "Is he grateful? is he modest? "Or, is he conceited and un-

"done?"* Nor could the un- easy little great actor bring him- self to make his journey home until he had privately sent on, for anonymous publica- tion at the moment of his arrival, a rhymed satirical fable in anticipation and forestalment of expected Grub-street attacks, wherein he humbly depicted him- self as *The Sick Monkey*, and the whole race of other animals as railing at the monkey and his travels. But it was labour all thrown away. The finessing and trick ** were of no use, the hearts of his admirers being already securely his without such miser- able help. Grub-street, when he came, showed no sign of dis- composure; and there was but one desire in London and West- minster, to see their favourite actor again.

Let us not be surprised if these intolerable vanities and self-distrusts weighed, with con- temporaries of his own grade, against the better qualities of this delightful man, and pressed down the scale. Johnson loved him, but could not always show it for hatred of his foppery;

"length fallen on my fortune." It was indeed but a transient gleam, for the ad- ministration passed away in a month!

* March 10, 1765. Peake's *Memoirs*, I. 141.

** "Powell," Sterne adds,—"good "heaven! give me some one with less "smoke and more fire. There are who, "like the Pharisees, still think they shall "be heard for *much* speaking. Come— "come away, my dear Garrick, and teach "us another lesson." Letter dated Bath, April 6, 1765.

* Letter dated 7th April, 1765. Peake's *Memoirs*, 1. 149-50.

** "Though secure of our hearts, yet confoundedly sick, If they were not his own by finess- ing and trick."
                              Retaliation.
See Colman's *Posthumous Letters*, 271-8, for the instructions to Colman to puff "our little stage hero" in his absence, received from the little stage hero him- self. See also Murphy's *Life*, II. 14, and Davies's, II. 332.

Goldsmith admired him, yet was always ready to join in any scheme for his mortification and annoyance. Two things had been done in his ab-sence to which he addressed himself with great anxiety on his return. The Covent-garden actors had established a voluntary benefit-subscription, to relieve their poorer fellows in distress; and, jealous of such a proposal without previous consultation with himself, he was now throwing all his energy into a similar fund at Drury-lane, which should excel and overrule the other. Without him, too, the Club had been established; but as he could not hope to succeed in setting up a rival to *that*, he was using every anxious means to secure his own immediate election. Johnson resolutely opposed it. Reynolds first conveyed to him Garrick's wish, to the effect that he liked the idea of the club excessively, and thought he should be of them. "He'll be of us!" exclaimed Johnson; "how does he "know we will permit him? The "first duke in England has no "right to hold such language."[*] To Thrale, the next intercessor, he threw out even threats of a black-ball; but this moved the worthy brewer to remonstrate warmly, and Johnson, thus hard-pressed, picked up somewhat

recklessly a line of Pope's, as in self-defence one might pick up a stone by the wayside, without regard to its form or fitness. "Why, sir, I love my little "David dearly, better than all or "any of his flatterers do; but "surely one ought to sit in a "society like ours

"Unelbow'd by a gamester, pimp or
    player."[*]

Still the subject was not suffered to let drop, and the next who undertook it was Hawkins. "He will disturb us, sir, by his "buffoonery," was the only and obdurate answer.[**] Garrick saw that for the present it was hopeless (though not long after, as will be seen, Percy, Chambers, and Colman obtained their election); and, with his happier tact and really handsome spirit,[***]

[*] *Boswell*, ii. 274-5. Boswell relates this by way of contradicting Hawkins, whose account, however, it plainly confirms.

[*] *Piozzi Letters*, ii. 387.
[**] *Life of Johnson*, 425.
[***] In the midst of Garrick's uneasy little vanities let me show him in his better character (also from an incident of the present year), as the benefactor and friend of worth and virtue. It will enable me too, as I have already illustrated Goldsmith's Doctor Marrowfat by comparison with a living dignitary of the church (*ante*, 192), to offer a not unworthy companion picture to Goldsmith's Doctor Primrose, in the person of a living vicar. Garrick is writing to one of his great friends on behalf of the Rev. Mr. Heighton, and "the worthy parson" is happily sketched by him. "The honest "vicar of Egham might be made the "happiest man upon earth with a small "addition to his present income. . . He is "gouty and turned of sixty, yet has not "only the severe duty of Egham upon "him, but is obliged to ride five or six "miles through much water, and often to "swim his horse, for the sake of about "thirty pounds a-year. I entered lately "into a very serious conversation with

visited Johnson as usual, and seemed to withdraw his claim. But he could not conceal his uneasiness. "He would often stop "at my gate," says his good-natured friend Hawkins, who lived at Twickenham, "in his "way to and from Hampton, with "messages from Johnson relat-"ing to his *Shakespeare*, then in "the press, and ask such ques-"tions as these: 'Were you at "'the Club on Monday night? "'What did you talk of? Was "'Johnson there? I suppose he "'said something of Davy?— "'that Davy was a clever fellow "'in his way, full of convivial "'pleasantry, but no poet, no "'writer, ha!'"* Hawkins might hear all this, however, with better grace than any one else; for that worthy magistrate took little interest in the club. In a letter to Langton, written shortly after, Johnson specially mentions him as remiss in attendance, while he admits that he is himself not over-diligent. "Dyer, Doc-"tor Nugent, Doctor Goldsmith, "and Mr. Reynolds," he adds, "are very constant."*

1765.
Æt. 37.

Without its dignified doctorial prefix, Goldsmith's name is now seldom mentioned; even Newbery is careful to preserve it in his memoranda of books lent for the purposes of compilation; and he does not seem, himself, to have again wholly laid it aside. Indeed, he now made a brief effort, at the suggestion of Reynolds, to make positive professional use of it. It was much to have a regular calling, said the successful painter; it gave a man social rank, and consideration in the world. Advantage should be taken of the growing popularity of the *Traveller*. To be at once physician and man of letters was the most natural thing possible: there were the Arbuthnots and Garths, to say nothing of Cowley himself, among the dead; there were the Akensides, Graingers, Armstrongs, and Smolletts, still among the living; and where was the degree in medicine belonging to any of them, to which the degree in poetry or wit had not given more glad acceptance? Out came Goldsmith accordingly

---

"him about his affairs, and he confessed "to me that he found a curate was neces-"sary for him; I made him an offer of "money for that purpose till something "might happen, but he absolutely refused "me. .. I assure you, upon my word and "honour, that this step is taken without "his knowledge or concurrence. .. My "friend is a great dabbler in curiosities, "and he has collected some few in his "little library and garden; but I defy "him to show me a greater rarity than "himself, for he is a generous, modest, "ingenious, and disinterested clergy-"man." Two years later, this application having failed, he wrote to the wife of the chancellor, Lord Camden, with better effect. "The good man," he writes to her, acknowledging her answer, "hap-"pened to dine with me at Hampton "when I had the honour of receiving "your Ladyship's letter. He could not "refrain from tears of joy." *Gar. Cor.* I. 190-1, 263.

* *Life of Johnson*, 427.

* *Boswell*, II. 321. In the same letter he writes, "Mr. Lye is printing his Saxon "and Gothic dictionary: all The Club "subscribes."

(in the June of this year, according to the account-books of Mr. William Filby the tailor),* in 1765. purple silk small-clothes, a handsome scarlet roque-laure buttoned close under the chin, and with all the additional importance derivable from a full dress professional wig, a sword, and a gold-headed cane. The style of the coat and small-clothes may be presumed from the "four guineas and a half" paid for them; and, as a child with its toy is uneasy without swift renewal of the pleasurable excitement, Goldsmith amazed his friends with no less than three similar suits, not less expensive, in the next six months. Yet greatly was the enjoyment of these fine clothes abridged by the dignity he was obliged to put on with them; and, easy as he had found it to blot from his now genteeler page the names of innocent but vulgar haunts once so familiar there, he had found it much harder to give up the actual reality of those old humble haunts, of his tea at the White-conduit, of his ale-house club at Islington, of his nights at the Wrekin or St. Giles's. In truth, he would say (*in truth* was a favourite phrase of his, inter-

poses Cooke, who relates the anecdote), one has to make vast sacrifices for good company's sake; "for here am I shut out of "several places where I used to "play the fool very agreeably."* Nor is it quite clear that the most moderate accession of good company, professionally speaking, rewarded this reluctant gravity. The only instance remembered of his practice was in the case of a Mrs. Sidebotham, described as one of his recent acquaintance of the better sort; whose waiting-woman was often afterwards known to relate with what a ludicrous assumption of dignity he would show off his cloak and his cane, as he strutted with his queer little figure, stuck through as with a huge pin by his wandering sword, into the sick-room of her mistress. At last it one day happened, that, his opinion differing somewhat from the apothecary's in attendance, the lady thought her apothecary the safer counsellor, and Goldsmith quitted the house in high indignation.** He would leave off prescribing for his friends, he said. "Do so, my "dear Doctor," observed Beau-clerc. "Whenever you under-"take to kill, let it only be your "enemies." Upon the whole this seems to have been the close of Doctor Goldsmith's professional practice.

* These account-books were communicated to Mr. Prior by the son of William Filby (miscalled John in *Boswell*), Mr. John Filby, "a respectable member of "the Corporation of London," and will hereafter be quoted in detail. They complete the picture of which I furnish the beginning on a previous page (38), in the extracts there first printed from the Edinburgh tailor's ledger.

* *Europ. Mag.* XXIV.
** Told on the relation of Mrs. Gwyn. *Prior,* ii. 105.

CHAPTER XII.

News for the Club from Various Places.
1765—1766.

THE literary engagements of Doctor Oliver Goldsmith were meanwhile going on with Newbery; and towards the close of the year he appears to have completed a compilation of a kind somewhat novel to him, induced in all probability by his concurrent professional attempts. It was "*A Survey of Experimental* "*Philosophy*, considered in its "present state of improvement;" and Newbery paid him sixty guineas for it.* He also took great interest at this time in the proceedings of the Society of Arts; and is supposed, from the many small advances entered in Newbery's memoranda as made in connection with that Society,**

to have contributed sundry reports and disquisitions on its proceedings and affairs to a new commercial and agricultural magazine in which the busy publisher had engaged. It was certainly not an idle year with him, though what remains in proof of his employment may be scant and indifferent enough. Johnson's blind pensioner, Miss Williams, had for several months been getting together a subscription volume of Miscellanies, to which Goldsmith had promised a poem; and she complains that she found him always too busy to redeem his promise, and was continually put off with a "Leave it to me." Nor was Johnson, who had made like promises, much better. "Well, we'll think about it." was his form of excuse.* With Johnson, in truth, a year of most unusual exertion had succeeded his year of visitings, and he had at last completed, nine years later than he promised it, his edition of *Shakespeare*. It came out in October, in eight octavo volumes; and was bitterly assailed (nor, it may be admitted, without a certain coarse smartness) by Kenrick, who, in one of the notes to his attack, coupling "learned

* I give the memorandum of books lent to Goldsmith for the purpose of this compilation. "Sent to Dr. Goldsmith, "Sept. 11th, 1765, from Canbury (Canon- "bury) House the Copy of the Philosophy "to be revised, with the Abbé Nollet's "Philosophy, and to have an account "added of Hale's Ventilator, together with "the following Books. 1. Pemberton's "Newton, Quarto. 2. Two pamphlets of "Mr. Franklin's on Electricity. 3. 1 of "Ferguson's Astronomy, Quarto. 4. "D'Alembert's Treatise of Fluids, Quarto. "5. Martin's Philosophy, 3 vols. 6. Fergu- "son's Lectures, Do. 7. Holsham's Do. "8. Kiel's Introduction, Do. 9. Kiel's "Astronomy, Do. 10. Nature Displayed, "7 vols, 12mo. 11. Nollet's Philosophy, "3 vols. 12mo." (Nollet is called Nola and Noletus, Ferguson figures as Furgason and Furgeson, and D'Alembert is transformed into Darlembort, in worthy Mr. Newbery's orthography). Newbery MSS, in Mr. Murray's possession.

** See *ante*, 284, note. Besides the entries there given, others exist having reference to 1765, as for example: "Lent "Dr. Goldsmith, at the Society of Arts, "and to pay arrears, 3*l*. 3*s*." And see *post*, one of the notes in chap. xix.

* *Boswell*, iii. 9. The poor old lady was more nervous about having received and spent her subscription half-crowns than Johnson felt about his subscription guineas (*ante*, 152).

"doctors of Dublin" with "doc-"torial dignities of Rheims and "Louvain," may have meant a sarcasm at Goldsmith. I have indicated the latter place as the probable source of his medical degree; and, three months before, Dublin University had conferred a doctorship on Johnson, though not until ten years later, when Oxford did him similar honour, did he consent to acknowledge the title.[*] He had now, I may add, left his Temple chambers, and become master of a house in one of the courts in Fleet-street which bore his own name; and where he was able to give lodging on the ground floor to Miss Williams, and in the garret to Robert Levett. It is remembered as a decent house, with stout old-fashioned mahogany furniture. Goldsmith appears meanwhile to have got into somewhat better chambers in the same (Garden) court [**] where his library stair-case chambers stood, which he

1765.
Æt. 37.

was able to furnish more comfortably; and to which we shortly trace (by the help of Mr. Filby's bills, and their memoranda of altered suits) the presence of a man-servant.

So passed the year 1765. It was the year in which he had first felt any advantage of rank arising from literature; and it closed upon him as he seems to have resolved to make the most of his growing importance, and enjoy it in all possible ways. Joseph Warton, now preparing for the head-mastership of Winchester school, was in London at the opening of 1766, and saw something of the so-ciety of the club. He had wished to see Hume; but Hume, though he had left Paris (where he had been secretary of the embassy to Lord Hertford, re-called and sent to Dublin by the new administration), was not yet in London. A strange Paris "season" it had been, and odd and ill-assorted its assemblage of visitors. There had Sterne, Foote, Walpole, and Wilkes been thrown together at the same din-ner-table. There had Hume, with his broad Scotch accent, his unintelligible French, his inex-pressive fat face, and his cor-pulent body, been the object of enthusiasm without example, and played the Sultan in pantomimic tableaux to the prettiest women of the time.[*]   There had the

1766.
Æt. 38.

---

* He never himself, however, actually assumed it; and it is not a little curious, remembering how world-famous the dignity became in his person, that he never called himself anything but "Mr. "Johnson" to the close of his life.

** Mr. Tom Taylor says (*Life of Reynolds*, i. 244) that "Goldsmith had this "summer (1765) reached his second stage "in the Temple. He had left the shabby "chambers which he shared with Jeffs "the butler on the library staircase, for "rooms in 3 King's Bench-walk, where I "find Reynolds engaged to dine with him "in July." I do not know the authority for this statement, unless Reynolds has himself given that address. Goldsmith changed his Temple chambers only twice.

* "They believe in Mr. Hume," writes Walpole, "the only thing in the world "that they believe implicitly; which they

author of the *Héloïse* and the *Contrat Social*, half crazed with the passionate admiration which had welcomed his *Emile*, and flattered out of the rest of his wits by the persecution that followed it, stalked about with all Paris at his heels, in a caftan and Armenian robes, and so enchanted the Scotch historian and sage, to whom he seemed a sort of better Socrates, that he had offered him a home in England.* There was the young painter-student, Barry, writing modest letters on his way to Rome, whither William and Edmund Burke had subscribed out of their limited means to send him. There was the young lion-hunter Boswell, more pompous and conceited than ever; as little laden with law from Utrecht, where he has studied since we saw him last, as with heroism from Corsica, where he has visited Pascal Paoli, or with wit from Ferney, where he has been to see Voltaire; pushing his way into every salon, inflicting himself on every celebrity, and ridiculed by all.* There, finally, was Horace Walpole, twinged with the gout and smarting from political slight, but revenging himself with laughter at everybody around him and beyond him: now with aspiring Geoffrin and the philosophers, now with blind Du Deffand and the wits** ("women

1766.
Æt. 38.

"must do; for I defy them to understand "any language that he speaks." "Il fit "son début chez Madame de T——; . . on "le place sur un sopha entre les deux "plus jolies femmes de Paris, il les re-"garde attentivement, il se frappe le "ventre et les genoux a' plusieurs re-"prises, et ne trouve jamais autre chose "a' leur dire que: 'Eh bien! mes de-"'moiselles . . . Eh bien! vous voilà "'donc . . Eh bien! vous voilà . . vous "'voilà ici?'" *Memoires et Correspondance de Madame d'Epinay*, III. 284.

* "I find him," says the too impressible philosopher, "mild, and gentle, and "modest, and good-humoured; and he "has more the behaviour of a man of the "world, than any of the learned here, "except M. de Buffon; who, in his figure, "and air, and deportment, answers your "idea of a marechal of France rather than "that of a philosopher. M. Rousseau is "of a small stature, and would rather be "ugly, had he not the finest physiognomy "in the world: I mean the most expres-"sive countenance. . . His Armenian "dress is not affectation. He has had an "infirmity from his infancy, which makes "brooches inconvenient for him." Burton's *Hume*, II. 299, 302. In connection with this passage it may be worth adding that Buffon was the only known French writer of this period whom Johnson declared he would care to cross the sea to visit, and (as his reason for *not* going) "I "can find in Buffon's book all that he can "say." *Boswell*, IV. 247. He never speaks of Voltaire without unconsciously betraying a sort of uneasy fear of his vivacity and scorn.

* "He is a strange being," writes Walpole of Boswell, "and, like Cambridge, "has a rage of knowing anybody that "ever was talked of. He forced himself "upon me at Paris in spite of my teeth "and my doors." *Coll. Lett.* v. 192.
** *Coll. Lett.* v. 123-4. I must give the reader a peep (from a letter in the *Selwyn Correspondence*) at one of the leading members of this distinguished society. "Madame de Deffand has filled up her "vacancies, and given me enough new "French. With one of them you would "be delighted, a Madame de Marchais. "She is not perfectly young, has a face "like a Jew pedlar, her person is about "four feet, her head about six, and her "*coiffure* about tou. Her forehead, chin, "and neck, are whiter than a miller's; "and she wears more festoons of natural "flowers than all the *figurantes* at the "Opera. Her eloquence is still more

"who violated all the duties of "life and gave very pretty sup-"pers"); lumping up in the same contempt, Wilkes and Foote, Boswell and Sterne;* proclaiming as impostors in their various ways, alike the jesuits, the methodists, the philosophers, the politicians, the encyclopedists, the hypocrite Rousseau, the scoffer Voltaire, the Humes, the Lytteltons, the Grenvilles, the atheist tyrant of Prussia, and the mountebank of history, Mr. Pitt; and counting a ploughman who sows, reads his almanack, and believes the stars but so many farthing candles created to prevent his falling into a ditch as he goes home at night, a wiser as well as more rational, and certainly an honester being than any of them.** Such

1766.
———
Æt. 38.

was the winter society of Paris; let Joseph Warton describe what he saw of literature in London. "I only dined with Johnson," he writes to his brother, "who "seemed cold and indifferent, "and scarce said anything to me. "Perhaps he has heard what I "said of his *Shakespeare*, or rather, "was offended at what I wrote "to him—as he pleases. Of all "solemn coxcombs, Goldsmith is "the first; yet sensible; but af-"fects to use Johnson's hard "words in conversation.* We "had a Mr. Dyer, who is a "scholar and a gentleman. Gar-"rick is entirely off from John-"son, and cannot, he says, for-"give him his insinuating that he "withheld his old editions, which "always were open to him, nor "I suppose his never mentioning "him in all his works."

What Garrick could with greater difficulty forgive (Warton's allusion is to that passage

---

"abundant, her *attentions* exuberant. "She talks volumes, writes folios—I mean "in *billets*; presides over the *Académie*, "inspires passions, and has not time "enough to heal a quarter of the wounds "she gives. She has a house in a nut-"shell, that is fuller of invention than a "fairy tale; her bed stands in the middle "of the room, because there is no other "space that would hold it; it is sur-"rounded by such a perspective of look-"ing-glasses, that you may see all that "passes in it from the first ante-cham-"ber."

   * *Coll. Lett.* v. 91, 113.

   ** *Coll. Lett.* v. 96, 101. Nor can I help quoting from the same volume (110) Walpole's shrewd anticipation as to Hume and his new friend. "Mr. Hume "carries this letter and Rousseau to Eng-"land. I wish the former may not re-"pent having engaged with the latter, "who contradicts and quarrels with all "mankind in order to obtain their ad-"miration. I think both his means and "his end below such a genius. If I had "talents like his, I should despise any

"suffrage below my own standard, and "should blush to owe any part of my "fame to singularities and affectations. "But great parts seem like high towers "erected on high mountains, the more "exposed to every wind, and readier to "tumble. Charles Townshend is blown "round the compass; Rousseau insists "that the north and south blow at the "same time; and Voltaire demolishes "the Bible to erect fatalism in its stead. "So compatible are the greatest abilities "and greatest absurdities!" Gray's anticipations were not less shrewd.

   * Wooll's *Warton*, 312-3. This charge, which the not very lively Joe Warton brings against Goldsmith, of affecting to use Johnson's hard words in conversation, and which Hawkins also brings against him, I have dealt with, *post*, Book IV. chap. IV.

in the *Preface* to his edition which regrets that he could not collate more copies, since he had not found the collectors of those rarities very communicative) was the studied absence of any mention of his acting. He had not withheld his old plays; he had been careful, through others, to let Johnson understand (too notoriously careless of books,* as he was, to be safely trusted with rare editions) that the books were at his service, and that in his absence abroad the keys of his library had, with that view solely, been intrusted to a servant: but this implied an overture from Johnson, who thought it Garrick's duty, on the contrary, to make overtures to him; who knew that the other course involved acknowledgments he was not prepared to make; and who laughed at nothing so much, on Davy's subsequent loan of all his plays to George Steevens,**

as when he read this year, in the first publication of that acute young Mephistophelean critic, that "Mr. Garrick's zeal "would not permit him to "withhold anything that "might ever so remotely tend "to show the perfections of that "author *who only could have enabled* "*him to display his own.*" Johnson could not have hit off a compliment of such satirical nicety; he must have praised honestly, if at all, and it went against his grain to do it. He let out the reason to Boswell eight years afterwards. "Garrick has been liber-"ally paid, sir, for anything he "has done for Shakespeare. If "I should praise him, I should "much more praise the nation "who paid him."* With better reason he used to laugh at his managerial preference of the player's text (which it is little to the credit of the stage that the last of the great actors, Mr. Macready, should have been the first to depart from**), and

* Cooke says (in his *Life of Foote*) his ordinary habit was to open a book so wide as almost to break the back of it, and then to flug it down. Cradock describes the same peculiarity; and adds that on one occasion, Johnson having been admitted to Garrick's room in Southampton-street to wait till its master should arrive, the latter found, on his arrival, all his most splendidly bound prosentation-volumes from various authors and writers of plays &c flung damaged on the floor as "stuff, trash, and non-"sense." Boswell, who refers to the circumstances mentioned in the text, adds that, "considering the slovenly and care-"less manner in which books were "treated by Johnson, it could not have "been expected that scarce and valuable "editions should have been lent to him." III. 229.

** *Correspondence of Garrick*, I. 216-17.

Oliver Goldsmith's Life and Times. I.

* *Boswell*, IV. 266. The real truth of his apparent inconsistencies about Garrick, of which so many instances are given in this biography, was admirably hit off by Reynolds in the remark, that in point of fact Johnson considered him to be as it were his *property*; and would allow no man either to blame or to praise Garrick in his presence, without contradicting him. In proof of this Sir Joshua himself compiled, from actual recollected scraps of his talk about Davy, two imaginary conversations, in the first of which Johnson attacks Garrick against Sir Joshua, and in the second defends him against Gibbon. These dialogues are to be found in Miss Hawkins's *Memoirs*, I. 110-128.

** The Fool in *Lear*, and other master-couple it with a doubt whether he had ever examined one of the original plays from the first scene to the last. Nor did Garrick take all this quietly. The king had commanded his reappearance in Benedict at the close of the year; and, though he did not think it safe to resume any part of which Powell was in possession, except Lusignan, Lothario, and Leon, his popularity had again shone forth unabated. It brought back his sense of power; and with it a disposition to use it, even against Johnson. The latter had not hesitated, notwithstanding their doubtful relations, to seek to "secure an honest prejudice" in favour of his book by formally asking the popular actor's "suf-"frage" for it on its appearance; yet the suffrage of the popular actor was certainly exerted against it; and that Johnson had not a taste for the finest productions of genius,* Garrick afterwards went about busily explaining. With Iago's ingenious mischief, with Hal's gay compliance in Falstaff's vices, such a critic might be at home; but from Lear in the storm, and from Macbeth on the blasted heath, he must be content to be far away. He could, there, but mount the high horse, and bluster about imperial tragedy. The tone was caught by the actor's friends; is perceptible in parts of his correspondence;* is in the letters of Warburton, and in such as I have quoted of the Wartons; and gradually, to the disturbance of even Johnson, passed from society into the press, and became a stock theme with the newspapers. Garrick went too far, however, when he suffered the libeller Kenrick, not many months after his published attack on Johnson, to exhibit upon his theatre a play called *Falstaff's Wedding;* and to make another attempt, the following season, with a piece called the *Widowed Wife.* The first was damned, and, till Shakespeare's fat Jack is forgotten, is not likely to be heard of again; the second passed into oblivion more slowly:** but

<hr>

pieces of the poet's original text, were first restored to the stage by Mr. Macready, after more than two centuries of discreditable exile.

* His extraordinary argument in support of the unapproached excellence of a passage in Congreve's *Mourning Bride* (which he held to be superior to anything in Shakespeare, because the latter "never "had six lines together without a fault," *Boswell*, III. 99) is well known; but notwithstanding this and other abundant proofs of his insensibility to the higher and more subtle parts of Shakespeare's genius, his edition was an excellent one, and did noble service to the poet's text— such was his knowledge of language, and the power of his strong common sense.

* It will suffice to refer to *Gar. Cor.* I. 205. But see what Mrs. Piozzi says, *Anecdotes*, 57-9.

** See Davies's *Life of Garrick*, II. 132; and Murphy's *Life*, II. 32, 33. "Who," asks Garrick (Colman's *Post. Lett.* 290), "wrote the *Answer* to Kenrick's *Review?* "Johnson sent it to me through Steevens "last week—but mum—it is not quite the "thing: by J.'s fondness for it, he must "have felt K——. What things we are! "and how little are we known!" Yet, on the other hand, see *Boswell*, IV. 305, for

Garrick was brought, by both, into personal relations with the writer which he lived to have reason to deplore. Meanwhile, and for some little time to come, what Joseph Warton had written was but too true. Garrick and Johnson were entirely off; and in a certain gloom of spirits, and disquietude of health, which were just now stealing over the latter, even his interest in the stage appeared to have passed away.

"I think, Mr. Johnson," said Goldsmith, as they sat talking together one evening in February, "you don't go near the theatres "now. You give yourself no "more concern about a new play, "than if you had never had any-"thing to do with the stage." Johnson avoided the question,[*] and his friend shifted the subject. He spoke of the public claim and expectation that the author of *Irene* should give them "something in some "other way;" on which Johnson began to talk of making verses, and said (very truly) that the great difficulty was to know when you had made good ones. He remarked that he had once written, in one day, a hundred lines of the *Vanity of Human Wishes;* and turning quickly to Goldsmith, added, "Doctor, I "am not quite idle; I made one "line t'other day; but I made "no more." Let us hear it," said the other, laughing; "we'll "put a bad one to it." "No,

$\overline{}$ 1766.　Æt. 38.

Johnson's amusing and contemptuous reiteration about *"the boy"* who answered Kenrick.

[*] In the dialogue that passed Johnson offered his excuse for the comparative scantiness of his writings in the later years of his life: JOHNSON: "Why, sir, "our tastes greatly alter. The lad does "not care for the child's rattle, and the "old man does not care for the young "man's whore." GOLDSMITH: "Nay, sir; "but your Muse was not a whore." JOHNSON: "Sir, I do not think she was. "But as we advance in the journey of "life, we drop some of the things which "have pleased us; whether it be that we "are fatigued and don't choose to carry "so many things any farther, or that we "find other things which we like better." BOSWELL: "But, sir, why don't you give "us something in some other way?" GOLDSMITH: "Ay, sir, we have a claim "upon you." JOHNSON: "No, sir, I am "not obliged to do any more. No man is "obliged to do as much as he can do. A "man is to have part of his life to him-"self. If a soldier has fought a good "many campaigns, he is not to be blamed "if he retires to ease and tranquillity. "A physician, who has practised long in "a great city, may be excused if he re-"tires to a small town, and takes less "practice. Now, sir, the good I can do "by my conversations bears the same "proportion to the good I can do by my "writings, that the practice of a phy-"sician, retired to a small town, does to "his practice in a great city." BOSWELL: "But I wonder, sir, you have not more "pleasure in writing than in not writ-"ing." JOHNSON: Sir, you *may* wonder." *Boswell*, II. 318-9. Seven years later the same subject was resumed, when Johnson, less disposed to be tolerant of him-self than in the present instance, told Boswell that he had been trying to cure his laziness all his life, and could not do it; upon which Boswell, with broad al-lusion to the great achievement of the *Dictionary*, interposed the remark, that if a man does in a shorter time what might be the labour of a life, there was nothing to be said against him; and elicited from Johnson this admirable and noble reply: "Suppose that flattery to be true, the "consequence would be that the world "would have no right to censure a man; "*but that will not justify him* TO HIMSELF." *Boswell*, IV. 251.

"sir," replied Johnson, "I have "forgot it."

Boswell was the reporter of this conversation. He had arrived from Paris a few days before, bringing with him Rousseau's old servant maid, Mademoiselle Le Vasseur. "She's "very homely and very awk- "ward," says Hume, "but more "talked of than the Princess of "Morocco or the Countess of "Egmont, on account of her "fidelity and attachment towards "him. His very dog, who is no "better than a collie, has a name "and reputation in the world!"* It was enough for Boswell, who clung to any rag of celebrity; nor, remembering how the an- cient widow of Cicero and Sal- lust had seduced a silly young patrician into thinking that her close connection with genius must have given her the secret of it, were Hume and Walpole quite secure of even the honour of the young Scotch escort of the ugly old Frenchwoman. They arrived safely and virtu- ously, notwithstanding; and Bos- well straightway went to John- son, whom, not a little to his discomfort, he found put by his doctors on a water regimen. Though they supped twice at the Mitre, it was not as in the old social time. On the night of the conversation just given, being then on the eve of his return to Scotland, he had taken Gold- smith with him to call again on

1766.
Æt. 38.

Johnson, "with the hope of pre- "vailing on him to sup with us "at the Mitre." But they found him indisposed, and resolved not to go abroad. "Come then," said Goldsmith gaily, "we will "not go to the Mitre to-night, "since we cannot have the big "man with us." Whereupon the big man, laughing at the jovial Irish phrase, called for a bottle of port; of which, adds Boswell, "Goldsmith and I partook, while "our friend, now a water drinker, "sat by us."*

One does not discover, in such anecdotes as these, what honest though somewhat dry Joe War- ton calls Goldsmith's solemn cox- combry. But beside Boswell's effulgence in that kind, any lesser light could hardly hope to shine. Even to the great commoner himself, at whose unapproach- able seclusion all London had so lately been amazed, and who at length, with little abatement of the haughty mystery, had reap- peared in the House of Com- mons, was "Bozzy" now re- solved, before leaving London, to force his way. With Corsican Paoli as his card he would play for this mighty Pam; and mys- terious intimation had already gone to Pitt of certain views of the struggling patriot, of the il- lustrious Paoli, which he desired to communicate to "the prime "minister of the brave, the secre- "tary of freedom and of spirit." Wonder reigned at the Club when they found the interview

---

* Burton's *Life*, II. 299. And see *Cor- respondence of Gray and Mason*, 387.

* *Boswell*, II. 318.

granted, and inextinguishable laughter when they heard of the interview itself. Profiting by Rousseau's Armenian example, Boswell went in Corsican robes. "He came in the Corsican dress," says Lord Buchan, who was present; "and Mr. Pitt smiled; but "received him very graciously, "in his pompous manner."* It was an advantage the young Scot followed up; very soon inflicting on Pitt a brief history of himself, in an elaborate epistle. He described his general love of great people, and how that Mr. Pitt's character in particular had filled many of his best hours with what he oddly called "that noble ad- "miration which a disinterested "soul can enjoy in the bower of "philosophy." He told him he was going to publish an account of Corsica, and of Paoli's gallant efforts against the tyrant Genoese; added that to please his father he had himself studied law, and was now fairly entered to the bar; and concluded thus: "I begin to like it. I can labour "hard; I feel myself coming for- "ward, and I hope to be useful "to my country. *Could you find time* "*to honour me now and then with a* "*letter?*" ** To no wiser man

than this, it should be always kept in mind, posterity became chiefly indebted for its laugh at Goldsmith's literary vanities, social absurdities, and so-called self-important ways.

1766.
————
Æt. 38.

With Pitt's reappearance had meanwhile been connected another event of not less mighty consequence. On the day (the 14th of January) when he rose to support Conway's repeal of the American stamp-act, and to resist his accompanying admission that such an act was not void in itself; when, in answer, to Nugent's furious denunciation of rebellious colonies, he rejoiced that Massachusetts had resisted, and affirmed that colonies unrepresented could not be taxed by parliament; Burke took his seat, by an arrangement with Lord Verney, for Wendover borough. A fortnight later he made his first speech, and divided the admiration of the house with Pitt himself.* Afterwards, and with

---

* "In consequence of this letter," wrote Lord Buchan on the back of one of Boswell's epistles, "I desired him to call "at Mr. Pitt's, and took care to be with "him when he was introduced. Mr. Pitt "was then in the Duke of Grafton's "house in Great-bond-street... Boswell "had genius, but wanted ballast to coun- "teract his whim. He preferred being a "showman to keeping a shop of his own."
** *Chatham Correspondence*, III. 247.

* In the best passages of his *Memoirs of George III*, Horace Walpole celebrates Pitt's farewell, and Burke's accession, to the House of Commons. "Two great "orators and statesmen," says Mr. Macaulay, speaking of the debates on Conway's motion, "belonging to two different "generations, repeatedly put forth all "their powers in defence of the bill. The "house of commons heard Pitt for the "last time, and Burke for the first time, "and was in doubt to which of them the "palm of eloquence should be assigned. "It was indeed a splendid sunset and a "splendid dawn." *Essays*, III. 517. Burke himself, as though unconscious of his own more commanding greatness, speaks in a precisely similar strain of the sudden burst of Charles Townshend on

increased effect, he spoke again; Pitt praising him, and telling his friends to set proper value on the "acquisition they had "made;" and when the struggle for the repeal was over, after the last victorious division on the memorable morning of the 22nd of February, and Pitt and Conway came out amid the huzzaings of the crowded lobby, where the leading merchants of the kingdom whom this great question so vitally affected had till "almost a winter's return "of light" tremblingly awaited the decision, Burke stood at their side, and received share of the same shouts and benedictions.*

1766.
——
Æt. 38.

Extraordinary news for the club, all this; and again the excellent Hawkins is in a state of wonder. "Sir," exclaimed Johnson, "there is no wonder at all. "We who know Mr. Burke, "know that he will be one of the "first men in the country."** But he had regrets with which to sober this admission. He disliked the Rockingham party, and

was zealous for more strict attendance at the club. "We have "the loss of Burke's company," he complained to Langton, "since he has been engaged in "the public business." Yet he cannot help adding (it was the first letter he had written to Langton from his new study in Johnson's-court, which he thinks "looks very pretty" about him) that it is well so great a man by nature as Burke should be expected soon to attain civil greatness. "He has gained more re-"putation than perhaps any man "at his first appearance ever "gained before. His speeches "have filled the town with "wonder."*

Ten days after the date of this letter came out an advertisement in the *St. James's Chronicle*, which affected the town with neither wonder nor curiosity, though not without matter for both to the members of the club. "In a few "days will be published," it said, "in two volumes, twelves, price "six shillings bound, or five shil-"lings sewed, *The Vicar of Wake-*"*field*. A tale, supposed to be "written by himself. Printed for "F. Newbery at the Crown in "Paternoster Row." This was the manuscript story sold to Newbery's nephew fifteen months before; and it seems impossible satisfactorily to account for the bookseller's delay. Johnson says that not till now had the *Traveller's* success made the publication worth while; but eight

the scene, as Pitt was magnificently retreating. "Even then, sir, even before "this splendid orb was entirely set, and "while the western horizon was in a "blaze with his descending glory, on the "opposite quarter of the heavens arose "another luminary, and for his hour be-"came lord of the ascendant." *Works*, I. 482. 1 may refer the reader who desires to have a notion of Burke's manner as he spoke in the House of Commons in later life, to a lively and minute description in Wraxall's *Hist. Mem.* II. 35, &c.

* Burke's *Works*, I. 473.
** *Boswell*, VI. 80.

* *Boswell*, II. 320-1.

months were passed, even now, since the *Traveller* had reached its fourth edition. We are left to conjecture; and the most likely supposition will probably be, that the delay was consequent on business arrangements between the younger and elder Newbery. Goldsmith had certainly not claimed the interval for any purpose of retouching his work;* and can hardly have failed to desire speedy publication, for what had been to him a labour of love as rare as the *Traveller* itself. But the elder Newbery may have interposed some claim to a property in the novel, and objected to its appearance contemporaneously with the *Traveller*. He often took part in this way in his nephew's affairs; and thus, for a translation of a French book on philosophy which the nephew published after the *Vicar*, and which Goldsmith at this very time was labouring at, we find, from the summer account handed in by the elder Newbery, that the latter had himself provided the payment.** He gave Goldsmith twenty pounds for it; and had also advanced him, at about the time when the *Vicar* was put in hand (it was printed at Salisbury, and was nearly three months in passing through the press), the sum of eleven guineas on his own promissory note.* The impression of a common interest between the booksellers is confirmed by what I find appended to all Mr. Francis Newbery's advertisements of the novel in the various papers of the day ("of "whom may be had *The Tra-* "*veller*, or a Prospect of Society, "a poem by Doctor Goldsmith. "Price 1*s.* 6*d.*"); and it seems further to strengthen the surmise of Mr. John Newbery's connection with the book, that he is himself niched into it. He is introduced as the philanthropic bookseller in St. Paul's-churchyard, who had written so many little books for children ("he "called himself their friend, but "he was the friend of all man- "kind"); and as having published for the vicar against the deuterogamists of the age.

So let the worthy bookseller, whose philanthropy was always under watchful care of

1766.

Æt. 38.

---

* My opinion on this point is strengthened by a communication of Doctor Farr's to Percy. The Doctor, mentioning some instances of haste or carelessness in the *Vicar*, was told by Goldsmith that it was not from want of time they had not been corrected ("as Newbery "kept it by him in manuscript two years "before he published it"), but for another reason. "'He gave me (I think he "'said) £60 for the copy; and had I "'made it over so perfect or correct, I "'should not have had a shilling more.'" *Percy Memoir*, 62.

** See a mention of "Translation of "Philosophy" in one of the notes, *post*, chap. xiv. The book was a *History of Philosophy and Philosophers*, by Formey, whose *Philosophical Miscellanies* Goldsmith already had noticed in the *Critical Review: see ante*, 129.

* I quote from the Newbery MSS. In Mr. Murray's possession. "Received "from Mr. Newbery eleven guineas "which I promise to pay. Oliver Gold- "smith, January 8th, 1766."

his prudence, continue to live with the Whistonian controversy; for the good Doctor Primrose, that courageous monogamist, has made both immortal.

1766.
——
Æt. 38.

CHAPTER XIII.

The *Vicar of Wakefield.*
1766.

NO book upon record has obtained a wider popularity than the *Vicar of Wakefield*, and none is more likely to endure. One who, on the day of its appearance, had not left the nursery, but who grew to be a popular poet and a man of fine wit, and who happily still survives with the experience of the seventy years over which his pleasures of memory extend, remarked lately to the present writer, that, of all the books which, through the fitful changes of three generations, he had seen rise and fall, the charm of the *Vicar of Wakefield* had alone continued as at first; and, could he revisit the world after an interval of many more generations, he should as surely look to find it undiminished. Such is the reward of simplicity and truth, and of not overstepping the modesty of nature.

It is not necessary that any critical judgment should be here gone into, of the merits or the defects of this charming tale. Every one is familiar with Goldsmith's *Vicar of Wakefield*. We read it in youth and in age. We return to it, as Walter Scott has said, again and again: "and we "bless the memory of an author "who contrives so well to re-"concile us to human nature." With its ease of style, its turns of thought so whimsical yet wise, and the humour and wit which sparkle freshly through its narrative, we have all of us profitably amused the idle or the vacant hour; from year to year we have had its tender or mirthful incidents, its forms so homely in their beauty, its pathos and its comedy, given back to us from the canvas of our Wilkies, Newtons, and Stothards, our Leslies, Maclises, and Mulreadys: but not in those graces of style, or even in that home-cherished gallery of familiar faces, can the secret of its extraordinary fascination be said to consist. It lies nearer the heart. A something which has found its way *there;* which, while it amused, has made us happier; which, gently inweaving itself with our habits of thought, has increased our good-humour and charity; which, insensibly it may be, has corrected wilful impatiences of temper, and made the world's daily accidents easier and kinder to us all: somewhat thus should be expressed, I think, the charm of the *Vicar of Wakefield.* It is our first pure example of the simple domestic novel. Though wide as it was various, and most minutely as well as broadly marked with passion, incident, and character, the field selected by Richardson, Fielding, and Smollett for the exercise of their genius and display of their powers, had hardly included this. Nor is it likely that Goldsmith would himself have chosen it, if his leading object had been to write a book. Rather as a refuge from the writing of books was this book undertaken. Simple to very baldness are the materials employed;—but he threw into the midst of them his own nature; his actual experience; the suffering, discipline, and sweet emotion of his chequered life; and so made them a lesson and a delight to all men.

Good predominant over evil, is briefly the purpose and moral of the little story. It is designed to show us that patience in suffering, that persevering reliance on the providence of God, that quiet labour, cheerful endeavour, and an indulgent forgiveness of the faults and infirmities of others, are the easy and certain means of pleasure in this world, and of turning pain to noble uses. It is designed to show us that the heroism and self-denial needed for the duties of life are not of the superhuman sort; that they may co-exist with many follies, with some simple weaknesses, with many harmless vanities; and that in the improvement of mankind, near and remote, in its progress through worldly content to final happiness, the humblest of men have their place

assigned them, and their part allotted them to play.

There had been, in light amusing fiction, no such scene as that where Doctor Primrose, surrounded by the mocking felons of the gaol into which his villainous creditor has thrown him, finds in even those wretched outcasts a common nature to appeal to, minds to instruct, sympathies to bring back to virtue, souls to restore and save. "In less than a fortnight "I had formed them into some-"thing social and humane." * Into how many hearts may this have planted a desire which had yet become no man's care!   Not

1766.
Æt. 38.

* One might suppose, in the subjoined passage, that the good Vicar was describing the experience of yesterday (1852) in one of those most humane of modern institutions, our *ragged schools.* It is the exact process familiar to all who have laboured in this field, where the plough now happily held by peers and dignitaries of state was first planted in the soil by a chimney-sweep of Windsor. "I read them a portion of the service, "with a loud unaffected voice, and "found my audience perfectly merry "upon the occasion. Lewd whispers, "groans of contrition burlesqued, wink-"ing and coughing, alternately excited "laughter. However, I continued with "my natural solemnity to read on, sen-"sible that what I did might amend some, "but could itself receive no contamina-"tion from any." The good man describes also his reward: "I took no "notice of all that this mischievous group "of little beings could do; but went on, "perfectly sensible that what was ridicu-"lous in my attempt, would excite mirth "only the first or second time, while "what was serious would be permanent. "My design succeeded, and, in less "than six days, some were penitent and "all were attentive." Chapters xxvi and xxvii.

yet had Howard turned his thoughts to the prison, Romilly was but a boy of nine years old, and Elizabeth Fry had not been born. In Goldsmith's day, as for centuries before it, the gaol only existed as the portal to the gallows: it was crime's high-school, where law presided over the science of law-breaking, and did its best to spread guilt abroad. This prison, argues Doctor Primrose, makes men guilty where it does not find them so; it encloses wretches for the commission of one crime, and returns them, if returned alive, fitted for the perpetration of thousands. With what consequence? New vices call for fresh restraints; "penal laws, "which are in the hands of the "rich, are laid upon the poor;" and all our paltriest possessions are hung round with gibbets. "When by indiscriminate penal "laws a nation beholds the same "punishment affixed to dissimilar "degrees of guilt, from perceiv-"ing no distinction in the penalty, "the people are led to lose all "sense of distinction in the "crime." It scares men now to be told of what no man then took heed. Deliberate and foul murders were committed by the State. It was but four years after this that the government which had reduced a young wife to beggary by pressing her husband to sea, sentenced her to death for entering a draper's shop in Ludgate-hill, taking some coarse linen off the counter, and

1766.
Æt. 38.

laying it down again as the shopman gazed at her; listened unmoved to a defence which might have penetrated stone, that inasmuch, since her husband was stolen from her, she had had no bed to lie upon, nothing to clothe her two baby children with, nothing to give them to eat, "per-"haps she might have done "something wrong, for she hardly "knew what she did;" and finally sent her to Tyburn, with her infant sucking at her breast.* Not without reason did Horace Walpole call the country "a "shambles."** Hardly a Mon-

* Speech of Sir William Meredith on the bill for the better securing dock-yards. The case so affectingly described was that of Mary Jones. "It is a cir-"cumstance not to be forgotten," added Sir William, "that she was very young "(under nineteen), and most remarkably "handsome. .. Her defence was (I have "the trial in my pocket) that she had "lived in credit, and wanted for nothing, "till a press-gang came and stole her "husband from her. .. It was at the time "when press-warrants were issued on "the alarm about Falkland Islands." *Parl. Hist.* xix. 237-8. It was not until 1790 that the act for *burning* women found guilty of coining, and subjecting the sheriff to a severe penalty for not enforcing it, was repealed. *Ibid,* xxix. 782-3.

** "It is shocking to think," he wrote, but a very few years before this date, "what a shambles this country has "grown. Seventeen were executed this "morning, after having murdered the "turnkey on Friday night, and almost "forced open Newgate. One is forced to "travel, even at noon, as if one was "going to battle." *Collected Letters,* ii. 418-19. Here, at one view, is the system of frequent executions and its result. Henry Fielding had strongly protested against it, more than ten years before the present date, in his admirable *Enquiry into the Causes of the late Increase of*

day passed that was not Black Monday at Newgate. An execution came round as regularly as any other weekly show; and when it was that "shocking "sight of fifteen men executed," whereof Boswell makes more than one mention,* the interest was of course the greater. Men, not otherwise hardened, found here a debasing delight. George Selwyn passed as much time at Tyburn as at White's; and Mr. Boswell had a special suit of execution-black, to make a decent appearance near the scaffold. Not uncalled for, therefore, though solitary and as yet unheeded, was the warning of the good Doctor Primrose. Nay, not uncalled for is it now, though a century has passed. Do not, he said, draw the cords of society so hard, that a convulsion must come to burst them; do not cut away wretches as useless, before you have tried their utility; make law the protector, not the tyrant of the people. You will then find that creatures, whose souls are held as dross, want only the hand of a refiner; and that "very little blood will "serve to cement our se- "curity."*

1766.
———
Æt. 38.

Resemblances have been found, and may be admitted to exist, between the Reverend Charles Primrose and the Reverend Abraham Adams. They arose from kindred genius; and from the manly habit which Fielding and Goldsmith shared, of discerning what was good and beautiful in the homeliest aspects of humanity. In the parson's saddle-bag of sermons would hardly have been found this prison sermon of the vicar; and there was in Mr. Adams not only a capacity for beef and pudding, but for beating and being beaten, which would ill have consisted with the simple dignity of Doctor Primrose. But unquestionable learning, unsuspecting simplicity, amusing traits of credulity and pedantry, and a most Christian purity and benevolence of heart, are common to both these master-pieces of English fiction; and are in each with such exquisite touch discriminated, as to leave no possible doubt of the originality of either. Anything like the charge of imitation is

Robbers, &c; where, after urging the necessity of a mitigation of the criminal code, while at the same time he shows that sufficiently severe measures had not been taken against the worst class of criminals, he gives many reasons of weight in support of his opinion that executions should be private. "The design "of those who first appointed executions "to be public, was to add the punishment "of shame to that of death; in order to "make the example an object of greater "terror. But experience has shown us "that the event is directly contrary to "this intention." See the whole of the argument in *Works* (Ed. 1801), x. 461-7. The wise alteration has at last been made. 1870.

* *Life*, III. 94; VIII. 331, &c.

* Greatly as our penal jurisprudence has been improved since Goldsmith's day, there yet remains too much still to do to enable us to dispense with the warning contained in the noble passage of the *Vicar of Wakefield* (chap. XXVII) to which I refer in the text, and which never can be read too often.

preposterous. Fielding's friend, Young, sat for the parson, as in Goldsmith's father, Charles, we *1766. Æt. 38.* have seen the original of the vicar;* and as long as nature pleases to imitate herself, will such simple-hearted spirits reveal kindred with each other. At the same time, and with peculiar mastery, art vindicates also in such cases her power and skill; and the general truth of resemblance is, after all, perceived to be much less striking than the local accidents of difference. Does it not well-nigh seem incredible, indeed, comparing the tone of language and incident in the two stories, that a space of twenty years should have comprised *Joseph Andrews* and the *Vicar of Wakefield?*

Little, it must be confessed, had past experience in fiction, from the days of De Foe to these of Smollett, prepared the age for a simple novel of English domestic life.* Least of all for that picture, so purely and delicately shaded, of the vicar, in his character of pastor, parent, and husband; of his helpmate, with her motherly cunning and housewifely prudence, loving and respecting him, "but at the "dictates of maternal vanity "counter - plotting his wisest "schemes;" of both, with their children around them, their quiet labour and domestic happiness, —which Walter Scott declares to be without a parallel, in all his novel-reading, as a fireside picture of perfect beauty. It may

* A confused and quite unfounded statement of Mr. Cradock's will hereafter be referred to (Book IV. Chap. xix.) to the effect that the *Vicar* was written "en-"tirely in a fortnight" in order to pay a journey of needful business to Wakefield, and hence the name. On the other hand, an American loyalist who took refuge in England, and had occasion to visit Wakefield, three years after Goldsmith's death, seems to have had curious proof of the anxiety of the good people of that prosperous town to claim a property in the vicar himself, as well as in the name of the vicarage. "Departed in a "stage-coach from Sheffield, and arrived "at Black Barnsley through a delightful "though uneven road; distance fourteen "miles. Here we took post-chaises, and "in two hours alighted at Wakefield, a "clothing town, wherein appeared evi-"dent tokens of taste in building, and of "wealth. .. The Westgate-street has the "noblest appearance of any I ever saw, "out of London. .. It has a very large "episcopal church, with a remarkably "lofty tower and spire. The principal "character in the novel called *The Vicar* "*of Wakefield* was taken from the late "vicar of this church, named Johnson, "whose peculiarly odd and singular hu-"mour has exposed his memory to the "ridicule of that satire." It is hardly necessary to remark that the worthy Boston trader whose diary I quote (Curwen's *Journal and Letters*, 131) could not himself have read the book which he thus characterises.

* I must always regard it as extraordinary, in such men, how much both Fielding and Smollett resorted in their novels to that sort of stimulus which the covert satire of individuals could alone supply to the generally false and depraved taste of the day, and which Goldsmith so steadily turned aside from. The truth is, as already I have hinted, that not many years before this date half the papers that issued from Grub-street were mere scandalous chronicles; and literature still suffered even less from the contempt into which the inferior talents of their writers had brought it, than from the dregs of the example they had left, and of the diseased taste to which they had so largely administered.

be freely admitted that there are many grave faults, many improbabilities, some even palpable absurdities, in the construction of the story.* Goldsmith knew this. "There are an hundred "faults in this Thing," he said, in his brief advertisement to it; "and an hundred things might "be said to prove them beauties. "But it is needless." (His meaning is, that to make beauties out of faults, be the proof ever so successful, does not mend the matter.) "A book may be amus- "ing with numerous errors, or it "may be very dull without a "single absurdity." He rested, with well-grounded faith, on the vital reality of his characters. It is wonderful with what nice variety the family likeness of each Primrose is preserved, and how little the defects of the story interfere with any of them. Cannot one see that there is a propriety, an eternal fitness, in even the historical family picture? Those rosy Flamborough girls, who do nothing but flaunt in red top-knots, hunt the slipper, burn nuts, play tricks, dance country dances, and scream with laughter; who have not the

least idea of high life or high-lived company, or such fashionable topics as pictures, taste, Shakespeare, and the musical-glasses, *—how should it be possible for *them* to

$\frac{1766.}{\text{Æt. 38.}}$

* Macaulay, who as usual states his objection to the fable very strongly, yet entertains no doubt that it is a tale "likely to last as long as our language. .. "It wants not merely that probability "which ought to be found in a tale of "common English life, but that con- "sistency which ought to be found even "in the wildest fiction about witches, "giants, and fairies. But the earlier "chapters have all the sweetness of "pastoral poetry, together with all the "vivacity of comedy." *Biog. Ess.* 62.

* Let me remark of this now famous allusion, that it may help in some degree to show us how long the little story had been in hand, and that there is no ground for supposing it, as Hawkins and others have called it, a mere occasional piece of writing to meet "a moment of pressure." An allusion to "the last *Auditor*," marking 1762 as about the time when the publication of Murphy's unsuccessful paper so called was in progress and would have suggested that reference, is borne out by "the musical-glasses." It was at the close of 1761 and in 1762 that musical-glasses were the temporary rage. Everybody's letters allude to them. Here is a charming one from Gray to Mason, which, being in one quaint sentence, I need not scruple to quote entire. "Pemb. "Hall, Dec. 8, 1761. Dear Mason, Of all "loves come to Cambridge out of hand, "for here is Mr. Delaval and a charm- "ing set of glasses that sing like night- "ingales; and we have concerts every "other night, and shall stay here this "month or two; and a vast deal of "good company, and a whale in pickle "just come from Ipswich; and the "man will not die, and Mr. Wood is "gone to Chatsworth; and there is no- "body but you and Tom and the curled "dog; and do not talk of the charge, for "we will make a subscription; besides, "we know you always come when you "have a mind. T. G." *Correspondence of Gray and Mason*, 283-4. They had been introduced some years before, with less effect, by a German composer, thus re- ferred to in a letter of Walpole's to Mann (*Coll. Lett.* II. 111). "The operas flourish "more than in any latter years; the "composer is Gluck, a German: he is to "have a benefit, at which he is to play on "a set of drinking-glasses, which he "modulates with water. I think I have "heard you speak of having seen some "such thing." I close this note with an advertisement from the *St. James's Chronicle* of Dec. 3rd, 1761: "At Mr. "Sheridan's lecture on elocution, Miss

have any other notion or desire than just to be painted in their red top-knots, each holding an orange? But Olivia Primrose! who, to her mother's knowledge, has a great deal to say upon every subject, and is very well skilled in controversy; who has read Thwackum and Square's disputes in *Tom Jones*, as well as the argument of man Friday and his master in *Robinson Crusoe*, and is not without hopes of converting her rake of a lover by means of the dialogues in *Religious Court-ship*;—is it not somehow quite as much in character with the flighty vivacity of this ambitious little Livy, that she should wish to be drawn as an Amazon sitting upon a bank of flowers, dressed in a green joseph richly laced with gold, a whip in her hand, and the young squire as Alexander the Great lying captive at her feet; as it certainly suits the more sober simplicity and prudent good sense of her sister Sophy, to figure in the same composition as a shepherdess, with as many sheep as the painter can put in for nothing? Mrs. Deborah Primrose triumphing in her lamb's-wool and gooseberry-wine, and claiming to be represented as the Mother of Love with plenty of diamonds in her hair and stomacher, is at first a little startling: but it admits of an excellent introduction of honest old Dick and chubby little Bill, by way of Cupids; and to what conceivable creature so much in need as Venus of conversion to monogamy could the Vicar "in his gown and band" have presented his books on the Whistonian controversy? There remains only Moses to complete the masterpiece; and is not his hat and white feather typical of both his arguments and his bargains, his sale of Dobbin the colt and his purchase of the gross of green spectacles? The simple, credulous, generous, inoffensive, family habits are common to all; but in each a separate identity is yet as broadly marked as in the Amazon, the Venus, or the Shepherdess of the immortal family picture.

Still, from all that touches and diverts us in these harmless vanities of the delightful group, we return to the primal source of what has given this glorious little story its unequalled popularity. It is not that we enjoy a secret charm of assumed superiority over the credulity and simplicity of almost every actor in it, being very certain that the sharper and his cosmogony would never have imposed on *us*, but that the better secret is laid open to us of the real superiority of such credulous ways over much of what the world mistakes for its shrewdest wisdom.* It is not

"Lloyd succeeds Miss Ford in perform-"ing on the musical-glasses for the "amusement of genteel company." It was eminently, we perceive, an amusement for "the genteel," the Skeggses and Blarneys of high life.

* "One way or another," says the sharp Mr. Jenkinson, "I generally

simply that a happy fireside is depicted there, but that it is one over which calamity and sorrow can only cast the most temporary shade. In his deepest distress, the Vicar has but to remember how much kinder Heaven is to us than we are to ourselves, and how few are the misfortunes of nature's making, to recover his cheerful patience. There never was a book in which indulgence and charity made virtue look so lustrous. Nobody is strait-laced: if we except Miss Carolina Wilelmina Amelia Skeggs, whose pretensions are summed up in Burchell's noble monosyllable. "Virtue, my dear Lady Blarney, "virtue is worth any price; but "where is that to be found?" "*Fudge*." When worldly reverses visit the good Doctor Primrose, they are of less account than the equanimity they cannot deprive him of; than the belief in good to which they only give wider scope; than the happiness which even in its worldliest sense they ultimately strengthen, by enlarged activity, and increased necessity for labour. It is only when struck through the sides of his children that for an instant his faith gives way. Most lovely is the pathos of that scene; so briefly and beautifully told. The little family at night are gathered round a charming fire, telling

"cheated simple neighbour Flamborough "once a year. Yet still the honest man "went forward without suspicion, and "grow rich, while I still continued "tricksy and cunning, and was poor."
Chap. XXVI.

stories of the past, laying schemes for the future, and listening to Moses's thoughtful opinion of matters and things in general, to the effect that all things, in his judgment, go on very well, and that he has just been thinking, when sister Livy is married to Farmer Williams, they'll get the loan of his cider-press and brewing-tubs for nothing. The best gooseberry-wine has been this night much in request. "Let us have one "bottle more, Deborah, my life," says the Vicar; "and Moses, "give us a good song. .. But "where is my darling Olivia?" Little Dick comes running in. "O pappa, pappa, she is gone "from us, she is gone from us, "my sister Livy is gone from us "for ever!" "Gone, child!" "Yes, she is gone off with two "gentlemen in a post-chaise, and "one of them kissed her, and "said he would die for her; and "she cried very much, and was "for coming back; but he per-"suaded her again, and she went "into the chaise, and said, *O* "*what will my poor pappa do when* "*he knows I am undone!*" "Now "then, my children, go and be "miserable; for we shall never "enjoy one hour more;" and the old man, struck to the heart, cannot help cursing the seducer. But Moses is mindful of happier teaching, and with a loving simplicity rebukes his father. .. "You should be my mother's "comforter, sir, and you increase "her pain. .. You should not

[margin: 1766. Æt. 38.]

"have curst him, villain as he is." "I did not curse him, child, did "I?" "Indeed, sir, you did; "you curst him twice." "Then may Heaven for- "give me and him if I "did." Charity resumes its place in his heart; with forgiveness, happiness half visits him again; by kindly patience, even Deborah's reproaches are subdued and stayed; he takes back with most affecting tenderness his penitent child; and the voices of all his children are heard once more in their simple concert on the honey-suckle bank. We feel that it is better than cursing; and are even content that the rascally young squire should have time and hope for a sort of shabby repentance, and be allowed the intermediate comfort (it seems after all, one hardly knows why or wherefore, the most appropriate thing he can do) of "blowing the French horn." Mr. Abraham Adams has infinite claims on respect and love, nor ever to be forgotten are his groans over Wilson's worldly narrative, his sermon on vanity, his manuscript Æschylus, his noble independence to Lady Booby, and his grand rebuke to Peter Pounce: but he is put to no such trial as this which has been illustrated here, and which sets before us, with such blended grandeur, simplicity, and pathos, the Christian heroism of the loving father, and forgiving ambassador of God to man.

It was not an age of particular

1766.
———
Æt. 38.

earnestness, this Hume and Walpole age: but no one can be in earnest himself without in some degree affecting others. "I re- "member a passage in the *Vicar* "*of Wakefield*," said Johnson, a few years after its author's death, "which Goldsmith was after- "wards fool enough to expunge. "*I do not love a man who is zealous* "*for nothing.*"* The words were

* VII. 247. Hereupon Boswell remarked that that was a fine passage. "Yes, sir: there was another fine pas- "sage too, which he struck out: 'When "'I was a young man, being anxious to "'distinguish myself, I was perpetually "'starting new propositions. But I soon "'gave this over; for I found that "'generally what was new was false.'" Substantially, however, the sentiment is left, though the particular expression is removed. It is where George Primrose describes his Grub-street career: "Find- "ing that the best things remained to be "said on the wrong side, I resolved to "write a book that should be wholly "new. ... The jewels of truth have been "so often imported by others, that no- "thing was left for me to import but "some splendid things that at a dis- "tance looked every bit as well." There is also a passage in Mrs. Piozzi's *Letters* (I. 247) which shows how Johnson must have talked of this among the set. "Well!" she writes to Johnson, 24th June, 1775, "Cræsus promised a reward, "you remember, for him who should "produce a new delight; but the prize "was never obtained, for nothing that "was new proved delightful; and Dr. "Goldsmith, 3000 years afterwards, found "out, that whoever did a new thing did "a bad thing, and whoever said a new "thing, said a false thing." I may add (as another instance of what I have frequent occasion to remark as to the many various and doubtful forms in which stories about Johnson and Goldsmith are apt to appear, when once we lose sight of the trustworthy Boswell) the following item from Dr. Burney's recollections: "Johnson told Dr. Burney, "that Goldsmith said, when he first

little, since the feeling was re-tained; for the very basis of the little tale was a sincerity and zeal for many things. This indeed it was, which, while all the world were admiring it for its mirth and sweetness, its bright and happy pictures, its simultaneous movement of the springs of laughter and tears, gave it a rarer value to a more select audience, and connected it with not the least memorable anecdote of modern literary history. It had been published little more than four years, when two Germans whose names became afterwards world-famous, one a student at that time in his twentieth, the other a graduate in his twenty-fifth year, met in the city of Strasburg. The younger, Johann Wolfgang Goethe, a law-scholar of the University with a passion for literature, sought knowledge from the elder, Johann Gottfried Herder, for the course on which he was moved to enter. Herder, a severe and masterly though somewhat cynical critic, laughed at the likings of the young aspirant, and roused him to other aspiration. Producing a German translation of the *Vicar of Wakefield*, he read it out aloud to Goethe in a manner which was peculiar to him; and,

as the incidents of the little story came forth in his serious simple voice, in one unmoved unaltering tone ("just as if no-"thing of it was present "before him, but all was "only historical; as if the "shadows of this poetical crea-"tion did not affect him in a life-"like manner, but only glided "gently by"), a new ideal of letters and of life arose in the mind of the listener.* Years passed on; and while that younger student raised up and re-established the literature of his country, and came at last, in his prime and in his age, to be acknowledged for the wisest of modern men, he never ceased throughout to confess what he owed to those old evenings at Strasburg. The strength which can conquer circumstance; the wisdom that lifts itself above every object, fortune and misfortune, good and evil, death and life, and attains to the possession of a poetical world; first visited Goethe in the tone with which Goldsmith's tale is told. The fiction became to him life's first reality; in country clergymen of Drusenheim, there started up vicars of Wakefield; for Olivias and Sophias of Alsace, first love fluttered at his heart;—and at every stage of his illustrious after-career its impression still vividly recurred to him. He remembered it when, at the height of his worldly honour and suc-

1766. Æt. 38.

"began to write, he determined to com-"mit to paper nothing but what was *new*; "but he afterwards found that what was "*new* was generally false, and from that "time was no longer solicitous about "novelty." This is obviously a more confused recollection of what is correctly told by Boswell.

* *Truth and Poetry from my Own Life*, translated by John Oxenford, i. 363.

cess, he made his written Life (*Wahrheit und Dichtung*) record what a blessing it had been to him; he had not forgotten it when, some twenty years ago,* standing at the age of eighty-one on the very brink of the grave, he told a friend that in the decisive moment of mental development the *Vicar of Wakefield* had formed his education, and that he had recently, with unabated delight, "read the "charming book again from be-"ginning to end, not a little af-"fected by the lively recollec-"tion" of how much he had been indebted to the author seventy years before.

1766.
Æt. 38.

Goldsmith was unconscious of this exalted tribute. He died as ignorant of Herder's friendly criticism, as of the gratitude of Goethe. The little book silently forced its way. I find upon examination of the periodicals of the day that no noise was made about it, no trumpets blown for it. The *St. James's Chronicle* did not condescend to notice its appearance, and the *Monthly Review* confessed frankly that nothing was to be made of it.** The better sort of newspapers as well as the more dignified reviews contemptuously left it to the patronage of *Lloyd's Evening Post*, the *London Chronicle*, and journals of that class; which simply informed their readers that a new novel, called the *Vicar of Wakefield*, had been published, that "the Editor "is Doctor Goldsmith, who has "affixed his name to an intro-"ductory advertisement," and that such and such were the incidents of the story. Several columns of the *Evening Post* and the *Chronicle*, between the dates of March and April, were filled in this way with bald recital of the plot; and with such extracts as the prison-scene, the account of the Primroses, and the brief episode of Matilda: but, in the way of praise or of criticism, not a word was said. Johnson, as I have remarked, took little interest in the story at any time but as the means of getting so much money for its author; and believing that "Harry Fielden" (as he called him) knew nothing but the shell of life,* may be

---

* Written in 1848.

** I subjoin the close of the notice which appeared in that respectable periodical: "Through the whole course "of our travels in the wild regions of "romance, we never met with anything "more difficult to characterise than the "*Vicar of Wakefield*. . . In brief, with all "its faults, there is much rational enter-"tainment to be met with in this very "singular tale." *Monthly Review*, xxxiv. 407, May 1766. Well might Southey say that the *Vicar of Wakefield* had proved "a "puzzler" to its critics!

* "Richardson had picked the kernel "of life (he said) while Fielding was con-"tented with the husk." Mrs. Piozzi's *Anecdotes*, 198. Fielding being mentioned, Johnson exclaimed, "He was a block-"head;" and upon Boswell expressing his astonishment at so strange an assertion, he said, "What I mean by his being "a blockhead is, that he was a barren "rascal." BOSWELL: "Will you not al-"low, sir, that he draws very natural "pictures of human life?" JOHNSON: "Why, sir, it is of very low life. "Richardson used to say, that had he not "known who Fielding was, he should "have believed he was an ostler." (So

excused for thinking the *Vicar* a "mere fanciful performance." It would seem that none of the club indeed, excepting Burke, cared much about it: and one may read, in the French letters of the time, how perfectly Madame Riccoboni agrees with her friend Garrick as to the little to be learned from it; and how surprised the lively lady is that the Burkes should have found it pathetic, or be able to approve of its arguments in favour of thieves and outcasts.* Admira-

tion, nevertheless, gathered slowly and steadily around it. A second edition* appeared at the close of May, and a third on the 25th of August; it reached its seventh edi-

1766.
———
Æt. 38.

much the worse, I would ask leave to say, for Richardson.) "Sir, there is "more knowledge of the heart in one "letter of Richardson's, than in all Tom "Jones! I, indeed, never read *Joseph* "*Andrews*." Erskine: "Surely, sir, "Richardson is very tedious." Johnson: "Why, sir, if you were to read Richard-"son for the story, your impatience "would be so much fretted that you "would hang yourself. But you must "read him for the sentiment." *Boswell*, III. 207, 208. (For an exception he would occasionally make in favour of *Amelia*, see Mrs. Piozzi's *Anecdotes*, 221-2.) This talk was at Sir Alexander Macdonald's in 1772, and "the Erskine" who finds Richardson tedious was a "young officer "in the regimentals of the Scots Royal, "who talked with a vivacity, fluency, "and precision so uncommon, that he at-"tracted particular attention;" who afterwards attracted more particular attention still as the first advocate of Westminster-hall, and ultimately lord high chancellor: and whose genuine sense of humour, and natural wit, must surely have resented very strongly this most astounding of all Johnson's heresies.

* The lively Frenchwoman's letter will be found in the *Garrick Correspondence*, II. 492-4. She had heard so much of the *Vicar* that she was dying to read it. But though everybody wrote to tell her that they had sent it, the little book never came. A Mr. Jenkinson was to have conveyed it to her, but the Mr. Jenkinson of the novel did not turn out a baser de-

ceiver. Then "peu de jours après, voilà "une lettre de Mr. Burke. Un style "charmant, des excuses de sa longue "négligence, mille politesses, un badi-"nage léger, de l'esprit, de l'agrément, "de la finesse; rien de plus joli. Il prend "la liberté de m'envoyer, il a l'honneur "de me présenter,—qui, quoi? devinez, "*Le Vicaire de Wakefield*. Un Irlandois "doit me le remettre, avec," &c. But the Irishman, alas, proved only another Jenkinson; and he ushered in still further disappointments, till at last the little lady, exasperated almost to despair, receives "un billet de Mr. Garrick, une "lettre de Mr. Becket, et ce *Vicaire* si dé-"siré, si longtemps attendu—je pousse "un cri de joie," &c. Then of course, as usual when expectation has been so highly wrought, disappointment succeeds. "Vous avez raison," she writes to Garrick, "de dire, qu'il ne m'apprendra rien. "C'est un homme qui va de malheurs en "malheurs assez rapidement, et de bon-"heurs en bonheurs tout aussi vite. Cela "ne ressemble guère à la vie du monde. "... Je ne suis pas un juge compétent du "style, mais le plan de l'ouvrage ne m'a "pas intéressé; le pathétique annoncé "par Mr. Burke ne m'a point frappée: "le plaidoyer en faveur des voleurs, "des petits larrons, des gens de mau-"vaises mœurs, est fort éloigné de me "plaire."

* I ought not to mention this second impression without adding that it contained some additions, such as Burchel's *repetition* of his famous monosyllable at each pause in the revelations of Miss Skeggs; and some omissions, as of a passage that Goldsmith may possibly have found in use against himself, in which he had said of Moses, "for he always "ascribed to his wit that laughter which "was lavished on his simplicity." We owe to Johnson, as I have shown in a previous note, the mention of two omissions made before publication, which he could hardly have remembered if he had not very carefully read the MS.

21*

1766.
———
Æt. 38.

tion in little more than seven years; and thus early it had been translated into several continental languages.* These were indications of success which its author lived to enjoy, but there were others in which he was not to share. He was not to know that the little story would make its way into every English home, and take its place as one of the half-dozen masterpieces of the language. While yet he lived, it had helped to form the character of the greatest man of modern days; but its writer was not to know it. When a French sovereign declared that it had been to him, in his English exile, a pleasure not equalled since the restoration of his throne,** Gold-smith had been dead nearly half a century. Nor were any solider enjoyments from it to be his, any more than these delights of fame. As it had been with the *Traveller* so it was with the *Vicar.* In the year of his death its seventh edition was published; but he went to his grave without receiving from the booksellers the least addition to that original sorry payment which Johnson himself thought "accidentally" less than it ought to have been. In this, as in so many other instances, his marked ill-fortune attended him. That people "made a "point" of not buying what he wrote, could not at least be said of the *Vicar*, either in Paul's-churchyard or Paternoster-row. Yet the very month when the appearance of its second edition may have brought this assurance to himself, was also that in which he was to receive assurance not less convincing, that, with even such a success following hard upon that of his poem, his troubles and toil were not to pass away.

* These have since multiplied to excess. I add a mention of one or two of the latest that have been sent to me. "Le Ministre de Wakefield. Précédé "d'un Essai sur la vie et les écrits "d'Oliver Goldsmith. Par M. Hennequin. "Paris, Brédrip, 1825." This is careful and good. "Le Vicaire de Wakefield. "Traduit par Charles Nodier. Paris, "Gorsclin, 1841." The notice by Nodier prefixed is charming. "Der Landpredi-"ger von Wakefield. Leipsic, 1835." Here a number of illustrations are reproduced from Westall. Another published in the same city, six years later, has an abundant series of woodcuts by Louis Richter, very humorous and pleasant. The list might be extended indefinitely.

** "The writer of these remarks," says the reviewer of the first edition of this biography in the *Morning Chronicle* of the 13th June, 1848, "is enabled to state "that, at the coronation of the late King "of France, Charles X, he told the Duke "of Northumberland that he had never "known, since the restoration of his "family, the pleasure he used to enjoy at "Hartwell-house in reading *The Vicar of* "*Wakefield.*"

APPENDIX TO VOLUME I.

A. (Page 9.)

DOCTOR STREAN AND THE REVEREND EDWARD MANGIN.

STREAN was a physician who had taken orders. He died eleven years ago, at nearly ninety years of age. He then held the perpetual cure of St. Peter's in Athlone; but had in his early life succeeded Henry Goldsmith in the curacy of Kilkenny West, which the latter occupied at the period of his death, and, as he is careful to tell us, in its emoluments of £40 a year, "which was "not only his salary, but con-"tinued to be the same when "I, a successor, was appointed "to that parish." His relative by marriage, the Rev. Edward Mangin, to whose intelligent inquiries (the results of which are published in an *Essay on Light Reading*, 12mo. 1808) we owe much of our knowledge of the poet's youth, still lives in Bath.

Since I thus wrote, in a note appended to my first edition, the life of Mr. Mangin closed on the 17th of October, 1852, at the ripe age of eighty-one. A "friend of "forty years" wrote of him in the *Standard* newspaper of a few evenings later:

"Descended from a Huguenot family, who took refuge in Ireland from the persecution in the time of Louis XIV, and who rose to opulent and important stations in their adopted country, Mr. Mangin had much of the manners of both France and Ireland—foreign acuteness of conversation, with a remarkable share of the pleasantry and good humour of the Irish gentleman.

"Educated at Oxford, for the Church, obtaining preferment in Ireland at an early age, and always disposed to literature and society, no man could commence his career under happier auspices, and no man enjoyed it with more manly gratification. Possessing all the allowable indulgences of life without trouble, and thus wanting the *great* stimulus to exertion, he published but little, and that little rather as the overflow of a remarkably ingenious mind, than as the labour of study or the effort of invention. The lightness of such works naturally destines them to float away with the current of authorship; but some of Mr. Mangin's publications on Manners, Travel and Character, will be preserved, and new form the melancholy pleasure of friends, who retrace in them the liveliness, point, and force of his conversation.

"Marrying early, but soon left a widower with an only daughter, worthy of him, and to whom he was affectionately attached through life; after a long interval he married again, and has left two sons, like himself educated at Oxford, and now in the Church.

"Residing for many years in Bath, writing occasionally, associating with all the intelligent in that intelligent city, easy in fortune, and scarcely visited by the common casualties of life, he rather glided through years than felt them.

"His death was like his life—tranquil. He walked out the day before, sat with his family during the evening, retired to rest with no appearance of an increase of illness, and slept undisturbed during the night. In that sleep, between seven and eight next morning, he expired."

It will not perhaps be thought unbecoming, notwithstanding its expressions complimentary to myself, to subjoin a letter on the subject of Goldsmith with which Mr. Mangin favoured me shortly after the publication of this book. Its personal information and anecdote may not be unwelcome to my readers.

"BATH, *Monday, April,* 24, 1848.

"SIR, I trust you will kindly "pardon my freedom in ventur- "ing to trouble you with this, "for which the least bad apology "I can offer is the circumstance "of your having kindly men- "tioned the writer in your lately "published delightful work *The* "*Life and Adventures of Oliver Gold-* "*smith.*

"Your book will, beyond doubt, "be generally sought for and re- "lished; and indeed cannot, I "should imagine, fail of a place "in the collection of every one "who has a taste for genuine "poetry, and discernment suf- "ficient to approve of your "labours in behalf of Goldsmith's "renown.

"Excuse my pointing out a "minute oversight in the early "part of your most interesting

"volume. I refer to a passage "in which you state my having "addressed my inquiries to Doc- "tor Strean 'twenty-five years "'ago.' I lament to say that "more than *forty* years have "passed since I put my queries "to the Doctor; whose letter in "reply is, I observe, dated on "the closing day of the year "1807, and was introduced into "a brief forgotten *Essay on Light* "*Reading* published in the spring "of 1808.

"Upon a different occasion, I "have said that when he died, "Strean's age was almost *ninety:* "this is probably not correct; "but I remember asking him "once how old he was, and his "saying that he could not an- "swer me exactly, but that what "he recollected longest was his "mother's giving him, when in a "child's dress, a black ribbon to "wear round his waist, and re- "peating to him that it signified "mourning for King George's "death. This, we know, oc- "curred in 1760, when we may "suppose the boy about seven "years old; so, if born in 1753, "or 1754, and living till 1837, he "was certainly above four-score. "He was a man of considerable "attainments, and sundry re- "sources; he was a well-grounded "Greek and Latin scholar, and, "which is more rare in Ireland, "a good prosodian. He had a "thoroughly mechanical genius; "he sometimes bound his own "books; and had made, in a "very workman-like manner, "many articles of furniture in his "parsonage-house. He was an "expert mathematician, and was "valued as such by the learned "Bishop Law of Elphin, with "whom he corresponded on "their favourite science. The "good bishop had, besides, a "high opinion of him as a re-"gular and conscientious pastor.

"Through Strean, I made ac-"quaintance, in 1798, with an old "friend of his, Anthony De-"venish, who had been, I be-"lieve, Goldsmith's school-fel-"low, and used to enlarge on "the Bard's dexterity in the craft "of ball-playing.

"I also, in those times, met at "Athlone a Doctor Nelligan, a "cheerful, shrewd little man, "with much humour; and of him "this story was in circulation:—"Some one argued in his hear-"ing, that Goldsmith must have "written the *Deserted Village* in "England, because the night-"ingale is sketched in as a "feature in his rural picture, and "it is supposed that there are "not any nightingales in Ireland. "Nelligan's retort was, that his "opponent's logic was defective; "for, by his mode of drawing an "inference, it might be shown "that when *Paradise Lost* was "written the immortal author "must have been in Hell.

"As to the name of the birth-"place of the poet of Auburn, it "is unquestionably *Pallis;* the "word, so spelled, was tran-"scribed from a leaf of the Gold-"smith family Bible; and the

"entry is concluded to be in the "hand-writing of Oliver's father.

"Your analysis of the Life and "'Strange surprising' Adven-"tures of Goldsmith appears to "me most ingeniously devised "and executed; the idea strikes "me as being eminently happy "and new; and your book might "well have been announced as "the history of Oliver Gold-"smith's *mind*, for such it really "is.

"You rather intimate, to my "great gratification, that you do "not conceive Goldsmith to have "been *understood* by the persons "among whom he usually moved; "I own I have always thought he "was not, and that his ordinary "deportment and powers of con-"versation are grossly misrepre-"sented by several who have "talked and scribbled so flip-"pantly about his peculiarities "and blunders. We had for-"merly at Upham's Library here "(once Bull's), an assistant in the "establishment of the name of "Crute or Croot. He had filled "the situation for many years, "and was a clear-headed, ob-"serving old man. He often "amused me and others with "anecdotes of the distinguished "individuals known to him as "frequenters of the Library; and "one day, speaking of Gold-"smith, he told us that the poet "was eagerly greeted on his en-"trance, and always conversed "so pleasantly, that he had be-"hind his chair a crowd of re-"spectful auditors and admirers.

"Your efforts to uphold the "fair fame of him who has be-"queathed to the national litera-"ture the undying *Vicar of Wake-"field*, &c, will, I hope, plead for "me, and prevail with you to "forgive this intrusion on the "part of
 "Sir,
  "Your most obt. humble
   "servant,
    "EDWARD MANGIN.
"JOHN FORSTER, ESQ."

B. (PAGES 31—33.)

The letter to Mrs. Anne Goldsmith, which must be read with the allowance mentioned in the text, is here subjoined.

"MY DEAR MOTHER,

"If you will sit down and calmly listen to what I say, you shall be fully resolved in every one of those many questions you have asked me. I went to Cork and converted my horse, which you prize so much higher than Fiddleback, into cash, took my passage in a ship bound for America, and, at the same time, paid the captain for my freight and all the other expenses of my voyage. But it so happened that the wind did not answer for three weeks; and you know, mother, that I could not command the elements. My misfortune was that when the wind served I happened to be with a party in the country, and my friend the captain never inquired after me, but set sail with as much indifference as if I had been on board. The remainder of my time I employed in the city and its environs, viewing everything curious, and you know no one can starve while he has money in his pocket.

"Reduced, however, to my last two guineas, I began to think of my dear mother and friends whom I had left behind me, and so bought that generous beast Fiddleback, and made adieu to Cork with only two shillings in my pocket. This to be sure was but a scanty allowance for man and horse towards a journey of above a hundred miles; but I did not despair, for I knew I must find friends on the road.

"I recollected particularly an old and faithful acquaintance I made at college, who had often and earnestly pressed me to spend a summer with him, and he lived but eight miles from Cork. This circumstance of vicinity he would expatiate on to me with peculiar emphasis. 'We shall,' says he, 'enjoy the delights of both city and country, and you shall command my stable and my purse.'

"However, upon the way I met a poor woman all in tears, who told me her husband had been arrested for a debt he was not able to pay, and that his eight children must now starve, bereaved as they were of his industry, which had been their only support. I thought myself at home, being not far from my good friend's house, and therefore parted with a moiety of all my store; and pray, mother, ought I not to have given her the other half-crown, for what she got would be of little use to her?—However, I soon arrived at the mansion of my affectionate friend, guarded by the vigilance of a huge mastiff, who flew at me and would have torn me to pieces out for the assistance of a woman, whose countenance was not less grim than that of the dog; yet she with great humanity relieved me from the jaws of this Cerberus, and was prevailed on to carry up my name to her master.

"Without suffering me to wait long, my old friend, who was then recovering from a severe fit of sickness, came down in his night-cap, night-gown, and slippers, and embraced me with the most cordial welcome, showed me in, and, after giving me a history of his indisposition, assured me that he considered himself peculiarly fortunate in having under his roof the man he most loved on earth, and whose stay with him must, above all things, contribute to his perfect recovery. I now repented sorely I had not given the poor woman the other half-crown, as I thought all my bills of humanity would be punctually answered by this worthy man. I revealed to him my whole soul;

I opened to him all my distresses; and freely owned that I had but one half-crown in my pocket; but that now, like a ship after weathering out the storm, I considered myself secure in a safe and hospitable harbour. He made no answer, but walked about the room, rubbing his hands as one in deep study. This I imputed to the sympathetic feelings of a tender heart, which increased my esteem for him, and, as that increased, I gave the most favourable interpretation to his silence. I construed it into delicacy of sentiment, as if he dreaded to wound my pride by expressing his commiseration in words, leaving his generous conduct to speak for itself.

"It now approached six o'clock in the evening, and as I had eaten no breakfast, and as my spirits were raised, my appetite for dinner grew uncommonly keen. At length the old woman came into the room with two plates, one spoon, and a dirty cloth, which she laid upon the table. This appearance, without increasing my spirits, did not diminish my appetite. My protectress soon returned with a small bowl of sago, a small porringer of sour milk, a loaf of stale brown bread, and the heel of an old cheese all over crawling with mites. My friend apologised that his illness obliged him to live on slops, and that better fare was not in the house; observing, at the same time, that a milk diet was certainly the most healthful. At eight o'clock he again recommended a regular life, declaring that for his part he would *lie down with the lamb and rise with the lark*. My hunger was at this time so exceedingly sharp that I wished for another slice of the loaf, but was obliged to go to bed without even that refreshment.

"This lenten entertainment I had received made me resolve to depart as soon as possible; accordingly next morning, when I spoke of going, he did not oppose my resolution; he rather commended my design, adding some very sage counsel upon the occasion. 'To be sure,' said he, 'the longer you stay away from your 'mother the more you will grieve her 'and your other friends; and possibly 'they are already afflicted at hearing of 'this foolish expedition you have made.' Notwithstanding all this, and without any hope of softening such a sordid heart, I again renewed the tale of my distress, and asking 'how he thought I 'could travel above a hundred miles 'upon one half-crown?' I begged to borrow a single guinea, which I assured him should be repaid with thanks. 'And 'you know, sir,' said I, 'it is no more 'than I have often done for you.' To which he firmly answered, 'Why look 'you, Mr. Goldsmith, that is neither here 'nor there. I have paid you all you ever 'lent me, and this sickness of mine has 'left me bare of cash. But I have be-'thought myself of a conveyance for you; 'sell your horse, and I will furnish you 'with a much better one to ride on.' I readily grasped at this proposal, and begged to see the nag, on which he led me to his bedchamber, and from under the bed he pulled out a stout oak stick. 'Here he is,' said he; 'take this in your 'hand, and it will carry you to your 'mother's with more safety than such a 'horse as you ride.' I was in doubt, when I got it into my hand, whether I should not, in the first place, apply it to his pate; but a rap at the street-door made the wretch fly to it, and when I returned to the parlour, he introduced me, as if nothing of the kind had happened, to the gentleman who entered, as Mr. Goldsmith, his most ingenious and worthy friend, of whom he had so often heard him speak with rapture. I could scarcely compose myself; and must have betrayed indignation in my mien to the stranger, who was a counsellor at law in the neighbourhood, a man of engaging aspect and polite address.

"After spending an hour, he asked my friend and me to dine with him at his house. This I declined at first, as I wished to have no further communication with my hospitable friend; but at the solicitation of both I at last consented, determined as I was by two motives; one, that I was prejudiced in favour of the looks and manner of the counsellor; and the other, that I stood in need of a comfortable dinner. And there indeed I found everything that I could wish, abundance without profusion, and elegance without affectation. In the evening, when my old friend, who had eaten very plentifully at his neighbour's table, but talked again of lying down with the lamb, made a motion to me for retiring, our generous host requested I should take a bed with him, upon which I plainly told my old friend that he might go home and take care of the horse he had given me, but that I should never re-enter his doors. He went away with a laugh, leaving me to add this to the other little things the counsellor already knew of his plausible neighbour.

"And now, my dear mother, I found sufficient to reconcile me to all my follies; for here I spent three whole days. The counsellor had two sweet girls to his daughters, who played enchantingly on the harpsichord: and yet it was but a melancholy pleasure I felt the first time I heard them; for that being the first time also that either of them had touched the instrument since their mother's death, I saw the tears in silence trickle down their father's cheeks. I every day endeavoured to go away, but every day was pressed and obliged to stay. On my going, the counsellor offered me his purse, with a horse and servant to convey me home; but the latter I declined, and only took a guinea to bear my necessary expenses on the road.

"OLIVER GOLDSMITH.

"*To* MRS. ANNE GOLDSMITH,
"*Ballymahon.*"

C. (PAGES 35, 36, 39, AND 41.)

LETTERS TO BRYANTON AND CONTARINE.

1. TO ROBERT BRYANTON.

This letter, to which I have alluded at p. 35, is dated Edinburgh, Sept. 26, 1753; and is addressed to Robert Bryanton, Esq. at Ballymahon, Ireland:

"MY DEAR BOB,

"How many good excuses (and you know I was ever good at an excuse) might I call up to vindicate my past shameful silence! I might tell how I wrote a long letter on my first coming hither, and seem vastly angry at my not receiving an answer: I might allege that business (with business you know I was always pestered) had never given me time to finger a pen;—but I suppress these and twenty more equally plausible, and as easily invented, since they might be attended with a slight inconvenience of being known to be lies. Let me then speak truth: an hereditary indolence (I have it from the mother's side) has hitherto prevented my writing to you, and still prevents my writing at least twenty-five letters more, due to my friends in Ireland. No turnspit dog gets up into his wheel with more reluctance than I sit down to write: yet no dog ever loved the roast meat he turns better than I do him I now address. Yet what shall I say now I'm entered? Shall I tire you with a description of this unfruitful country, where I must lead you over their hills all brown with heath, or their vallies scarce able to feed a rabbit? Man alone seems to be the only creature who has arrived to the natural size in this poor soil. Every part of the country presents the same dismal landscape. No grove nor brook lend their music to cheer the stranger, or make the inhabitants forget their poverty: yet with all these disadvantages, enough to call him down to humility, a Scotchman is one of the proudest things alive. The poor have pride ever ready to relieve them. If mankind should happen to despise them, they are masters of their own admiration; and *that* they can plentifully bestow upon themselves.

"From their pride and poverty, as I take it, results one advantage this country enjoys, namely, the gentlemen here are much better bred than amongst us. No such characters here as our fox-hunters; and they have expressed great surprise when I informed them, that some men in Ireland of 1000*l.* a year spend their whole lives in running after a hare, drinking to be drunk, and getting every girl that will let them with child: and truly, if such a being, equipped in his hunting dress, came among a circle of Scotch gentry, they would behold him with the same astonishment that a countryman would King George on horseback.

"The men here have generally high cheek-bones, and are lean and swarthy, fond of action, dancing in particular. Though now I mention dancing, let me say something of their balls which are very frequent here. When a stranger enters the dancing-hall, he sees one end of the room taken up with the ladies, who sit dismally in a groupe by themselves. On the other end stand their pensive partners, that are to be: but no more intercourse between the sexes than there is between two countries at war:—the ladies, indeed, may ogle, and the gentlemen sigh, but an embargo is laid on any closer commerce. At length, to interrupt hostilities, the lady directress or intendant, or what you will, pitches on a gentleman and lady to 'walk a minuet; which they perform with a formality that approaches to despondence. After five or six couple have thus walked the gauntlet, all stand up to country dances; each gentleman furnished with a partner from the aforesaid lady directress; so they dance much and say nothing, and thus concludes our assembly. I told a Scotch gentleman that such profound silence resembled the ancient procession of the Roman matrons in honour of Ceres; and the Scotch gentleman told me (and 'faith, I believe he was right) that I was a very great pedant for my pains.

"Now I am come to the ladies; and to show that I love Scotland, and everything that belongs to so charming a country, I insist on it, and will give him leave to break my head that denies it, that the Scotch ladies are ten thousand times handsomer and finer than the Irish:—to be sure now I see your sisters Betty and Peggy vastly surprised at my partiality, but tell them flatly, I don't value them, or their fine skins, or eyes, or good sense, or ——, a potato; for I say it, and will maintain it, and as a convincing proof (I'm in a very great passion) of what I assert, the Scotch ladies say it themselves. But to be less serious; where will you find a language so pretty become a pretty mouth as the broad Scotch? and the women here speak it in its highest purity; for instance, teach one of their young ladies to pronounce 'Whoar 'wull I gong?' with a becoming wideness of mouth, and I'll lay my life they will wound every hearer.

"We have no such character here as a coquet; but, 'alas! how many envious prudes! Some days ago I walked into my Lord Kilcoubry's (don't be surprised, my lord is but a glover) when the Duchess of Hamilton (that fair who sacri-ficed her beauty to ambition, and her inward peace to a title and gilt equipage) passed by in her chariot; her battered husband, or more properly the guardian of her charms, sat by her side. Straight envy began, in the shape of no less than three ladies who sat with me, to find faults in her faultless form.—'For my 'part,' says the first, 'I think, what I al-'ways thought, that the Duchess has too 'much red in her complexion.' 'Madam, 'I'm of your opinion,' says the second; 'I 'think her face has a palish cast too much 'on the delicate order.' 'And let me tell 'you,' adds the third lady, whose mouth was puckered up to the size of an issue, 'that the Duchess has fine lips, but she 'wants a mouth.' At this every lady drew up her mouth as if going to pronounce the letter P.

"But how ill, my Bob, does it become me to ridicule women with whom I have scarce any correspondence! There are, 'tis certain, handsome women here; and 'tis as certain there are handsome men to keep them company. An ugly and a poor man is society for himself; and such society the world lets me enjoy in great abundance. Fortune has given you circumstances, and nature a person to look charming in the eyes of the fair world. Nor do I envy my dear Bob such blessings while I may sit down and laugh at the world, and at myself, the most ridiculous object in it.—But I begin to grow splenetic; and perhaps, the fit may continue till I receive an answer to this. I know you can't send news from B[ally]-mahon, but such as it is send it all; everything you write will be agreeable and entertaining to me. Has George Conway put up a sign yet; or John Finecly* left off drinking drams; or Tom Allen got a new wig? But I leave to your own choice what to write.—While Oliver Goldsmith lives, know you have a friend!

"P.S. Give my sincere regards (not compliments, do you mind) to your agreeable family, and give my service to my mother if you see her; for, as you express it in Ireland, I have a sneaking kindness for her still.

"Direct to me, ——, Student in Physic, in Edinburgh."

---

* Mr. Prior prints the name as John Binely (i. 145).

II. TO THE REV. THOMAS CONTARINE.

The first letter to the Reverend Mr. Contarine mentioned in the text (p. 36) is dated 8th May, 1753, and runs thus:

"MY DEAR UNCLE,

"In your letter (the only one I received from Kilmore), you call me the philosopher who carries all his goods about him. Yet how can such a character fit me, who have left behind in Ireland everything I think worth possessing; friends that I loved, and a society that pleased while it instructed? Who but must regret the loss of such enjoyments? Who but must regret his absence from Kilmore, that ever knew it as I did? Here, as recluse as the Turkish Spy at Paris, I am almost unknown to everybody, except some few who attend the professors of physic as I do.

"Apropos, I shall give you the professors' names, and, as far as occurs to me, their characters; and first, as most deserving, Mr. Munro, professor of Anatomy. This man has brought the science he teaches to as much perfection as it is capable of; and not content with barely teaching anatomy, he launches out into all the branches of physic, when all his remarks are new and useful. 'Tis he, I may venture to say, that draws hither such a number of students from most parts of the world, even from Russia. He is not only a skilful physician, but an able orator, and delivers things in their nature obscure in so easy a manner, that the most unlearned may understand him. Plume, professor of Chemistry, understands his business well, but delivers himself so ill, that he is but little regarded. Alston, professor of Materia Medica, speaks much, but little to the purpose. The professors of Theory and Practice (of physic) say nothing but what we may find in books laid before us; and speak that in so drowsy and heavy a manner, that their hearers are not many degrees in a better state than their patients.

"You see then, dear sir, that Munro is the only great man among them; so that I intend to hear him another winter, and go then to hear Albinus, the great professor at Leyden. I read (with satisfaction) a science the most pleasing in nature, so that my labours are but a relaxation, and, I may truly say, the only thing here that gives me pleasure. How I enjoy the pleasing hope of returning with skill, and to find my friends stand in no need of my assistance! How many happy years do I wish you! and nothing but want of health can take from you happiness, since you so well pursue the paths that conduct to virtue.

"I am, my dear Uncle, your most obliged,
"Most affectionate nephew,
"OLIVER GOLDSMITH.

"P.S. I draw this time for 6l, and will draw next October but for 4l, as I was obliged to buy everything since I came to Scotland, shirts not even excepted. I am a little more early the first year than I shall be for the future, for I absolutely will not trouble you before the time hereafter.

"My best love attend Mr. and Mrs. Lawder, and Heaven preserve them! I am again your dutiful nephew, O. G.

"I have been a month in the Highlands. I set out the first day on foot, but an ill-natured corn I have got on my toe has for the future prevented that cheap method of travelling; so the second day I hired a horse of about the size of a ram, and he walked away (trot he could not) as pensive as his master. In three days we reached the Highlands. This letter would be too long if it contained the description I intend giving of that country, so shall make it the subject of my next."

III. TO THE REV. THOMAS CONTARINE.

The second letter to Mr. Contarine, referred to at p. 39, is not dated, but was undoubtedly written at the close of 1753:

"MY DEAR UNCLE,

"After having spent two winters in Edinburgh, I now prepare to go to France the 10th of next February. I have seen all that this country can exhibit in the medical way, and therefore intend to visit Paris, where the great Mr. Farhein, Petit, and Du Hammel de Moncean instruct their pupils in all the branches of medicine. They speak French, and consequently I shall have much the advantage of most of my countrymen, as I am perfectly acquainted with that language, and few who leave Ireland are so.

"Since I am upon so pleasing a topic as self-applause, give me leave to say that the circle of science which I have run through, before I undertook the study of physic, is not only useful, but absolutely necessary to the making a skilful physician. Such sciences enlarge our understanding, and sharpen our sagacity; and what is a practitioner without both but an empiric, for never yet was a disorder found entirely the same in two patients. A quack, unable to distinguish the particularities in each disease, prescribes at a venture: if he finds such a disorder may be called by the general name of fever for instance, he has a set of remedies which he applies to cure it, nor does he desist till his medicines are run out, or his patient has lost his life. But the skilful physician distinguishes the symptoms; manures the sterility of nature, or prunes her luxuriance; nor does he depend so much on the efficacy of medicines as on their proper application. I shall spend this spring and summer in Paris, and the beginning of next winter go to Leyden. The great Albinus is still alive there, and 'twill be proper to go, though only to have it said that we have studied in so famous an university.

"As I shall not have another opportunity of receiving money from your bounty till my return to Ireland, so I have drawn for the last sum that I hope I shall ever trouble you for; 'tis 20*l*. And, now, dear Sir, let me here acknowledge the humility of the station in which you found me; let me tell how I was despised by most, and hateful to myself. Poverty, hopeless poverty, was my lot, and Melancholy was beginning to make me her own. When you—but I stop here, to inquire how your health goes on. How does my dear cousin Jenny, and has she recovered her late complaint? How does my poor Jack Goldsmith? I fear his disorder is of such a nature as he won't easily recover. I wish, my dear Sir, you would make me happy by another letter before I go abroad, for there I shall hardly hear from you. I shall carry just 33*l*. to France, with good store of clothes, shirts, &c. &c. and that with economy will serve.

"I have spent more than a fortnight every second day at the Duke of Hamilton's, but it seems they like me more as a *jester* than as a companion; so I disdained so servile an employment; 'twas unworthy my calling as a physician.

"I have nothing new to add from this country; and I beg, dear Sir, you will excuse this letter, so filled with egotism. I wish you may be revenged on me, by sending an answer filled with nothing but an account of yourself.

"I am, dear Uncle,
"Your most devoted
"OLIVER GOLDSMITH.

"Give my —— how shall I express it? Give my earnest love to Mr. and Mrs. Lawder."

Finally, I subjoin the whole of the third letter to Mr. Contarine described at p. 41, written from Leyden, but without any other date.

"LEYDEN [Date wanting].
"DEAR SIR,

"I suppose by this time I am accused of either neglect or ingratitude, and my silence imputed to my usual slowness of writing. But believe me, Sir, when I say, that till now I had not an opportunity of sitting down with that ease of mind which writing required. You may see by the top of the letter that I am at Leyden; but of my journey hither you must be informed. Sometime after the receipt of your last, I embarked for Bourdeaux, on board a Scotch ship called the St. Andrews, Capt. John Wall, master. The ship made a tolerable appearance, and as another inducement, I was let to know that six agreeable passengers were to be my company. Well, we were but two days at sea when a storm drove us into a city of England called Newcastle-upon-Tyne. We all went ashore to refresh us after the fatigue of our voyage. Seven men and I were one day on shore, and on the following evening as we were all very merry, the room door bursts open: enters a serjeant and twelve grenadiers with their bayonets screwed: and puts us all under the King's arrest. It seems my company were Scotchmen in the French service, and had been in Scotland to enlist soldiers for the French army. I endeavoured all I could to prove my innocence; however, I remained in prison with the rest a fortnight, and with difficulty got off even then. Dear sir, keep this all a secret, or at least say it was for debt; for if it were once known at the university, I should hardly get a degree. But hear how Providence interposed in my favour: the ship was gone on to Bourdeaux before I got from prison, and was wrecked at the mouth of the Garonne, and every one of the crew were drowned. It happened the last great storm. There was a ship at that time ready for Holland: I embarked, and in nine days, thank my God, I arrived save at Rotterdam; whence I travelled by land to Leyden; and whence I now write.

"You may expect some account of this country, and though I am not well qualified for such an undertaking, yet shall I endeavour to satisfy some part of your expectations. Nothing surprised me more than the books every day published, descriptive of the manners of this country. Any young man who takes it into his head to publish his travels, visits the countries he intends to describe; passes through them with as much inattention as his valet de chambre; and consequently not having a fund himself to fill a volume, he applies to those who wrote before him, and gives us the manners of a country, not as he must have seen them, but such as they might have been fifty years before. The modern Dutchman is quite a different creature from him of former times: he in everything imitates a Frenchman, but in his easy disengaged air, which is the result of keeping polite company. The Dutchman is vastly ceremonious, and is perhaps exactly what a Frenchman might have been in the reign of Louis XIV. Such are the better bred. But the downright Hollander is one of the oddest figures in nature. Upon a head of lank hair he wears a half-cocked narrow hat laced with black ribbon: no coat, but seven waistcoats, and nine pairs of breeches; so that his hips reach almost up to his arm-pits. This well-clothed vegetable is now fit to see company, or make love. But what a pleasing creature is the object of his appetite? Why she wears a large fur cap with a deal of Flan-

ders lace: and for every pair of breeches he carries, she puts on two petticoats.

"A Dutch lady burns nothing about her phlegmatic admirer but his tobacco. You must know, sir, every woman carries in her hand a stove with coals in it, which, when she sits, she snugs under her petticoats; and at this chimney dozing Strephon lights his pipe. I take it that this continual smoking is what gives the man the ruddy healthful complexion he generally wears, by draining his superfluous moisture, while the woman, deprived of this amusement, overflows with such viscidities as tint the complexion, and give that paleness of visage which low fenny grounds and moist air conspire to cause. A Dutch woman and Scotch will well bear an opposition. The one is pale and fat, the other lean and ruddy: the one walks as if she were straddling after a go-cart, and the other takes too masculine a stride. I shall not endeavour to deprive either country of its share of beauty; but must say, that of all objects on this earth, an English farmer's daughter is most charming. Every woman there is a complete beauty, while the higher class of women want many of the requisites to make them even tolerable. Their pleasures here are very dull, though very various. You may smoke, you may doze; you may go to the Italian comedy, as good an amusement as either of the former. This entertainment always brings in Harlequin, who is generally a magician, and in consequence of his diabolical art performs a thousand tricks on the rest of the persons of the drama, who are all fools. I have seen the pit in a roar of laughter at this humour, when with his sword he touches the glass from which another was drinking. 'Twas not his face they laughed at, for that was masked. They must have seen something vastly queer in the wooden sword, that neither I, nor you, sir, were you there, could see.

"In winter, when their canals are frozen, every house is forsaken, and all people are on the ice; sleds drawn by horses, and skaiting, are at that time the reigning amusements. They have boats here that slide on the ice, and are driven by the winds. When they spread all their sails they go more than a mile and a half a minute, and their motion is so rapid the eye can scarcely accompany them. Their ordinary manner of travelling is very cheap and very convenient: they sail in covered boats drawn by horses; and in these you are sure to meet people of all nations. Here the Dutch slumber, the French chatter, and the English play at cards. Any man who likes company may have them to his taste. For my part I generally detached myself from all society, and was wholly taken up in observing the face of the country. Nothing can equal its beauty; wherever I turn my eye, fine houses, elegant gardens, statues, grottos, vistas, presented themselves; but when you enter their towns you are charmed beyond description. No misery is to be seen here; every one is usefully employed.

"Scotland and this country bear the highest contrast. There hills and rocks intercept every prospect: here 'tis all a continued plain. There you might see a well-dressed duchess issuing from a dirty close; and here a dirty Dutchman inhabiting a palace. The Scotch may be compared to a tulip planted in dung; but I never see a Dutchman in his own house but I think of a magnificent Egyptian temple dedicated to an ox. Physic is by no means taught here so well as in Edinburgh; and in all Leyden there are but four British students, owing to all necessaries being so extremely dear and the professors so very lazy (the chemical professor excepted), that we don't much care to come hither. I am not certain how long my stay here may be; however I expect to have the happiness of seeing you at Kilmore, if I can, next March.

"Direct to me, if I am honoured with a letter from you, to Madame Diallion's at Leyden.

"Thou best of men, may Heaven guard and preserve you, and those you love.

"OLIVER GOLDSMITH."

D. (PAGE 153, 154.)

THE PLAY OF *GISIPPUS*.

In brief justification of the opinion I have expressed of this tragedy, and of the interest I feel in its writer's memory, I subjoin one short scene. The period of the action is the reign of Augustus Cæsar, and the subject is the friendship borne by the philosophic Greek, Gisippus, to the ambitious Roman, Fulvius, to secure whose happiness he surrenders his own. Having made unequalled sacrifices for his friend; having passed, for his sake, from honoured love and worldly esteem into solitude and beggary; he finds himself at last, his friend apparently heedless or forgetful of his sufferings, a slave. The lessons of the Academy and the Porch (so often taught in unison in the later Athenian day) on this desert their old follower, and the character takes colouring from that middle-ages romance which furnished Boccacio with the subject on which the play is written. Fulvius meanwhile, moving on from conquest to conquest with the old Roman stride, heedless of what he has while there is anything he has not, has mounted nearly to the top of the ladder of fortune. He is Praetor and in the midst of an Ovation, with neither contented, when his former friend, in squalid ragged wretchedness, planting himself in the streets before him, fixes upon him a glance, which, though steadily returned, leads to no recognition; and, on the seeming miserable beggar persisting still in his desire to have audience of the Praetor, he is struck by the Lictors' fasces. The result is that, deliberately resolving to place himself in the way of death, he is

sentenced to execution by Fulvius on the false charge of a
murder he has taken on himself.
What follows is at the scene of
execution. It is brief, and in mere
writing not of the highest order;
but infinite feeling and suffering
are crowded into it. The laugh
with which it closes tells us this;
and in the thought "not worth
the notice" of the Roman soldier,
there is all that the Greek had
studied by the Porch and in the
Grove, on appearance and the
realities.

Decius. Remove his chains.
Gisippus.   Let it be ever thus—
The generous still be poor; the niggard
    thrive;
Fortune still pave the ingrate's path with
    gold;
Death dog the innocent still; and surely
    those
Who now uplift their streaming eyes and
    murmur
Against oppressive fate, will own its
    justice.
Invisible ruler! should man meet thy
    trials
With silent and lethargic sufferance,
Or lift his hands and ask heaven for a
    reason?
Our hearts must speak—the sting, the
    whip is on them!
We rush in madness forth to tear away
The veil that blinds us to the cause—in
    vain.
The hand of that Eternal Providence
Still holds it there, unmoved, impene-
    trable.
We can but pause, and turn away
    again
To mourn—to wonder—and endure.
Decius. My duty
Compels me to disturb you, prisoner.

Gisippus. I am glad you do so, for my
    thoughts were growing
Somewhat unfriendly to me.—World,
    farewell;
And thou whose image never left his
    heart,
Sweet vision of my memory, fare thee
    well!
Pray walk this way.
This Fulvius, your young Practor, by
    whose sentence
My life stands forfeit has the reputation
Of a good man amongst you?
Decius. Better breathes not.
Gisippus. A just man, and a grateful.
    One who thinks
Upon his friends sometimes; a liberal
    man,
Whose wealth is not for his own use; a
    kind man,
To his clients and his household?
Decius. He is all this.
Gisippus. A gallant soldier too?
Decius. I've witnessed that
In many a desperate fight.
Gisippus. In short; there lives not
A man of fairer fame in Rome?
Decius. Nor out of it.
Gisippus. Good.—Look on me now, look
    on my face!
I am a villain, am I not!—nay, speak!
Decius. You are found a murderer.
Gisippus. A coward murderer:
A secret, sudden stabber. 'Tis not pos-
    sible
That you can find a blacker, fouler cha-
    racter,
Than this of mine?
Decius. The Gods must judge your
    guilt,
But it is such as man should shudder at.
Gisippus. This is a wise world, too,
    friend, is it not?
Men have eyes, ears, and (sometime
    judgment.
Have they not?
Decius. They are not all fools.
Gisippus. Ha! ha!
Decius. You laugh!
Gisippus. A thought
Not worth your notice, sir.

END OF VOL. I.

PRINTING OFFICE OF THE PUBLISHER.